Get the eBook FREE!
(PDF, ePub, Kindle, and liveBook all included)

We believe that once you buy a book from us, you should be able to read it in any format we have available. To get electronic versions of this book at no additional cost to you, purchase and then register this book at the Manning website.

Go to https://www.manning.com/freebook and follow the instructions to complete your pBook registration.

That's it!
Thanks from Manning!

Istio in Action

Istio in Action

CHRISTIAN E. POSTA
RINOR MALOKU
FOREWORD BY ERIC BREWER

MANNING
SHELTER ISLAND

For online information and ordering of this and other Manning books, please visit
www.manning.com. The publisher offers discounts on this book when ordered in quantity.
For more information, please contact

    Special Sales Department
    Manning Publications Co.
    20 Baldwin Road
    PO Box 761
    Shelter Island, NY 11964
    Email: orders@manning.com

Manning Publications Co.	Development editor:	Elesha Hyde
20 Baldwin Road	Technical development editor:	Brent Stains
PO Box 761	Review editor:	Aleksandar Dragosavljević
Shelter Island, NY 11964	Production editor:	Andy Marinkovich
	Copy editor:	Tiffany Taylor
	Proofreader:	Jason Everett
	Technical proofreaders:	Gregory Reshetniak
	Typesetter and cover designer:	Marija Tudor

ISBN 9781617295829
Printed in the United States of America

I dedicate this book to my wife and daughters.
—Christian Posta

I dedicate this book to everybody
who shares knowledge on the web.
—Rinor Maloku

brief contents

contents

foreword

A service mesh can maximize the development speed of your whole organization by enabling thousands of independent microservices that are automatically compliant with a wide range of evolving policies. This book discusses many other benefits of Istio, but they largely follow from this premise.

This brings us to the central question, "What is a service mesh, and why do I need one?" I'm asked this question frequently, and the answer is not trivial. It is not about security or telemetry or most of the benefits some people claim. Nor is it automatically the case that you need a service mesh for your application, especially if it is a monolith.

The real answer has to do with decoupling applications from infrastructure. Istio is the third major step in that direction. First, Docker provided a way to package an application (and its library choices) separately from the machine on which it runs. Next, Kubernetes made it easy to create a service with automation to help with auto-scaling and management. Together, Docker and Kubernetes enabled the practical movement to fine-grain services, often called *microservices*. This book guides you through implementing a service mesh with Istio to achieve this third step: application decoupling.

Microservices allow greater overall velocity by enabling teams to be more autonomous. Ideally, your team can update its microservice(s) without deep interactions with other teams. The top-level goal for Istio is to enable this at scale—to make it easy to have thousands of microservices (Google has more than a million!).

But enabling velocity for a service is not just about decoupling it from the machine; the service must also be decoupled from shared policies. Every enterprise has policies that apply to all services, and we must be able to change those policies quickly if needed. Traditionally, such policies are embedded inside services as part of the code or as libraries that services are expected to use. Either way, such policies are hard to update and enforce.

Istio moves a wide range of such policies (primarily those involving an API) out of the service and into the service mesh, which is essentially a proxy that sits in front of the service and implements the policies. When this is done correctly, all services meet the policies with no work—and, conversely, policy changes do not require updating the services. This is the decoupling we are after.

In *Istio in Action,* Christian and Rinor present a clear-headed vision of how to achieve the goal of decoupling applications from infrastructure. I hope you'll enjoy this book as much as I have.

— ERIC BREWER
VP INFRASTRUCTURE AND GOOGLE FELLOW

preface

Building software is hard. Connecting different services across a network is harder. Any time you put a packet, message, or request on the network, there are no guarantees about its outcome. Will the request make it? How long will it take? Will anyone know if the communication fails?

Docker and Kubernetes have done a lot to support distributed services architectures like microservices, but they exacerbate the existing communication problems. One misbehaving service might take down everything.

While working with organizations worldwide that are trying to adopt microservices, I find that getting teams to consistently think about and solve these communication problems is very difficult. There are many questions: How will they do service discovery? Timeouts? Retries? Circuit breaking? Tracing? Authentication? Large cloud companies like Netflix, Twitter, and Google pioneered some of the early, successful microservices architectures. These companies had to build a lot of their own developer tooling and infrastructure to solve these problems, and fortunately, they open sourced much of it. Could other organizations use the NetflixOSS stack or Twitter Finagle? They could, and some did, but doing so created a new operational nightmare.

For example, the NetflixOSS stack was primarily written for Java developers. What about NodeJS, Golang, and Python teams? Teams had to either build libraries themselves or hack together the functionality with various bits they found on the internet. They also had to intermingle this "networking" code into their business logic. This approach added transitive dependencies, cluttered the code, and made revisions more difficult. Operating a service architecture with these application networking libraries, upgrading, patching, and doing this consistently across many different languages was extremely complex and error prone.

A service mesh is a cleaner solution to this application-networking problem. With a service mesh, we abstract away the application-networking logic into a dedicated piece of infrastructure and apply it to all services regardless of what languages they are written in.

Istio is a scalable, mature, powerful service-mesh implementation that originally came out of a project from IBM and Google. I was introduced to the Istio team in January 2017 and began working on the project very early. At the end of 2018, I went to work as global field CTO at a startup, Solo.io, to focus full-time on service mesh technology and advancing the state of application networking.

Building a startup from the ground up, pushing the boundaries on this technology, and writing an in-depth book on this topic is not an easy combination. I needed someone with dedication and passion to help me move the book forward; so, when I was halfway through, the Manning team and I invited Rinor Maloku to join the effort. Thanks to the time we both spend in the community and working with our customers at Solo.io, some of which are the largest deployments of Istio in the world, Rinor and I have been able to compile an excellent resource for Istio based on real-world experience. We hope this book will show you the value and power of Istio and make you comfortable adopting this technology into production, as many others have.

acknowledgments

Writing this book has been possible only due to the support of many people.

Special thanks to our personal friends Gentrina Gashi, Dimal Zeqiri, and Taulant Mehmeti, who provided such valuable feedback.

Thank you to the Manning Early Access Program (MEAP) readers who posted comments in the online forum—Takahiko Suzuki, George Tseres, Amol Nayak, Mark O'Crally—and the forum moderator, Ayush Singh.

Sincere gratitude to our editor, Elesha Hyde, who was always patient when responding to our questions and concerns. Most important, thank you for being understanding and supportive when we missed deadlines, and for keeping our focus on writing a better book for our readers.

A big thank you also goes to our technical editors, Gregor Zurowski and Brent Stains, as well as our technical proofreader, Gregory Reshetniak.

Thank you to all the reviewers: Alceu Rodrigues de Freitas Junior, Alessandro Campeis, Allan Makura, Amitabh Cheekoth, Andrea Cosentino, Andrea Tarocchi, Andres Sacco, Borko Djurkovic, Christoph Schubert, Dinkar Gupta, Eriks Zelenka, Ernesto Cardenas, Fotis Stamatelopoulos, Giuseppe Catalano, James Liu, Javier Muñoz, Jeff Hajewski, Karthikeyan Mohan, Kelum Prabath Senanayake, Kent R. Spillner, Leonardo Jose Gomes da Silva, Maciej Drożdżowski, Michael Bright, Michael J Haller, Morgan Nelson, Paolo Antinori, Salvatore Campagna, Satadru Roy, Stanley Anozie, Taylor Dolezal, Vijay Thakorlal, and Yogesh Shetty. Your excellent suggestions made this a better book.

Thank you to key people in the Istio community, including Louis Ryan (Google), Shriram Rajagopalan (Google), and Sven Mawson (Google) who are the three founders of the Istio project; along with Dan Berg (Digital.ai), Lin Sun (Solo.io), Dan Ciruli (Zuora), Idit Levine (Solo.io), John Howard (Google), Kevin Connor (Red Hat),

Jason McGee (IBM), Zack Butcher (Tetrate), Ram Vennam (Solo.io), and Neeraj Poddar (Solo.io).

Finally, we thank the entire Istio community, who are working to build an amazing technology that is a joy to work on and write about on a daily basis.

I am extremely fortunate to work on technology, which has been my passion since I was young. I wouldn't have been able to get here without the love and support of my family. My father, Cask Posta, immigrated to the United States in the early 1970s; he provided me and my sister with a strong foundation and taught me the value of hard work. My beautiful wife Jackie has been by my side through all the unknowns and uncertainties and has shown nothing but unwavering support and love. Thank you, Jackie: without you, we wouldn't have been able to accomplish all we've done.

Finally, I'm thankful for my two lovely daughters, Maddie and Claire, who can put a smile on my face no matter how the day has been and for whom my wife and I work so hard.

—CHRISTIAN E. POSTA

I'd like to thank my parents, Sahadi and Sheride, and my brothers, Aurel and Drilon, for giving me a worry-less childhood that allowed me to explore my many hobbies. One of those, programming, turned into a joyful career; and another, writing, contributed to this book. I'd also like to thank my girlfriend, Rinora, for her endless love and support. To Christian Posta, I'd like to express my eternal gratitude for the trust you put in me. It was crucial in enabling me to do my best work as a first-time writer.

—RINOR MALOKU

about this book

Who should read this book

This book is meant for developers, architects, and or service operators who operate or are planning to operate distributed services such as user-facing web applications, APIs, and backend services and want to provide highly available services to their end users. If you are a member of a platform engineering team and provide infrastructure and other supporting components such as log management, monitoring, container orchestration, and so on to many development teams within your organization, this book will show you how to give your users the tools to make their apps resilient, secure, and observable as well as reduce the risk of shipping new features.

If you are already using Istio in a testing or staging environment but many of its workings are a mystery to you, this book will demystify Istio's components. The latter chapters, in particular, will show you how to scale the service mesh in your organization, troubleshoot it when its behavior doesn't match your expectations, and customize it to meet your enterprise's needs.

If you are already an Istio expert, you may still find this book useful, as we took great care to ingrain into this book what we've learned from working in the field over the last three years.

If building a container is new to you, or you are unsure what a Kubernetes deployment, pod, or service is, this book may not be for you—yet. There are a lot of resources to get you started. We highly recommend *Kubernetes in Action* by Marko Lukša (Manning, 2017); in addition to being a thorough introduction to this topic, the book is a real page-turner. Once you understand the foundation of Kubernetes and its resources and how Kubernetes controllers work, you can return here and dive into the Istio service mesh.

You should also have a basic understanding of networking, and we do mean *basic*. If you are familiar with the network layer (layer 3), the transport layer (layer 4), and how they differ from the application (layer 7) according to the Open Systems Inter-connection model, you are ready for this book.

How this book is organized: A roadmap

This book has four parts and 14 chapters. Part 1 of the book introduces the concept of a service mesh and explains how Istio implements it. These three chapters cover the architecture of Istio, how Envoy fits into it, and how it can benefit your organization:

- Chapter 1 introduces the benefits of Istio and the value that adopting service meshes can bring to an organization.
- Chapter 2 is a hands-on tutorial for installing Istio in a Kubernetes cluster. You deploy and integrate your first application into the mesh and configure it with Istio's custom resources. Using the demo application, this chapter provides an overview of what you get out of the box with Istio and covers traffic management, observability, and security.
- Chapter 3 is all about Envoy: how it came to be, what problems it solves, and how it fits within the service mesh architecture.

Part 2 is a deep dive into Istio. The focus switches to practical examples, and we answer key operational questions: how to secure traffic coming into your cluster, make services more resilient, and make your system observable using the telemetry generated by the service proxies. This part contains six chapters:

- Chapter 4 teaches you how to use and configure the Istio *ingress gateway* to route traffic securely from the public network to your services (what we call north-south traffic).
- Chapter 5 proceeds after traffic is admitted into the cluster. It shows how `VirtualServices` and `DestinationRules` are used to route traffic in a fine-grained manner, enabling complex deployment patterns to reduce risk when you release new software.
- Chapter 6 explores how Istio benefits application teams. We discuss making services robust by implementing retries, circuit-breaking, load balancing across regions, and locality-aware load balancing right in the service mesh.
- Chapter 7 teaches you how Istio makes services observable by generating metrics, traces, and logs. Here we dive deeper into the metrics generated by service proxies, what information the metrics record, and how the recorded information can be customized.
- Chapter 8 shows you how to use telemetry visualization tools to make sense of the collected data. You use Prometheus to collect metrics and Grafana to visualize them. You use Jaeger to stitch together the traces of a request traveling through your services. And we show how Kiali intertwines this information to make troubleshooting services in the mesh a breeze.

- Chapter 9 elaborates on how Istio secures service-to-service traffic, how services receive their identity, and how the identity is used to implement access control and reduce the potential attack scope.

Part 3 is all about day-2 operations. It shows you how to troubleshoot issues in the data plane and maintain the control plane's stability and performance. By the end of this part, you will have a firm understanding of Istio's internals, and you will be able to discover and fix issues on your own:

- Chapter 10 shows you how to troubleshoot issues in the data plane using tools such as Istioctl, Kiali, and telemetry that is collected and visualized.
- Chapter 11 discusses Istio's performance factors. It shows how Istio can be configured to make the control plane more performant—the foundation of a robust service mesh.

The fourth and final part of the book shows you how to make Istio yours. Enterprises have services running across boundaries, such as different clusters, different networks, or a mixture of cloud-native and legacy workloads. By the end of part 4, you will know how to join your workloads into a single mesh and customize the mesh's behavior using WebAssembly to meet your unique requirements:

- Chapter 12 shows you how to connect workloads in different Kubernetes clusters wherever they are running, such as different cloud providers, on premises, or in a hybrid cloud.
- Chapter 13 shows how to integrate legacy workloads running in virtual machines into the mesh and extend to those workloads the mesh's capabilities of resiliency and high availability.
- Chapter 14 teaches you how to extend and customize Istio's capabilities with existing Envoy functionality or your code using Lua scripting and WebAssembly.

About the code

This book contains many examples of source code in numbered listings and in line with normal text. In both cases, source code is formatted in a `fixed-width font like this` to separate it from ordinary text. Sometimes code is also **in bold** to highlight code that has changed from previous steps in the chapter, such as when a new feature adds to an existing line of code.

In many cases, the original source code has been reformatted; we've added line breaks and reworked indentation to accommodate the available page space in the book. In rare cases, even this was not enough, and listings include line-continuation markers (➥). Additionally, comments in the source code have often been removed from the listings when the code is described in the text. Code annotations accompany many of the listings, highlighting important concepts.

You can get executable snippets of code from the liveBook (online) version of this book at https://livebook.manning.com/book/istio-in-action. The complete code for the examples in the book is available for download from the Manning website at www.manning.com, and from GitHub at https://github.com/istioinaction/book -source-code.

liveBook discussion forum

Purchase of *Istio in Action* includes free access to liveBook, Manning's online reading platform. Using liveBook's exclusive discussion features, you can attach comments to the book globally or to specific sections or paragraphs. It's a snap to make notes for yourself, ask and answer technical questions, and receive help from the authors and other users. To access the forum, go to https://livebook.manning.com/book/istio-in -action/discussion. You can also learn more about Manning's forums and the rules of conduct at https://livebook.manning.com/discussion.

Manning's commitment to our readers is to provide a venue where a meaningful dialogue between individual readers and between readers and the authors can take place. It is not a commitment to any specific amount of participation on the part of the authors, whose contribution to the forum remains voluntary (and unpaid). We suggest you try asking the authors some challenging questions lest their interests stray! The forum and the archives of previous discussions will be accessible from the pub- lisher's website as long as the book is in print.

about the authors

CHRISTIAN POSTA (@christianposta) is VP, Global Field CTO at Solo.io. He is well known in the cloud-native community for being an author, blogger (https://blog.christianposta.com), speaker, and contributor to various open-source projects in the service mesh and cloud-native ecosystem. Christian has spent time at enterprises and web-scale companies and now helps organizations create and deploy large-scale, cloud-native, resilient, distributed architectures. He enjoys mentoring, training, and leading teams to be successful with distributed systems concepts, microservices, DevOps, and cloud-native application design.

RINOR MALOKU (@rinormaloku) is an engineer at Solo.io, where he consults clients adopting application networking solutions, such as service meshes. Previously, he worked at Red Hat, where he built middleware software that enabled teams to ensure the high availability of their services. As a freelancer, he consulted multiple DAX 30 members in their endeavor to fully utilize the potential of cloud computing technologies.

about the cover illustration

The figure on the cover of *Istio in Action* is "Femme Islandoise," or "Icelandic woman," taken from a collection by Jacques Grasset de Saint-Sauveur, published in 1797. Each illustration is finely drawn and colored by hand.

In those days, it was easy to identify where people lived and what their trade or station in life was just by their dress. Manning celebrates the inventiveness and initiative of the computer business with book covers based on the rich diversity of regional culture centuries ago, brought back to life by pictures from collections such as this one.

Part 1

Understanding Istio

What programming language do you use to implement your microservices or applications? Java? NodeJS? Golang? Whichever language or framework you use will eventually have to communicate with services over the network. The network is a perilous place for applications. What do you do for service discovery? timeouts? retries? circuit-breaking? security?

Istio is an open source service mesh that helps solve service-to-service connectivity challenges in your cloud and microservices environment regardless of what language or framework you use. In chapters 1-3, we explain why a service mesh is critical infrastructure for a microservices and cloud-native application architecture, how Istio helps, and what you can expect from the rest of the book. Istio is built on an open source proxy named Envoy, which we cover in detail to set the foundations for the rest of the Istio functionality covered in future chapters.

Introducing
the Istio service mesh

1

This chapter covers

- Addressing the challenges of service-oriented architectures with service meshes
- Introducing Istio and how it helps solve microservice issues
- Comparing service meshes to earlier technologies

Software is the lifeblood of today's companies. As we move to a more digital world, consumers will expect convenience, service, and quality when interacting with businesses, and software will be used to deliver these experiences. Customers don't conform nicely to structure, processes, or predefined boxes. Customers' demands and needs are fluid, dynamic, and unpredictable, and our companies and software systems will need to have these same characteristics. For some companies (such as startups), building software systems that are agile and able to respond to unpredictability will be the difference between surviving or failing. For others (such as existing companies), the inability to use software as a differentiator will mean slower growth, decay, and eventual collapse.

As we explore how to go faster and take advantage of newer technology like cloud platforms and containers, we'll encounter an amplification of some past problems. For example, the network is not reliable and when we start to build larger, more distributed systems, the network must become a central design consideration in our applications. Should applications implement network resilience like retries, timeouts, and circuit breakers? What about consistent network observability? Application-layer security?

Resilience, security, and metrics collection are cross-cutting concerns and not application-specific. Moreover, they are not processes that differentiate your business. Developers are critical resources in large IT systems, and their time is best spent writing capabilities that deliver business value in a differentiating way. Application networking, security, and metrics collection are necessary practices, but they aren't differentiating. What we'd like is a way to implement these capabilities in a language- and framework-agnostic way and apply them as policy.

Service mesh is a relatively recent term used to describe a decentralized application-networking infrastructure that allows applications to be secure, resilient, observable, and controllable. It describes an architecture made up of a data plane that uses application-layer proxies to manage networking traffic on behalf of an application and a control plane to manage proxies. This architecture lets us build important application-networking capabilities outside of the application without relying on a particular programming language or framework.

Istio is an open source implementation of a service mesh. It was created initially by folks at Lyft, Google, and IBM, but now it has a vibrant, open, diverse community that includes individuals from Lyft, Red Hat, VMWare, Solo.io, Aspen Mesh, Salesforce, and many others. Istio allows us to build reliable, secure, cloud-native systems and solve difficult problems like security, policy management, and observability in most cases with no application code changes. Istio's data plane is made up of service proxies, based on the Envoy proxy, that live alongside the applications. Those act as intermediaries between the applications and affect networking behavior according to the configuration sent by the control plane.

Istio is intended for microservices or service-oriented architecture (SOA)-style architectures, but it is not limited to those. The reality is, most organizations have a lot of investment in existing applications and platforms. They'll most likely build services architectures around their existing applications, and this is where Istio really shines. With Istio, we can implement these application-networking concerns without forcing changes in existing systems. Since the service proxies live outside of the application, any application for any architecture is a welcome first-class citizen in the service mesh. We'll explore more of this in a hybrid *brownfield* application landscape.

This book introduces you to Istio, helps you understand how all this is possible, and teaches you how to use Istio to build more resilient applications that you can monitor and operate in a cloud environment. Along the way, we explore Istio's design principles, explain why it's different from past attempts to solve these problems, and discuss when Istio is not the solution for your problem.

But we certainly don't want to start using new technology just because it's "new," "hip," or "cool." As technologists, we find ourselves easily getting excited about technology; however, we'd be doing ourselves and our organizations a disservice by not fully understanding when and when not to use a technology. Let's spend a few moments understanding why you would use Istio, what problems it solves, what problems to avoid, and why this technology is exciting going forward.

1.1 Challenges of going faster

The technology teams at ACME Inc. have bought into microservices, automated testing, containers, and continuous integration and delivery (CI/CD). They decided to split out module A and B from ACMEmono, their core revenue-generation system, into their own standalone services. They also needed some new capabilities that they decided to build as service C, resulting in the services shown in figure 1.1.

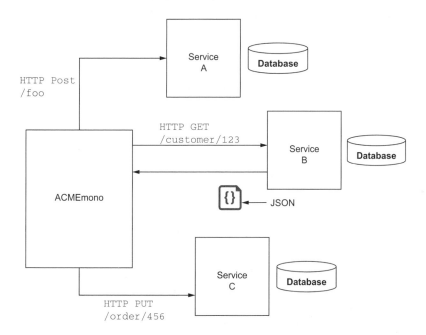

Figure 1.1 ACMEMono modernization with complementary services

They packaged their new services in containers and used a Kubernetes-based platform into which to deploy. As they began to implement these approaches, they quickly experienced some challenges.

The first thing ACME noticed was that sometimes services in the architecture were very inconsistent in how long they took to process requests. During peak customer usage, some services experienced intermittent issues and were unable to serve any traffic. Furthermore, ACME identified that if service B experienced trouble processing requests, service A also did, but only for certain requests.

The second thing ACME noticed was that when they practiced automated deployments, at times they introduced bugs into the system that weren't caught by automated testing. They practiced a deployment approach called *blue-green* deployment, which means they brought up the new deployment (the *green* deployment) in its own cluster and then at some point cut over the traffic from the old cluster (the *blue* deployment) to the new cluster. They had hoped the blue-green approach would lower the risk of doing deployments, but instead they experienced more of a "big bang" release, which is what they wanted to avoid.

Finally, ACME found that the teams implementing services A and B were handling security completely differently. Team A favored secure connections with certificates and private keys, while team B created their own custom framework built on passing tokens and verifying signatures. The team operating service C decided they didn't need any additional security since these were "internal" services behind the company firewall.

These challenges are not unique to ACME, nor is the extent of the challenges limited to what they encountered. The following things must be addressed when moving to a services-oriented architecture:

- Keeping faults from jumping isolation boundaries
- Building applications/services capable of responding to changes in their environment
- Building systems capable of running in partially failed conditions
- Understanding what's happening to the overall system as it constantly changes and evolves
- Inability to control the runtime behaviors of the system
- Implementing strong security as the attack surface grows
- Lowering the risk of making changes to the system
- Enforcing policies about who or what can use system components, and when

As we dig into Istio, we'll explore these in more detail and explain how to deal with them. These are core challenges to building services-based architectures on any cloud infrastructure. In the past, non-cloud architectures did have to contend with some of these problems; but in today's cloud environments, they are highly amplified and can take down your entire system if not taken into account correctly. Let's look a little bit closer at the problems encountered with unreliable infrastructure.

1.1.1   *Our cloud infrastructure is not reliable*

Even though, as consumers of cloud infrastructure, we don't see the actual hardware, clouds are made up of millions of pieces of hardware and software. These components form the compute, storage, and networking virtualized infrastructure that we can provision via self-service APIs. Any of these components can, and do, fail. In the past, we did everything we could to make infrastructure highly available, and we built our applications on top of it with assumptions of availability and reliability. In the cloud, we have to build our apps assuming the infrastructure is ephemeral and will be unavailable at times. This ephemerality must be considered upfront in our architectures.

Let's take a very simple example. Let's say a Preference service is in charge of managing customer preferences and ends up making calls to a Customer service. In figure 1.2, the Preference service calls the Customer service to update some customer data and experiences severe slowdowns when it sends a message. What does it do? A slow downstream dependency can wreak havoc on the Preference service, including causing it to fail (thus initiating a cascading failure). This scenario can happen for any number of reasons, such as these:

- The Customer service is overloaded and running slowly.
- The Customer service has a bug.
- The network has firewalls that are slowing the traffic.
- The network is congested and is slowing traffic.
- The network experienced some failed hardware and is rerouting traffic.
- The network card on the Customer service hardware is experiencing failures.

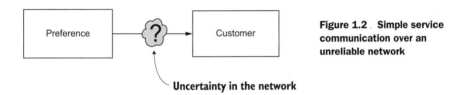

Figure 1.2 Simple service communication over an unreliable network

The problem is, the Preference service cannot distinguish whether this is a failure of the Customer service. Again, in a cloud environment with millions of hardware and software components, these types of scenarios happen all the time.

1.1.2 Making service interactions resilient

The Preference service can try a few things. It can retry the request, although in a scenario where things are overloaded, that might just add to the downstream issues. If it does retry the request, it cannot be sure that previous attempts didn't succeed. It can time out the request after some threshold and throw an error. It can also retry to a different instance of the Customer service, maybe in a different availability zone. If the Customer service experiences these or similar issues for an extended period of time, the Preference service may opt to stop calling the Customer service altogether for a *cool-off period* (a form of *circuit breaking*, which we'll cover in more depth in later chapters).

Some patterns have evolved to help mitigate these types of scenarios and help make applications more resilient to unplanned, unexpected failures:

- *Client-side load balancing*—Give the client the list of possible endpoints, and let it decide which one to call.
- *Service discovery*—A mechanism for finding the periodically updated list of healthy endpoints for a particular logical service.

- *Circuit breaking*—Shed load for a period of time to a service that appears to be misbehaving.
- *Bulkheading*—Limit client resource usage with explicit thresholds (connections, threads, sessions, and so on) when making calls to a service.
- *Timeouts*—Enforce time limitations on requests, sockets, liveness, and so on when making calls to a service.
- *Retries*—Retry a failed request.
- *Retry budgets*—Apply constraints to retries: that is, limit the number of retries in a given period (for example, only retry 50% of the calls in a 10-second window).
- *Deadlines*—Give requests context about how long a response may still be useful; if outside the deadline, disregard processing the request.

Collectively, these types of patterns can be thought of as *application networking*. They have a lot of overlap with similar constructs at lower layers of the networking stack, except that they operate at the layer of messages instead of packets.

1.1.3   Understanding what's happening in real time

A very important aspect of going faster is making sure we're going in the right direction. We try to get deployments out quickly, so we can test how customers react to them, but they will not have an opportunity to react (or will avoid our service) if it's slow or not available. As we make changes to our services, do we understand what impact (positive or negative) they will have? Do we know how things are running before we make changes?

It is critical to know things about our services architecture like which services are talking to each other, what typical service load looks like, how many failures we expect to see, what happens when services fail, service health, and so on. Each time we make a change by deploying new code or configuration, we introduce the possibility of negatively impacting our key metrics. When network and infrastructure unreliability rear their ugly heads, or if we deploy new code with bugs in it, can we be confident we have enough of a pulse on what's really happening to trust that the system isn't on verge of collapse? Observing the system with metrics, logs, and traces is a crucial part of running a services architecture.

1.2   Solving these challenges with application libraries

The first organizations to figure out how to run their applications and services in a cloud environment were the large internet companies, many of which pioneered cloud infrastructure as we know it today. These companies invested massive amounts of time and resources into building libraries and frameworks for a select set of languages that everyone had to use, which helped solve the challenges of running services in a cloud-native architecture. Google built frameworks like Stubby, Twitter built Finagle, and, in 2012, Netflix open sourced its microservices libraries to the open source community. For example, with NetflixOSS, libraries targeted for Java developers handle cloud-native concerns:

- *Hystrix*—Circuit breaking and bulkheading
- *Ribbon*—Client-side load balancing
- *Eureka*—Service registration and discovery
- *Zuul*—Dynamic edge proxy

Since these libraries were targeted for Java runtimes, they could only be used in Java projects. To use them, we'd have to create an application dependency on them, pull them into our classpath, and then use them in our application code. The following example of using NetflixOSS Hystrix pulls a dependency on Hystrix into your dependency control system:

```
<dependency>
    <groupId>com.netflix.hystrix</groupId>
    <artifactId>hystrix-core</artifactId>
    <version>x.y.z</version>
</dependency>
```

To use Hystrix, we wrap our commands with a base Hystrix class, `HystrixCommand`.

```
public class CommandHelloWorld extends HystrixCommand<String> {

    private final String name;

    public CommandHelloWorld(String name) {
        super(HystrixCommandGroupKey.Factory.asKey("ExampleGroup"));
        this.name = name;
    }

    @Override
    protected String run() {
        // a real example would do work like a network call here
        return "Hello " + name + "!";
    }
}
```

If each application is responsible for building resilience into its code, we can distribute the handling of these concerns and eliminate central bottlenecks. In large-scale deployments on unreliable cloud infrastructure, this is a desirable system trait.

1.2.1 Drawbacks to application-specific libraries

Although we've mitigated a concern about large-scale services architectures when we decentralize and distribute the implementation of application resiliency into the applications themselves, we've introduced some new challenges. The first challenge is around the expected assumptions of any application. If we wish to introduce a new service into our architecture, it will be constrained to implementation decisions made by other people and other teams. For example, to use NetflixOSS Hystrix, you must use Java or a JVM-based technology. Typically, circuit breaking and load balancing go together, so you'd need to use both of those resilience libraries. To use Netflix Ribbon for load balancing, you'd need some kind of registry to discover service endpoints, which might mean using Eureka. Going down this path of using libraries introduces implicit constraints around a very undefined protocol for interacting with the rest of the system.

The second issue is around introducing a new language or framework to implement a service. You may find that NodeJS is a better fit for implementing user-facing APIs but the rest of your architecture uses Java and NetflixOSS. You may opt to find a different set of libraries to implement resilience patterns. Or you may try to find analogous packages like `resilient` (www.npmjs.com/package/resilient) or `hystrixjs` (www.npmjs.com/package/hystrixjs). And you'll need to search for each language you wish to introduce (microservices enable a polyglot development environment, although standardizing on a handful of languages is usually best), certify it, and introduce it to your development stack. Each of these libraries will have a different implementation making different assumptions. In some cases you may not be able to find analogous replacements for each framework/language combination. You end up with a partial implementation for some languages and overall inconsistency in the implementation that is very difficult to reason about in failure scenarios and possibly contributes to obscuring/propagating failures. Figure 1.3 shows how services end up implementing the same set of libraries to manage application networking.

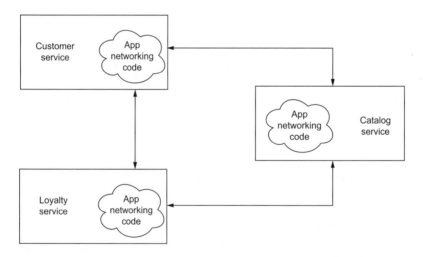

Figure 1.3 Application networking libraries commingled with an application

Finally, maintaining a handful of libraries across a bunch of programming languages and frameworks requires a lot of discipline and is very hard to get right. The key is ensuring that all of the implementations are consistent and correct. One deviation, and you've introduced more unpredictability into your system. Pushing out updates and changes across a fleet of services all at the same time can be a daunting task as well.

Although the decentralization of application networking is better for cloud architectures, the operational burden and constraints this approach puts on a system in exchange will be difficult for most organizations to swallow. Even if they take on that challenge, getting it right is even harder. What if there was a way to get the benefits of decentralization without paying the price of massive overhead in maintaining and operating these applications with embedded libraries?

1.3 *Pushing these concerns to the infrastructure*

These basic application-networking concerns are not specific to any particular application, language, or framework. Retries, timeouts, client-side load balancing, circuit breaking, and so on are also not differentiating application features. They are critical concerns to have as part of your service, but investing massive time and resources into language-specific implementations for each language you intend to use (including the other drawbacks from the previous section) is a waste of time. What we really want is a technology-agnostic way to implement these concerns and relieve applications from having to do so themselves.

1.3.1 *The application-aware service proxy*

Using a *proxy* is a way to move these horizontal concerns into the infrastructure. A proxy is an intermediate infrastructure component that can handle connections and redirect them to appropriate backends. We use proxies all the time (whether we know it or not) to handle network traffic, enforce security, and load balance work to backend servers. For example, HAProxy is a simple but powerful reverse proxy for distributing connections across many backend servers. mod_proxy is a module for the Apache HTTP server that also acts as a reverse proxy. In our corporate IT systems, all outgoing internet traffic is typically routed through forwarding proxies in a firewall. These proxies monitor traffic and block certain types of activities.

What we want for this problem, however, is a proxy that's *application aware* and able to perform application networking on behalf of our services (see figure 1.4). To do so, this *service proxy* will need to understand application constructs like messages and requests, unlike more traditional infrastructure proxies, which understand connections and packets. In other words, we need a layer 7 proxy.

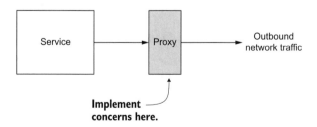

Figure 1.4 Using a proxy to push horizontal concerns such as resilience, traffic control, and security out of the application implementation

1.3.2   *Meet the Envoy proxy*

Envoy (http://envoyproxy.io) is a service proxy that has emerged in the open source community as a versatile, performant, and capable application-layer proxy. Envoy was developed at Lyft as part of the company's SOA infrastructure and is capable of implementing networking concerns like retries, timeouts, circuit breaking, client-side load balancing, service discovery, security, and metrics collection without any explicit language or framework dependencies. Envoy implements all of that out-of-process from the application, as shown in figure 1.5.

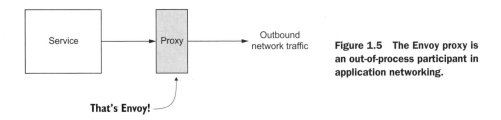

Figure 1.5   The Envoy proxy is an out-of-process participant in application networking.

The power of Envoy is not limited to these application-layer resilience aspects. Envoy also captures many application-networking metrics like requests per second, number of failures, circuit-breaking events, and more. By using Envoy, we can automatically get visibility into what's happening between our services, which is where we start to see a lot of unanticipated complexity. The Envoy proxy forms the foundation for solving cross-cutting, horizontal reliability and observability concerns for a services architecture and allows us to push these concerns outside of the applications and into the infrastructure. We'll cover more of Envoy in ensuing sections and chapters.

We can deploy service proxies alongside our applications to get these features (resilience and observability) out-of-process from the application, but at a fidelity that is very application specific. Figure 1.6 shows how in this model, applications that wish to communicate with the rest of the system do so by passing their requests to Envoy first, which then handles the communication upstream.

Service proxies can also do things like collect distributed tracing spans so we can stitch together all the steps taken by a particular request. We can see how long each step took and look for potential bottlenecks or bugs in our system. If all applications talk through their own proxy to the outside world, and all incoming traffic to an application goes through our proxy, we gain some important capabilities for our application without changing any application code. This proxy + application combination forms the foundation of a communication bus known as a *service mesh*.

We can deploy a service proxy like Envoy along with every instance of our application as a single atomic unit. For example, in Kubernetes, we can co-deploy a service proxy with our application in a single Pod. Figure 1.7 visualizes the *sidecar* deployment pattern in which the service proxy is deployed to complement the main application instance.

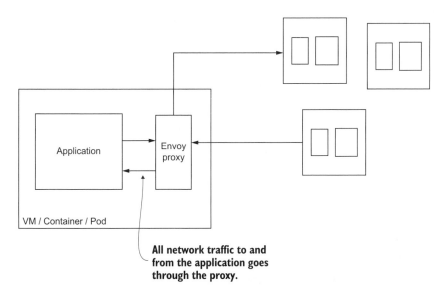

All network traffic to and from the application goes through the proxy.

Figure 1.6 The Envoy proxy out-of-process from the application

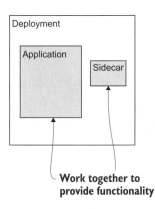

Figure 1.7   A sidecar deployment is an additional process that works cooperatively with the main application process to deliver a piece of functionality.

Work together to provide functionality

1.4   What's a service mesh?

Service proxies like Envoy help add important capabilities to our services architecture running in a cloud environment. Each application can have its own requirements or configurations for how a proxy should behave, given its workload goals. With an increasing number of applications and services, it can be difficult to configure and manage a large fleet of proxies. Moreover, having these proxies in place at each application instance opens opportunities for building interesting higher-order capabilities that we would otherwise have to do in the applications themselves.

A *service mesh* is a distributed application infrastructure that is responsible for handling network traffic on behalf of the application in a transparent, out-of-process manner. Figure 1.8 shows how service proxies form the *data plane* through which all traffic is handled and observed. The data plane is responsible for establishing, securing, and controlling the traffic through the mesh. The data plane behavior is configured by the *control plane*. The control plane is the brains of the mesh and exposes an API for operators to manipulate network behaviors. Together, the data plane and the control plane provide important capabilities necessary in any cloud-native architecture:

- Service resilience
- Observability signals
- Traffic control capabilities
- Security
- Policy enforcement

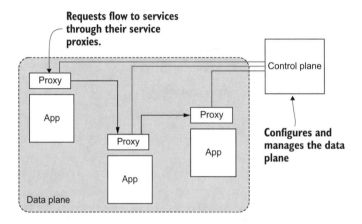

Figure 1.8   A service mesh architecture with co-located application-layer proxies (data plane) and management components (control plane)

The service mesh takes on the responsibility of making service communication resilient to failures by implementing capabilities like retries, timeouts, and circuit breakers. It's also capable of handling evolving infrastructure topologies by handling things like service discovery, adaptive and zone-aware load balancing, and health checking. Since all the traffic flows through the mesh, operators can control and direct traffic explicitly. For example, if we want to deploy a new version of our application, we may want to expose it to only a small fraction, say 1%, of live traffic. With the service mesh in place, we have the power to do that. Of course, the converse of control in the service mesh is understanding its current behavior. Since traffic flows through the mesh, we're able to capture detailed signals about the behavior of the network by tracking metrics like request spikes, latency, throughput, failures, and so on. We can use this telemetry to paint a picture of what's happening in our system. Finally, since the service mesh controls both ends of the network communication between applications, it can enforce strong security like transport-layer encryption with mutual authentication: specifically, using the mutual Transport Layer Security (mTLS) protocol.

The service mesh provides all of these capabilities to service operators with very few or no application code changes, dependencies, or intrusions. Some capabilities require minor cooperation with the application code, but we can avoid large, complicated library dependencies. With a service mesh, it doesn't matter what application framework or programming language you've used to build your application; these capabilities are implemented consistently and correctly and allow service teams to move quickly, safely, and confidently when implementing and delivering changes to systems to test their hypotheses and deliver value.

1.5 *Introducing the Istio service mesh*

Istio is an open source implementation of a service mesh founded by Google, IBM, and Lyft. It helps you add resilience and observability to your services architecture in a transparent way. With Istio, applications don't have to know that they're part of the service mesh: whenever they interact with the outside world, Istio handles the networking on their behalf. It doesn't matter if you're using microservices, monoliths, or anything in between—Istio can bring many benefits. Istio's data plane uses the Envoy proxy and helps you configure your application to have an instance of the service proxy (Envoy) deployed alongside it. Istio's control plane is made up of a few components that provide APIs for end users/operators, configuration APIs for the proxies, security settings, policy declarations, and more. We'll cover these control-plane components in future sections of this book.

Istio was originally built to run on Kubernetes but was written from the perspective of being deployment-platform agnostic. This means you can use an Istio-based service mesh across deployment platforms like Kubernetes, OpenShift, and even traditional deployment environments like virtual machines (VMs). In later chapters, we'll take a look at how powerful this can be for hybrid deployments across combinations of clouds, including private data centers.

> **NOTE** *Istio* is Greek for "sail," which goes along nicely with the rest of the Kubernetes nautical words.

With a service proxy next to each application instance, applications no longer need language-specific resilience libraries for circuit breaking, timeouts, retries, service discovery, load balancing, and so on. Moreover, the service proxy also handles metrics collection, distributed tracing, and access control.

Since traffic in the service mesh flows through the Istio service proxy, Istio has control points at each application to influence and direct its networking behavior. This allows a service operator to control traffic flow and implement fine-grained releases with canary releases, dark launches, graduated roll outs, and A/B style testing. We'll explore these capabilities in later chapters.

Figure 1.9 shows the following:

1 Traffic comes into the cluster from a client outside the mesh through the Istio ingress gateway.

2 Traffic goes to the Shopping Cart service. The traffic first passes through its service proxy. The service proxy can apply timeouts, metric collection, security enforcement, and so on, for the service.

3 As the request makes its way through various services, Istio's service proxy can intercept the request at various steps and make routing decisions (for example, to route some requests intended for the Tax service to v1.1 of the Tax service, which may have a fix for certain tax calculations).

4 Istio's control plane (istiod) is used to configure the Istio proxies, which handle routing, security, telemetry collection, and resilience.

5 Request metrics are periodically sent back to various collection services. Distributed tracing spans (like Jaeger or Zipkin) are sent back to a tracing store, which can be used later to track the path and latency of a request through the system.

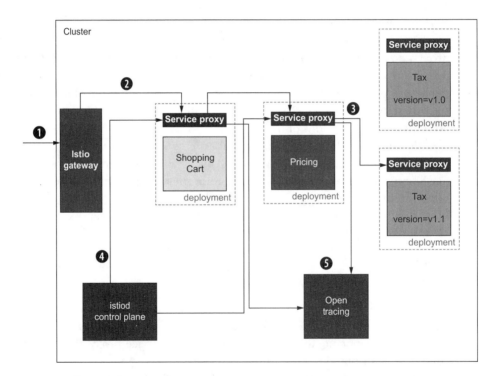

Figure 1.9 Istio is an implementation of a service mesh with a data plane based on Envoy and a control plane.

An important requirement for any services-based architecture is security. Istio has security enabled by default. Since Istio controls each end of the application's networking path, it can transparently encrypt the traffic by default. In fact, to take it a step further, Istio can manage key and certificate issuance, installation, and rotation so that services get mutual TLS out of the box. If you've ever experienced the pain of installing and configuring certificates for mutual TLS, you'll appreciate both the simplicity of operation and how powerful this capability is. Istio can assign a workload identity and embed that into the certificates. Istio can also use the identities of different workloads to further implement powerful access-control policies.

Finally, but no less important than the previous capabilities, with Istio you can implement quotas, rate limiting, and organizational policies. Using Istio's policy enforcement, you can create very fine-grained rules about what services are allowed to interact with each other, and which are not. This becomes especially important when deploying services across clouds (public and on premises).

Istio is a powerful implementation of a service mesh. Its capabilities allow you to simplify running and operating a cloud-native services architecture, potentially across a hybrid environment. Throughout the rest of this book, we'll show you how to take advantage of Istio's functionality to operate your microservices in a cloud-native world.

1.5.1 How a service mesh relates to an enterprise service bus

An enterprise service bus (ESB) from SOA days has some similarities to a service mesh, at least in spirit. If we take a look at how the ESB was originally described in the early days of SOA, we even see some similar language:

> *The enterprise service bus (ESB) is a silent partner in the SOA logical architecture. Its presence in the architecture is transparent to the services of your SOA application. However, the presence of an ESB is fundamental to simplifying the task of invoking services—making the use of services wherever they are needed, independent of the details of locating those services and transporting service requests across the network to invoke those services wherever they reside within your enterprise.* (http://mng.bz/5K7D)

In this description of an ESB, we see that it's supposed to be a *silent partner*, which means applications should not know about it. With a service mesh, we expect similar behavior. The service mesh should be transparent to the application. An ESB also is "fundamental to simplifying the task of invoking services." For an ESB, this included things like protocol mediation, message transformation, and content-based routing. A service mesh is not responsible for all the things an ESB does, but it does provide request resilience through retries, timeouts, and circuit breaking, and it does provide services like service discovery and load balancing.

Overall, there are a few significant differences between a service mesh and an ESB:

- The ESB introduced a new silo in organizations that was the gatekeeper for service integrations within the enterprise.
- It was a very centralized deployment/implementation.
- It mixed application networking and service mediation concerns.
- It was often based on complicated proprietary vendor software.

Figure 1.10 shows how ESB integrated applications by placing itself in the center and then comingled application business logic with application routing, transformation, and mediation.

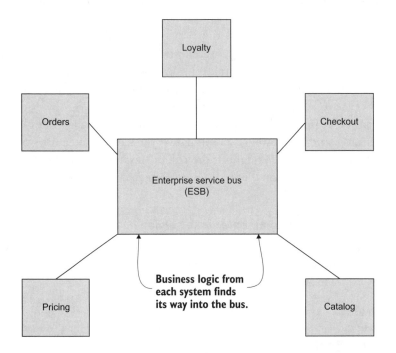

Figure 1.10   An ESB as a centralized system that integrates applications

A service mesh's role is only in application networking concerns. Complex business transformations (such as X12, EDI, and HL7), business process orchestration, process exceptions, service orchestration, and so on do not belong in a service mesh. Additionally, the service mesh data plane is highly distributed, with its proxies collocated with applications. This eliminates single points of failure or bottlenecks that often appear with an ESB architecture. Finally, both operator and service teams are responsible for establishing service-level objectives (SLOs) and configuring the service mesh to support them. The responsibility for integration with other systems is no longer the purview of a centralized team; all service developers share that duty.

1.5.2   *How a service mesh relates to an API gateway*

Istio and service-mesh technology also have some similarities to and differences from API gateways. API gateway infrastructure (not the microservices pattern from http://microservices.io/patterns/apigateway.html) is used in API management suites to provide a public-facing endpoint for an organization's public APIs. Its role is to provide security, rate limiting, quota management, and metrics collection for these public

APIs and tie into an overall API management solution that includes API plan specification, user registration, billing, and other operational concerns. API gateway architectures vary wildly but have been used mostly at the edge of architectures to expose public APIs. They have also been used for internal APIs to centralize security, policy, and metrics collection. However, this creates a centralized system through which traffic travels, which can become a source of bottlenecks, as described for the ESB and messaging bus.

Figure 1.11 shows how all internal traffic between services traverses the API gateway when used for internal APIs. This means for each service in the graph, we're taking two hops: one to get to the gateway and one to get to the actual service. This has implications not just for network overhead and latency but also for security. With this multi-hop architecture, the API gateway cannot secure the transport mechanism with the application unless the application participates in the security configuration. And in many cases, an API gateway doesn't implement resilience capabilities like circuit breakers or bulkheading.

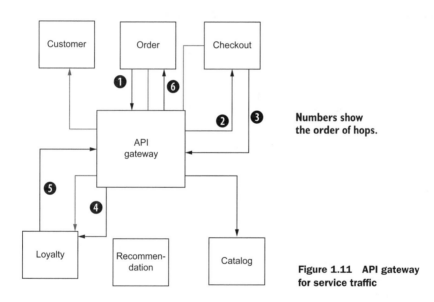

**Figure 1.11   API gateway
for service traffic**

In a service mesh, proxies are collocated with the services and do not take on additional hops. They're also decentralized so each application can configure its proxy for its particular workloads and not be affected by noisy neighbor scenarios.[1] Since each proxy lives with its corresponding application instance, it can secure the transport mechanism from end to end without the application knowing or actively participating.

---

[1] The term *noisy neighbor* describes the scenario where a service is degraded due to the activity of another service. Learn more at http://mng.bz/mxvM.

Figure 1.12 shows how the service proxies are becoming a place to enforce and implement API gateway functionality. As service mesh technologies like Istio continue to mature, we'll see API management built on top of the service mesh and not need specialized API gateway proxies.

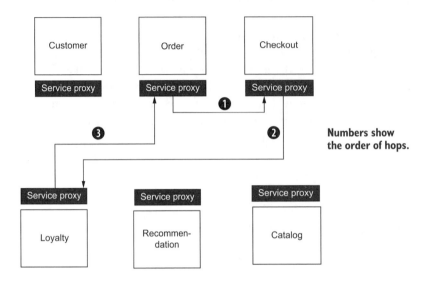

Figure 1.12 The service proxies implement ESB and API gateway functionalities.

1.5.3 *Can I use Istio for non-microservices deployments?*

Istio's power shines as you move to architectures that experience large numbers of services, interconnections, and networks over unreliable cloud infrastructure, potentially spanning clusters, clouds, and data centers. Furthermore, since Istio runs out-of-process from the application, it can be deployed to existing legacy or brownfield environments as well, thus incorporating those into the mesh.

For example, if you have existing monolith deployments, the Istio service proxy can be deployed alongside each monolith instance and will transparently handle network traffic for it. At a minimum, this can add request metrics that become very useful for understanding the application's usage, latency, throughput, and failure characteristics. Istio can also participate in higher-level features like policy enforcement about what services are allowed to talk to it. This capability becomes highly important in a hybrid-cloud deployment with monoliths running on premises and cloud services potentially running in a public cloud. With Istio, we can enforce policies such as "cloud services cannot talk to and use data from on-premises applications."

You may also have an older vintage of microservices implemented with resilience libraries like NetflixOSS. Istio brings powerful capabilities to these deployments as well. Even if both Istio and the application implement functionality like a circuit breaker, you can feel secure, knowing that the more restrictive policies will kick in and everything should work fine. Scenarios with timeouts and retries may conflict, but using Istio, you can test your service and find these conflicts before you ever make it to production.

1.5.4 *Where Istio fits in distributed architectures*

You should pick the technology you use in your implementations based on the problems you have and the capabilities you need. Technologies like Istio, and service meshes in general, are powerful infrastructure capabilities and touch a lot of areas of a distributed architecture—but they are not right for and should not be considered for every problem you may have. Figure 1.13 shows how an ideal cloud architecture would separate different concerns from each layer in the implementation.

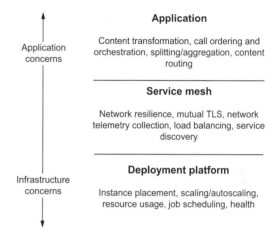

At the lower level of your architecture is your deployment automation infrastructure. This is responsible for getting code deployed onto your

Figure 1.13 An overview of separation of concerns in cloud-native applications. Istio plays a supporting role to the application layer and sits above the lower-level deployment layer.

platform (containers, Kubernetes, public cloud, VMs, and so on). Istio does not encroach on or prescribe what deployment automation tools you should use.

At a higher level, you have application business logic: the differentiating code that a business must write to stay competitive. This code includes the business domain as well as knowing which services to call and in what order, what to do with service interaction responses (such as how to aggregate them together), and what to do when there are process failures. Istio does not implement or replace any business logic. It does not do service orchestration, business payload transformation, payload enrichment, splitting/aggregating, or rules computation. These capabilities are best left to libraries and frameworks inside your applications.

Istio plays the role of connective tissue between the deployment platform and the application code. Its role is to facilitate taking complicated networking code out of the application. It can do content-based routing based on external metadata that is part of the request (HTTP headers, and so on). It can do fine-grained traffic control and routing based on service and request metadata matching. It can also secure the transport and offload security token verification and enforce quota and usage policies defined by service operators.

Now that we have a basic understanding of what Istio is, the best way to get further acquainted with its power is to use it. In chapter 2, we'll look at using Istio to achieve basic metrics collection, reliability, and traffic control.

1.5.5   *What are the drawbacks to using a service mesh?*

We've talked a lot about the problems of building a distributed architecture and how a service mesh can help, but we don't want to give the impression that a service mesh is the one and only way to solve these problems or that a service mesh doesn't have drawbacks. Using a service mesh does have a few drawbacks you must be aware of.

First, using a service mesh puts another piece of middleware, specifically a proxy, in the request path. This proxy can deliver a lot of value; but for those unfamiliar with the proxy, it can end up being a black box and make it harder to debug an application's behavior. The Envoy proxy is specifically built to be very debuggable by exposing a lot about what's happening on the network—more so than if it wasn't there—but for someone unfamiliar with operating Envoy, it could look very complex and inhibit existing debugging practices.

Another drawback of using a service mesh is in terms of tenancy. A mesh is as valuable as the services running in the mesh. That is, the more services in the mesh, the more valuable the mesh becomes for operating those services. However, without proper policy, automation, and forethought going into the tenancy and isolation models of the physical mesh deployment, you could end up in a situation where misconfiguring the mesh impacts many services.

Finally, a service mesh becomes a fundamentally important piece of your services and application architecture since it's on the request path. A service mesh can expose a lot of opportunities to improve security, observability, and routing control posture. The downside is that a mesh introduces another layer and another opportunity for complexity. It can be difficult to understand how to configure, operate, and, most importantly, integrate it within your existing organizational processes and governance and between existing teams.

In general, a service mesh brings a lot of value—but not without trade-offs. Just as with any tool or platform, you should evaluate these trade-offs based on your context and constraints, determine whether a service mesh makes sense for your scenarios, and, if so, make a plan to successfully adopt a mesh.

Overall, we love service meshes; and now that Istio is mature, it is already improving the operations of many businesses. With the continuous stream of contributions to both Istio and Envoy, it is exciting to see where it's going next. Hopefully, this chapter has passed some of the excitement on to you and given you ideas about how Istio can improve the security and reliability of your services.

Summary

- Operating microservices in the cloud involves many challenges: network unreliability, service availability, traffic flow that is hard to understand, traffic encryption, application health, and performance, to name a few.

- Those difficulties are alleviated by patterns (such as service discovery, client-side load balancing, and retries) that are implemented using libraries within every application.
- Additional libraries and services are required to create and distribute metrics and traces to gain observability over the services.
- A service mesh is an infrastructure that implements those cross-cutting concerns on behalf of applications in a transparent, out-of-process manner.
- Istio is an implementation of a service mesh composed of the following:
  - The data plane, which is composed of service proxies that are deployed alongside applications and complement them by implementing policies, managing traffic, generating metrics and traces, and much more.
  - The control plane, which exposes an API for operators to manipulate the data plane's network behavior.
- Istio uses Envoy as its service proxy due to its versatility and because it can be dynamically configured.

First steps with Istio

This chapter covers

- Installing Istio on Kubernetes
- Understanding the Istio control-plane components
- Deploying an application with the Istio proxy
- Controlling traffic with the Istio `VirtualService` resource
- Exploring complementary components for tracing, metrics, and visualization

Istio solves some of the difficult challenges of service communication in cloud environments and provides a lot of capabilities to both developers and operators. We'll cover these capabilities and how it all works in subsequent chapters; but to help you get a feel for some of the features of Istio, in this chapter we do a basic installation (more advanced installation options can be found in appendix A) and deploy a few services. The services and examples come from the book's source code, which you can find at https://github.com/istioinaction/book-source-code. From there, we explore the components that make up Istio and what functionality we can provide to our example services. Finally, we look at how to do basic traffic routing, metrics collection, and resilience. Further chapters will dive deeper into the functionality.

2.1 *Deploying Istio on Kubernetes*

We're going to deploy Istio and our example applications using containers, and we'll use the Kubernetes container platform to do that. Kubernetes is a very powerful container platform capable of scheduling and orchestrating containers over a fleet of host machines known as Kubernetes *nodes*. These nodes are host machines capable of running containers, but Kubernetes handles those mechanisms. As we'll see, Kubernetes is a great place to initially kick the tires with Istio—although we should be clear that Istio is intended to support multiple types of workloads, including those running on virtual machines (VMs).

2.1.1 *Using Docker Desktop for the examples*

To get started, we need access to a Kubernetes distribution. For this book, we use Docker Desktop (www.docker.com/products/docker-desktop), which provides a slim VM on your host computer that's capable of running Docker and Kubernetes.

> **Allocating the recommended resources to Docker Desktop**
>
> Although Istio won't require many resources on your local machine for Docker Desktop, we install many other supporting components in some chapters. It may be worth giving Docker 8 GB of memory and four CPUs. You can do that under the advanced settings in Docker Desktop's preferences.

Docker Desktop also has nice integration between the host machine and the VM. You're not constrained to using Docker Desktop to run these examples and follow along in this book: these examples should run well on any variant of Kubernetes, including Google Kubernetes Engine (GKE), OpenShift, or your own self-bootstrapped Kubernetes distribution. To set up Kubernetes, see the Docker Desktop documentation (www.docker.com/products/docker-desktop) for your machine. After successfully setting up Docker Desktop and enabling Kubernetes, you should be able to connect to your Kubernetes clusters as shown next:

```
$  kubectl get nodes
NAME              STATUS    ROLES     AGE    VERSION
docker-desktop    Ready     master    15h    v1.21.1
```

> **NOTE** Istio 1.13.0, used in this book, requires a minimum of Kubernetes version 1.19.x.

2.1.2 *Getting the Istio distribution*

Next, we want to install Istio into our Kubernetes distribution. We use the `istioctl` command-line tool to install Istio. To do that, download the Istio 1.13.0 distribution from the Istio release page at https://github.com/istio/istio/releases and download the distribution for your operating system. You can choose Windows, macOS/Darwin, or Linux. Alternatively, you can run this handy script:

```
curl -L https://istio.io/downloadIstio | ISTIO_VERSION=1.13.0 sh -
```

After downloading the distribution for your operating system, extract the compressed file to a directory. If you use the `downloadIstio` script, the archive is extracted automatically. From there, you can explore the contents of the distribution, including examples, installation resources, and a binary command-line interface for your OS. This example explores the Istio distribution for macOS:

```
$  cd istio-1.13.0
$  ls -l
total 48
-rw-r--r--    1 ceposta   staff   11348 Mar 19 15:33 LICENSE
-rw-r--r--    1 ceposta   staff    5866 Mar 19 15:33 README.md
drwxr-x---    3 ceposta   staff      96 Mar 19 15:33 bin
-rw-r-----    1 ceposta   staff     853 Mar 19 15:33 manifest.yaml
drwxr-xr-x    5 ceposta   staff     160 Mar 19 15:33 manifests
drwxr-xr-x   20 ceposta   staff     640 Mar 19 15:33 samples
drwxr-x---    6 ceposta   staff     192 Mar 19 15:33 tools
```

Browse the distribution directories to get an idea of what comes with Istio. For example, in the samples directory, you'll see a handful of tutorials and applications to help you get your feet wet with Istio. Going through each of these will give you a good initial idea of what Istio can do and how to interact with its components. We take a deeper look in the next section. The tools directory contains a few tools for troubleshooting Istio deployments, as well as bash-completion for `istioctl`. And the manifests directory contains Helm charts and `istioctl` profiles for customizing the installation of Istio for your specific platform. You likely won't need to use these directly (as we'll see), but they're there for customization purposes.

Of particular interest is the bin directory, where you'll find a simple command-line interface (CLI) `istioctl` tool for interacting with Istio. This binary is similar to `kubectl` for interacting with the Kubernetes API, but it includes a handful of commands to enhance the user experience of using Istio. Run the `istioctl` binary to verify that everything works as expected:

```
$  ./bin/istioctl version
no running Istio pods in "istio-system"
1.13.0
```

At this point, you can add the `istioctl` CLI to your path, so it's available wherever you navigate on the command line. This is platform specific and up to you to figure out.

Finally, let's verify that any prerequisites have been met in our Kubernetes cluster (such as the version) and identify any issues we may have *before* we begin the installation. We can run the following command to do that:

```
$ istioctl x precheck

✓ No issues found when checking the cluster.
➥Istio is safe to install or upgrade!
  To get started, check out
  ➥https://istio.io/latest/docs/setup/getting-started/
```

At this point, we've downloaded the distribution files and verified that the `istioctl` CLI tools are a fit for our operating system and Kubernetes cluster. Next, let's do a basic installation of Istio to get hands-on with its concepts.

2.1.3 *Installing the Istio components into Kubernetes*

In the distribution you just downloaded and unpacked, the manifests directory contains a collection of charts and resource files for installing Istio into the platform of your choice. The official method for any real installation of Istio is to use `istioctl`, `istio-operator`, or Helm. Appendix A guides you through installing and customizing Istio using `istioctl` and `istio-operator`.

For this book, we use `istioctl` and various pre-curated profiles to take a step-by-step, incremental approach to adopting Istio. To perform the demo install, use the `istioctl` CLI tool as shown next:

```
$ istioctl install --set profile=demo -y

✓ Istio core installed
✓ Istiod installed
✓ Ingress gateways installed
✓ Egress gateways installed
✓ Installation complete
```

After running this command, you may have to wait a few moments for the Docker images to properly download and the deployments to succeed. Once things have settled in, you can run the `kubectl` command to list all of the Pods in the `istio-system` namespace. You may also see a notification that your cluster doesn't support third-party JSON Web Token (JWT) authentication. This is fine for local development, but not for production. If the error appears during the installation in a production cluster, follow the Istio documentation on how to configure third-party service account tokens (http://mng.bz/Vl7G), which is the default with most cloud providers and shouldn't be necessary.

The `istio-system` namespace is special in that the control plane is deployed into it and can act as a cluster-wide control plane for Istio. Let's see what components are installed into the `istio-system` namespace:

```
$ kubectl get pod -n istio-system
NAME                                        READY   STATUS    RESTARTS   AGE
istio-egressgateway-55d547456b-q2ldq        1/1     Running   0          92s
istio-ingressgateway-7654895f97-2pb62       1/1     Running   0          93s
istiod-5b9d44c58b-vvrpb                     1/1     Running   0          99s
```

What exactly did we install? In chapter 1, we introduced the concept of a service mesh and said that Istio is an open source implementation of a service mesh. We also said that a service mesh comprises data-plane (that is, service proxies) and control-plane components. After installing Istio into a cluster, you should see the control plane and the ingress and egress gateways. As soon as we install applications and inject the service proxies into them, we will have a data plane as well.

The astute reader may notice that for each component of the Istio control plane, there is only a single replica or instance. You may also be thinking, "This appears to be a single point of failure. What happens if these components fail or go down?" That's a great question and one we'll cover throughout the book. For now, know that the Istio control plane is intended to be deployed in a highly available architecture (with multiple replicas of each component). In the event of failures of the control-plane components or even the entire control plane, the data plane is resilient enough to continue for periods of disconnection from the control plane. Istio is implemented to be highly resilient to the myriad of failures that can occur in a distributed system.

The last thing we want to do is verify the installation. We can run the `verify-install` command post-install to verify that it has completed successfully:

```
$ istioctl verify-install
```

This command compares the install manifest with what is actually installed and alerts us to any deviations. We should see a listing of the output ending with

```
✓ Istio is installed and verified successfully
```

Finally, we need to install the control-plane supporting components. These components are not strictly required but should be installed for any real deployment of Istio. The versions of the supporting components we install here are recommended for demo purposes only, not production usage. From the root of the Istio distribution you downloaded, run the following to install the example supporting components:

```
$ kubectl apply -f ./samples/addons
```

Now, if we check the `istio-system` namespace, we see the supporting components installed:

```
$ kubectl get pod -n istio-system

NAME                                        READY   STATUS
grafana-784c89f4cf-8w8f4                     1/1     Running      ◁──  Visualizes metrics
                                                                      generated by the
                                                                      proxies and collected
                                                                      by Prometheus
istio-egressgateway-96cf6b468-9n65h          1/1     Running
istio-ingressgateway-57b94d999-48vmn         1/1     Running
istiod-58c5fdd87b-lr4jf                      1/1     Running           Distributed tracing system
                                                                      to visualize request flow
jaeger-7f78b6fb65-rvfr7                      1/1     Running      ◁──  through the mesh
```

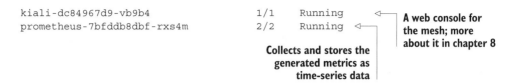

```
kiali-dc84967d9-vb9b4              1/1     Running
prometheus-7bfddb8dbf-rxs4m        2/2     Running
```

> A web console for the mesh; more about it in chapter 8

> Collects and stores the generated metrics as time-series data

2.2 Getting to know the Istio control plane

In the previous section, we did a demo installation of Istio that deployed all of the control-plane components and supporting components to Kubernetes. The control plane provides a way for users of the service mesh to control, observe, manage, and configure the mesh. For Istio, the control plane provides the following functions:

- APIs for operators to specify desired routing/resilience behavior
- APIs for the data plane to consume their configuration
- A service discovery abstraction for the data plane
- APIs for specifying usage policies
- Certificate issuance and rotation
- Workload identity assignment
- Unified telemetry collection
- Service-proxy sidecar injection
- Specification of network boundaries and how to access them

The bulk of these responsibilities is implemented in a single control-plane component called `istiod`. Figure 2.1 shows `istiod` along with gateways responsible for ingress traffic and egress traffic. We also see supporting components that are typically integrated with a service mesh to support observability or security use cases. We'll take a closer look at all of these components in the forthcoming chapters. Now, let's examine the control-plane components.

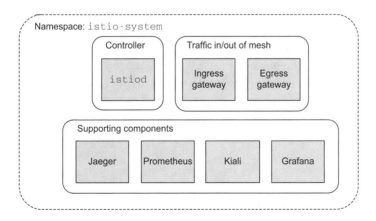

Figure 2.1   Istio control plane and supporting components

2.2.1   *Istiod*

Istio's control-plane responsibilities are implemented in the `istiod` component. `istiod`, sometimes referred to as Istio Pilot, is responsible for taking higher-level Istio configurations specified by the user/operator and turning them into proxy-specific configurations for each data-plane service proxy (see figure 2.2).

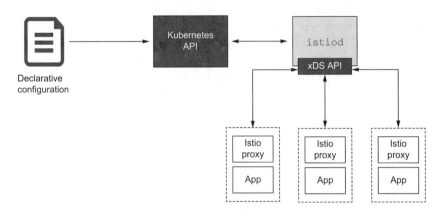

Figure 2.2   Istio control plane: understanding how `istiod` takes configuration from operators and exposes it to the data plane (Istio proxies)

> **NOTE**   We will learn more about the xDS API in chapter 3. For now, it suffices to know that it enables the control plane to dynamically configure the service proxies.

For example, through configuration resources, we can specify how traffic is allowed into the cluster, how it is routed to specific versions of services, how to shift traffic when doing a new deployment, and how callers of a service should treat resiliency aspects like timeouts, retries, and circuit breaking. `istiod` takes these configurations, interprets them, and exposes them as service-proxy-specific configurations. Istio uses Envoy as its service proxy, so these configurations are translated to Envoy configurations. For example, for a service trying to talk to a `catalog` service, we may wish to send traffic to v2 of the service if it has the header `x-dark-launch` in its request. We can express that for Istio with the following configuration:

```
apiVersion: networking.istio.io/v1alpha3
kind: VirtualService
metadata:
  name: catalog-service
spec:
  hosts:
  - catalog.prod.svc.cluster.local
  http:                              ⟵————————  Request
  - match:                                       matching
```

```
    - headers:
        x-dark-launch:              Exact match
          exact: "v2"        ◁──┘  of header
    route:
    - destination:           ◁─────────────────┐  Where to route
        host: catalog.prod.svc.cluster.local   │  on match
        subset: v2              Where to route
  - route:                  ┌─ all other traffic
    - destination:       ◁──┘
        host: catalog.prod.svc.cluster.local
        subset: v1
```

For the moment, don't worry about the specifics, as this example is just to illustrate that this YAML configuration is translated to the data plane as a proxy-specific configuration. The configuration specifies that, based on header matching, we would like to route a request to the v2 deployment of the catalog service when there is a header x-dark-launch that equals v2; and that for all other requests, we will route to v1 of the catalog service. As an operator of Istio running on Kubernetes, we would create this configuration using a tool like kubectl. For example, if this configuration is stored in a file named catalog-service.yaml, we can create it as follows:

```
kubectl apply -f catalog-service.yaml
```

We'll dig deeper into what this configuration does later in the chapter. For now, just know that configuring Istio traffic routing rules will use a similar pattern: describe intent in Istio resource files (YAML) and pass it to the Kubernetes API.

Istio uses Kubernetes custom resources when deployed on Kubernetes

Istio's configuration resources are implemented as Kubernetes custom resource definitions (CRDs). CRDs are used to extend the native Kubernetes API to add new functionality to a Kubernetes cluster without having to modify any Kubernetes code. In the case of Istio, we can use Istio's custom resources (CRs) to add Istio functionality to a Kubernetes cluster and use native Kubernetes tools to apply, create, and delete the resources. Istio implements a controller that watches for these new CRs to be added and reacts to them accordingly.

Istio reads Istio-specific configuration objects, like VirtualService in the previous configuration, and translates them into Envoy's native configuration. istiod exposes this configuration intent to the service proxies as Envoy configuration through its data-plane API:

```
"domains": [
  "catalog.prod.svc.cluster.local"
],
"name": "catalog.prod.svc.cluster.local:80",
"routes": [
  {
```

```
  "match": {
    "headers": [
      {
        "name": "x-dark-launch",
        "value": "v2"
      }
    ],
    "prefix": "/"
  },
  "route": {
      "cluster":
      "outbound|80|v2|catalog.prod.svc.cluster.local",
      "use_websocket": false
  }
},
{
  "match": {
    "prefix": "/"
  },
  "route": {
    "cluster":
    "outbound|80|v1|catalog.prod.svc.cluster.local",
    "use_websocket": false
  }
}
}
]
```

This data-plane API exposed by istiod implements Envoy's *discovery APIs*. These discovery APIs, like those for service discovery (listener discovery service [LDS]), endpoints (endpoint discovery service [EDS]), and routing rules (route discovery service [RDS]) are known as the *xDS APIs*. These APIs allow the data plane to separate how it is configured and dynamically adapt its behavior without having to stop and reload. We'll cover these xDS APIs from the perspective of the Envoy proxy in chapter 3.

IDENTITY MANAGEMENT

With the Istio service mesh, service proxies run alongside each application instance, and all application traffic goes through these proxies. When an application wishes to issue a request to another service, the proxies on the sender and receiver talk to each other directly.

One of Istio's core features is the ability to assign an identity to each workload instance and encrypt the transport for calls between services since it sits at both ends (origination and termination) of the request path. To do this, Istio uses X.509 certificates to encrypt the traffic. Workload identity is embedded in these certificates following the SPIFFE (Secure Production Identity Framework For Everyone; https://spiffe.io) specification. This gives Istio the ability to provide strong mutual authentication (mTLS) without the applications being aware of certificates, public/private keys, and so on. istiod handles attestation, signing, and delivery of the certificates and rotation of the certificates used to enable this form of security (see figure 2.3). We'll cover security in chapter 9.

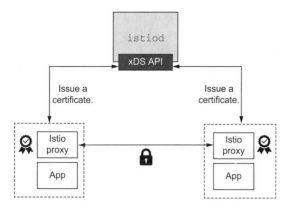

Figure 2.3 Istio control plane issues certificates to each workload.

2.2.2 *Ingress and egress gateway*

For our applications and services to provide anything meaningful, they need to inter-act with applications that live outside of our cluster. Those could be existing monolith applications, off-the-shelf software, messaging queues, databases, and third-party part-ner systems. To do this, operators need to configure Istio to allow traffic into the clus-ter and be very specific about what traffic is allowed to leave the cluster. Modeling and understanding what traffic is allowed into and out of the cluster is good practice and improves our security posture.

Figure 2.4 shows the Istio components that provide this functionality: `istio-ingressgateway` and `istio-egressgateway`. We saw those when we printed out the control plane components.

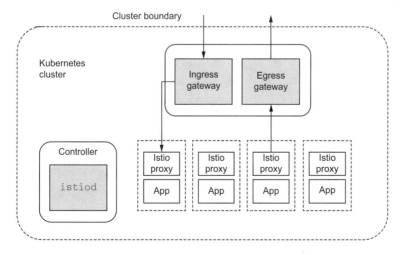

Figure 2.4 Incoming and outgoing traffic flow through Istio gateways

These components are really Envoy proxies that can understand Istio configurations. Although they are not technically part of the control plane, they are instrumental in any real-world usage of a service mesh. These components reside in the data plane and are configured very similarly to Istio service proxies that live with the applications. The only actual difference is that they're independent of any application workload and are just to let traffic into and out of the cluster. In future chapters, we'll see how these components play a role in combining clusters and even clouds.

2.3   Deploying your first application in the service mesh

The ACME company is redoing its website and the systems that power inventory and checkout. The company has decided to use Kubernetes as the core of its deployment platform and to build its applications to the Kubernetes API and not a specific cloud vendor. ACME is looking to solve some of the challenges of service communication in a cloud environment, so when its head architect found out about Istio, the company decided to use it. ACME's application is an online web store that consists of typical enterprise application services (see figure 2.5). We'll walk through the components that make up the store, but for this first look at Istio's functionality, we focus on a smaller subset of the components.

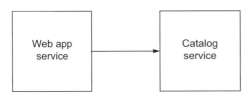

Figure 2.5   Example application consisting of web app and catalog services

To get the source code for this example, download it from http://istioinaction.io or clone it from https://github.com/istioinaction/book-source-code. In the services directory, you should see the Kubernetes resource files that describe the deployment of our components. The first thing to do is create a namespace in Kubernetes in which we'll deploy our services:

```
$ kubectl create namespace istioinaction
$ kubectl config set-context $(kubectl config current-context) \
  --namespace=istioinaction
```

Now that we're in the istioinaction namespace, let's take a look at what we're going to deploy. The Kubernetes resource files for catalog-service can be found in the $SRC_BASE/services/catalog/kubernetes/catalog.yaml file and looks similar to this:

```
apiVersion: v1
kind: Service
metadata:
  labels:
    app: catalog
  name: catalog
```

```
spec:
  ports:
  - name: http
    port: 80
    protocol: TCP
    targetPort: 3000
  selector:
    app: catalog
---
apiVersion: apps/v1
kind: Deployment
metadata:
  labels:
    app: catalog
    version: v1
  name: catalog
spec:
  replicas: 1
  selector:
    matchLabels:
      app: catalog
      version: v1
  template:
    metadata:
      labels:
        app: catalog
        version: v1
    spec:
      containers:
      - env:
        - name: KUBERNETES_NAMESPACE
          valueFrom:
            fieldRef:
              fieldPath: metadata.namespace
        image: istioinaction/catalog:latest
        imagePullPolicy: IfNotPresent
        name: catalog
        ports:
        - containerPort: 3000
          name: http
          protocol: TCP
        securityContext:
          privileged: false
```

Before we deploy this, however, we want to inject the Istio service proxy so that this service can participate in the service mesh. From the root of the source code, run the `istioctl` command we introduced earlier:

```
$ istioctl kube-inject -f services/catalog/kubernetes/catalog.yaml
```

The `istioctl kube-inject` command takes a Kubernetes resource file and enriches it with the sidecar deployment of the Istio service proxy and a few additional components (elaborated on in appendix B). Recall from chapter 1 that a *sidecar* deployment packages a complementing container alongside the main application container: they work together to deliver some functionality. In the case of Istio, the sidecar is the service proxy, and the main application container is your application code. If you look through the previous command's output, the YAML now includes a few extra containers as part of the deployment. Most notably, you should see the following:

```
- args:
  - proxy
  - sidecar
  - --domain
  - $(POD_NAMESPACE).svc.cluster.local
  - --serviceCluster
  - catalog.$(POD_NAMESPACE)
  - --proxyLogLevel=warning
  - --proxyComponentLogLevel=misc:error
  - --trust-domain=cluster.local
  - --concurrency
  - "2"
  env:
  - name: JWT_POLICY
    value: first-party-jwt
  - name: PILOT_CERT_PROVIDER
    value: istiod
  - name: CA_ADDR
    value: istiod.istio-system.svc:15012
  - name: POD_NAME
    valueFrom:
      fieldRef:
        fieldPath: metadata.name
...
  image: docker.io/istio/proxyv2:{1.13.0}
  imagePullPolicy: Always
  name: istio-proxy
```

In Kubernetes, the smallest unit of deployment is called a *Pod*. A Pod can be one or more containers deployed atomically together. When we run `kube-inject`, we add another container named `istio-proxy` to the Pod template in the `Deployment` object, although we haven't actually deployed anything yet. We could deploy the YAML file created by the `kube-inject` command directly; however, we are going to take advantage of Istio's ability to automatically inject the sidecar proxy.

To enable automatic injection, we label the `istioinaction` namespace with `istio-injection=enabled`:

```
$ kubectl label namespace istioinaction istio-injection=enabled
```

Now let's create the `catalog` deployment:

```
$ kubectl apply -f services/catalog/kubernetes/catalog.yaml
```

```
serviceaccount/catalog created
service/catalog created
deployment.apps/catalog created
```

If we ask Kubernetes what Pods are deployed, we see something like this:

```
$ kubectl get pod
NAME                      READY   STATUS    RESTARTS   AGE
catalog-7c96f7cc66-flm8g  2/2     Running   0          1m
```

If the Pods are not ready, it may take a few moments to download the Docker images. After things come to a steady state, you should see the Pod with `Running` in the `Status` column, as in the previous snippet. Also note the `2/2` in the `Ready` column: this means there are two containers in the Pod, and two of them are in the `Ready` state. One of those containers is the application container, `catalog` in this case. The other container is the `istio-proxy` sidecar.

At this point, we can query the `catalog` service *from within* the Kubernetes cluster with the hostname `catalog.istioinaction`. Run the following command to verify everything is up and running properly. If you see the following JSON output, the service is up and running correctly:

```
$ kubectl run -i -n default --rm --restart=Never dummy \
--image=curlimages/curl --command -- \
sh -c 'curl -s http://catalog.istioinaction/items/1'

{
  "id": 1,
  "color": "amber",
  "department": "Eyewear",
  "name": "Elinor Glasses",
  "price": "282.00"
}
```

Next we deploy the `webapp` service, which aggregates the data from the other services and displays it visually in the browser. This service also exposes an API that ends up calling the `catalog` service, which we just deployed and verified. This means `webapp` is like a facade of the other backend services:

```
$ kubectl apply -f services/webapp/kubernetes/webapp.yaml

serviceaccount/webapp created
service/webapp created
deployment.apps/webapp created
```

If we list the Pods in our Kubernetes cluster, we see our new `webapp` deployment with 2/2 containers running:

```
$ kubectl get pod

NAME                       READY   STATUS    RESTARTS   AGE
catalog-759767f98b-mcqcm   2/2     Running   0          3m59s
webapp-8454b8bbf6-b8g7j    2/2     Running   0          50s
```

Finally, let's call the new `webapp` service and verify that it works:

```
$ kubectl run -i -n default --rm --restart=Never dummy \
--image=curlimages/curl --command -- \
sh -c 'curl -s http://webapp.istioinaction/api/catalog/items/1'
```

If this command completes correctly, you should see the same JSON response as when we called the `catalog` service directly. Additionally, we can visualize the content of all the services behind the `webapp` service by accessing it through the browser. To do so, port-forward the application to your localhost:

```
$  kubectl port-forward deploy/webapp 8080:8080
```

You can open the web application UI on your browser at http://localhost:8080, as shown in figure 2.6.

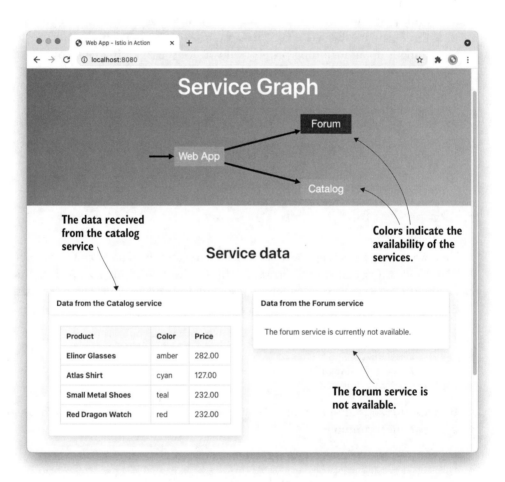

Figure 2.6   The web app user interface presents the data queried from the other services.

So far, all we've done is deploy the `catalog` and `webapp` services with the Istio service proxies. Each service has its own sidecar proxy, and all traffic to or from the individual services goes through the respective sidecar proxy (see figure 2.7).

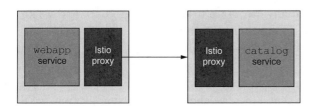

Figure 2.7   The `webapp` **service calling the** `catalog` **service both with** `istio-proxy` **injected**

2.4 *Exploring the power of Istio with resilience, observability, and traffic control*

In the previous example, we had to port-forward the `webapp` service locally because, so far, we have no way of getting traffic into the cluster. With Kubernetes, we typically use an ingress controller like Nginx or a dedicated API gateway like Solo.io's Gloo Edge to do that. With Istio, we can use an Istio ingress gateway to get traffic into the cluster, so we can call our web application. In chapter 4, we'll look at why the out-of-the-box Kubernetes ingress resource is not sufficient for typical enterprise workloads and how Istio has the concepts of `Gateway` and `VirtualService` resources to solve those challenges. For now, we'll use the Istio ingress gateway to expose our `webapp` service:

```
$  kubectl apply -f ch2/ingress-gateway.yaml
```

```
gateway.networking.istio.io/coolstore-gateway created
virtualservice.networking.istio.io/webapp-virtualservice created
```

At this point, we've made Istio aware of the `webapp` service at the edge of the Kubernetes cluster, and we can call into it. Let's see whether we can reach our service. First we need to get the endpoint on which the Istio gateway is listening. On Docker Desktop, it defaults to http://localhost:80:

```
$  curl http://localhost:80/api/catalog/items/1
```

If you're running on your own Kubernetes cluster—for example, on a public cloud— you can find the public cloud's external endpoint by listing the Kubernetes services in the `istio-system` namespace :

```
$  URL=$(kubectl -n istio-system get svc istio-ingressgateway \
-o jsonpath='{.status.loadBalancer.ingress[0].ip}')
```

```
$  curl $URL/api/catalog/items/1
```

If you cannot use a load balancer, an alternative approach is to port-forward to your local machine using `kubectl`, as follows (updating the URL to `localhost:8080`):

```
$  kubectl port-forward deploy/istio-ingressgateway \
-n istio-system 8080:8080
```

After hitting the endpoint with `curl` as we did here, you should see the same output as in the previous steps where we hit the services individually.

If you have encountered any errors up to this point, go back and make sure you successfully complete all of the steps. If you still encounter errors, ensure that the Istio ingress gateway has a route to our `webapp` service set up properly. To do that, you can use Istio's debugging tools to check the configuration of the ingress gateway proxy. You can use the same technique to check any Istio proxy deployed with any application, but we'll come back to that. For now, check whether your gateway has a route:

```
$ istioctl proxy-config routes \
  deploy/istio-ingressgateway.istio-system
```

You should see something similar to this:

```
NOTE: This output only contains routes loaded via RDS.
NAME        DOMAINS  MATCH              VIRTUAL SERVICE
http.80     *        /*                 webapp-virtualservice.istioinaction
            *        /healthz/ready*
            *        /stats/prometheus*
```

If you don't, your best bet is to double-check that the gateway and virtual service resources were installed:

```
$ kubectl get gateway
$ kubectl get virtualservice
```

Additionally, make sure they are applied in the `istioinaction` namespace: in the virtual service definition, we use the abbreviated hostname (`webapp`), which lacks the namespace and defaults to the namespace the virtual service is applied to. You can also add the namespace by updating the virtual service to route traffic to the host `webapp.istioinaction`.

2.4.1   *Istio observability*

Since the Istio service proxy sits in the call path on both sides of the connection (each service has its own service proxy), Istio can collect a lot of telemetry and insight into what's happening between applications. Istio's service proxy is deployed as a sidecar alongside each application, so the insight it collects is from "out of process" of the application. For the most part, this means applications do not need library- or framework-specific implementations to accomplish this level of observability. The application is a black box to the proxy, and telemetry is focused on the application's behavior as observed through the network.

Istio creates telemetry for two major categories of observability. The first is top-line metrics or things like requests per second, number of failures, and tail-latency percentiles. Knowing these values can provide great insight into where problems are starting to arise in a system. Second, Istio can facilitate distributed tracing like OpenTracing.io. Istio can send spans to distributed-tracing backends without applications having to worry about it. This way, we can dig into what happened during a particular service interaction, see where latency occurred, and get information about overall call latency. Let's explore these capabilities hands-on with our example application.

TOP-LEVEL METRICS

We'll first look at some Istio observability features we can get out of the box. In the previous section, we added two Kubernetes deployments and injected them with the Istio sidecar proxies. Then we added an Istio ingress gateway, so we could reach our service from outside the cluster. To get metrics, we will use Prometheus and Grafana.

Istio by default comes with some sample add-ons or supporting components that we installed earlier. As noted in the previous sections, these components from the Istio installation are intended for demo purposes only. For a production setup, you should install each supporting component following its respective documentation. Referring again to the diagram of the control plane (figure 2.8), we can see how these components fit in.

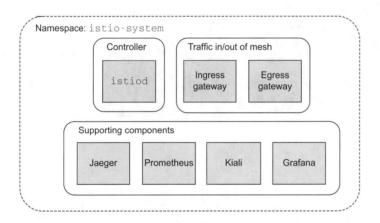

Figure 2.8   Istio control plane and supporting components

Let's use `istioctl` to port-forward Grafana to our local machine, so we can see the dashboards:

```
$  istioctl dashboard grafana
http://localhost:3000
```

This should automatically open your default browser; if it doesn't, open a browser and go to http://localhost:3000. You should arrive at the Grafana home screen, as shown in figure 2.9. In the upper-left corner, select the Home dashboard to expose a drop-down list of other dashboards we can switch to.

Istio has a set of out-of-the-box dashboards that give some basic details about the services running in Istio (see figure 2.10). With these dashboards, we can see the services we have installed and running in the mesh and some of the Istio control-plane components. In the list of dashboards, click Istio Service Dashboard. (If you don't see it in Recents, click to expand the Istio section under Recents.)

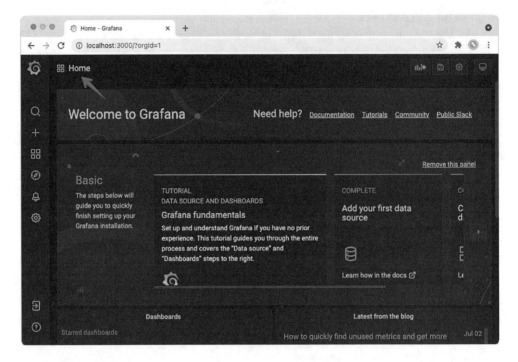

Figure 2.9   Grafana home screen

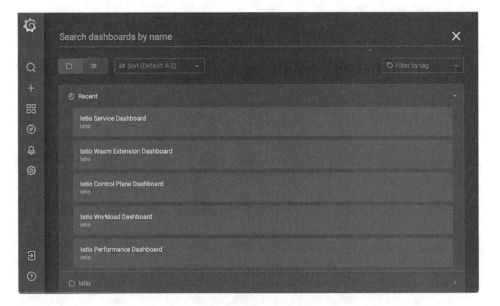

Figure 2.10   List of installed Grafana dashboards, including the Istio out-of-the-box dashboards

The dashboard should show some top-level metrics of the particular service selected. In the Service drop-down box toward the top of the dashboard, make sure the `webapp.istioinaction.svc.cluster.local` service is selected. It should look similar to figure 2.11.

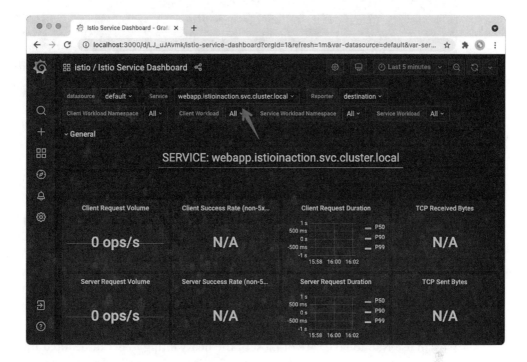

Figure 2.11   Dashboard for the `webapp` service

We see metrics like Client Request Volume and Client Success Rate, but the values are mostly empty or "N/A". In your command-line shell, let's send some traffic to the services and watch what happens:

```
$  while true; do curl http://localhost/api/catalog; sleep .5; done
```

Press Ctrl-C to exit this `while` loop. Now, if you look at the Grafana dashboard, you should see some interesting traffic, as shown in figure 2.12 (you may have to refresh the dashboard).

Our service received some traffic, we had a 100% success rate, and we experienced P50, P90, and P99 tail latencies. Scroll down the dashboard, and you can see other interesting metrics about what services and clients are calling the `webapp` service and what that behavior looks like.

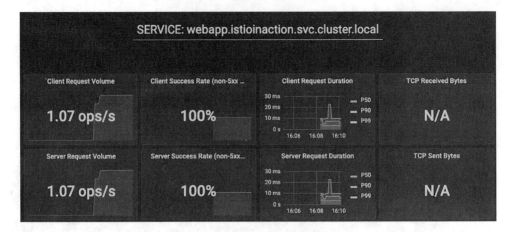

Figure 2.12   Top-level metrics for our web app as seen in Grafana

You will notice we have not added any instrumentation to our application code. Although we should always heavily instrument our applications, what we see here is what the application actually did over the network regardless of what the application *thinks* happened. From a black-box perspective, we can observe how the applications and their collaborators are behaving in the mesh—and all we did was add the Istio sidecar proxies. To get a more holistic view of individual calls through the cluster, we can look at things like distributed tracing to follow a single request as it hits multiple services.

DISTRIBUTED TRACING WITH OPEN TRACING

We can use Istio to take care of most of the heavy lifting to get distributed tracing out of the box. One of the add-ons that comes with Istio's installation is the Jaeger tracing dashboard, which we can open like this:

```
$  istioctl dashboard jaeger

http://localhost:16686
```

Now, let's use our web browser to navigate to http://localhost:16686, which should take us to the Jaeger web console (see figure 2.13). The service in the Service drop-down in the upper-left pane should be `istio-ingressgateway.istio-system`. If it isn't, click the drop-down and select `istio-ingressgateway.istio-system`. Then click Find Traces at the lower left in the side pane. You should see some distributed tracing entries. If you don't, re-run the traffic-generation client from your command line:

```
$  while true; do curl http://localhost/api/catalog; sleep .5; done
```

Press Ctrl-C to exit the `while` loop.

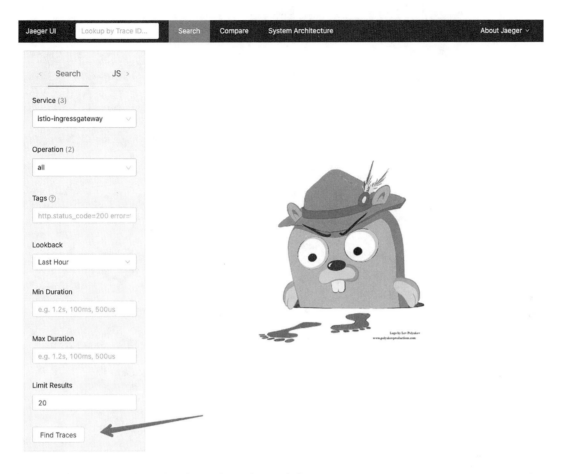

Figure 2.13 Jaeger distributed-tracing engine web console home page

You should see the most recent calls that came into the cluster and the distributed tracing spans they generated (see figure 2.14). Clicking one of the span entries displays the details of a particular call. Figure 2.15 shows that from `istio-ingressgate-way`, the call went to the `webapp` service and then the `catalog` service.

In subsequent chapters, we'll explore how all this works. For now, you should understand that the Istio service proxy propagated the tracing IDs and metadata between services and also sent tracing span information to a tracing engine (like Zipkin or Jaeger). However, we don't want to gloss over the fact that the application plays a small part in this overall capability.

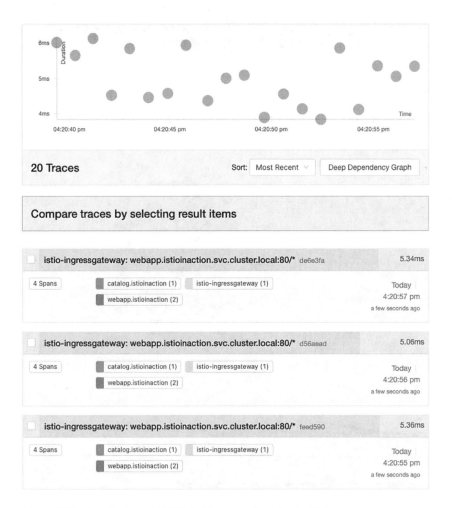

Figure 2.14   A collection of distributed traces gathered using Istio

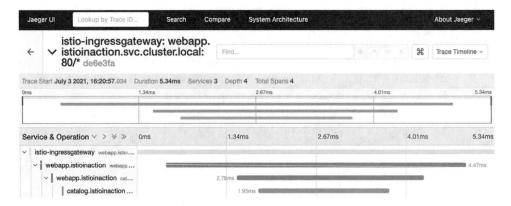

Figure 2.15   Detailed spans for a specific call

Although Istio can propagate the traces *between* services and to the tracing engine, the applications are responsible for propagating the tracing metadata *inside* themselves. The tracing metadata usually consists of a set of HTTP headers (for HTTP and HTTPS traffic), and it's up to the application to correlate the incoming headers with any outgoing requests. Said another way, Istio cannot know what happens inside a particular service or application, so it cannot know that a specific request that comes in should be associated with a specific outgoing request (causation). It relies on the application to know that and to properly inject the headers into any outgoing request. From there, Istio can capture those spans and send them to the tracing engine.

2.4.2 Istio for resiliency

As we've discussed, applications that communicate over the network to help complete their business logic must be aware of and account for the fallacies of distributed computing: they need to deal with network unpredictability. In the past, we tried to include a lot of this networking workaround code in our applications by doing things like retries, timeouts, circuit-breaking, and so on. Istio can save us from having to write this networking code directly into our applications and provide a consistent, default expectation of resilience for all the applications in the service mesh.

One such resiliency aspect is retrying requests amid intermittent/transient network errors. For example, if the network experiences failures, our application may see these errors and continue by just retrying the request. In our example architectures, we'll simulate this by driving the behavior from our `catalog` service.

If we make a call to our `webapp` service endpoint, as we did in the previous section, the call returns successfully. However, if we want all calls to fail, we can use a script that injects bad behavior into the application (see figure 2.16). Running the following command from the root of our source code causes all calls to fail with an HTTP 500 error response 100% of the time:

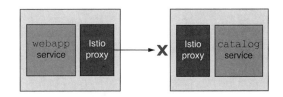

```
$  ./bin/chaos.sh 500 100
```

If you query the `catalog` items now, HTTP 500 is returned:

Figure 2.16 The `catalog` service can be provoked to fail by injecting bad behavior.

```
$  curl -v http://localhost/api/catalog

*   Trying 192.168.64.67...
* TCP_NODELAY set
* Connected to 192.168.64.67 (192.168.64.67) port 31380 (#0)
> GET /api/catalog HTTP/1.1
> Host: 192.168.64.67:31380
> User-Agent: curl/7.54.0
> Accept: */*
>
< HTTP/1.1 500 Internal Server Error
< content-type: text/plain; charset=utf-8
```

```
< x-content-type-options: nosniff
< date: Wed, 17 Apr 2019 00:13:16 GMT
< content-length: 30
< x-envoy-upstream-service-time: 4
< server: istio-envoy
<
error calling Catalog service
* Connection #0 to host 192.168.64.67 left intact
```

To demonstrate Istio's ability to automatically perform a retry for an application, let's configure the `catalog` service to generate errors 50% of the time when we call our webapp service endpoint:

```
$ ./bin/chaos.sh 500 50
```

Now we can test the service responses:

```
$ while true; do curl http://localhost/api/catalog ; \
sleep .5; done
```

Press Ctrl-C to exit this `while` loop.

The output from this command should be intermittent successes and failures from the `webapp` service. Actually, the failures are caused when `webapp` talks with `catalog` service (the `catalog` service is misbehaving). Let's see how we can use Istio to make the network more resilient between `webapp` and `catalog`.

Using an Istio `VirtualService`, we can specify rules about interacting with services in the mesh. The following is an example of the `catalogVirtualService` definition:

```
apiVersion: networking.istio.io/v1alpha3
kind: VirtualService
metadata:
  name: catalog
spec:
  hosts:
  - catalog
  http:
  - route:
    - destination:
        host: catalog
    retries:
      attempts: 3
      perTryTimeout: 2s
```

With this definition, we specify that requests to the `catalog` service are eligible for retry up to three times, with each try having a timeout of two seconds. If we put this rule into place, we can use Istio to automatically retry when we experience failures (as we did in the previous step). Let's create this rule and re-run our test client script:

```
$ kubectl apply -f ch2/catalog-virtualservice.yaml
```

```
virtualservice.networking.istio.io/catalog created
```

Now try running the client script again:

```
$ while true; do curl http://localhost/api/catalog ; \
sleep .5; done
```

Press Ctrl-C to exit this `while` loop.

You should see fewer exceptions bubbling up to the client. Using Istio, and without touching any application code, we can add a level of resilience when communicating over the network.

Let's disable the failures in the `catalog` service:

```
$ ./bin/chaos.sh 500 delete
```

This should stop any misbehaving responses from `catalog`.

2.4.3 *Istio for traffic routing*

The last Istio capability we'll look at in this chapter is the ability to have very fine-grained control over requests in the service mesh no matter how deep they are in a call graph. So far, we've looked at a simple architecture consisting of the `webapp` service providing a facade over any of the services it communicates with in the backend. The one service it talks to at the moment is `catalog`. Let's say we want to add some new functionality to the `catalog` service. For this example, we'll add a flag to the payload to indicate whether an image is available for a particular item in the catalog. We want to expose this information to end callers (like a user interface capable of understanding this flag, or a service that can then use the flag to decide whether to enrich an item with more image information, and so on) that can handle this change.

V1 of the `catalog` service has the following properties in its response:

```
{
  "id": 1,
  "color": "amber",
  "department": "Eyewear",
  "name": "Elinor Glasses",
  "price": "282.00"
}
```

For v2 of `catalog`, we have added a new property named `imageUrl`:

```
{
  "id": 1,
  "color": "amber",
  "department": "Eyewear",
  "name": "Elinor Glasses",
  "price": "282.00"
  "imageUrl": "http://lorempixel.com/640/480"
}
```

When we make requests to the `catalog` service, for version v2, we'll expect this new `imageUrl` field in the response.

In principle, we want to deploy the new version of `catalog`, but we also want to finely control to whom it is exposed (released). It's important to be able to separate *deployment* from *release* in such a way as to reduce the chances of breaking things in production and having paying customers be at the forefront of our risky behavior. Specifically, a *deployment* is when we bring new code to production. When it's in production, we can run tests against it and evaluate whether it's fit for production usage. When we *release* code, we bring live traffic to it. We can exercise a phased approach to a release wherein we route only certain classes of users to the new deployment. One such strategy could be to only route internal employees to new deployments and watch how the deployment and overall system behave. We could then graduate the traffic up to non-paying customers, silver-level customers, and so on. We'll cover more of this principle in chapter 5 when we look deeper at Istio's request-routing functionality.

Using Istio, we can finely control which traffic goes to v1 of our service and which requests go to v2. We use a concept from Istio called a `DestinationRule` to split up our services by version, as follows:

```
apiVersion: networking.istio.io/v1alpha3
kind: DestinationRule
metadata:
  name: catalog
spec:
  host: catalog
  subsets:
  - name: version-v1
    labels:
      version: v1
  - name: version-v2
    labels:
      version: v2
```

With this `DestinationRule`, we denote two different versions of the `catalog` service. We specify the group based on the labels of the deployments in Kubernetes. Any Kubernetes Pods labeled with `version: v2` belong to the v2 group of the `catalog` service that Istio knows about. Before we create the `DestinationRule`, let's deploy a second version of `catalog`:

```
$  kubectl apply \
      -f services/catalog/kubernetes/catalog-deployment-v2.yaml
deployment.extensions/catalog-v2 created
```

When the new deployment is ready, we see a second `catalog` Pod:

```
$  kubectl get pod
```

NAME	READY	STATUS	RESTARTS	AGE
webapp-bd97b9bb9-q9g46	2/2	Running	0	17m
catalog-5dc749fd84-fwcl8	2/2	Running	0	10m
catalog-v2-64d758d964-rldc7	2/2	Running	0	38s

If we call our service a handful of times, some of the responses have our new `imageUrl` field in the response, and some do not. By default, Kubernetes can do a limited form of load balancing between the two versions:

```
$ while true; do curl http://localhost/api/catalog; sleep .5; done
```

Press Ctrl-C to exit this `while` loop.

However, we want to safely deploy software to production without impacting end users, and we also have the option to test it in production before releasing it. So we will restrict traffic to the v1 version of `catalog` for now.

The first thing we do is let Istio know how to identify different versions of our catalog service. We use the `DestinationRule` to do that:

```
$ kubectl apply -f ch2/catalog-destinationrule.yaml
destinationrule.networking.istio.io/catalog created
```

Next, we create a rule in the `catalog` `VirtualService` that says to route all traffic to v1 of `catalog`:

```
apiVersion: networking.istio.io/v1alpha3
kind: VirtualService
metadata:
  name: catalog
spec:
  hosts:
  - catalog
  http:
  - route:
    - destination:
        host: catalog
        subset: version-v1
```

Let's update the `catalogVirtualService` with our new traffic routing rule:

```
$ kubectl apply -f ch2/catalog-virtualservice-all-v1.yaml

virtualservice.networking.istio.io/catalog created
```

Now, if we send traffic to our `webapp` endpoint, we see only v1 responses:

```
$ while true; do curl http://localhost/api/catalog; sleep .5; done
```

Press Ctrl-C to exit this `while` loop.

Let's say that for certain users, we want to expose the functionality of v2 of the catalog service. Istio gives us the power to control the routing for individual requests and match on things like request path, headers, cookies, and so on. If users pass in a specific header, we will allow them to hit the new catalog v2 service. Using a revised `VirtualService` definition for `catalog`, let's match on a header called x-dark-launch. We'll send any requests with that header to catalog v2:

```
apiVersion: networking.istio.io/v1alpha3
kind: VirtualService
```

```
metadata:
  name: catalog
spec:
  hosts:
  - catalog
  http:
  - match:          ⟵┐ A match
    - headers:         └ clause
        x-dark-launch:
          exact: "v2"    ┐ A route to v2 that is
    route:          ⟵┘ activated when matched
    - destination:
        host: catalog
        subset: version-v2
  - route:          ┐ Default
    - destination:  ⟵┘ route
        host: catalog
        subset: version-v1
```

Let's create this new routing rule in our `VirtualService`:

```
$ kubectl apply -f ch2/catalog-virtualservice-dark-v2.yaml
virtualservice.networking.istio.io/catalog configured
```

Try calling the `webapp` endpoint again. You should see only v1 responses from the `catalog` service in the response:

```
$ while true; do curl http://localhost/api/catalog; sleep .5; done
```

Now, let's call the endpoint with our special header `x-dark-launch`:

```
$ curl http://localhost/api/catalog -H "x-dark-launch: v2"
[
  {
    "id": 0,
    "color": "teal",
    "department": "Clothing",
    "name": "Small Metal Shoes",
    "price": "232.00",
    "imageUrl": "http://lorempixel.com/640/480"
  }
]
```

When we include the `x-dark-launch: v2` header in our call, we see the response from the `catalog-v2` service; all other traffic goes to `catalog-v1`. Here we've used Istio to finely control the traffic to our services based on individual requests.

Before we move on, delete the example applications. We'll reinstall the individual components as we go:

```
$ kubectl delete deployment,svc,gateway,\
virtualservice,destinationrule --all -n istioinaction
```

In the next chapter, we take a deeper look at the Envoy proxy, Istio's default dataplane proxy, to understand it as a standalone component. Then we show how Istio uses Envoy to achieve the functionality desired by a service mesh.

Summary

- We can use `istioctl` to install Istio and `istioctl x precheck` to verify that Istio can be installed in a cluster.
- Istio's configuration is implemented as Kubernetes custom resources.
- To configure proxies, we describe the intent in YAML (according to the Istio custom resources) and apply it to the cluster.
- The control plane watches for Istio resources, converts them to Envoy configuration, and uses the xDS API to dynamically update Envoy proxies.
- Inbound and outbound traffic to and from the mesh is managed by ingress and egress gateways.
- The sidecar proxy can be injected manually into YAML using `istioctl kube-inject`.
- In namespaces labeled with `istio-injection=enabled`, the proxies are automatically injected into newly created Pods.
- We can use the `VirtualService` API to manipulate application network traffic, such as implementing retries on failed requests.

Istio's data plane: The Envoy proxy

This chapter covers

- Understanding the standalone Envoy proxy and how it contributes to Istio
- Exploring how Envoy's capabilities are core to a service mesh like Istio
- Configuring Envoy with static configuration
- Using Envoy's Admin API to introspect and debug it

When we introduced the idea of a service mesh in chapter 1, we established the concept of a service proxy and how this proxy understands application-level constructs (for example, application protocols like HTTP and gRPC) and enhances an application's business logic with non-differentiating application-networking logic. A service proxy runs collocated and out of process with the application, and the application talks through the service proxy whenever it wants to communicate with other services.

With Istio, the Envoy proxies are deployed collocated with all application instances participating in the service mesh, thus forming the service-mesh data plane. Since Envoy is such a critical component in the data plane and in the overall service-mesh architecture, we spend this chapter getting familiar with it. This should give you a better understanding of Istio and how to debug or troubleshoot your deployments.

3.1 *What is the Envoy proxy?*

Envoy was developed at Lyft to solve some of the difficult application networking problems that crop up when building distributed systems. It was contributed as an open source project in September 2016, and a year later (September 2017) it joined the Cloud Native Computing Foundation (CNCF). Envoy is written in C++ in an effort to increase performance and, more importantly, to make it more stable and deterministic at higher load echelons.

Envoy was created following two critical principles:

> *The network should be transparent to applications. When network and application problems do occur it should be easy to determine the source of the problem.*

> —Envoy announcement

Envoy is a proxy, so before we go any further, we should make very clear what a proxy is. We already mentioned that a *proxy* is an intermediary component in a network architecture that is positioned in the middle of the communication between a client and a server (see figure 3.1). Being in the middle enables it to provide additional features like security, privacy, and policy.

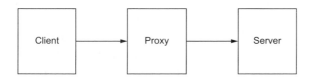

Figure 3.1 A proxy is an intermediary that adds functionality to the flow of traffic.

Proxies can simplify what a client needs to know when talking to a service. For example, a service may be implemented as a set of identical instances (a cluster), each of which can handle a certain amount of load. How should the client know which instance or IP address to use when making requests to that service? A proxy can stand in the middle with a single identifier or IP address, and clients can use that to talk to the instances of the service. Figure 3.2 shows how the proxy handles load balancing across the instances of the service without the client knowing any details of how things are actually deployed. Another common function of this type of reverse proxy is checking the health of instances in the cluster and routing traffic around failing or misbehaving backend instances. This way, the proxy can protect the client from having to know and understand which backends are overloaded or failing.

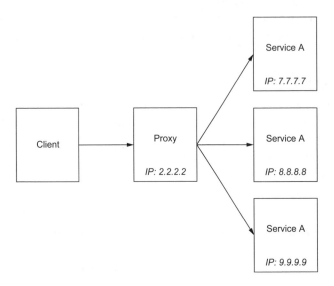

Figure 3.2   A proxy can hide backend topology from clients and implement algorithms to fairly distribute traffic (load balancing).

The Envoy proxy is specifically an application-level proxy that we can insert into the request path of our applications to provide things like service discovery, load balancing, and health checking, but Envoy can do more than that. We've hinted at some of these enhanced capabilities in earlier chapters, and we'll cover them more in this chapter. Envoy can understand layer 7 protocols that an application may speak when communicating with other services. For example, out of the box, Envoy understands HTTP 1.1, HTTP 2, gRPC, and other protocols and can add behavior like request-level timeouts, retries, per-retry timeouts, circuit breaking, and other resilience features. Something like this cannot be accomplished with basic connection-level (L3/L4) proxies that only understand connections.

Envoy can be extended to understand protocols in addition to the out-of-the-box defaults. Filters have been written for databases like MongoDB, DynamoDB, and even asynchronous protocols like Advanced Message Queuing Protocol (AMQP). Reliability and the goal of network transparency for applications are worthwhile endeavors, but just as important is the ability to quickly understand what's happening in a distributed architecture, especially when things are not working as expected. Since Envoy understands application-level protocols and application traffic flows through Envoy, the proxy can collect lots of telemetry about the requests flowing through the system, such as how long they're taking, how many requests certain services are seeing (throughput), and what error rates the services are experiencing. We will cover Envoy's telemetry-collection capabilities in chapter 7 and its extensibility in chapter 14.

As a proxy, Envoy is designed to shield developers from networking concerns by running out-of-process from applications. This means any application written in any programming language or with any framework can take advantage of these features. Moreover, although services architectures (SOA, microservices, and so on) are the architecture *de jour*, Envoy doesn't care if you're doing microservices or if you have monoliths and legacy applications written in any language. As long as they speak protocols that Envoy can understand (like HTTP), Envoy can provide benefits.

Envoy is a very versatile proxy and can be used in different roles: as a proxy at the edge of your cluster (as an ingress point), as a shared proxy for a single host or group of services, and even as a per-service proxy as we see with Istio. With Istio, a single Envoy proxy is deployed per service instance to achieve the most flexibility, performance, and control. Just because you use one type of deployment pattern (a sidecar service proxy) doesn't mean you cannot also have the edge served with Envoy. In fact, having the proxy be the same implementation at the edge as well as located within the application traffic can make your infrastructure easier to operate and reason about. As we'll see in chapter 4, Envoy can be used at the edge for ingress and to tie into the service mesh to give full control and observe traffic from the point it enters the cluster all the way to the individual services in a call graph for a particular request.

3.1.1 Envoy's core features

Envoy has many features useful for inter-service communication. To help understand these features and capabilities, you should be familiar with the following Envoy concepts at a high level:

- *Listeners*—Expose a port to the outside world to which applications can connect. For example, a listener on port 80 accepts traffic and applies any configured behavior to that traffic.
- *Routes*—Routing rules for how to handle traffic that comes in on *listeners*. For example, if a request comes in and matches /catalog, direct that traffic to the catalog cluster.
- *Clusters*—Specific upstream services to which Envoy can route traffic. For example, catalog-v1 and catalog-v2 can be separate clusters, and routes can specify rules about how to direct traffic to either v1 or v2 of the catalog service.

This is a conceptual understanding of what Envoy does for L7 traffic. We will go into more detail in chapter 14.

Envoy uses terminology similar to that of other proxies when conveying traffic directionality. For example, traffic comes into a *listener* from a *downstream* system. This traffic is routed to one of Envoy's *clusters*, which is responsible for sending that traffic to an *upstream* system (as shown in figure 3.3). Traffic flows through Envoy from downstream to upstream. Now, let's move on to some of Envoy's features.

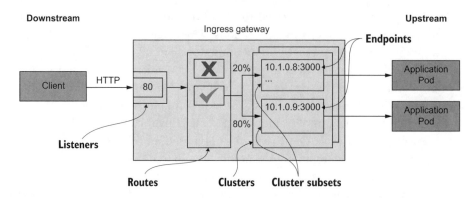

Figure 3.3   A request comes in from a downstream system through the listeners, goes through the routing rules, and ends up going to a cluster that sends it to an upstream service.

SERVICE DISCOVERY

Instead of using runtime-specific libraries for client-side service discovery, Envoy can do this automatically for an application. By configuring Envoy to look for service endpoints from a simple discovery API, applications can be agnostic to how service endpoints are found. The discovery API is a simple REST API that can be used to wrap other common service-discovery APIs (like HashiCorp Consul, Apache ZooKeeper, Netflix Eureka, and so on). Istio's control plane implements this API out of the box.

Envoy is specifically built to rely on *eventually consistent* updates to the service-discovery catalog. This means in a distributed system we cannot expect to know the *exact* status of all services with which we can communicate and whether they're available. The best we can do is use the knowledge at hand, employ active and passive health checking, and expect that those results may not be the most up to date (nor could they be).

Istio abstracts away a lot of this detail by providing a higher-level set of resources that drives the configuration of Envoy's service-discovery mechanisms. We'll look more closely at this throughout the book.

LOAD BALANCING

Envoy implements a few advanced load-balancing algorithms that applications can take advantage of. One of the more interesting capabilities of Envoy's load-balancing algorithms is the *locality-aware load balancing*. In this situation, Envoy is smart enough to keep traffic from crossing any locality boundaries unless it meets certain criteria and will provide a better balance of traffic. For example, Envoy makes sure that service-to-service traffic is routed to instances in the same locality unless doing so would create a failure situation. Envoy provides out-of-the-box load-balancing algorithms for the following strategies:

- Random
- Round robin
- Weighted, least request
- Consistent hashing (sticky)

TRAFFIC AND REQUEST ROUTING

Because Envoy can understand application protocols like HTTP 1.1 and HTTP 2, it can use sophisticated routing rules to direct traffic to specific backend clusters. Envoy can do basic reverse-proxy routing like mapping virtual hosts and context-path routing; it can also do header- and priority-based routing, retries and timeouts for routing, and fault injection.

TRAFFIC SHIFTING AND SHADOWING CAPABILITIES

Envoy supports percentage-based (that is, weighted) traffic splitting/shifting. This enables agile teams to use continuous delivery techniques that mitigate risk such as canary releases. Although they mitigate risk to a smaller user pool, canary releases still deal with live user traffic.

Envoy can also make copies of the traffic and *shadow* that traffic in a *fire and forget* mode to an Envoy cluster. You can think of this shadowing capability as something like traffic splitting, but the requests that the upstream cluster sees are a copy of the live traffic; thus we can route shadowed traffic to a new version of a service without really acting on live production traffic. This is a very powerful capability for testing service changes with production traffic without impacting customers. We'll see more of this in chapter 5.

NETWORK RESILIENCE

Envoy can be used to offload certain classes of resilience problems, but note that it's the application's responsibility to fine-tune and configure these parameters. Envoy can automatically do request timeouts as well as request-level retries (with per-retry timeouts). This type of retry behavior is very useful when a request experiences intermittent network instability. On the other hand, retry amplification can lead to cascading failures; Envoy allows you to limit retry behavior. Also note that application-level retries may still be needed and cannot be completely offloaded to Envoy. Additionally, when Envoy calls upstream clusters, it can be configured with bulkheading characteristics like limiting the number of connections or outstanding requests in flight and to fast-fail any that exceed those thresholds (with some jitter on those thresholds). Finally, Envoy can perform *outlier detection*, which behaves like a circuit breaker, and eject endpoints from the load-balancing pool when they misbehave.

HTTP/2 AND gRPC

HTTP/2 is a significant improvement to the HTTP protocol that allows multiplexing requests over a single connection, server-push interactions, streaming interactions, and request backpressure. Envoy was built from the beginning to be an HTTP/1.1 and HTTP/2 proxy with proxying capabilities for each protocol both downstream and upstream. This means, for example, that Envoy can accept HTTP/1.1 connections and proxy to HTTP/2—or vice versa—or proxy incoming HTTP/2 to upstream HTTP/2 clusters. gRPC is an RPC protocol using Google Protocol Buffers (Protobuf) that lives on top of HTTP/2 and is also natively supported by Envoy. These are powerful features (and difficult to get correct in an implementation) and differentiate Envoy from other service proxies.

OBSERVABILITY WITH METRICS COLLECTION

As we saw in the Envoy announcement from Lyft back in September 2016, one of the goals of Envoy is to help make the network understandable. Envoy collects a large set of metrics to help achieve this goal. It tracks many dimensions around the downstream systems that call it, the server itself, and the upstream clusters to which it sends requests. Envoy's stats are tracked as counters, gauges, or histograms. Table 3.1 lists some examples of the types of statistics tracked for an upstream cluster.

Table 3.1 Some of the stats that the Envoy proxy collects

Statistic	Description
`downstream_cx_total`	Total connections
`downstream_cx_http1_active`	Total active HTTP/1.1 connections
`downstream_rq_http2_total`	Total HTTP/2 requests
`cluster.<name>.upstream_cx_overflow`	Total number of times that the cluster's connection circuit breaker overflowed
`cluster.<name>.upstream_rq_retry`	Total number of request retries
`cluster.<name>.ejections_detected_consecutive_5xx`	Number of detected consecutive 5xx ejections (even if unenforced)

Envoy can emit stats using configurable adapters and formats. Out of the box, Envoy supports the following:

- StatsD
- Datadog; DogStatsD
- Hystrix formatting
- Generic metrics service

OBSERVABILITY WITH DISTRIBUTED TRACING

Envoy can report trace spans to OpenTracing (http://opentracing.io) engines to visualize traffic flow, hops, and latency in a call graph. This means you don't have to install special OpenTracing libraries. On the other hand, the application is responsible for propagating the necessary Zipkin headers, which can be done with thin wrapper libraries.

Envoy generates a `x-request-id` header to correlate calls across services and can also generate the initial `x-b3*` headers when tracing is triggered. The headers that the application is responsible for propagating are as follows:

- `x-b3-traceid`
- `x-b3-spanid`
- `x-b3-parentspanid`
- `x-b3-sampled`
- `x-b3-flags`

AUTOMATIC TLS TERMINATION AND ORIGINATION

Envoy can terminate Transport Level Security (TLS) traffic destined for a specific service both at the edge of a cluster and deep within a mesh of service proxies. A more interesting capability is that Envoy can be used to *originate* TLS traffic to an upstream cluster on behalf of an application. For enterprise developers and operators, this means we don't have to muck with language-specific settings and keystores or truststores. By having Envoy in our request path, we can automatically get TLS and even mutual TLS.

RATE LIMITING

An important aspect of resiliency is the ability to restrict or limit access to resources that are protected. Resources like databases or caches or shared services may be protected for various reasons:

- Expensive to call (per-invocation cost)
- Slow or unpredictable latency
- Fairness algorithms needed to protect against starvation

Especially as services are configured for retries, we don't want to magnify the effect of certain failures in the system. To help throttle requests in these scenarios, we can use a global rate-limiting service. Envoy can integrate with a rate-limiting service at both the network (per connection) and HTTP (per request) levels. We'll show how to do that in chapter 14.

EXTENDING ENVOY

At its core, Envoy is a byte-processing engine on which protocol (layer 7) codecs (called *filters*) can be built. Envoy makes building additional filters a first-class use case and an exciting way to extend Envoy for specific use cases. Envoy filters are written in C++ and compiled into the Envoy binary. Additionally, Envoy supports Lua (www.lua.org) scripting and WebAssembly (Wasm) for a less invasive approach to extending Envoy functionality. Extending Envoy is covered in chapter 14.

3.1.2 Comparing Envoy to other proxies

Envoy's sweet spot is playing the role of application or service proxy, where Envoy facilitates applications talking to each other through the proxy and solves the problems of reliability and observability. Other proxies have evolved from load balancers and web servers into more capable and performant proxies. Some of these communities don't move all that fast or are closed source and have taken a while to evolve to the point that they can be used in application-to-application scenarios. In particular, Envoy shines with respect to other proxies in these areas:

- Extensibility with WebAssembly
- Open community
- Modular codebase built for maintenance and extension
- HTTP/2 support (upstream and downstream)
- Deep protocol metrics collection
- C++ / non-garbage-collected
- Dynamic configuration, no need for hot restarts

For a more specific and detailed comparison, see the following:

- Envoy documentation and comparison: http://bit.ly/2U2g7zb
- Turbine Labs' switch from Nginx to Envoy: http://bit.ly/2nn4tPr
- Cindy Sridharan's initial take on Envoy: http://bit.ly/2OqbMkR
- Why Ambassador chose Envoy over HAProxy and Nginx: http://bit.ly/2OVbsvz

3.2   Configuring Envoy

Envoy is driven by a configuration file in either JSON or YAML format. The configuration file specifies listeners, routes, and clusters as well as server-specific settings like whether to enable the Admin API, where access logs should go, tracing engine configuration, and so on. If you are already familiar with Envoy or Envoy configuration, you may know that there are different versions of the Envoy config. The initial versions, v1 and v2, have been deprecated in favor of v3. We look only at v3 configuration in this book, as that's the go-forward version and is what Istio uses.

Envoy's v3 configuration API is built on gRPC. Envoy and implementers of the v3 API can take advantage of streaming capabilities when calling the API and reduce the time required for Envoy proxies to converge on the correct configuration. In practice, this eliminates the need to poll the API and allows the server to push updates to the Envoys instead of the proxies polling at periodic intervals.

3.2.1   Static configuration

We can specify listeners, route rules, and clusters using Envoy's configuration file. The following is a very simple Envoy configuration:

```
static_resources:
  listeners:                          ◁─── Listener definitions
  - name: httpbin-demo
    address:
      socket_address: {
        address: 0.0.0.0, port_value: 15001 }
    filter_chains:
    - filters:
      - name: envoy.http_connection_manager      ◁─── HTTP filter
        config:
          stat_prefix: egress_http
          route_config:                   ◁─── Route rules
            name: httpbin_local_route
            virtual_hosts:
            - name: httpbin_local_service
              domains: ["*"]              ◁─── Wildcard virtual hosts
              routes:
              - match: { prefix: "/" }
                route:
                  auto_host_rewrite: true
                  cluster: httpbin_service      ◁─── Route to a cluster
          http_filters:
          - name: envoy.router
```

```
clusters:
  - name: httpbin_service              <──┤ Upstream cluster
    connect_timeout: 5s
    type: LOGICAL_DNS
    # Comment out the following line to test on v6 networks
    dns_lookup_family: V4_ONLY
    lb_policy: ROUND_ROBIN
    hosts: [{ socket_address: {
      address: httpbin, port_value: 8000 }}]
```

This simple Envoy configuration file declares a listener that opens a socket on port 15001 and attaches a chain of filters to it. The filters configure the http_connection _manager in Envoy with routing directives. The simple routing directive in this example is to match on the wildcard * for all virtual hosts and route all traffic to the httpbin _service cluster. The last section of the configuration defines the connection properties to the httpbin_service cluster. This example specifies LOGICAL_DNS for endpoint service discovery and ROUND_ROBIN for load balancing when talking to the upstream httpbin service. See Envoy's documentation (http://mng.bz/xvJY) for more.

This configuration file creates a listener to which incoming traffic can connect and routes *all* traffic to the httpbin cluster. It also specifies what load-balancing settings to use and what kind of connect timeout to use. If we call this proxy, we expect our request to be routed to an httpbin service.

Notice that much of the configuration is specified explicitly (what listeners there are, what the routing rules are, what clusters we can route to, and so on). This is an example of a fully static configuration file. In previous sections, we pointed out that Envoy can dynamically configure its various settings. For the hands-on section of Envoy, we'll use the static configurations, but we'll first cover the dynamic services and how Envoy uses its xDS APIs for dynamic configuration.

3.2.2 *Dynamic configuration*

Envoy can use a set of APIs to do inline configuration updates without any downtime or restarts. It just needs a simple bootstrap configuration file that points the configuration to the correct discovery service APIs; the rest is configured dynamically. Envoy uses the following APIs for dynamic configuration:

- *Listener discovery service (LDS)*—An API that allows Envoy to query what listeners should be exposed on this proxy.
- *Route discovery service (RDS)*—Part of the configuration for listeners that specifies which routes to use. This is a subset of LDS for when static and dynamic configuration should be used.
- *Cluster discovery service (CDS)*—An API that allows Envoy to discover what clusters and respective configuration for each cluster this proxy should have.
- *Endpoint discovery service (EDS)*—Part of the configuration for clusters that specifies which endpoints to use for a specific cluster. This is a subset of CDS.
- *Secret discovery service (SDS)*—An API used to distribute certificates.

- *Aggregate discovery service (ADS)*—A serialized stream of all the changes to the rest of the APIs. You can use this single API to get all of the changes in order.

Collectively, these APIs are referred to as the *xDS* services. A configuration can use one or some combination of them; you don't have to use them all. Note that Envoy's xDS APIs are built on a premise of eventual consistency and that correct configurations eventually converge. For instance, Envoy could get an update to RDS with a new route that routes traffic to a cluster *foo* that has not yet been updated in CDS yet. The route could introduce routing errors until the CDS is updated. Envoy introduced ADS to account for this ordering race condition. Istio implements ADS for proxy configuration changes.

For example, to dynamically discover the listeners for an Envoy proxy, we can use a configuration like the following:

```
dynamic_resources:
  lds_config:                     ◁──────────┐  Configuration for
    api_config_source:                       │  listeners (LDS)
      api_type: GRPC
      grpc_services:
        - envoy_grpc:             ◁──────────┐  Go to this cluster for
            cluster_name: xds_cluster        │  the listener API.

clusters:
- name: xds_cluster              ◁──────────┐  gRPC cluster that
  connect_timeout: 0.25s                     │  implements LDS
  type: STATIC
  lb_policy: ROUND_ROBIN
  http2_protocol_options: {}
  hosts: [{ socket_address: {
    address: 127.0.0.3, port_value: 5678 }}]
```

With this configuration, we don't need to explicitly configure each listener in the configuration file. We're telling Envoy to use the LDS API to discover the correct listener configuration values at run time. We do, however, configure one cluster explicitly: the cluster where the LDS API lives (named xds_cluster in this example).

For a more concrete example, Istio uses a `bootstrap` configuration for its service proxies, similar to the following:

```
bootstrap:
  dynamicResources:
    ldsConfig:
      ads: {}        ◁──┤ ADS for listeners
    cdsConfig:
      ads: {}              ◁──┤ ADS for clusters
    adsConfig:
      apiType: GRPC
      grpcServices:
      - envoyGrpc:
          clusterName: xds-grpc    ◁──────┐  Uses a cluster
        refreshDelay: 1.000s              │  named xds-grpc
  staticResources:
```

```
clusters:
- name: xds-grpc                    Defines the xds-
  type: STRICT_DNS                  grpc cluster
  connectTimeout: 10.000s
  hosts:
  - socketAddress:
      address: istio-pilot.istio-system
      portValue: 15010
  circuitBreakers:                  Reliability and circuit-
    thresholds:                     breaking settings
    - maxConnections: 100000
      maxPendingRequests: 100000
      maxRequests: 100000
    - priority: HIGH
      maxConnections: 100000
      maxPendingRequests: 100000
      maxRequests: 100000
  http2ProtocolOptions: {}
```

Let's tinker with a simple static Envoy configuration file to see Envoy in action.

3.3 *Envoy in action*

Envoy is written in C++ and compiled to a native/specific platform. The best way to get started with Envoy is to use Docker and run a Docker container with it. We've been using Docker Desktop for this book, but access to any Docker daemon can be used for this section. For example, on a Linux machine, you can directly install Docker.

Start by pulling in three Docker images that we'll use to explore Envoy's functionality:

```
$ docker pull envoyproxy/envoy:v1.19.0
$ docker pull curlimages/curl
$ docker pull citizenstig/httpbin
```

To begin, we'll create a simple httpbin service. If you're not familiar with httpbin, you can go to http://httpbin.org and explore the different endpoints available. It basically implements a service that can return headers that were used to call it, delay an HTTP request, or throw an error, depending on which endpoint we call. For example, navigate to http://httpbin.org/headers. Once we start the httpbin service, we'll start up Envoy and configure it to proxy all traffic to the httpbin service. Then we'll start up a client app and call the proxy. The simplified architecture of this example is shown in figure 3.4.

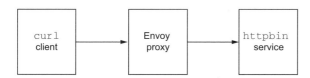

Figure 3.4 The example applications we'll use to exercise some of Envoy's functionality

Run the following command to set up the `httpbin` service running in Docker:

```
$  docker run -d --name httpbin citizenstig/httpbin
787b7ec9365ff01841f2525cdd4e74e154e9d345f633a4004027f7ff1926e317
```

Let's test that our new `httpbin` service was correctly deployed by querying the `/head-ers` endpoint:

```
$  docker run -it --rm --link httpbin curlimages/curl \
curl -X GET http://httpbin:8000/headers

{
  "headers": {
    "Accept": "*/*",
    "Host": "httpbin:8000",
    "User-Agent": "curl/7.80.0"
  }
}
```

You should see similar output; the response returns with the headers we used to call the `/headers` endpoint.

Now let's run our Envoy proxy, pass `--help` to the command, and explore some of its flags and command-line parameters:

```
$  docker run -it --rm envoyproxy/envoy:v1.19.0 envoy --help
```

Some of the interesting flags are `-c` for passing in a configuration file, `--service-zone` for specifying the availability zone into which the proxy is deployed, and `--service-node` for giving the proxy a unique name. You may also be interested in the `--log-level` flag, which controls how verbose the logging is from the proxy.

Let's try to run Envoy:

```
$  docker run -it --rm envoyproxy/envoy:v1.19.0 envoy

[2021-11-21 21:28:37.347] [1] [info] [main]
  [source/server/server.cc:855] exiting
At least one of --config-path or --config-yaml or
  Options::configProto() should be non-empty
```

What happened? We tried to run the proxy, but we did not pass in a valid configuration file. Let's fix that and pass in a simple configuration file based on the sample configuration we saw earlier. It has this structure:

```
static_resources:
  listeners:
  - name: httpbin-demo          ◁──  A listener on
    address:                          port 15001
      socket_address:
        address: 0.0.0.0
        port_value: 15001
    filter_chains:
    - filters:
      - name:  envoy.filters.network.http_connection_manager
```

```
    typed_config:
      "@type": type.googleapis.com/envoy.extensions.filters.
      ➥network.http_connection_manager.v3.HttpConnectionManager
      stat_prefix: ingress_http
      http_filters:
      - name: envoy.filters.http.router
      route_config:
        name: httpbin_local_route
        virtual_hosts:
        - name: httpbin_local_service
          domains: ["*"]
          routes:
          - match: { prefix: "/" }
            route:                        ◁────┐ A simple
              auto_host_rewrite: true           │ route rule
              cluster: httpbin_service
  clusters:
    - name: httpbin_service            ◁──┐ A cluster
      connect_timeout: 5s                  │ for httpbin
      type: LOGICAL_DNS
      dns_lookup_family: V4_ONLY
      lb_policy: ROUND_ROBIN
      load_assignment:
        cluster_name: httpbin
        endpoints:
        - lb_endpoints:
          - endpoint:
              address:
                socket_address:
                  address: httpbin
                  port_value: 8000
```

Basically, we're exposing a single listener on port 15001, and we route all traffic to our httpbin cluster. Let's start up Envoy with this configuration file (ch3/simple.yaml) located at the root of the source code:

```
$  docker run --name proxy --link httpbin envoyproxy/envoy:v1.19.0 \
   --config-yaml "$(cat ch3/simple.yaml)"

5d32538c078a6e14ba0d4072d6ff10592a8a439714e7c9ac9c69e1ff71aa54f2

$ docker logs proxy
[2018-08-09 22:57:50.769] [5] [info] [config]
➥all dependencies initialized. starting workers
[2018-08-09 22:57:50.769] [5] [info] [main]
➥starting main dispatch loop
```

The proxy starts successfully and is listening on port 15001. Let's use a simple command-line client, curl, to call the proxy:

```
$  docker run -it --rm --link proxy curlimages/curl \
   curl  -X GET http://proxy:15001/headers

{
  "headers": {
```

```
            "Accept": "*/*",
            "Content-Length": "0",
            "Host": "httpbin",
            "User-Agent": "curl/7.80.0",
            "X-Envoy-Expected-Rq-Timeout-Ms": "15000",
            "X-Request-Id": "45f74d49-7933-4077-b315-c15183d1da90"
      }
}
```

The traffic was correctly sent to the `httpbin` service even though we called the proxy. We also have some new headers:

- `X-Envoy-Expected-Rq-Timeout-Ms`
- `X-Request-Id`

It may seem insignificant, but Envoy is already doing a lot for us. It generated a new `X-Request-Id`, which can be used to correlate requests across a cluster and potentially multiple hops across services to fulfill the request. The second header, `X-Envoy-Expected-Rq-Timeout-Ms`, is a hint to upstream services that the request is expected to time out after 15,000 ms. Upstream systems, and any other hops the request takes, can use this hint to implement a *deadline*. A deadline allows us to communicate time-out intentions to upstream systems and lets them cease processing if the deadline has passed. This frees up resources after a timeout has been executed.

Now, let's alter this configuration a little and try to set the expected request time-out to one second. In our configuration file, we update the `route` rule:

```
- match: { prefix: "/" }
  route:
      auto_host_rewrite: true
      cluster: httpbin_service
      timeout: 1s
```

For this example, we've already updated the configuration file, and it's available in the Docker image: simple_change_timeout.yaml. We can pass it as an argument to Envoy. Let's stop our existing proxy and restart it with this new configuration file:

```
$  docker rm -f proxy
proxy

$  docker run --name proxy --link httpbin envoyproxy/envoy:v1.19.0 \
   --config-yaml "$(cat ch3/simple_change_timeout.yaml)"

26fb84558165ae9f9d9afb67e9dd7f553c4d412989904542795a82cc721f1ce5
```

Now, let's call the proxy again:

```
$  docker run -it --rm --link proxy curlimages/curl \
curl  -X GET http://proxy:15001/headers

{
  "headers": {
    "Accept": "*/*",
```

```
    "Content-Length": "0",
    "Host": "httpbin",
    "User-Agent": "curl/7.80.0",
    "X-Envoy-Expected-Rq-Timeout-Ms": "1000",
    "X-Request-Id": "c7e9212a-81e0-4ac2-9788-2639b9898772"
  }
}
```

The expected request timeout value has changed to 1000. Next, let's do something a little more exciting than changing the deadline hint headers.

3.3.1 Envoy's Admin API

To explore more of Envoy's functionality, let's first get familiar with Envoy's Admin API. The Admin API gives us insight into how the proxy is behaving, access to its metrics, and access to its configuration. Let's start by running curl against http://proxy:15000/stats:

```
$ docker run -it --rm --link proxy curlimages/curl \
curl -X GET http://proxy:15000/stats
```

The response is a long list of statistics and metrics for the listeners, clusters, and server. We can trim the output using grep and only show those statistics that include the word retry:

```
$ docker run -it --rm --link proxy curlimages/curl \
curl -X GET http://proxy:15000/stats | grep retry

cluster.httpbin_service.retry_or_shadow_abandoned: 0
cluster.httpbin_service.upstream_rq_retry: 0
cluster.httpbin_service.upstream_rq_retry_overflow: 0
cluster.httpbin_service.upstream_rq_retry_success: 0
```

If you call the Admin API directly, without the /stats context path, you should see a list of other endpoints you can call. Some endpoints to explore include the following:

- /certs—Certificates on the machine
- /clusters—Clusters Envoy is configured with
- /config_dump—A dump of the Envoy configuration
- /listeners—Listeners Envoy is configured with
- /logging—Lets you view and change logging settings
- /stats—Envoy statistics
- /stats/prometheus—Envoy statistics formatted as Prometheus records

3.3.2 Envoy request retries

Let's cause some failures in our request to httpbin and watch how Envoy can automatically retry a request for us. First we update the configuration file to use a retry_policy:

```
- match: { prefix: "/" }
  route:
    auto_host_rewrite: true
```

```
cluster: httpbin_service
retry_policy:
    retry_on: 5xx        <——| Retry on 5xx
    num_retries: 3       <——┐ Number
                           | of times
```

Just as in the previous example, you don't have to update the configuration file: an updated version named simple_retry.yaml is available on the Docker image. Let's pass in the configuration file this time when we start Envoy:

```
$  docker rm -f proxy
proxy

$  docker run --name proxy --link httpbin envoyproxy/envoy:v1.19.0 \
   --config-yaml "$(cat ch3/simple_retry.yaml)"
4f99c5e3f7b1eb0ab3e6a97c16d76827c15c2020c143205c1dc2afb7b22553b4
```

Now we call our proxy with the /status/500 context path. Calling httpbin (which the proxy does) with that context path forces an error:

```
$  docker run -it --rm --link proxy curlimages/curl \
curl -v http://proxy:15001/status/500
```

When the call completes, we shouldn't see any response. What happened? Let's ask Envoy's Admin API:

```
$  docker run -it --rm --link proxy curlimages/curl \
curl -X GET http://proxy:15000/stats | grep retry

cluster.httpbin_service.retry.upstream_rq_500: 3
cluster.httpbin_service.retry.upstream_rq_5xx: 3
cluster.httpbin_service.retry_or_shadow_abandoned: 0
cluster.httpbin_service.upstream_rq_retry: 3
cluster.httpbin_service.upstream_rq_retry_overflow: 0
cluster.httpbin_service.upstream_rq_retry_success: 0
```

Envoy encountered an HTTP 500 response when talking to the upstream cluster httpbin. This is as we expected. Envoy also automatically retried the request for us, as indicated by the stat cluster.httpbin_service.upstream_rq_retry: 3.

We just demonstrated some very basic capabilities of Envoy that automatically give us reliability in our application networking. We used static configuration files to reason about and demonstrate these capabilities; but as we saw in the previous section, Istio uses dynamic configuration capabilities. Doing so allows Istio to manage a large fleet of Envoy proxies, each with its own potentially complex configuration. Refer to the Envoy documentation (www.envoyproxy.io) or the "Microservices Patterns with Envoy Sidecar Proxy" series of blog posts (http://bit.ly/2M6Yld3) for more detail about Envoy's capabilities.

3.4　*How Envoy fits with Istio*

Envoy provides the bulk of the heavy lifting for most of the Istio features we covered in chapter 2 and throughout this book. As a proxy, Envoy is a great fit for the service-mesh use case; however, to get the most value out of Envoy, it needs supporting infrastructure or components. The supporting components that allow for user configuration, security policies, and runtime settings, which Istio provides, create the control plane. Envoy also does not do all the work in the data plane and needs support. To learn more about that, see appendix B.

Let's illustrate the need for supporting components with a few examples. We saw that due to Envoy's capabilities, we can configure a fleet of service proxies using static configuration files or a set of *xDS discovery services* for discovering listeners, endpoints, and clusters at run time. Istio implements these xDS APIs in the `istiod` control-plane component.

Figure 3.5 illustrates how `istiod` uses the Kubernetes API to read Istio configurations, such as virtual services, and then dynamically configures the service proxies.

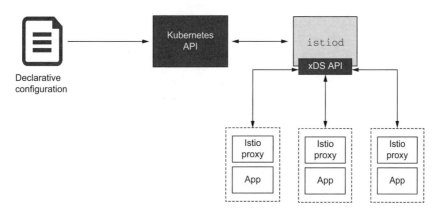

Figure 3.5　Istio abstracts away the service registry and provides an implementation of Envoy's xDS API.

A related example is Envoy's service discovery, which relies on a service registry of some sort to discover endpoints. `istiod` implements this API but also abstracts Envoy away from any particular service-registry implementation. When Istio is deployed on Kubernetes, Istio uses Kubernetes' service registry for service discovery. The Envoy proxy is completely shielded from those implementation details.

Here's another example: Envoy can emit a lot of metrics and telemetry. This telemetry needs to go somewhere, and Envoy must be configured to send it. Istio configures the data plane to integrate with time-series systems like Prometheus. We also saw how Envoy can send distributed-tracing spans to an OpenTracing engine—and Istio can configure Envoy to send its spans to that location (see figure 3.6). For example, Istio integrates with the Jaeger tracing engine (www.jaegertracing.io); Zipkin can be used as well (https://zipkin.io).

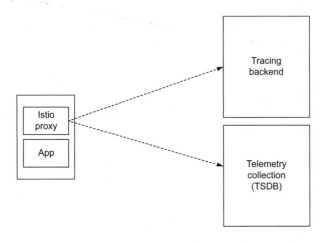

Figure 3.6 **Istio helps configure and integrate with metrics-collection and distributed-tracing infrastructure.**

Finally, Envoy can terminate and originate TLS traffic to services in our mesh. To do this, we need supporting infrastructure to create, sign, and rotate certificates. Istio provides this with the `istiod` component (see figure 3.7).

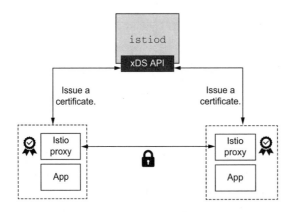

Figure 3.7 `istiod` **delivers application-specific certificates that can be used to establish mutual TLS to secure traffic between services.**

Together, Istio's components and the Envoy proxies make for a compelling service-mesh implementation. Both have thriving, vibrant communities and are geared toward next-generation services architectures. The rest of the book assumes Envoy as a data plane, so all of your learning from this chapter is transferable to the remaining chapters. From here on, we refer to Envoy as the *Istio service proxy*, and its capabilities are seen through Istio's APIs—but understand that many actually come from and are implemented by Envoy.

In the next chapter, we look at how we can begin to get traffic into our service-mesh cluster by going through an edge gateway/proxy that controls traffic. When client applications outside of our cluster wish to communicate with services running inside our cluster, we need to be very clear and explicit about what traffic is and is not allowed in. We'll look at Istio's gateway and how it provides the functionality we need to establish a controlled ingress point. All the knowledge from this chapter will apply: Istio's default gateway is built on the Envoy proxy.

Summary

- Envoy is a proxy that applications can use for application-level behavior.
- Envoy is Istio's data plane.
- Envoy can help solve cloud reliability challenges (network failures, topology changes, elasticity) consistently and correctly.
- Envoy uses a dynamic API for runtime control (which Istio uses).
- Envoy exposes many powerful metrics and information about application usage and proxy internals.

Part 2

Securing, observing, and controlling your service's network traffic

A single misbehaving service has the potential to take down your entire system. We've seen it time and time again: maybe a thread pool fills up, a database slows down, or a rare bug triggers and causes a service to spin out of control. How do we build resilience into our services to expect and correctly deal with these scenarios? How do we consistently monitor golden signals to detect failure situations? How do we secure the communication between services?

Istio helps solve these challenges. Chapters 4-9 look at handling traffic from ingress to deep within a call graph. How do load-balancing algorithms coupled with resilience strategies help the overall system stay available even in the face of service failures? How do you observe throughput, latency, saturation, and error rates for all of the services consistently in your architecture? Can you trace specific service calls to help pinpoint issues in the network? Can you write policies about which services can communicate and, when they do, verify that peers on both side of the connection are certain they are communicating with whom they think they are? All of these topics are covered in this part of the book.

Istio gateways: Getting traffic into a cluster

This chapter covers
- Defining entry points into a cluster
- Routing ingress traffic to deployments in your cluster
- Securing ingress traffic
- Routing non HTTP/S traffic

We usually run interesting services and applications inside our cluster. And as we'll see throughout the book, Istio allows us to solve some difficult challenges in service-to-service communication. It is this intra-service communication where Istio shines (within a cluster or across clusters).

Before services communicate with each other, something must trigger the interactions. For example, an end user purchasing an item, a client querying our API, and so on. What each of these triggers have in common is that they originate outside of the cluster. This raises the question: how do we get traffic from the outside of the cluster and into it (see figure 4.1)? In this chapter, we will answer the question by opening an entry point for clients that live *outside* the cluster to connect securely to services running *inside* the cluster.

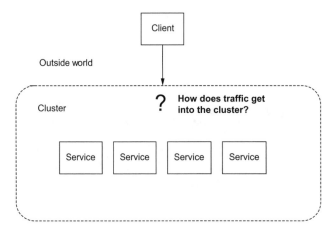

Figure 4.1   We want to connect networks by connecting clients running outside of our cluster to services running inside our cluster.

4.1   *Traffic ingress concepts*

The networking community has a term for connecting networks via well-established entry points: *ingress points. Ingress* refers to traffic that originates outside the network and is intended for an endpoint within the network. The traffic is first routed to an ingress point that acts as a gatekeeper for traffic coming into the network. The ingress point enforces rules and policies about what traffic is allowed into the local network. If the ingress point allows the traffic, it proxies the traffic to the correct endpoint in the local network. If the traffic is not allowed, the ingress point rejects the traffic.

4.1.1   *Virtual IPs: Simplifying service access*

At this point, it's useful to dig a little further into how traffic is routed to a network's ingress points—at least, how it relates to the type of clusters we look at in this book. Let's say we have a service that we wish to expose at api.istioinaction.io/v1/products for external systems to get a list of products in our catalog. When our client tries to query that endpoint, the client's networking stack first tries to resolve the api.istioinaction.io domain name to an IP address. This is done with DNS servers. The networking stack queries the DNS servers for the IP addresses for a particular hostname. So the first step in getting traffic into our network is to map our service's IP to a hostname in DNS. For a public address, we could use a service like Amazon Route 53 or Google Cloud DNS and map a domain name to an IP address. In our own datacenters, we'd use internal DNS servers to do the same thing. But to what IP address should we map the name?

Figure 4.2 visualizes why we should not map the name directly to a single instance or endpoint of our service (single IP), as that approach can be very fragile. What would happen if that one specific service instance went down? Clients would see many errors until we changed the DNS mapping to a new IP address with a working endpoint. But doing this any time a service goes down is slow, error-prone, and low availability.

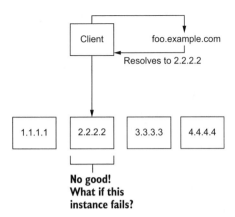

Figure 4.2 We don't want to map domain names to specific instances and IPs of a service.

Figure 4.3 shows how mapping the domain name to a *virtual IP* address that *represents* our service and forwards traffic to our actual service instances, provides us with higher-availability and flexibility. The virtual IP is bound to a type of ingress point known as a *reverse proxy*. The reverse proxy is an intermediary component that's responsible for distributing requests to backend services and does not correspond to any specific service. The reverse proxy can also provide capabilities like load balancing so requests don't overwhelm any one backend.

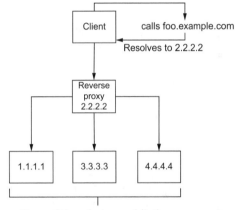

Figure 4.3 Let's map a virtual IP to a reverse proxy that handles load balancing across service instances.

4.1.2 Virtual hosting: Multiple services from a single access point

In the previous section, we saw how a single virtual IP can be used to address a service that may consist of many service instances with their own IPs; however, the client only uses the virtual IP. We can also represent multiple different hostnames using a single virtual IP. For example, we could have both prod.istioinaction.io and api.istioinaction.io resolve to the same virtual IP address. This would mean requests for both hostnames would end up going to the same virtual IP, and thus the same ingress reverse proxy would route the request. If the reverse proxy was smart enough, it could use the Host HTTP header to further delineate which requests should go to which group of services (see figure 4.4).

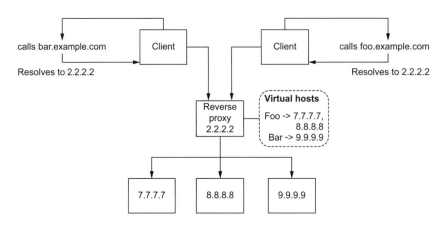

Figure 4.4   Virtual hosting lets us map multiple services to a single virtual IP.

Hosting multiple different services at a single entry point is known as *virtual hosting.* We need a way to decide which virtual host group a particular request should be routed to. With HTTP/1.1, we can use the `Host` header; with HTTP/2, we can use the `:authority` header; and with TCP connections, we can rely on Server Name Indication (SNI) with TLS. We'll take a closer look at SNI later in this chapter. The important thing to note is that the edge ingress functionality we see in Istio uses virtual IP routing and virtual hosting to route service traffic into the cluster.

4.2   *Istio ingress gateways*

Istio has the concept of an *ingress gateway* that plays the role of the network ingress point and is responsible for guarding and controlling access to the cluster from traffic that originates outside of the cluster. Additionally, Istio's ingress gateway handles load balancing and virtual-host routing.

Figure 4.5 shows Istio's ingress gateway component allowing traffic into the cluster and performing reverse proxy functionality. Istio uses a single Envoy proxy as the ingress gateway. We saw in chapter 3 that Envoy is a capable service-to-service proxy, but it can also be used to load balance and route traffic from outside the service mesh to services running inside it. All the features of Envoy that we discussed in the previous chapter are also available in an ingress gateway.

Let's take a closer look at how Istio uses Envoy to implement its ingress gateway component. As we saw when we installed Istio in chapter 2, figure 4.6 shows the list of components that make up the control plane and additional components that support the control plane.

> **NOTE**   In figure 4.6, next to the `istio-ingressgateway` Pod, notice the `istio-egressgateway` component. This component is responsible for routing traffic *out* of the cluster. The egress gateway is configured with the same resources as the ingress gateway which we'll see in this chapter.

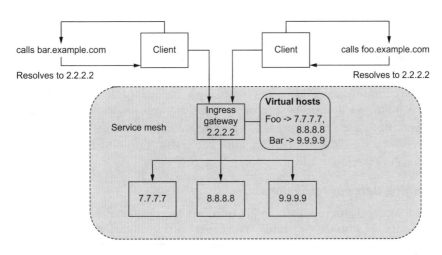

Figure 4.5 An Istio ingress gateway plays the role of a network ingress point and uses an Envoy proxy to do routing and load balancing.

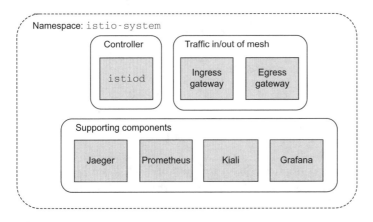

Figure 4.6 Review of the components installed in chapter 2; some form the Istio control plane, and others support it.

If you'd like to verify that the Istio service proxy (Envoy proxy) is indeed running in the Istio ingress gateway, you can run something like this from the root directory of the book's source code:

```
$ kubectl -n istio-system exec \
deploy/istio-ingressgateway -- ps

  PID TTY          TIME CMD
    1 ?        00:00:04 pilot-agent
   14 ?        00:00:24 envoy
   44 ?        00:00:00 ps
```

You should see a process listing as the output, showing the Istio service proxy command line with both `pilot-agent` and `envoy` as the running processes. The `pilot-agent` process initially configures and bootstraps the Envoy proxy; and as we'll see in chapter 13, it implements a DNS proxy as well.

To configure Istio's ingress gateway to allow traffic into the cluster and through the service mesh, we'll start by exploring two Istio resources: `Gateway` and `VirtualService`. Both are fundamental for getting traffic to flow in Istio, but we'll look at them only within the context of allowing traffic into the cluster. We will cover `VirtualService` more fully in chapter 5.

4.2.1 Specifying Gateway resources

To configure an ingress gateway in Istio, we use the `Gateway` resource and specify which ports we wish to open and what virtual hosts to allow for those ports. The example `Gateway` resource we'll explore is quite simple and exposes an HTTP port on port 80 that accepts traffic destined for virtual host `webapp.istioinaction.io`:

```
apiVersion: networking.istio.io/v1alpha3
kind: Gateway
metadata:
  name: coolstore-gateway          ◁── Name of the gateway
spec:
  selector:
    istio: ingressgateway          ◁── Which gateway implementation
  servers:
  - port:                          ◁── Ports to expose
      number: 80
      name: http
      protocol: HTTP
    hosts:                         ◁── Host(s) for this port
    - "webapp.istioinaction.io"
```

Our `Gateway` resource configures Envoy to listen on port 80 and expect HTTP traffic. Let's create that resource and see what it does. In the root of the book's source code is a ch4/coolstore-gw.yaml file. To create the configuration, run the following:

```
$ kubectl -n istioinaction apply -f ch4/coolstore-gw.yaml
```

Let's see whether our settings took effect:

```
$ istioctl -n istio-system proxy-config \
listener deploy/istio-ingressgateway

ADDRESS PORT  MATCH DESTINATION
0.0.0.0 8080  ALL   Route: http.80
0.0.0.0 15021 ALL   Inline Route: /healthz/ready*
0.0.0.0 15090 ALL   Inline Route: /stats/prometheus*
```

If you see this output, you've exposed the HTTP port (port 80) correctly! Looking at the routes for virtual services, we see that the gateway doesn't have any at the moment (you may see another route for Prometheus, but you can ignore it for now):

NOTE If you are not using Docker Desktop, the name of the listener (in this instance "http.8080") may be different. Update the command below accordingly.

```
$  istioctl proxy-config route deploy/istio-ingressgateway \
-o json --name http.8080  -n istio-system

[
    {
        "name": "http.8080",
        "virtualHosts": [
            {
                "name": "blackhole:80",
                "domains": [
                    "*"
                ],
            }
        ],
        "validateClusters": false
    }
]
```

Our listener is bound to a `blackhole` default route that routes everything to HTTP 404. In the next section, we set up a virtual host to route traffic from port 80 to a service within the service mesh.

Before we go on, there's an important last point to be made. The Pod running the gateway, whether that's the default `istio-ingressgateway` or your own custom gateway, must be able to listen on a port or IP that is exposed outside the cluster. For example, on the local Docker Desktop that we're using for these examples, the ingress gateway is listening on port 80. If you're deploying on a cloud service like Google Container Engine (GKE), make sure you use a service of type `LoadBalancer`, which gets an externally routable IP address. You can find more information at https://istio.io/ v1.13/docs/tasks/traffic-management/ingress/.

Additionally, the default `istio-ingressgateway` does not need privileged access to open any ports, as it does not listen on any system ports (80 for HTTP). `istio-ingressgateway` by default listens on port 8080; however, whatever service or load balancer you use to expose the gateway is the actual port. In our examples with Docker Desktop, we expose the service on port 80.

4.2.2 *Gateway routing with virtual services*

So far, all we've done is configure an Istio gateway to expose a specific port, expect a specific protocol on that port, and define specific hosts to serve from the port/protocol pair. When traffic comes into the gateway, we need a way to get it to a specific service within the service mesh; and to do that, we'll use the `VirtualService` resource. In Istio, a `VirtualService` resource defines how a client talks to a specific service through its fully qualified domain name, which versions of a service are available, and other routing properties (like retries and request timeouts). We'll cover Virtual-Service in more depth in the next chapter when we explore traffic routing; in this chapter, it's sufficient to know that VirtualService allows us to route traffic from the ingress gateway to a specific service.

An example of a VirtualService that routes traffic for the virtual host webapp.istioinaction.io to services deployed in our service mesh looks like this:

```
apiVersion: networking.istio.io/v1alpha3
kind: VirtualService
metadata:
  name: webapp-vs-from-gw        ◄──┘  Name of the
                                        virtual service
spec:
  hosts:                               Virtual host name(s)
  - "webapp.istioinaction.io"   ◄──┘  to match
  gateways:
  - coolstore-gateway           ◄──┐  Gateways to which
  http:                               this applies
  - route:
    - destination:              ◄──┐  Destination service
        host: webapp                   for this traffic
        port:
          number: 8080
```

With this VirtualService resource, we define what to do with traffic when it comes into the gateway. In this case, as you can see from the spec.gateways field, these traffic rules apply only to traffic coming from the coolstore-gateway gateway definition, which we created in the previous section. Additionally, we specify the virtual host webapp.istioinaction.io for which traffic must be destined for these rules to match. An example of matching this rule is a client querying http://webapp.istioinaction.io, which resolves to an IP that the Istio gateway is listening on. Additionally, a client can explicitly set the Host header in the HTTP request to be webapp.istioinaction.io, as we'll show through an example.

Again, verify that you're in the root directory of the source code:

```
$  kubectl apply -n istioinaction -f ch4/coolstore-vs.yaml
```

After a few moments (the configuration needs to sync; recall that configuration in the Istio service mesh is *eventually consistent*), we can re-run our commands to list the listeners and routes:

```
$  istioctl proxy-config route deploy/istio-ingressgateway \
-o json --name http.8080  -n istio-system

[
  {
    "name": "http.8080",
    "virtualHosts": [
      {
```

```
            "name": "webapp-vs-from-gw:80",
            "domains": [
                "webapp.istioinaction.io"        <——| Domains to match
            ],
            "routes": [
              {
                "match": {
                    "prefix": "/"
                },
                "route": {          <——| Where to route
                    "cluster":
                    "outbound|8080||webapp.istioinaction.svc.cluster.local",
                    "timeout": "0.000s"
                }
              }
            ]
          }
        ]
      }
]
```

The output for route should look similar to the previous listing, although it may contain other attributes and information. The critical part is that we can see how defining a VirtualService created an Envoy route in our Istio gateway that routes traffic matching domain webapp.istioinaction.io to webapp in our service mesh.

We have the routing set up for our services, but we should deploy the services for them to work. The following commands are meant to be run from the root of the book's source code:

```
$  kubectl config set-context $(kubectl config current-context) \
 --namespace=istioinaction
$  kubectl apply -f services/catalog/kubernetes/catalog.yaml
$  kubectl apply -f services/webapp/kubernetes/webapp.yaml
```

Once all the Pods are ready, you should see something like this:

```
$  kubectl get pod
NAME                       READY    STATUS     RESTARTS    AGE
webapp-bd97b9bb9-q9g46     2/2      Running    18          19d
catalog-786894888c-8lbk4   2/2      Running    8           6d
```

Verify that your Gateway and VirtualService resources are installed correctly:

```
$  kubectl get gateway
NAME                CREATED AT
coolstore-gateway   2h

$  kubectl get virtualservice
NAME               GATEWAYS                  HOSTS
webapp-vs-from-gw  ["coolstore-gateway"]     ["webapp.istioinaction.io"]
```

Now, let's try to call the gateway and verify that the traffic is allowed into the cluster. Remember that we are using the Docker Desktop approach, where the Istio ingress gateway is available on port 80 on localhost. If you're using a cloud service or Node-Port service, you'll need to figure out what that external IP is. For example, in chapter 2, we saw that one way to get the correct host for the ingress gateway exposed on a public load balancer looks like this:

```
$  URL=$(kubectl -n istio-system get svc istio-ingressgateway \
-o jsonpath='{.status.loadBalancer.ingress[0].ip}')
```

Once you have the correct endpoint, you can run something similar to this (remember, localhost is on Docker Desktop):

```
$  curl http://localhost/api/catalog
```

You should see no response. Why is that? If we take a closer look at the call by printing the headers, we see that the Host header we sent in is *not* a host that the gateway recognizes:

```
$  curl -v http://localhost/api/catalog
*    Trying ::1...
* TCP_NODELAY set
* Connected to localhost (::1) port 80      ⊲─┤ Host
> GET /api/catalog HTTP/1.1
> Host: localhost
> User-Agent: curl/7.54.0
> Accept: */*
>
< HTTP/1.1 404 Not Found                    ⊲─┤ Not found
< date: Tue, 21 Aug 2018 16:08:28 GMT
< server: envoy
< content-length: 0
<
* Connection #0 to host 192.168.64.27 left intact
```

Neither the Istio gateway nor any of the routing rules we declared in the Virtual-Service knows anything about Host: localhost:80, but it does know about the virtual host webapp.istioinaction.io. Let's override the Host header on our command line, and then the call should work:

```
$ curl http://localhost/api/catalog -H "Host: webapp.istioinaction.io"
```

Now you should see a successful response.

4.2.3   *Overall view of traffic flow*

In the previous sections, we got hands-on with the Gateway and VirtualService resources from Istio. The Gateway resource defines ports, protocols, and virtual hosts that we wish to listen for at the edge of our service-mesh cluster. VirtualService resources define where traffic should go once it's allowed in at the edge. Figure 4.7 shows the full end-to-end flow.

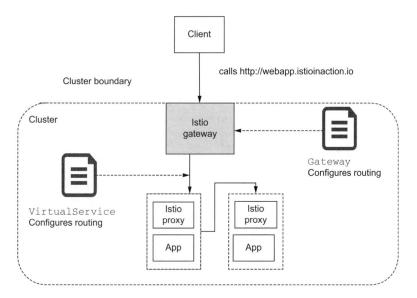

Figure 4.7   Flow of traffic from a client outside the service mesh/cluster to services inside the service mesh through the ingress gateway

4.2.4   Istio ingress gateway vs. Kubernetes Ingress

When running on Kubernetes, you may ask, "Why doesn't Istio just use the Kubernetes Ingress v1 resource to specify ingress?" Istio does support the Kubernetes Ingress v1 resource, but there are significant limitations with the Kubernetes Ingress v1 specification.

The first limitation is that Kubernetes Ingress v1 is a very simple specification geared toward HTTP workloads. There are implementations of Kubernetes Ingress (like Nginx and Traefik); however, each is geared toward HTTP traffic. In fact, the Ingress specification only considers port 80 and port 443 as ingress points. This severely limits the types of traffic a cluster operator can allow into the service mesh. For example, if you have Kafka or NATS.io workloads, you may wish to expose direct TCP connections to these messaging systems. Kubernetes Ingress doesn't allow for that.

Second, the Kubernetes Ingress v1 resource is severely underspecified. There is no common way to specify complex traffic routing rules, traffic splitting, or things like traffic shadowing. The lack of specification in this area causes each vendor to reimagine how best to implement configurations for each type of Ingress implementation (HAProxy, Nginx, and so on).

Finally, since things are underspecified, most vendors have chosen to expose configuration through bespoke annotations on deployments. The annotations between vendors vary and are not portable, and if Istio had continued that trend, there would have been many more annotations to account for all the power of Envoy as an edge gateway.

Ultimately, Istio decided on a clean slate for building ingress patterns and specifically separated out the layer 4 (transport) and layer 5 (session) properties from the layer 7 (application) routing concerns. Istio `Gateway` handles the L4 and L5 concerns, while `VirtualService` handles the L7 concerns. Many mesh and gateway providers have also built their own APIs for ingress, and the Kubernetes community is working on a revised Ingress API.

Kubernetes Gateway API

At the time of this writing, the Kubernetes community is hard at work on the Gateway API to supplant the Ingress v1 API. You can find more information at https://gateway-api.sigs.k8s.io. This is different from the Istio `Gateway` and `VirtualService` resources covered in this book. Istio's implementation and resources came before the Gateway API and in many ways inspired the Gateway API.

4.2.5   *Istio ingress gateway vs. API gateways*

An API gateway allows an organization to abstract a client that consumes a set of services in a boundary (either network-wise or architectural) from the details of the implementation of those services. For example, clients may call a set of APIs that are expected to be well documented, evolve with backward- and forward-compatible semantics, and offer self-service and other mechanisms for usage. To accomplish this, the API gateway needs to be able to identify clients using different security challenges (OpenID Connect [OIDC], OAuth 2.0, Lightweight Directory Access Protocol [LDAP]), transform messages (SOAP to REST, gRPC to Rest, body and header text-based transformations, and so on), provide sophisticated business-level rate limiting, and have a self-signup or developer portal. Istio's ingress gateway does not do these things out of the box. For a more capable API gateway—even one built on an Envoy proxy—that can play this role inside and outside your mesh, take a look at something like Solo.io Gloo Edge (https://docs.solo.io/gloo-edge/latest).

4.3   *Securing gateway traffic*

So far, we've shown how to expose basic HTTP services with an Istio gateway using the `Gateway` and `VirtualService` resources. When connecting services from outside a cluster (let's say, the public internet) to those running inside a cluster, one of the basic capabilities of the ingress gateway in a system is to secure traffic and help establish trust in the system. We can begin to secure our traffic by giving clients confidence that the service they're hoping to communicate with is indeed the service it claims to be. Additionally, we want to exclude anyone from eavesdropping on our communication, so we should encrypt the traffic.

Istio's gateway implementation allows us to terminate incoming TLS/SSL traffic, pass it through to the backend services, redirect any non-TLS traffic to the proper TLS ports, and implement mutual TLS. We'll look at each of these capabilities in this section.

4.3.1 HTTP traffic with TLS

To prevent man-in-the-middle (MITM) attacks and encrypt all traffic coming into the service mesh, we can set up TLS on the Istio gateway so that any incoming traffic is served over HTTPS (for HTTP traffic; we'll cover non-HTTP traffic in later sections). MITM attacks occur when a client intends to connect to a service but instead connects to an impostor service claiming to be the intended service. The impostor service can gain access to the communication, including sensitive information. TLS helps to mitigate this attack.

To enable HTTPS for ingress traffic, we need to specify the correct private keys and certificates that the gateway should use. As a quick reminder, the certificate that the server presents is how it announces its identity to any clients. The certificate is basically the server's public key, which has been signed by a reputable authority, also known as a certificate authority (CA). Figure 4.8 visualizes how a client can trust that the server's certificate is indeed valid. First, it must have installed the CA issuer's certificate, which means this is a trusted CA and certificates issued by it are trusted too. With the CA certificate installed, the client can verify that the certificate is signed by a CA that it trusts. It proceeds to encrypt traffic sent to the server using the public key within the certificate. The server can then decrypt the traffic using the private key.

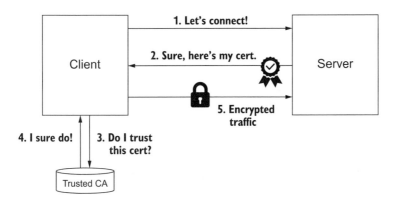

Figure 4.8 Basic model of how TLS is established between a client and server

NOTE The previous statement wasn't entirely correct: the TLS handshake includes a more sophisticated protocol that combines the public/private keys (asymmetric) for initial communication and then creates a session key (symmetric) that is used for the TLS session to encrypt and decrypt traffic. See appendix C for a more complete explanation of TLS.

Before we can configure the default `istio-ingressgateway` to use certificates and keys, we need to create them as Kubernetes secrets.

> **NOTE** Kubernetes secrets are *not* secret: they're effectively stored as clear text. You may wish to consider a more appropriate approach for storing keys and certs.

Let's start by creating the `webapp-credential` secret. Run the following from within the root of the repository:

```
$ kubectl create -n istio-system secret tls webapp-credential \
--key ch4/certs/3_application/private/webapp.istioinaction.io.key.pem \
--cert ch4/certs/3_application/certs/webapp.istioinaction.io.cert.pem

secret/webapp-credential created
```

In this step, we create the secret in the `istio-system` namespace. At the time of writing (Istio 1.13.0), the secret used for TLS in the gateway can only be retrieved if it's in the same namespace as the Istio ingress gateway. The default gateway is run in the `istio-system` namespace, so that's where we put the secret. We could run the ingress gateway in a different namespace, but the secret would still have to be in that namespace. For production, you should run the ingress gateway component in its own namespace, separate from `istio-system`.

Now we can configure our Istio `Gateway` resource to use the certificates and keys:

```
apiVersion: networking.istio.io/v1alpha3
kind: Gateway
metadata:
  name: coolstore-gateway
spec:
  selector:
    istio: ingressgateway
  servers:
  - port:
      number: 80          ◁──┐ Admits
      name: http              HTTP traffic
      protocol: HTTP
    hosts:
    - "webapp.istioinaction.io"
  - port:
      number: 443     ◁─────────┐ Admits secured
      name: https                 HTTPS traffic
      protocol: HTTPS
    tls:
      mode: SIMPLE    ◁──┐ A secure
                           connection
      credentialName: webapp-credential   ◁──┐ The name of the Kubernetes secret
    hosts:                                      containing the TLS certificates
    - "webapp.istioinaction.io"
```

In the `Gateway` resource, we open port 443 on our ingress gateway and specify its protocol to be HTTPS. Additionally, we add a `tls` section to our gateway configuration, where we specify the locations of the certificates and keys to use for TLS. Note that these are the same locations mounted into the `istio-ingressgateway` that we saw earlier.

Let's replace our gateway with this new `Gateway` resource. Run this from the root of the source code:

```
$  kubectl apply -f ch4/coolstore-gw-tls.yaml

gateway.networking.istio.io/coolstore-gateway replaced
```

Use the correct host and ports for your environment

The commands in this book assume we're using Docker Desktop, but if you're using your own Kubernetes cluster (or a public-cloud hosted one), you can use those values directly. For example, on GKE, you can figure out the HOST IP by using the cloud load balancer's public IP, as shown when looking at the Kubernetes services:

```
$  kubectl get svc -n istio-system

NAME                   TYPE           CLUSTER-IP     EXTERNAL-IP
istio-ingressgateway   LoadBalancer   10.12.2.78     35.233.243.32
istio-pilot            ClusterIP      10.12.15.206   <none>
```

In this case, 35.233.243.32 is used for HTTPS_HOST. You can then use the real ports (80 and 443) for HTTP and HTTPS, respectively.

If we call the service as we did in the previous section, by passing in the proper `Host` header, we see something like this (note that we use https:// in the URL):

```
$  curl -v -H "Host: webapp.istioinaction.io" https://localhost/api/catalog

*    Trying 192.168.64.27...
* TCP_NODELAY set
* Connected to 192.168.64.27 (192.168.64.27) port 31390 (#0)
* ALPN, offering http/1.1
* Cipher selection: ALL:!EXPORT:!EXPORT40:!EXPORT56:!aNULL:!LOW:!RC4:@STRENGTH
* successfully set certificate verify locations:
*    CAfile: /usr/local/etc/openssl/cert.pem          ◁──────────┐  Default
  CApath: /usr/local/etc/openssl/certs                           │  certificate chain
* TLSv1.2 (OUT), TLS header, Certificate Status (22):
* TLSv1.2 (OUT), TLS handshake, Client hello (1):
* OpenSSL SSL_connect: SSL_ERROR_SYSCALL in connection to 192.168.64.27:31390
* Closing connection 0
curl: (35) OpenSSL SSL_connect: SSL_ERROR_SYSCALL in connection to
192.168.64.27:31390
```

This means the certificate presented by the server cannot be verified using the default CA certificate chains. Let's pass in the proper CA certificate chain to our `curl` client:

```
$  curl -v -H "Host: webapp.istioinaction.io" https://localhost/api/catalog \
--cacert ch4/certs/2_intermediate/certs/ca-chain.cert.pem

*    Trying 192.168.64.27...
* TCP_NODELAY set
* Connected to 192.168.64.27 (192.168.64.27) port 31390 (#0)
```

```
* ALPN, offering http/1.1
* Cipher selection: ALL:!EXPORT:!EXPORT40:
  !EXPORT56:!aNULL:!LOW:!RC4:@STRENGTH
* successfully set certificate verify locations:
*   CAfile: certs/2_intermediate/certs/ca-chain.cert.pem
  CApath: /usr/local/etc/openssl/certs
* TLSv1.2 (OUT), TLS header, Certificate Status (22):
* TLSv1.2 (OUT), TLS handshake, Client hello (1):
* OpenSSL SSL_connect: SSL_ERROR_SYSCALL in
  connection to 192.168.64.27:31390
* Closing connection 0
curl: (35) OpenSSL SSL_connect: SSL_ERROR_SYSCALL in connection to
192.168.64.27:31390
```

The client still cannot verify the certificate! This is because the server certificate is issued for webapp.istioinaction.io, and we're calling the Docker Desktop host (localhost, in this case). We can use a curl parameter called --resolve that lets us call the service as though it were at webapp.istioinaction.io but then tell curl to use localhost:

```
$ curl -H "Host: webapp.istioinaction.io" \
https://webapp.istioinaction.io:443/api/catalog \
--cacert ch4/certs/2_intermediate/certs/ca-chain.cert.pem \
--resolve webapp.istioinaction.io:443:127.0.0.1
```

Now we see a proper HTTP/1.1 200 response and the JSON payload for the products list. As a client, we're verifying that the server is who it says it is by trusting the CA that signed the certificate, and we're able to encrypt the traffic to the server by using this certificate.

Note that we use the --resolve flag to map the hostname and port in the certificate to the real IP we're using. With Docker Desktop, the ingress runs on localhost, as we've seen. If you are using a cloud-provided load balancer, you can replace 127.0.0.1 with the appropriate IP.

Will curl work for you?

Note that for curl to work in this section, you need to make sure it supports TLS, and you can add your own CA certificates to override the default. Not all builds of curl support TLS. For example, in some versions of curl on macOS, CA certificates can only come from the Apple keychain. Newer builds of curl should have the proper SSL libraries and should work for you, but you need to see something about your SSL library (OpenSSL, LibreSSL, and so on) when you type this:

```
curl --version | grep -i SSL
```

Figure 4.9 visualizes that we have achieved end-to-end encryption. We've secured traffic by encrypting it to the Istio ingress gateway, which terminates the TLS connection and then sends the traffic to the backend webapp service running in our service mesh. The hop between the `istio-ingressgateway` component and the `webapp` service is encrypted using the identities of the services. We will elaborate that further in chapter 9.

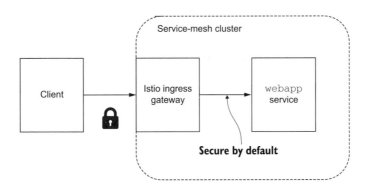

Figure 4.9 Secured traffic from the outside world to the Istio ingress gateway component. Traffic within the mesh is not secured yet.

NOTE You will likely want to integrate your certificate workflows with an external CA or your own internal PKI. You can use something like cert-manager to help with that integration. See https://cert-manager.io/docs for more.

4.3.2 *HTTP redirect to HTTPS*

We set up TLS in the previous section, but what if we want to force all traffic to always use TLS? We could have used both http:// and https:// to access our service through the ingress gateway, but in this section, we force all traffic to use HTTPS. To do that, we have to modify our `Gateway` resource slightly to force a redirect for HTTP traffic:

```
apiVersion: networking.istio.io/v1alpha3
kind: Gateway
metadata:
  name: coolstore-gateway
spec:
  selector:
    istio: ingressgateway
  servers:
  - port:
      number: 80
      name: http
      protocol: HTTP
    hosts:
    - "webapp.istioinaction.io"
    tls:
      httpsRedirect: true       ⊲──┐  Redirects HTTP
  - port:                          │  to HTTPS
      number: 443
```

```
  name: https
  protocol: HTTPS
tls:
  mode: SIMPLE
  credentialName: webapp-credential
hosts:
- "webapp.istioinaction.io"
```

If we update our Gateway to use this configuration, we can limit all traffic to only HTTPS:

```
$ kubectl apply -f ch4/coolstore-gw-tls-redirect.yaml
```

```
gateway.networking.istio.io/coolstore-gateway configured
```

Now, if we call the ingress gateway on the HTTP port, we should see something like this:

```
$ curl -v http://localhost/api/catalog \
  -H "Host: webapp.istioinaction.io"

*   Trying 192.168.64.27...
* TCP_NODELAY set
* Connected to 192.168.64.27 (192.168.64.27) port 31380 (#0)
> GET /api/catalog HTTP/1.1
> Host: webapp.istioinaction.io
> User-Agent: curl/7.61.0
> Accept: */*
>                                            │ HTTP 301
< HTTP/1.1 301 Moved Permanently      ◁──┘   redirect
< location: https://webapp.istioinaction.io/api/catalog
< date: Wed, 22 Aug 2018 21:01:29 GMT
< server: envoy
< content-length: 0
<
* Connection #0 to host 192.168.64.27 left intact
```

This redirect instructs the client to call the HTTPS version of this API. Now we can expect all traffic going to our ingress gateway to always be encrypted.

4.3.3   *HTTP traffic with mutual TLS*

In the previous section, we used standard TLS to allow the server to prove its identity to the client. But what if we want our cluster to verify who the clients are before we accept any traffic from outside the cluster? In the simple TLS scenario, the server sends its public certificate to the client, and the client verifies that it trusts the CA that signed the server's certificate. We want to have the client send its public certificate and let the server verify that it trusts it. Figure 4.10 visualizes how with the mutual TLS (mTLS) protocol both the client and the server verify each other's certificates, in other words mutually authenticate. And the certificates are used to encrypt traffic.

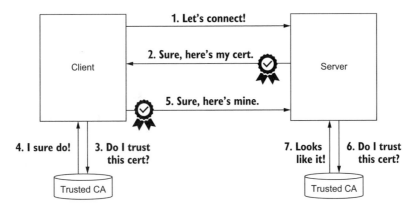

Figure 4.10   Basic model of how mTLS is established between a client and server

To configure the default `istio-ingressgateway` to participate in a mutual TLS connection, we need to give it a set of CA certificates to use to verify a client's certificate. Just as we did in the previous section, we need to make this CA certificate (or certificate chain, more specifically) available to the `istio-ingressgateway` with a Kubernetes secret.

Let's start by configuring the `istio-ingressgateway-ca-certs` secret with the proper CA certificate chain:

```
$  kubectl create -n istio-system secret \
generic webapp-credential-mtls --from-file=tls.key=\
ch4/certs/3_application/private/webapp.istioinaction.io.key.pem \
--from-file=tls.crt=\
ch4/certs/3_application/certs/webapp.istioinaction.io.cert.pem \
--from-file=ca.crt=ch4/certs/2_intermediate/certs/ca-chain.cert.pem

secret/webapp-credential-mtls created
```

Now let's update the Istio `Gateway` resource to point to the location of the CA certificate chain and configure the expected protocol to be mutual TLS:

```
apiVersion: networking.istio.io/v1alpha3
kind: Gateway
metadata:
  name: coolstore-gateway
spec:
  selector:
    istio: ingressgateway
  servers:
  - port:
      number: 80
      name: http
      protocol: HTTP
    hosts:
```

```
     - "webapp.istioinaction.io"
  - port:
      number: 443
      name: https
      protocol: HTTPS
    tls:                                    Configured
      mode: MUTUAL                          for mTLS
      credentialName: webapp-credential-mtls      Credentials with a
    hosts:                                          trusted CA configured
    - "webapp.istioinaction.io"
```

Let's replace the Gateway configuration with this new updated version. Run this from the root of the source code:

```
$  kubectl apply -f ch4/coolstore-gw-mtls.yaml

gateway.networking.istio.io/coolstore-gateway configured
```

Now, if we try to call the ingress gateway the same way we did in the previous section (assuming simple TLS), the call is rejected:

```
$  curl -H "Host: webapp.istioinaction.io" \
https://webapp.istioinaction.io:443/api/catalog \
--cacert ch4/certs/2_intermediate/certs/ca-chain.cert.pem \
--resolve webapp.istioinaction.io:443:127.0.0.1

curl: (35) error:14094410:SSL routines:ssl3_read_bytes:sslv3 alert
handshake failure
```

Istio gateway SDS

An Istio gateway gets the certificates from the secret discovery service (SDS) built into the `istio-agent` process that's used to start the `istio-proxy`. SDS is a dynamic API that should automatically propagate the updates. The same is true for service proxies.

You can check the status of certificates delivered via SDS with the following command:

```
istioctl pc secret -n istio-system deploy/istio-ingressgateway
```

Note that if you don't see the new certificate configuration take effect, you may wish to "bounce" the `istio-ingressgateway` Pod:

```
kubectl delete po -n istio-system -l app=istio-ingressgateway
```

This call is rejected because the SSL handshake wasn't successful. We are only passing the CA certificate chain to the `curl` command; we need to also pass the client's certificate and private key. With `curl`, we can do so by passing the `--cert` and `--key` parameters like this:

```
$  curl -H "Host: webapp.istioinaction.io" \
https://webapp.istioinaction.io:443/api/catalog \
--cacert ch4/certs/2_intermediate/certs/ca-chain.cert.pem \
```

```
--resolve webapp.istioinaction.io:443:127.0.0.1 \
--cert ch4/certs/4_client/certs/webapp.istioinaction.io.cert.pem \
--key ch4/certs/4_client/private/webapp.istioinaction.io.key.pem
```

Now we should see a proper HTTP/1.1 200 response and the JSON payload for the products list. The client is validating the server's certificate and sending its own certificate for validation to achieve mutual TLS.

4.3.4 *Serving multiple virtual hosts with TLS*

Istio's ingress gateway can serve multiple virtual hosts, each with its own certificate and private key from the same HTTPS port (port 443). To do that, we add multiple entries for the same port and the same protocol. For example, we can add multiple entries for both the webapp.istioinaction.io and catalog.istioinaction.io services, each with its own certificate and key pair. An Istio Gateway resource that describes multiple virtual hosts served with HTTPS looks like this:

```
apiVersion: networking.istio.io/v1alpha3
kind: Gateway
metadata:
  name: coolstore-gateway
spec:
  selector:
    istio: ingressgateway
  servers:
  - port:
      number: 443           ◁—| First entry
      name: https-webapp
      protocol: HTTPS
    tls:
      mode: SIMPLE
      credentialName: webapp-credential
    hosts:
    - "webapp.istioinaction.io"
  - port:
      number: 443           ◁—| Second entry
      name: https-catalog
      protocol: HTTPS
    tls:
      mode: SIMPLE
      credentialName: catalog-credential
    hosts:
    - "catalog.istioinaction.io"
```

Notice that both entries listen on port 443 and serve the HTTPS protocol, but they have different names: https-webapp and https-catalog. Each has unique certificates and keys that are used for the specific virtual host it serves. To put this into action, we need to add these new certificates and keys. Let's create them. From the root of the book source, run the following command:

```
$ kubectl create -n istio-system secret tls catalog-credential \
--key ch4/certs2/3_application/private/catalog.istioinaction.io.key.pem \
--cert ch4/certs2/3_application/certs/catalog.istioinaction.io.cert.pem
```

Now let's update the gateway configuration. From the root of the source code, run the following:

```
$ kubectl apply -f ch4/coolstore-gw-multi-tls.yaml
gateway.networking.istio.io/coolstore-gateway replaced
```

Finally, we need to add a `VirtualService` resource for the `catalog` service we'll expose through this ingress gateway:

```
$ kubectl apply -f ch4/catalog-vs.yaml
```

Now that we've updated the `istio-ingressgateway`, let's give it a try. Calling `webapp.istioinaction.io` should work just as it did for the simple TLS:

```
$ curl -H "Host: webapp.istioinaction.io" \
https://webapp.istioinaction.io:443/api/catalog \
--cacert ch4/certs/2_intermediate/certs/ca-chain.cert.pem \
--resolve webapp.istioinaction.io:443:127.0.0.1
```

When we call the `catalog` service through the Istio gateway, let's use different certificates:

```
$ curl -H "Host: catalog.istioinaction.io" \
https://catalog.istioinaction.io:443/items \
--cacert ch4/certs2/2_intermediate/certs/ca-chain.cert.pem \
--resolve catalog.istioinaction.io:443:127.0.0.1
```

Both calls should succeed with the same response. You may wonder how the Istio ingress gateway knows which certificate to present, depending on who's calling. There's only a single port opened for these connections: how does it know which service the client is trying to access and which certificate corresponds with that service? The answer lies in an extension to TLS called Server Name Indication (SNI). Basically, when an HTTPS connection is created, the client first identifies which service it's trying to reach using the `ClientHello` part of the TLS handshake. Istio's gateway (Envoy, specifically) implements SNI on TLS, which is how it can present the correct cert and route to the correct service.

   In this section, we successfully exposed the different virtual hosts through the ingress gateway and served each with its own unique certificate through the same HTTPS port. In the next section, we look at TCP traffic.

4.4 *TCP traffic*

Istio's gateway is powerful enough to serve not only HTTP/HTTPS traffic but also any traffic accessible via TCP. For example, we can expose a database (like MongoDB) or a message queue, like Kafka, through the ingress gateway. When Istio treats the traffic as plain TCP, we do not get as many useful features like retries, request-level circuit breaking, complex routing, and so on. This is simply because Istio cannot tell what protocol is being used (unless a specific protocol that Istio understands is used, like MongoDB). Let's take a look at how to expose TCP traffic through an Istio gateway so that clients outside the cluster can communicate with those running inside the cluster.

4.4.1 Exposing TCP ports on an Istio gateway

The first thing we need to do is create a TCP-based service within our service mesh. For this example, we use the `echo` service from https://github.com/cjimti/go-echo. This TCP service will allow us to log in with a simple TCP client like Telnet and issue commands that should be displayed back to us.

Let's deploy the TCP service and inject the Istio service proxy next to it. Recall that we're pointing to the `istioinaction` namespace:

```
$ kubectl config set-context $(kubectl config current-context) \
  --namespace=istioinaction
$ kubectl apply -f ch4/echo.yaml

deployment.apps/tcp-echo-deployment created
service/tcp-echo-service created
```

Next, we create an Istio `Gateway` resource that exposes a specific non-HTTP port for this service. In the following example, we expose port 31400 on the default `istio-ingressgateway`. Just as with the HTTP ports (80 and 443), TCP port 31400 must be made available either as a `NodePort` or as a cloud `LoadBalancer`. In our examples running on Docker Desktop, it is exposed as a `NodePort` running on port 31400:

```
apiVersion: networking.istio.io/v1alpha3
kind: Gateway
metadata:
  name: echo-tcp-gateway
spec:
  selector:
    istio: ingressgateway
  servers:
  - port:
      number: 31400        ◁—— Port to expose
      name: tcp-echo
      protocol: TCP        ◁—— Expected protocol
    hosts:
    - "*"        ◁—— For any hosts
```

You can find the port in which the `istio-ingressgateway` service is listening for TCP traffic using the following command:

```
$ kubectl get svc -n istio-system istio-ingressgateway \
    -o jsonpath='{.spec.ports[?(@.name == "tcp")]}'

{"name":"tcp","nodePort":30851,"port":31400,
➥"protocol":"TCP","targetPort":31400}
```

Let's create the gateway:

```
$ kubectl apply -f ch4/gateway-tcp.yaml

gateway.networking.istio.io/echo-tcp-gateway created
```

Now that we've exposed a port on our ingress gateway, we need to route the traffic to the `echo` service. To do that, we use the `VirtualService` resource as we did in the previous sections. Note that for TCP traffic, we must match on the incoming port—in this case, port 31400:

```
apiVersion: networking.istio.io/v1alpha3
kind: VirtualService
metadata:
  name: tcp-echo-vs-from-gw
spec:
  hosts:
  - "*"
  gateways:
  - echo-tcp-gateway      <──| Which gateway
  tcp:
  - match:
    - port: 31400         <──| Match on the port
    route:
    - destination:
        host: tcp-echo-service    <──| Where to route
        port:
          number: 2701
```

Let's create the virtual service:

```
$  kubectl apply -f ch4/echo-vs.yaml
```

```
virtualservice.networking.istio.io/tcp-echo-vs-from-gw created
```

> **NOTE** If you're running in a public cloud or a cluster that creates a Load-Balancer for the istio-ingressgateway service, and you can't connect as shown next, you may need to explicitly add a port to the istio-ingressgateway service on port 31400 and use targetPort 31400 for this to work correctly. By default, Istio 1.13.0 adds this port to the istio-ingressgateway service, but you may want to double-check.

Now that we have exposed a port on our ingress gateway and set up routing, we should be able to connect with a very simple telnet command:

```
$  telnet localhost 31400

Trying 192.168.64.27...
Connected to kubebook.
Escape character is '^]'.
Welcome, you are connected to node docker.
Running on Pod tcp-echo-deployment-6fbccd8485-m4mqq.
In namespace istioinaction.
With IP address 172.17.0.11.
Service default.
```

When you type anything into the console and press Return/Enter, your text is replayed back to you:

```
hello there
hello there
by now
by now
```

To quit Telnet, press Ctrl-], type `quit`, and press Return/Enter.

4.4.2 *Traffic routing with SNI passthrough*

In the previous section, we learned how to use the Istio gateway functionality to accept and route non-HTTP traffic: specifically, applications that may communicate over a TCP protocol that is very application-specific. Earlier, we saw how to route HTTPS traffic and present certain certificates depending on the SNI hostname. In this section, we look at a combination of these two capabilities: routing TCP traffic based on SNI hostname without terminating the traffic on the Istio ingress gateway. All the gateway will do is inspect the SNI headers and route the traffic to the specific backend, which will then terminate the TLS connection. The connection will "pass through" the gateway and be handled by the actual service, not the gateway.

This opens the door for a much wider swath of applications that can participate in the service mesh, including TCP over TLS services like databases, message queues, caches, and so on—even legacy applications that expect to handle and terminate HTTPS/TLS traffic. To see this in action, let's look at a `Gateway` definition that is configured to use `PASSTHROUGH` as its routing mechanism:

```
apiVersion: networking.istio.io/v1alpha3
kind: Gateway
metadata:
  name: sni-passthrough-gateway
spec:
  selector:
    istio: ingressgateway
  servers:
  - port:
      number: 31400        ◁─┐ Opens a specific
      name: tcp-sni          │ non-HTTP port
      protocol: TLS
                                        │ Associates this host
    hosts:                              │ with the port
    - "simple-sni-1.istioinaction.io"  ◁─┘
    tls:                     Treats this as
      mode: PASSTHROUGH   ◁──┘ passthrough traffic
```

In our example application, we configure the application to terminate TLS for the HTTPS connection using certificates. This means we don't need the ingress gateway to do anything with the connection. We won't need to configure any certificates on the gateway as we did in the previous section.

Let's get started by deploying our example application that terminates TLS. Switch to the root directory of the book's source code, and default to the `istioinaction` namespace in Kubernetes:

```
$ kubectl apply -f ch4/sni/simple-tls-service-1.yaml
```

Next, let's deploy our `Gateway` resource that opens port 31400. But before we do that, since we're using the same port as in section 4.4, let's make sure to delete the gateway that's already using that port:

```
$ kubectl delete gateway echo-tcp-gateway -n istioinaction
```

Now let's apply the passthrough gateway:

```
$ kubectl apply -f ch4/sni/passthrough-sni-gateway.yaml
```

At this point, we've opened port 31400 on the Istio ingress gateway. As you'll recall from previous sections, we also need to specify routing rules with a `VirtualService` resource to get the traffic from the gateway to the service. Here's the `VirtualService`:

```
apiVersion: networking.istio.io/v1alpha3
kind: VirtualService
metadata:
  name: simple-sni-1-vs
spec:
  hosts:
  - "simple-sni-1.istioinaction.io"
  gateways:
  - sni-passthrough-gateway
  tls:
  - match:                          ◁─── Matching clause on a
    - port: 31400                        specific port and host
      sniHosts:
      - simple-sni-1.istioinaction.io
    route:
    - destination:                  ◁─── Routing destination
        host: simple-tls-service-1       if traffic matched
        port:
          number: 80   ◁─── Routes to the
                            service port
```

Let's create the `VirtualService`:

```
$ kubectl apply -f ch4/sni/passthrough-sni-vs-1.yaml
```

Now let's call the Istio ingress gateway on port 31400:

```
$ curl -H "Host: simple-sni-1.istioinaction.io" \
 https://simple-sni-1.istioinaction.io:31400/ \
 --cacert ch4/sni/simple-sni-1/2_intermediate/certs/ca-chain.cert.pem \
 --resolve simple-sni-1.istioinaction.io:31400:127.0.0.1

{
  "name": "simple-tls-service-1",
  "uri": "/",
  "type": "HTTP",
  "ip_addresses": [
    "10.1.0.63"
  ],
  "start_time": "2020-09-03T20:09:08.129404",
  "end_time": "2020-09-03T20:09:08.129846",
  "duration": "441.5µs",
  "body": "Hello from simple-tls-service-1!!!",
  "code": 200
}
```

Our call from `curl` went to the Istio ingress gateway, traversed through without termination, and ended up on the example service `simple-tls-service-1`. To make the routing more apparent, let's deploy a second service with different certificates and routes based on the SNI host:

```
$  kubectl apply -f ch4/sni/simple-tls-service-2.yaml
```

Let's see what the `Gateway` resource looks like:

```
apiVersion: networking.istio.io/v1alpha3
kind: Gateway
metadata:
  name: sni-passthrough-gateway
spec:
  selector:
    istio: ingressgateway
  servers:
  - port:
      number: 31400
      name: tcp-sni-1
      protocol: TLS
    hosts:
    - "simple-sni-1.istioinaction.io"
    tls:
      mode: PASSTHROUGH
  - port:
      number: 31400
      name: tcp-sni-2
      protocol: TLS
    hosts:
    - "simple-sni-2.istioinaction.io"
    tls:
      mode: PASSTHROUGH
```

Let's apply this `Gateway` and `VirtualService`:

```
$  kubectl apply -f ch4/sni/passthrough-sni-gateway-both.yaml
$  kubectl apply -f ch4/sni/passthrough-sni-vs-2.yaml
```

Next we call again to the same ingress gateway port with a different hostname, and watch how the request is routed to the correct service:

```
$  curl -H "Host: simple-sni-2.istioinaction.io" \
 https://simple-sni-2.istioinaction.io:31400/ \
 --cacert ch4/sni/simple-sni-2/2_intermediate/certs/ca-chain.cert.pem \
 --resolve simple-sni-2.istioinaction.io:31400:127.0.0.1

{
  "name": "simple-tls-service-2",
  "uri": "/",
  "type": "HTTP",
  "ip_addresses": [
    "10.1.0.64"
  ],
  "start_time": "2020-09-03T20:14:13.982951",
  "end_time": "2020-09-03T20:14:13.984547",
  "duration": "1.5952ms",
```

```
  "body": "Hello from simple-tls-service-2!!!",
  "code": 200
}
```

Notice how this response in the body field indicates this request is served by the `simple-tls-service-2` service.

4.5   *Operational tips*

In this section, we leave you with some tips for using Istio's gateway capabilities in your environment. Although we deployed the out-of-the-box demo installation of Istio, which includes an ingress gateway and egress gateway deployment, the gateways are just Envoy proxies and can be configured and used as simple Envoy proxy deployments for a variety of use cases. Let's see how we can configure and tune them to meet our needs.

4.5.1   *Split gateway responsibilities*

We focused on the ingress use case in this chapter, but as stated previously, Istio's gateway is really just a simple Envoy proxy that's not deployed as a sidecar. This means you can use the gateway for various use cases such as ingress (covered here), egress, shared-gateway functionality, multi-cluster proxying, and so on. Although we positioned the ingress gateway as the single point of ingress, you can (and sometimes should) have multiple points of ingress.

You may want to deploy another ingress point to split up traffic and isolate traffic paths among various services (see figure 4.11). Some services may be more sensitive to performance or need to be more highly available or isolated for compliance reasons. Sometimes you want to let individual teams own their gateways and configuration without impacting other teams.

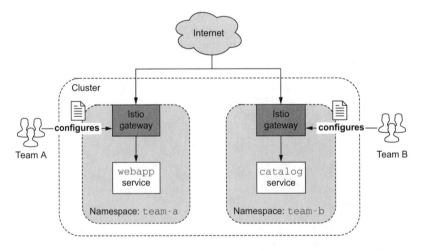

Figure 4.11   Multiple gateways allow teams to manage their configuration without impacting others.

Whatever the reason, it may be a good idea to allow multiple ingress gateways aligned to various boundaries (compliance, domain, team, and so on). Here's an example of how to define and install a new custom gateway:

```
apiVersion: install.istio.io/v1alpha1
kind: IstioOperator
metadata:
  name: my-user-gateway-install
  namespace: istioinaction
spec:
  profile: empty
  values:
    gateways:
      istio-ingressgateway:
        autoscaleEnabled: false
  components:
    ingressGateways:
    - name: istio-ingressgateway
      enabled: false
    - name: my-user-gateway
      namespace: istioinaction
      enabled: true
      label:
        istio: my-user-gateway
```

We could deploy this gateway with the following `istioctl` command:

```
$ istioctl install -y -n istioinaction -f ch4/my-user-gateway.yaml
```

This would install a new gateway just for the `istioinaction` namespace.

Keep in mind that when you create new ingress gateways, they likely need to be exposed outside of the cluster with a load balancer or other networking configuration. For example, in a public cloud, using the type `LoadBalancer` for the Kubernetes service that exposes the gateway incurs a cost per load balancer.

4.5.2 Gateway injection

Another way to allow users to create their own gateways without having to give them full access to `IstioOperator` resources (which can modify an existing Istio installation) is through gateway injection. With gateway injection, you deploy a stubbed-out gateway deployment, and Istio fills in the rest, similar to how sidecar injection is done. This way, you can give a team a stubbed-out gateway deployment resource and have Istio auto-configure the rest of it. Let's see an example:

```
apiVersion: apps/v1
kind: Deployment
metadata:
  name: my-user-gateway-injected
  namespace: istioinaction
spec:
  selector:
    matchLabels:
      ingress: my-user-gateway-injected
```

```
template:
  metadata:
    annotations:
      sidecar.istio.io/inject: "true"      ⟵┘  Enables
                                               injection
      inject.istio.io/templates: gateway   ⟵┐
    labels:                                   │  Uses the gateway
      ingress: my-user-gateway-injected      │  template
  spec:
    containers:                     ┌ Must be
    - name: istio-proxy    ⟵┘      named
      image: auto    ⟵┤ Stubbed-out image
```

The Kubernetes deployment specified is stubbed out and annotated with instructions for how Istio should do the injection. Specifically, we configure the template used for injection to be the `gateway` template. You can see which templates are available in the `istio-sidecar-injector` configmap in the `istio-system` namespace.

Let's apply this stubbed-out gateway:

```
$  kubectl apply -f ch4/my-user-gw-injection.yaml
```

```
deployment.apps/my-user-gateway-injected created
service/my-user-gateway-injected created
role.rbac.authorization.k8s.io/my-user-gateway-injected-sds created
rolebinding.rbac.authorization.k8s.io/my-user-gateway-injected-sds created
```

If you review which Pods exist in the `istioinaction` namespace, you should see the full gateway correctly filled out by Istio injection.

4.5.3   *Ingress gateway access logs*

A common feature for a proxy is logging every individual request that it processes. These *access logs* are helpful for troubleshooting issues. Istio's proxy (Envoy) can generate access logging. In the *demo* installation profile, the ingress gateways and service proxies are configured to print access logs to the standard output stream. To view the access logs, you only have to print the container logs:

```
kubectl -n istio-system logs deploy/istio-ingressgateway
```

This command prints the access logs of the ingress gateway. You should see the records of the traffic generated when we executed the earlier examples. It might surprise you to learn that access logging is disabled for the *production* Istio installation when using the *default* profile. However, you can change this by setting the `accessLogFile` property to print to the standard output stream:

```
$  istioctl install --set meshConfig.accessLogFile=/dev/stdout
```

Access logs are turned off by default, which makes sense given that production clusters have hundreds or thousands of workloads, each of which processes a lot of traffic. Additionally, because each request makes multiple hops from one service to another, the amount of access logging generated would strain any logging system. A better approach is to enable access logging only for the workloads for which you are interested in using the (new in Istio 1.12 as Alpha level) `Telemetry` API. For example, to show the access logs of only the ingress gateway workloads, you can use the following `Telemetry` configuration:

```
apiVersion: telemetry.istio.io/v1alpha1
kind: Telemetry
metadata:
  name: ingress-gateway
  namespace: istio-system
spec:
  selector:
    matchLabels:
      app: istio-ingressgateway        ⟵⎤ Pods matching the label get
  accessLogging:                          ⎦ the telemetry configuration.
  - providers:                   ⎤ The provider configuration
    - name: envoy         ⟵⎦ for access logging      ⎤ Enable by setting
      disabled: false         ⟵─────────────────⎦ disabled to false
```

This telemetry definition enables access logs for the Pods matching the selector in the `istio-system` namespace. If you have configured the Istio installation to print access logs to standard output, there is no need for access logging because all workloads are already printing to the console. However, to test it, you can set the `disabled` property to `true` and observe that the ingress gateway doesn't write access logs.

Istio configuration such as telemetry, sidecars, peer authentication, and so on can be applied in different scopes and have different precedence:

- *Mesh-wide*—Configurations are applied to workloads in the entire mesh. Mesh-wide configs must be applied in the Istio installation namespace and lack workload selectors.
- *Namespace-wide*—Configurations are applied to all workloads in a namespace. Namespace-wide configurations are applied in the namespace of the workloads we want to configure and also lack a workload selector. This overrides any mesh-wide configuration applied to the workloads.
- *Workload-specific*—Configurations apply only to workloads matching the workload selector in the namespace where the configuration is applied (as shown in the previous code). Workload-specific configuration overrides both mesh-wide and namespace-wide configuration.

NOTE Istio defines the following default providers: `prometheus`, `stackdriver`, and `envoy`. You can define custom providers using the `ExtensionProvider` API in the mesh configuration (http://mng.bz/REKP).

4.5.4 *Reducing gateway configuration*

Out of the box, Istio configures every proxy to know about every service in the mesh. If you have a mesh with many services, the configuration of the data-plane proxies can become very large. This large configuration can lead to resource bloat, performance issues, and scalability concerns. To deal with this, you can optimize the configuration for both the data plane and the control plane. See chapter 11 for more on using the Sidecar resource to trim down this configuration.

However, the Sidecar resource does not apply to gateways. When you deploy a new gateway (ingress gateway, for example), the proxy is configured with all of the services available for routing in the mesh. As mentioned, this can contribute to a very large configuration and put stress on the gateway.

The trick is to trim out any additional configurations for the proxy by including only configuration that's relevant to the gateway. Until recently, this functionality was turned off by default. In more recent versions, you can double-check whether it's enabled. In either case, you can explicitly enable configuration trimming for the gateways with the following configuration:

```
apiVersion: install.istio.io/v1alpha1
kind: IstioOperator
metadata:
  name: control-plane
spec:
  profile: minimal
  components:
    pilot:
      k8s:
        env:
        - name: PILOT_FILTER_GATEWAY_CLUSTER_CONFIG
          value: "true"
  meshConfig:
    defaultConfig:
      proxyMetadata:
        ISTIO_META_DNS_CAPTURE: "true"
    enablePrometheusMerge: true
```

The important part of this configuration is the PILOT_FILTER_GATEWAY_CLUSTER_CONFIG feature flag. It trims down the clusters in the gateway's proxy configuration to only those that are actually referenced in a VirtualService that applies to the particular gateway.

In the next chapter, we expand on our understanding of VirtualService resources for the purpose of more powerful routing within the service mesh and how this control helps us control new deployments, route around failures, and implement powerful testing capabilities.

Summary

- Ingress gateways provide fine-grained control over what traffic enters our service mesh.
- Using the Gateway resource, we can configure the type of traffic admitted into the mesh for a specific host.
- Just as with any service in the mesh, it uses VirtualService resources to route the traffic.

- TLS mode is configurable per host with one of the following modes:
  - Encrypt and prevent man-in-the-middle attacks with the SIMPLE TLS mode.
  - Mutually authenticate both server and client with the MUTUAL TLS mode.
  - Admit and reverse proxy encrypted traffic using the SNI header with the PASSTHROUGH TLS mode.
- Plain TCP traffic is supported in Istio for L7 protocols that are currently not supported. However, many features are not possible with plain TCP, such as retries, complex routing, and so on.
- We can enable teams to manage their own gateways by using gateway injection.

Traffic control: Fine-grained traffic routing

This chapter covers
- Traffic routing basics
- Shifting traffic during a new release
- Mirroring traffic to reduce the risk of a new release
- Controlling traffic as it leaves a cluster

In the previous chapter, we saw how to get traffic into a cluster and what considerations we needed to account for when doing so. Once a request makes it into our cluster, how is it routed to the appropriate service to handle the request? How do services that live within the cluster communicate with other services that live within the same cluster or outside the cluster? Finally, and most importantly, when we make changes to a service and introduce new versions, how do we safely expose our clients and customers to these changes with minimal disruption and impact?

As we've seen, Istio service proxies intercept the communication between services within the service-mesh cluster and give us a point of control for traffic. Istio allows us to finely control traffic flowing between applications down to the individual request. In this chapter, we look at why you might want to do that, how to do it, and what benefits you should achieve when utilizing these capabilities.

5.1 Reducing the risk of deploying new code

In chapter 1, we introduced the scenario of ACME Inc. moving to a cloud platform and adopting practices that helped reduce the company's risk of deploying code. One of the patterns ACME tried was *blue / green* deployments to introduce changes to applications. With a blue/green deployment, ACME took v2 (green) of the service they wanted to change and deployed it in production next to v1 (blue), as shown in figure 5.1.

When ACME wanted to release to customers, it cut the traffic over to v2 (green). This approach helped reduce outages during deployments because if there were any issues, ACME could cut back to v1 (blue) of the service.

Blue/green deployments help, but when we cut over from v1 to v2, we still experience a "big bang" in

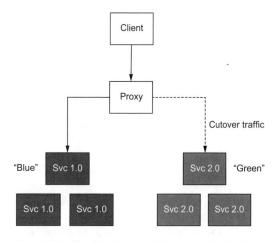

Figure 5.1 In a blue/green deployment, blue is the currently released software. When we release the new software, we cut over traffic to the green version.

which we release all the code changes at once. Let's see how we can further reduce the risk of doing deployments. First, we should clarify what we mean by *deployment* and *release*.

5.1.1 Deployment vs. release

Let's use our fictitious `catalog` service to help illustrate the differences between a *deployment* and a *release*. Suppose v1 of the `catalog` service is running in production at the moment. If we want to introduce a code change to the `catalog` service, we expect to build it using our continuous-integration system, tag it with a new version (let's say v1.1), and then deploy it and test it in pre-production environments. Once we can validate these changes in pre-production and have the necessary approvals, we can begin to bring the new version v1.1 to production.

When we do a *deployment* to production, we install the new code onto production resources (servers, containers, and so on), but we do not send any traffic to it. Doing a deployment to production should *not* impact users running in production because it doesn't take any user requests. At this point, we can run tests on the new deployment running in production to verify that it works as we expect (see figure 5.2). We should have metrics and log collection enabled, so we can use these signals to inform our confidence that our new deployment is behaving as expected.

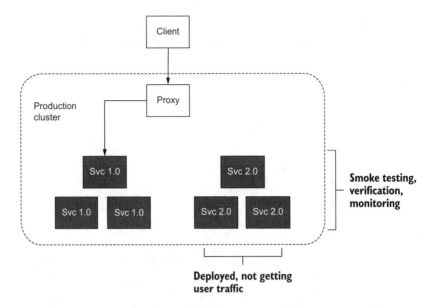

Figure 5.2   A *deployment* is code that is installed into production but does not take any live production traffic. While the deployment is installed into production, we do smoke tests and validate it.

Once we have code deployed into production, we can make a business decision about how to *release* it to our users. *Releasing* code means bringing live traffic over to our new deployment. But this is not an all-or-nothing proposition. This is where a decoupling between *deployment* and *release* becomes crucial to reduce the risk of bringing

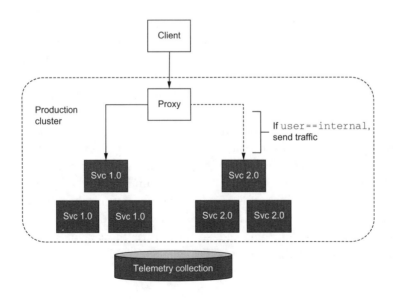

Figure 5.3   A release is when we start to bring production traffic over to the deployment, ideally in an incremental way.

new code to production. We can decide to release new software only to internal employees (see figure 5.3). Those internal employees can control the traffic such that they are exposed to the new version of the software. As operators of the software, they can then observe (using logging and metrics collection) and verify that the code change had the intended effect.

Now the old version of our software is taking the bulk of the live traffic, and the newer version is taking a small fraction of the traffic. This approach is known as *canarying* or a *canary release* (using the metaphor of a canary in a coal mine). Basically, we choose a small group of users to expose to the new version of our code and watch how it behaves. If it has unintended behaviors, we can back out the release and redirect traffic to the previous version of our service.

If we're comfortable with the behavior and performance of the new code changes, we can further open the aperture of the release (see figure 5.4). We may wish to allow non-paying customers or silver-level (versus gold or platinum) customers to see these changes now.

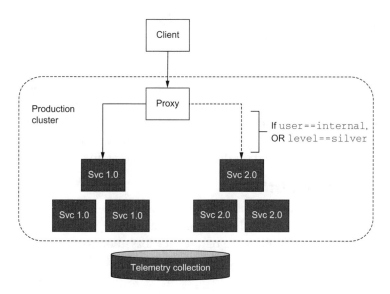

Figure 5.4   We can graduate the release to more of our user base by opening the criteria for which users should be routed to our new deployment.

We continue this iterative approach to release and observe until all of our customers are exposed to these new code changes (see figure 5.5). At any point in this process, we may find that the new code doesn't deliver the functionality, behavior, or performance we expected and validated through real user interaction. We can then roll back the release by directing traffic back to the previous version.

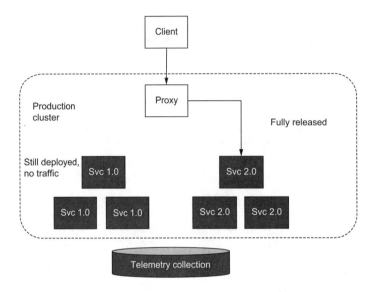

Figure 5.5   We can continue to shift traffic over to our new deployment until it's fully released. A rollback shifts traffic back to the original deployment.

In the past, ACME combined the two ideas of *deployment* and *release*. To bring code changes to production, the company initiated a rolling upgrade that effectively replaced old versions of a service with a new version. As soon as the new version was introduced to the cluster, it received production traffic. This approach exposed users to the new version of the code and any bugs or issues that it brought along.

Decoupling deployment and release allows us to more finely control how and which users are exposed to the new changes. This allows us to reduce the risk of bringing new code to production. Let's see how Istio can help lower the risk of doing a release by controlling traffic based on the requests that come into the system.

5.2   *Routing requests with Istio*

In chapter 2, we used Istio to control traffic to the `catalog` service. We used the Istio `VirtualService` resource to specify how to route the traffic. Let's take a closer look at how that works. We'll control the route of a request based on its content (by evaluating its headers). In this way, we can make a deployment available to certain users with a technique called a *dark launch*. In a dark launch, a large percentage of users are sent to a known working version of a service, while certain classes of users are sent to a newer version. Thus we can expose new functionality in a controlled way to a specific group without affecting everyone else.

5.2.1   *Cleaning up our workspace*

Before we dive in, let's clean up our environment, so we can start from a clean slate. If you're not already in the `istioinaction` namespace in your Kubernetes cluster, switch to the `istioinaction` namespace like this:

```
$  kubectl config set-context $(kubectl config current-context) \
 --namespace=istioinaction
```

Now clean up any resources:

```
$ kubectl delete deployment,svc,gateway,\
virtualservice,destinationrule --all -n istioinaction
```

5.2.2 Deploying v1 of the catalog service

Let's deploy v1 of our `catalog` service. From the root of the book's source code, run the following command:

```
$ kubectl apply -f services/catalog/kubernetes/catalog.yaml

serviceaccount/catalog created
service/catalog created
deployment.extensions/catalog created
```

Give it a few moments to start up. You can watch the progress with the following command:

```
$ kubectl get pod -w

NAME                    READY   STATUS    RESTARTS   AGE
catalog-98cfcf4cd-xnv79 2/2     Running   0          33s
```

At this point, we can only reach the `catalog` service from within the cluster. Run the following command to verify that we can reach the `catalog` service and that it responds correctly:

```
$ kubectl run -i -n default --rm --restart=Never dummy \
--image=curlimages/curl --command -- \
sh -c 'curl -s http://catalog.istioinaction/items'
```

Now, let's expose the `catalog` service to clients that live outside the cluster. Recalling what we learned in chapter 4, we use an Istio `Gateway` resource to do this (note that the domain we're using is `catalog.istioinaction.io`):

```
apiVersion: networking.istio.io/v1alpha3
kind: Gateway
metadata:
  name: catalog-gateway
spec:
  selector:
    istio: ingressgateway
  servers:
  - port:
      number: 80
      name: http
      protocol: HTTP
    hosts:
    - "catalog.istioinaction.io"
```

Run the following command:

```
$ kubectl apply -f ch5/catalog-gateway.yaml

gateway.networking.istio.io/catalog-gateway created
```

Next, just as we saw in chapter 4, we need to create a `VirtualService` resource that routes traffic to our `catalog` service. The `VirtualService` resource looks like this:

```
apiVersion: networking.istio.io/v1alpha3
kind: VirtualService
metadata:
  name: catalog-vs-from-gw
spec:
  hosts:
  - "catalog.istioinaction.io"
  gateways:
  - catalog-gateway
  http:
  - route:
    - destination:
        host: catalog
```

Let's create this `VirtualService`:

```
$  kubectl apply -f ch5/catalog-vs.yaml
```

```
virtualservice.networking.istio.io/catalog-vs-from-gw created
```

We can now reach the `catalog` service from outside the cluster by calling into the Istio gateway. We are using Docker Desktop, which publishes the Istio ingress gateway on `localhost:80`, so we can run the following command:

```
$  curl http://localhost/items -H "Host: catalog.istioinaction.io"
```

You should see the same output as when we called the service from inside the cluster. In this case, we're going through the gateway and calling the `catalog` service from outside the cluster (see figure 5.6).

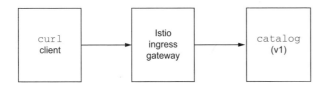

Figure 5.6   In this initial example, we're calling the `catalog` service directly through the gateway.

5.2.3   *Deploying v2 of the catalog service*

To see the traffic-control features of Istio, let's deploy v2 of the `catalog` service. This command assumes you're at the root of the source code directory:

```
$  kubectl apply -f services/catalog/kubernetes/catalog-deployment-v2.yaml
```

```
deployment.extensions/catalog-v2 created
```

List the Pods in your cluster:

```
$ kubectl get pod
```

```
NAME                          READY   STATUS    RESTARTS   AGE
catalog-98cfcf4cd-xnv79       2/2     Running   0          14m
catalog-v2-598b8cfbb5-6vw84   2/2     Running   0          36s
```

If you call the catalog service multiple times, some responses have an additional field in the response. v2 responses have a field called imageUrl, while v1 responses do not:

```
$ for in in {1..10}; do curl http://localhost/items \
-H "Host: catalog.istioinaction.io"; printf "\n\n"; done

[
  {
    "id": 0,
    "color": "teal",
    "department": "Clothing",
    "name": "Small Metal Shoes",
    "price": "232.00",
    "imageUrl": "http://lorempixel.com/640/480"
  }
]
[
  {
    "id": 0,
    "color": "teal",
    "department": "Clothing",
    "name": "Small Metal Shoes",
    "price": "232.00"
  }
]
```

5.2.4   *Routing all traffic to v1 of the catalog service*

As we did in chapter 2, let's route all traffic to v1 of the catalog service. This is the usual traffic pattern before beginning the dark launch. We need to give Istio a hint about how to identify which workloads are v1 and which are v2. In our Kubernetes Deployment resource for v1 of the catalog service, we use the labels app: catalog and version: v1. For the Deployment that specifies v2 of catalog, we use the labels app: catalog and version: v2. For Istio, we create a DestinationRule that specifies these different versions as subsets:

```
apiVersion: networking.istio.io/v1alpha3
kind: DestinationRule
metadata:
  name: catalog
spec:
  host: catalog
  subsets:
  - name: version-v1
    labels:
      version: v1
```

```
  - name: version-v2
    labels:
      version: v2
```

Let's create this `DestinationRule`. Run the following:

```
$ kubectl apply -f ch5/catalog-dest-rule.yaml

destinationrule.networking.istio.io/catalog created
```

Now that we've specified to Istio how to break up the different versions of our `catalog` service, let's update our `VirtualService` to route all traffic to v1 of `catalog`:

```
apiVersion: networking.istio.io/v1alpha3
kind: VirtualService
metadata:
  name: catalog-vs-from-gw
spec:
  hosts:
  - "catalog.istioinaction.io"
  gateways:
  - catalog-gateway
  http:
  - route:
    - destination:
        host: catalog
        subset: version-v1        <───┐ Specify
                                       │ subset
```

Let's update this `VirtualService`:

```
$ kubectl apply -f ch5/catalog-vs-v1.yaml

virtualservice.networking.istio.io/catalog-vs-from-gw configured
```

Now, when we call our `catalog` service, we see only v1 responses:

```
$ for i in {1..10}; do curl http://localhost/items \
-H "Host: catalog.istioinaction.io"; printf "\n\n"; done
```

At this point, all traffic is routed to v1 of the `catalog` service, as depicted in figure 5.7. Now, suppose we want to route specific requests to v2 in a controlled manner. Let's see how in the next section.

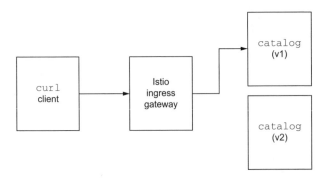

Figure 5.7   Routing all traffic to v1 of `catalog`

5.2.5 Routing specific requests to v2

Maybe we wish to route any traffic that includes the HTTP header x-istio-cohort: internal to v2 of catalog. We can specify this request routing in the Istio Virtual-Service resource like this:

```
apiVersion: networking.istio.io/v1alpha3
kind: VirtualService
metadata:
  name: catalog-vs-from-gw
spec:
  hosts:
  - "catalog.istioinaction.io"
  gateways:
  - catalog-gateway
  http:
  - match:
    - headers:
        x-istio-cohort:
          exact: "internal"
    route:
    - destination:
        host: catalog
        subset: version-v2
  - route:
    - destination:
        host: catalog
        subset: version-v1
```

Let's update this VirtualService:

```
$  kubectl apply -f ch5/catalog-vs-v2-request.yaml
```

```
virtualservice.networking.istio.io/catalog-vs-from-gw configured
```

When we call our service, we still see v1 responses. However, if we send a request with the x-istio-cohort header equal to internal, we are routed to v2 of the catalog service and see the expected response, as shown in figure 5.8:

```
$  curl  http://localhost/items \
-H "Host: catalog.istioinaction.io" -H "x-istio-cohort: internal"
```

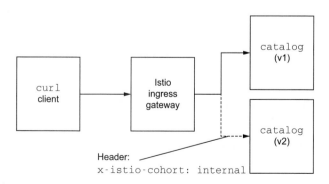

Figure 5.8 Fine-grained request routing for requests with certain content

5.2.6   *Routing deep within a call graph*

Up to this point, we've seen how we can use Istio to do request routing, but we've been doing the routing from the edge/gateway. These traffic rules can also be applied deep within a call graph (see figure 5.9). We did this in chapter 2, so let's re-create the process and verify that it works as expected.

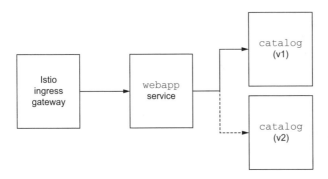

Figure 5.9   **Fine-grained request routing for requests with certain content deep within a call graph**

> **NOTE** Istio's routing capabilities derive from Envoy's capabilities. For request-specific routing, teams may opt to use application injected headers, as we see in this example of using x-istio-cohort, or rely on known headers like Agent or a value from a cookie. In practice, you can also use decision engines to decide what headers to inject and subsequently make routing decisions on.

First, remove all the Istio resources in our istioinaction namespace:

```
$  kubectl delete gateway,virtualservice,destinationrule --all
```

Let's restore the architecture we had in chapter 2 with the webapp and catalog services (and an Istio gateway directing traffic to webapp):

```
$  kubectl apply -f \
services/webapp/kubernetes/webapp.yaml

serviceaccount/webapp created
service/webapp created
deployment.extensions/webapp created
```

Now, set up the Istio ingress gateway to route to the webapp service:

```
$  kubectl apply -f services/webapp/istio/webapp-catalog-gw-vs.yaml

gateway.networking.istio.io/coolstore-gateway created
virtualservice.networking.istio.io/webapp-virtualservice created
```

Wait until the Pods come up correctly:

```
$ kubectl get pod -w

NAME                          READY    STATUS     RESTARTS    AGE
catalog-98cfcf4cd-t1lnl       2/2      Running    0           13m
catalog-v2-598b8cfbb5-5m65c   2/2      Running    0           28s
webapp-86b9cf46d6-5vzrg       2/2      Running    0           13m
```

If you issue calls again to the webapp service, you should see alternating responses to
v1 and v2 of catalog as we saw earlier when accessing catalog directly:

```
$ curl -H "Host: webapp.istioinaction.io" http://localhost/api/catalog
```

Let's create VirtualService and DestinationRule resources that route all traffic to
v1 of the catalog service:

```
$ kubectl apply -f ch5/catalog-dest-rule.yaml

destinationrule.networking.istio.io/catalog created

$ kubectl apply -f ch5/catalog-vs-v1-mesh.yaml

virtualservice.networking.istio.io/catalog created
```

Now, if you hit the webapp service endpoint again, you should only see v1 catalog
responses:

```
$ curl http://localhost/api/catalog -H "Host: webapp.istioinaction.io"
```

Finally, we add request-based routing specifying that routing depends on whether the
x-istio-cohort header is present and equals internal:

```
apiVersion: networking.istio.io/v1alpha3
kind: VirtualService
metadata:
  name: catalog
spec:
  hosts:
  - catalog
  gateways:              ┐ The virtual service applies to
  - mesh        ◁──┘ all sidecars in the mesh.
  http:
  - match:
    - headers:
        x-istio-cohort:
          exact: "internal"
    route:
    - destination:
        host: catalog
        subset: version-v2
  - route:
    - destination:
        host: catalog
        subset: version-v1
```

Let's update the `VirtualService`:

```
$  kubectl apply -f ch5/catalog-vs-v2-request-mesh.yaml
```

Pass in the `x-istio-cohort` header, and you see the traffic routed to v2 of the catalog service in the call graph:

```
$  curl http://localhost/api/catalog -H "Host: webapp.istioinaction.io" \
-H "x-istio-cohort: internal"
```

5.3   *Traffic shifting*

In this section, we look at another way to "canary" or incrementally release a deployment. In the previous section, we showed routing based on header matching to achieve a dark launch for certain user groups. In this section, we distribute all live traffic to a set of versions for a particular service based on weights. For example, if we've dark-launched v2 of our `catalog` service to internal employees, and we'd like to slowly release this version to everyone, we can specify a routing weight of 10% to v2: 10% of all traffic destined for `catalog` will go to v2, and 90% of the traffic will still go to v1. This way, we can further reduce the risk of doing a release by controlling how much of the total traffic would be affected by any negative impacts of the v2 code.

As with the dark launch, we want to monitor and observe our service for any errors and roll back the release if there are issues. In this case, rolling back is as simple as changing the routing weights so that v2 of the `catalog` service gets a reduced percentage of total traffic (all the way back to 0%, if needed). Let's take a look at using Istio to perform weighted traffic shifting.

From the previous section, the following services are running (including v1 and v2 of catalog):

```
$  kubectl get pod
```

```
NAME                          READY    STATUS    RESTARTS    AGE
webapp-86b9cf46d6-5vzrg       2/2      Running   58          12h
catalog-98cfcf4cd-tllnl       1/2      Running   60          12h
catalog-v2-598b8cfbb5-5m65c   1/2      Running   58          11h
```

Let's reset all traffic to v1 of the catalog service:

```
$  kubectl apply -f ch5/catalog-vs-v1-mesh.yaml

virtualservice.networking.istio.io/catalog configured
```

If we call our service, we see only responses from v1, as expected:

```
$  for i in {1..10}; do curl http://localhost/api/catalog \
-H "Host: webapp.istioinaction.io"; done
```

Let's route 10% of the traffic to v2 of catalog:

```
apiVersion: networking.istio.io/v1alpha3
kind: VirtualService
metadata:
```

```
  name: catalog
spec:
  hosts:
  - catalog
  gateways:
  - mesh
  http:
  - route:
    - destination:
        host: catalog
        subset: version-v1
      weight: 90
    - destination:
        host: catalog
        subset: version-v2
      weight: 10
```

Most traffic goes to v1.

Some traffic goes to v2.

Now we update the routing for `catalog`:

```
$  kubectl apply -f ch5/catalog-vs-v2-10-90-mesh.yaml

virtualservice.networking.istio.io/catalog configured
```

If we call our service, approximately 1 out of 10 calls have the v2 response:

```
$  for i in {1..100}; do curl -s http://localhost/api/catalog \
-H "Host: webapp.istioinaction.io"  \
| grep -i imageUrl; done | wc -l
```

In this command, we call the /api/catalog endpoint 100 times. When the command returns, a result close to 10 (10% of 100 items) should be printed on the screen.

If we want to split traffic 50/50, we just need to update the weights on the routing:

```
apiVersion: networking.istio.io/v1alpha3
kind: VirtualService
metadata:
  name: catalog
spec:
  hosts:
  - catalog
  gateways:
    - mesh
  http:
  - route:
    - destination:
        host: catalog
        subset: version-v1
      weight: 50
    - destination:
        host: catalog
        subset: version-v2
      weight: 50
```

```
$  kubectl apply -f ch5/catalog-vs-v2-50-50-mesh.yaml

virtualservice.networking.istio.io/catalog configured
```

Try calling the service again:

```
$  for i in {1..100}; do curl -s http://localhost/api/catalog \
-H "Host: webapp.istioinaction.io"  \
| grep -i imageUrl; done | wc -l
```

A value of approximately 50 is returned from that command, which means about half the calls returned with a response from v2 of our backend `catalog` service.

You can shift the traffic between 1 and 100 for each version of your service, but the sum of all the weights must equal 100. If it doesn't, unpredictable traffic routing can occur. Also note that if you have versions other than just v1 and v2, they must be declared as `subsets` in the `DestinationRule`. See ch5/catalog-dest-rule.yaml for an example.

For the steps in this chapter, we've manually shifted traffic between different versions. Ideally, we want to automate this traffic shifting behind some tooling or a deployment pipeline in the continuous integration / continuous delivery (CI/CD) pipeline. In the next section, we look at a tool that can help automate this canary release process.

> **WARNING** As you slowly release a new software version, you should monitor and observe both the new and old versions to verify things like stability, performance, and correctness. If you spot any signs of impact, you can easily roll back to the older version of the service by shifting the weights. Also keep in mind that your services need to be built to support multiple versions running concurrently when you use this approach. The more stateful a service is (even if it depends on external state), the more difficult this can be. See our blog posts at http://bit.ly/2NSE2gf and http://bit.ly/2oJ86jc for more thoughts on this topic.

5.3.1   Canary releasing with Flagger

Istio gives operators some powerful features to control traffic routing, as we saw in the previous sections, but we had to manually make the routing changes and apply new configuration from the CLI. We also created multiple versions of the configuration, which means more work and opportunities for misconfiguration.

We wish to avoid this manual human intervention when driving the canary since hundreds of releases may be going on simultaneously, and we want to reduce the chance for errors. We can automate the release of a service by using something like Flagger (https://flagger.app). Flagger is a canary-automation tool written by Stefan Prodan that allows you to specify parameters about how to perform the release, when to open the release to more users, and when to roll back if a release introduces issues. Flagger creates all of the appropriate configuration to drive the release.

Let's see how to use Flagger with Istio. In the previous section, we deployed `catalog-v2` and a `VirtualService` resource to explicitly control the traffic routing. Let's remove those and let Flagger handle the routing and the deployment changes:

```
$  kubectl delete vs catalog
virtualservice.networking.istio.io "catalog" deleted
```

```
$ kubectl delete deploy catalog-v2
deployment.apps "catalog-v2" deleted

$ kubectl delete service catalog
service "catalog" deleted

$ kubectl delete destinationrule catalog
destinationrule.networking.istio.io "catalog" deleted
```

Flagger relies on metrics to determine the health of a service, especially as a canary release is introduced. For Flagger to use any of the success metrics, we need to have Prometheus installed and scraping the Istio data plane. If you've been following along with the examples in this book, the Prometheus sample should already be installed. If not, quickly install the Prometheus add-on that comes with Istio:

```
$ kubectl apply -f istio-1.13.0/samples/addons/prometheus.yaml \
  -n istio-system
```

Next we want to install Flagger. Flagger uses Helm for installation, so verify that you have Helm 3.x on your system path:

```
$ helm repo add flagger https://flagger.app
$ kubectl apply -f \
https://raw.githubusercontent.com/fluxcd/\
flagger/main/artifacts/flagger/crd.yaml

$ helm install flagger flagger/flagger \
    --namespace=istio-system \
    --set crd.create=false \
    --set meshProvider=istio \
    --set metricsServer=http://prometheus:9090
```

NOTE See the Flagger documentation at https://docs.flagger.app/install/ flagger-install-on-kubernetes for more complete installation options and steps.

After installation, you should see the Prometheus and Flagger deployments in the istio-system namespace:

```
$ kubectl get po -n istio-system
NAME                                    READY   STATUS    RESTARTS   AGE
flagger-6764c647ff-w6jqz                1/1     Running   0          27h
istio-ingressgateway-7576658c9b-vcx7n   1/1     Running   0          5d4h
istiod-c85d85ddd-vtrlz                  1/1     Running   0          7d21h
prometheus-7d76687994-nh9bf             2/2     Running   0          27h
```

We're going to use the Flagger Canary resource to specify the parameters of our canary release, and we'll let Flagger create the appropriate resources to orchestrate this release as shown in the following listing.

Listing 5.1 Flagger Canary resource to configure canary automation

```
apiVersion: flagger.app/v1beta1
kind: Canary
```

```
metadata:
  name: catalog-release
  namespace: istioinaction
spec:
  targetRef:
    apiVersion: apps/v1        ◁──┐  Which deployment
    kind: Deployment              │  to canary
    name: catalog
  progressDeadlineSeconds: 60
  # Service / VirtualService Config
  service:                     ◁──┐  Configuration
    name: catalog                │  for the service
    port: 80
    targetPort: 3000
    gateways:
    - mesh
    hosts:
    - catalog
  analysis:              ◁──┐  Canary progression
    interval: 45s           │  parameters
    threshold: 5
    maxWeight: 50
    stepWeight: 10
    metrics:
    - name: request-success-rate
      thresholdRange:
        min: 99
      interval: 1m
    - name: request-duration
      thresholdRange:
        max: 500
      interval: 30s
```

In this Canary resource, we specify which Kubernetes Deployment should be the target of the canary, what Kubernetes Service and Istio VirtualService should be automatically created, and how to proceed with the canary. The last part of the Canary resource describes how quickly to promote the canary, what metrics to watch to determine viability, and the thresholds for determining success. We evaluate the canary steps every 45 seconds and increase the traffic by 10% at each step; when we get to 50% traffic, we cut over traffic to 100%.

We also specify that for the success-rate metric, we will tolerate only 99% success checking over a period of 1 minute. We also allow only a 500 ms request duration at P99 (the 99th percentile). If these metrics deviate from what we've specified for more than five intervals, the canary will be halted and rolled back.

Let's apply the configuration from listing 5.1 and begin the process of canarying the catalog service to v2 automatically. From the ch5 folder, run the following:

```
$ kubectl apply -f ch5/flagger/catalog-release.yaml

canary.flagger.app/catalog-release created
```

It may take a few moments, but during that time you can check the status of the canary as follows:

```
$  kubectl get canary catalog-release -w
NAME               STATUS         WEIGHT    LASTTRANSITIONTIME
catalog-release    Initializing   0         2021-01-20T22:50:16Z
catalog-release    Initialized    0         2021-01-20T22:51:11Z
```

At this point, Flagger has automatically created some of the Kubernetes resources necessary to drive a canary release, such as the Deployment, Service, and Virtual-Service objects. For example, if we examine the Istio VirtualService set up by Flagger, we'll get an idea of the routing rules.

Run the following command:

```
$  kubectl get virtualservice catalog -o yaml
```

Flagger automatically creates the corresponding VirtualService:

```
apiVersion: networking.istio.io/v1beta1
kind: VirtualService
metadata:
  name: catalog
  namespace: istioinaction
spec:
  gateways:
  - mesh
  hosts:
  - catalog
  http:
  - route:
    - destination:
        host: catalog-primary
      weight: 100
    - destination:
        host: catalog-canary
      weight: 0
```

From this VirtualService, we can see that traffic destined for the catalog service will be routed 100% to the catalog-primary service and 0% to the canary. Up to this point, all we've done is set up the base configuration; we haven't actually done the canary. Flagger watches for changes to the original deployment target (in this case, the catalog deployment), creates the canary deployment (catalog-canary) and service (catalog-canary), and adjusts the VirtualService weights.

Let's introduce v2 of catalog and see how Flagger automates it through a release and makes decisions based on metrics. Let's also generate load to the service through Istio, so Flagger has a baseline of what the metrics look like when healthy. In a new terminal window, run the following to loop through calling the services:

```
$  while true; do curl "http://localhost/api/catalog" \
-H "Host: webapp.istioinaction.io" ; sleep 1; done
```

Next, run the following command to deploy the `catalog-v2` service:

```
$ kubectl apply -f ch5/flagger/catalog-deployment-v2.yaml
deployment.apps/catalog configured
```

We can watch the evolution and progress of the canary with the following command:

```
$ kubectl get canary catalog-release -w
```

While the canary progresses and we see weight being shifted to the `catalog-v2` service, we can check the `VirtualService` resource config and verify that it matches with the traffic shifting expected:

```
$ kubectl get virtualservice catalog -o yaml
```

Flagger controls the weights of the `VirtualService`:

```
apiVersion: networking.istio.io/v1beta1
kind: VirtualService
metadata:
  name: catalog
  namespace: istioinaction
spec:
  gateways:
  - mesh
  hosts:
  - catalog
  http:
  - route:
    - destination:
        host: catalog-primary
      weight: 90
    - destination:
        host: catalog-canary
      weight: 10
```

We expect progression to happen for the canary every 45 seconds, as configured in the `Canary` object. Steps are made in 10% increments until 50% of the traffic is shifted to the canary. If Flagger sees that the metrics look good and there are no deviations, the process will progress until all traffic goes to the canary and it is promoted to the primary service. If things misbehave, Flagger will automatically roll back the canary release.

After a time, the output for the canary status looks something like this:

```
$ kubectl get canary catalog-release -w
NAME              STATUS         WEIGHT   LASTTRANSITIONTIME
catalog-release   Initializing   0        2021-01-20T22:50:16Z
catalog-release   Initialized    0        2021-01-20T22:51:11Z
catalog-release   Progressing    0        2021-01-20T22:58:41Z
catalog-release   Progressing    10       2021-01-20T22:59:26Z
catalog-release   Progressing    20       2021-01-20T23:00:11Z
catalog-release   Progressing    30       2021-01-20T23:00:56Z
catalog-release   Progressing    40       2021-01-20T23:01:41Z
```

```
catalog-release    Progressing    50    2021-01-20T23:02:26Z
catalog-release    Promoting       0    2021-01-20T23:03:11Z
catalog-release    Finalising      0    2021-01-20T23:03:56Z
catalog-release    Succeeded       0    2021-01-20T23:04:41Z
```

We used Flagger to automatically control the canary release using Istio's APIs and removed the need to manually configure resources or introduce any manual behavior that could cause configuration errors. Flagger can also do dark-launch testing, traffic mirroring (discussed in the next section), and more; see https://flagger.app.

To clean up this exercise and get the configuration into a state to continue the chapter, let's remove the Flagger `Canary` resource, reset the `catalog` deployment, and deploy `catalog-v2` as a separate deployment:

```
$ kubectl delete canary catalog-release
$ kubectl delete deploy catalog
$ kubectl apply -f services/catalog/kubernetes/catalog-svc.yaml
$ kubectl apply -f services/catalog/kubernetes/catalog-deployment.yaml
$ kubectl apply -f services/catalog/kubernetes/catalog-deployment-v2.yaml
$ kubectl apply -f ch5/catalog-dest-rule.yaml
```

Finally, remove Flagger:

```
$  helm uninstall flagger -n istio-system
```

5.4   *Reducing risk even further: Traffic mirroring*

Using the previous two techniques of request-level routing and traffic shifting, we can lower the risk of doing releases. Both techniques use live traffic and requests and can impact users even though you can control how widespread a potentially negative effect may be. Another approach is to mirror production traffic to a new deployment that copies the production traffic and sends it to the new deployment out of band of any customer traffic, as shown in figure 5.10. Using the mirroring approach, we can direct real production traffic to our deployment and get real feedback about how new code will behave without impacting users. Istio supports mirroring traffic, which can reduce the risk of doing a deployment and release even more than the other two approaches. Let's take a look.

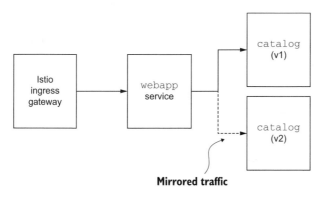

Figure 5.10   Traffic mirrored to the `catalog-v2` service out of band from the request path

To mirror traffic to v2 of our `catalog` service, let's first reset all traffic to v1. From the ch5 folder, run the following:

```
$  kubectl apply -f ch5/catalog-vs-v1-mesh.yaml
```

Now, let's look at the `VirtualService` we need to do the mirroring:

```
apiVersion: networking.istio.io/v1alpha3
kind: VirtualService
metadata:
  name: catalog
spec:
  hosts:
  - catalog
  gateways:
    - mesh
  http:
  - route:
    - destination:
        host: catalog
        subset: version-v1
      weight: 100          ⎤ Mirroring
    mirror:        ◄────────⎦ clause
      host: catalog                  ⎤ Subset of the
      subset: version-v2   ◄─────────⎦ catalog service
```

With this `VirtualService` definition, we route 100% of live traffic to v1 of the catalog service, but we also mirror the traffic to v2. As mentioned earlier, mirroring is done in a fire-and-forget manner in which a copy of the request is created and sent to the mirrored cluster (in this case, v2 of catalog). This mirrored request cannot affect the real request because the Istio proxy that does the mirroring ignores any responses (success/failure) from the mirrored cluster. Let's create this `VirtualService` resource:

```
$  kubectl apply -f ch5/catalog-vs-v2-mirror.yaml
```

```
virtualservice.networking.istio.io/catalog created
```

Now, if we send traffic to our service, we should see a response only from v1 of the catalog service:

```
$ curl http://localhost/api/catalog -H "Host: webapp.istioinaction.io"
```

We can check the log of the v1 service to verify that we're getting traffic:

```
$  CATALOG_V1=$(kubectl get pod -l app=catalog -l version=v1 \
-o jsonpath={.items..metadata.name})
$  kubectl logs $CATALOG_V1 -c catalog
```

The log entries look like this:

```
request path: /items
blowups: {}
number of blowups: 0
```

```
GET catalog.istioinaction:80 /items 200 502 - 2.363 ms
GET /items 200 2.363 ms - 502
```

If we get the log of v2 of the `catalog` service, we also see logging entries:

```
$  CATALOG_V2=$(kubectl get pod -l app=catalog -l version=v2 \
-o jsonpath={.items..metadata.name})
$  kubectl logs $CATALOG_V2 -c catalog

request path: /items
blowups: {}
number of blowups: 0
GET catalog.istioinaction-shadow:80 /items 200 698 - 2.517 ms
GET /items 200 2.517 ms - 698
```

For each request we send into our service, a request goes to v1 of `catalog` as well as v2. The request that makes it to v1 is the live request, and that's the response we see. The request that makes it to v2 is mirrored and sent as fire-and-forget.

Note that when the mirrored traffic makes it to `catalog` v2, the `Host` header has been modified to indicate that it is mirrored/shadowed traffic: instead of `Host: catalog:8080`, it is `Host: catalog-shadow:8080`. A service that receives a request with the `-shadow` postfix can identify that request as a mirrored request and take that into consideration when processing it (for example, the response will be discarded, so either roll back a transaction or don't make any calls that are resource-intensive).

Mirroring traffic is one part of the story to lower the risk of doing releases. Just as with request routing and traffic shifting, our applications should be aware of this context and be able to run in both live and mirrored modes, run as multiple versions, or both. See our blog posts at http://bit.ly/2NSE2gf and http://bit.ly/2oJ86jc to learn more.

5.5   Routing to services outside your cluster by using Istio's service discovery

By default, Istio allows any traffic out of the service mesh. For example, if an application tries to talk with external websites or services not managed by the service mesh, Istio allows this traffic out. Since all traffic first passes through the service-mesh sidecar proxy (Istio proxy), and we can control traffic routing, we can change Istio's default policy and deny all traffic that tries to leave the mesh.

Blocking all traffic leaving the mesh is a basic defense-in-depth posture to prevent bad actors from phoning home if a service or application within the mesh becomes compromised. Blocking external traffic using Istio is not sufficient, however. A compromised Pod could bypass the proxy. Therefore, you need a defense-in-depth approach with additional traffic blocking mechanisms such as layer 3 and layer 4 protection.

For example, if a vulnerability allows an attacker to take control of a particular service, they can try to inject code or otherwise manipulate the service to reach out to servers they control. If they can do this and further control the compromised service, they can exfiltrate company-sensitive data and intellectual property.

Let's configure Istio to block external traffic, leaving the mesh providing a simple layer of protection (see figure 5.11). Run the following command to change Istio's default from `ALLOW_ANY` to `REGISTRY_ONLY`. This means we'll allow traffic to leave the mesh only if it's explicitly whitelisted in the service-mesh registry:

```
$  istioctl install --set profile=demo \
 --set meshConfig.outboundTrafficPolicy.mode=REGISTRY_ONLY
```

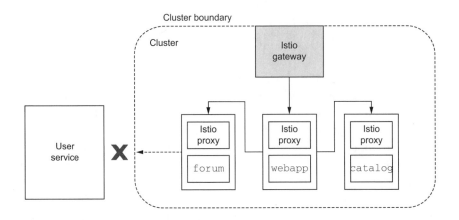

Figure 5.11 Let's block any traffic trying to leave the service by default.

> **NOTE** Here we update the Istio installation and set the `outboundTraffic-Policy` setting to `REGISTRY_ONLY`. For this book and experimentation purposes, that is fine. However, in a real deployment, you'd likely make changes to the Istio installation with `IstioOperator` or update the `istio` configmap in `istio-system` directly.

Since not all services live in the service mesh, we need a way for services inside the mesh to communicate with those outside the mesh. Those could be existing HTTP services or, more likely, infrastructure services like databases or caches. We can still implement sophisticated routing for services that reside outside Istio, but first we have to introduce the concept of a `ServiceEntry`.

Istio builds up an internal service registry of all the services that are known by the mesh and that can be accessed within the mesh. You can think of this registry as the canonical representation of a service-discovery registry that services within the mesh can use to find other services. Istio builds this internal registry by making assumptions about the platform on which the control plane is deployed. For example, in this book, we're deploying the control plane onto Kubernetes. Istio uses the default Kubernetes API to build its catalog of services (based on Kubernetes `Service` objects; see https://kubernetes.io/docs/concepts/services-networking/service), as depicted in figure

5.12. For our services within the mesh to communicate with those outside the mesh, we need to let Istio's service-discovery registry know about this external service.

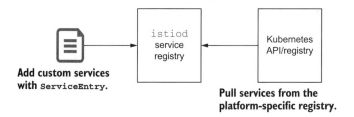

Figure 5.12 We can specify `ServiceEntry` **resources that augment and insert external services into the Istio service registry.**

In our fictitious store, we want to provide the best possible customer service and allow customers to give feedback or share thoughts directly with each other. To do that, we'll connect our users with an online forum that is built and deployed outside of our service-mesh cluster. In this case, our forum lives at the URL jsonplaceholder.typicode.com.

The Istio `ServiceEntry` resource encapsulates registry metadata that we can use to insert an entry into Istio's service registry. Here's an example:

```
apiVersion: networking.istio.io/v1alpha3
kind: ServiceEntry
metadata:
  name: jsonplaceholder
spec:
  hosts:
  - jsonplaceholder.typicode.com
  ports:
  - number: 80
    name: http
    protocol: HTTP
  resolution: DNS
  location: MESH_EXTERNAL
```

This `ServiceEntry` resource inserts an entry into Istio's service registry, which makes explicit that clients within the mesh are allowed to call JSON Placeholder using host `jsonplaceholder.typicode.com`. The JSON Placeholder service exposes a sample REST API that we can use to simulate talking with services that live outside our cluster. Before we create this service entry, let's install a service that talks to the `jsonplaceholder.typicode.com` REST API and observe that Istio indeed blocks any outbound traffic.

To install an example `forum` application that uses `jsonplaceholder.typicode.com`, run the following command from the root of the book's source code:

```
$ kubectl apply -f services/forum/kubernetes/forum-all.yaml
```

Give that a few moments to come up. The output should be similar to this:

```
$ kubectl get pod -w

NAME                          READY   STATUS    RESTARTS   AGE
catalog-b56cf7fdd-4smrk       2/2     Running   0          8m10s
catalog-v2-86854b8c7-blfp7    2/2     Running   0          8m6s
forum-7476c4f789-j5hqg        2/2     Running   0          30s
webapp-f7bdbcbb5-gkvpn        2/2     Running   0          25m
```

Let's try calling our new `forum` service from within the mesh:

```
$ curl http://localhost/api/users -H "Host: webapp.istioinaction.io"

error calling Forum service
```

To allow this call to go through, we can create an Istio `ServiceEntry` resource to the `jsonplaceholder.typicode.com` host. Doing so inserts an entry into Istio's service registry and makes it known to the service mesh. From the ch5 folder, run the following:

```
$ kubectl apply -f ch5/forum-serviceentry.yaml

serviceentry.networking.istio.io/jsonplaceholder created
```

Now try calling the `forum` service again:

```
$ curl http://localhost/api/users -H "Host: webapp.istioinaction.io"

...

  {
    "id": 10,
    "name": "Clementina DuBuque",
    "username": "Moriah.Stanton",
    "email": "Rey.Padberg@karina.biz",
    "address": {
      "street": "Kattie Turnpike",
      "suite": "Suite 198",
      "city": "Lebsackbury",
      "zipcode": "31428-2261",
      "geo": {
        "lat": "-38.2386",
        "lng": "57.2232"
      }
    },
    "phone": "024-648-3804",
    "website": "ambrose.net",
    "company": {
      "name": "Hoeger LLC",
      "catchPhrase": "Centralized empowering task-force",
      "bs": "target end-to-end models"
    }
  }
```

The call goes through and returns a `users` list, as shown in figure 5.13.

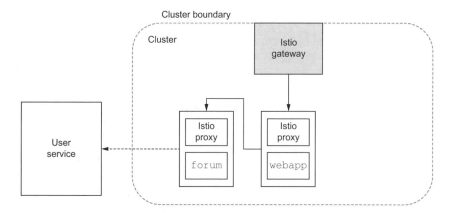

Figure 5.13   We can call external services from within the service mesh once we explicitly add the `ServiceEntry` resource.

In this chapter, we explored how to reduce the risk of deploying new code by using traffic mirroring, traffic shifting, and traffic routing to slowly introduce changes to our users. In the next chapter, we look at making application interactions more resilient by implementing timeouts, retries, and circuit breakers.

Summary

- Workloads can be separated into smaller subsets, such as version v1 and version v2, using `DestinationRules`.
- `VirtualServices` use these subsets to route traffic in a fine-grained manner.
- `VirtualServices` configure routing decisions based on application layer information such as HTTP headers. This enables the dark-launch technique, which sends a specific set of users (such as beta testers) to new versions of a service to test it.
- Service proxies using weighted routing (configured with `VirtualService` resources) can gradually route traffic to new deployments, enabling methods such as canary deployments (aka traffic shifting).
- Traffic shifting can be automated using Flagger, an open source solution that uses collected metrics to gradually increase traffic routed to a new deployment.
- Setting `outboundTrafficPolicy` to `REGISTRY_ONLY` prevents bad actors from phoning home by blocking all traffic that leaves the cluster.
- When outbound traffic is set to `REGISTRY_ONLY`, a `ServiceEntry` can permit traffic to external services.

Resilience: Solving application networking challenges

6

This chapter covers

- Understanding the importance of resilience
- Leveraging client-side load balancing
- Implementing request timeouts and retries
- Circuit breaking and connection pooling
- Migrating from application libraries used for resilience

Once we have traffic coming into our cluster through the Istio ingress gateway (covered in chapter 4), we can manipulate the traffic at the request level and control exactly where to route the request. In the previous chapter, we covered traffic control for weighted routing, request-match-based routing, and certain types of release patterns that can then be enabled. We can also use this traffic control to route around problems in the event of application errors, network partitions, and other major issues.

The problem with distributed systems is that they often fail in unpredictable ways, and we cannot manually take traffic-shifting actions. We need a way to build sensible behaviors *into* the application so they can respond on their own when they encounter problems. We can do that with Istio, including adding timeouts, retries, and circuit breaking, without having to alter application code. In this chapter, we look at how to do this and the implications for the rest of the system.

6.1 Building resilience into the application

Microservices must be built with resilience as a first-class concern. The world of "just build it so it won't fail" is not real; and when failure strikes, we risk taking down all of our services. When we build distributed systems with services communicating over the network, we risk creating even more failure points and face the possibility of catastrophic failures. Service owners should adopt a few resilience patterns consistently across their applications and services.

If service A calls service B, as depicted in figure 6.1, and experiences latency in requests sent to particular endpoints of service B, we want it to proactively identify this and route to other endpoints, other availability zones, or even other regions. If service B experiences intermittent errors, we may want to retry a failed request. Simi-

Figure 6.1 Service A, calling service B, can experience network issues.

larly, if we experience issues calling service B, we may wish to back off until it can recover from whatever problems it may be experiencing. If we keep putting load on service B (and, in some cases, amplifying the load as we retry the request), we risk overloading the service. This overload could ripple to service A and anyone that depends on these services and cause significant cascading errors.

The solution is to build our applications to *expect* failures and have a way for them to automatically attempt remediation or fall back to alternative paths when servicing a request. For example, when service A calls service B and starts to experience issues, we could retry a request, time out our request, or cancel any further outgoing requests using a circuit-breaking pattern. In this chapter, we explore how Istio can be used to solve these problems transparently so that applications have a correct and consistent implementation for resilience concerns regardless of what programming language the application is written in.

6.1.1 Building resilience into application libraries

Before service-mesh technology was widely available, as service developers we had to write a lot of these basic resilience patterns into our application code. Some frameworks emerged in the open source community that helped solve these problems. Twitter open sourced its resilience framework Finagle in 2011 (http://mng.bz/q2X6). Twitter Finagle is a Scala/Java/JVM application library that can be used to implement various remote procedure call (RPC) resilience patterns such as timeouts, retries, and circuit breaking. Shortly afterward, Netflix open sourced components of its resilience framework including Hystrix (http://mng.bz/7Wz7) and Ribbon (http://mng.bz/mx4W), which provided circuit-breaking and client-side load balancing, respectively. Both of these libraries were very popular in the Java community, including the Spring Framework adopting the NetflixOSS stack in its Spring Cloud framework (https://spring.io/projects/spring-cloud-netflix).

The problem with these frameworks is that across different permutations of languages, frameworks, and infrastructure, we will have varying implementations. Twitter Finagle and NetflixOSS were great for Java developers, but Node.js, Go, and Python developers had to find or implement their own variants of these patterns. In some cases, these libraries were also invasive to the application code, so networking code was sprinkled around and obscured the actual business logic. Finally, maintaining these libraries across multiple languages and frameworks strains operational aspects of running microservices: we have to try to patch and maintain functionality parity with all of the combinations at the same time.

6.1.2   *Using Istio to solve these problems*

As we've seen in previous chapters, Istio's service proxy sits next to the application and handles all network traffic to and from the application (see figure 6.2). With Istio, since the service proxy understands application-level requests and messages (such as HTTP requests), we can implement resilience features within the proxy.

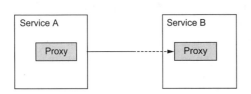

Figure 6.2   We can use Istio's service proxy to help add resilience.

For example, we can configure Istio to *retry* a failed request up to three times when we experience an HTTP 503 error on a service call. We can configure exactly what failures to retry on, the number of retries we would want, and the per-retry timeouts. Since the service proxy is deployed per service instance, we can have very fine-grained retry behavior that's customized to fit the specific needs of the application. The same is true for all of Istio's resilience settings. Istio's service proxy implements these basic resilience patterns out of the box:

- Client-side load balancing
- Locality-aware load balancing
- Timeouts and retries
- Circuit breaking

6.1.3   *Decentralized implementation of resilience*

Using Istio, we see that the data-plane proxy, through which an application's requests traverse, is co-located with the application instance, and no centralized gateway is needed. We get the same architecture if we use application libraries that co-locate the handling of these resilience patterns into the code. In previous iterations of solving for some of these cross-cutting distributed systems, we've placed expensive, difficult-to-change, centralized hardware appliances and other software middleware into the path of the request (hardware load balancers, messaging systems, Enterprise Service Bus, API management, and so on). These earlier implementations, built for more static environments, do not scale or respond well to highly dynamic, elastic cloud architectures and infrastructure. When solving for some of these resilience patterns, we should opt for distributed implementations.

In the following sections, we explore the resilience patterns that Istio can help with. We use a different set of sample applications, to get finer-grained control over how the services behave: a project called Fake Service (https://github.com/nicholas jackson/fake-service) by Nic Jackson, who created this project to illustrate how services may behave in more realistic production environments. In these following examples, we'll see a `simple-web` service call a set of `simple-backend` backends, as shown in figure 6.3.

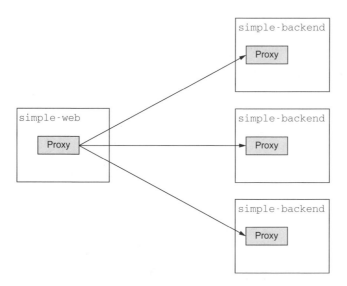

Figure 6.3 Example services: a web service calls a backend service.

6.2 *Client-side load balancing*

Client-side load balancing is the practice of informing the client about the various endpoints available for a service and letting the client pick specific load-balancing algorithms for the best distribution of requests over the endpoints. This reduces the need to rely on centralized load balancing, which could create bottlenecks and failure points, and allows the client to make direct, deliberate requests to specific endpoints without having to take unnecessary extra hops. Thus our clients and services can scale better and deal with a changing topology.

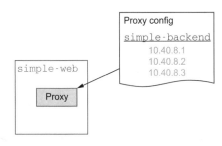

Figure 6.4   The `simple-web` proxy knows about `simple-backend` endpoints.

Istio uses service and endpoint discovery to equip the *client-side* proxy of service-to-service communication with the correct and most up-to-date information, as illustrated in figure 6.4. Developers and operators of the services can then configure this client-side load-balancing behavior through the Istio configuration.

Service operators and developers can configure what load-balancing algorithm a client uses by defining a `DestinationRule` resource. Istio's service proxy is based on Envoy and supports Envoy's load-balancing algorithms, some of which include:

- Round robin (default)
- Random
- Weighted least request

Let's take a look at a quick example.

6.2.1 *Getting started with client-side load balancing*

Before we begin, let's clean up our `istioinaction` namespace by deleting any resources from previous chapters. Be sure you're in the right namespace, delete the appropriate resources, and double-check that the namespace is labeled for sidecar injection:

```
$  kubectl config set-context $(kubectl config current-context) \
 --namespace=istioinaction
$  kubectl delete virtualservice,deployment,service,\
destinationrule,gateway --all
```

Navigate to the root folder of the source code for the book. We deploy two example services with the appropriate Istio `VirtualService` and `Gateway` resources so we can call the service (for more information on `Gateway` and `VirtualService` for ingress routing, see chapter 4):

```
$  kubectl apply -f ch6/simple-backend.yaml
$  kubectl apply -f ch6/simple-web.yaml
$  kubectl apply -f ch6/simple-web-gateway.yaml
```

It takes a few moments for the Pods to come up in the `istioinaction` namespace. When they're running, you should see something similar to this:

```
$  kubectl get pod
NAME                                READY   STATUS    RESTARTS   AGE
simple-backend-1-54856d64fc-59dz2   2/2     Running   0          29h
simple-backend-2-64f898c7fc-bt4x4   2/2     Running   0          29h
simple-backend-2-64f898c7fc-kx88m   2/2     Running   0          29h
simple-web-56d955b6f5-7nflr         2/2     Running   0          29h
```

Let's specify the load balancing for any client calling the `simple-backend` service to be `ROUND_ROBIN` with an Istio `DestinationRule` resource. A destination rule specifies policies for clients in the mesh calling the specific destination. Our starting destination rule for `simple-backend` looks like the following:

```
apiVersion: networking.istio.io/v1beta1
kind: DestinationRule
metadata:
  name: simple-backend-dr
spec:
  host: simple-backend.istioinaction.svc.cluster.local
  trafficPolicy:
    loadBalancer:
      simple: ROUND_ROBIN
```

Let's apply this destination rule:

```
$ kubectl apply -f ch6/simple-backend-dr-rr.yaml
destinationrule.networking.istio.io/simple-backend-dr configured
```

We have `simple-web`, which calls `simple-backend`, but there are multiple replicas of the `simple-backend` service. This is intentional, as we'll modify some of the endpoints at runtime.

If all is successful, you should be able to call the example service. We've been using Docker Desktop in our examples thus far, and for Docker Desktop, it looks similar to the following:

```
$ curl -s -H "Host: simple-web.istioinaction.io" http://localhost/

{
  "name": "simple-web",
  "uri": "/",
  "type": "HTTP",
  "ip_addresses": [
    "10.1.0.45"
  ],
  "start_time": "2020-09-15T20:39:29.270499",
  "end_time": "2020-09-15T20:39:29.434684",
  "duration": "164.184432ms",
  "body": "Hello from simple-web!!!",
  "upstream_calls": [
    {
      "name": "simple-backend",
      "uri": "http://simple-backend:80/",
      "type": "HTTP",
      "ip_addresses": [
        "10.1.0.64"
      ],
      "start_time": "2020-09-15T20:39:29.282673",
      "end_time": "2020-09-15T20:39:29.433141",
      "duration": "150.468571ms",
      "headers": {
        "Content-Length": "280",
```

```
          "Content-Type": "text/plain; charset=utf-8",
          "Date": "Tue, 15 Sep 2020 20:39:29 GMT",
          "Server": "envoy",
          "X-Envoy-Upstream-Service-Time": "155"
        },
        "body": "Hello from simple-backend-1",
        "code": 200
      }
    ],
    "code": 200
}
```

In this set of example services, we get a JSON response that shows a chain of calls. The `simple-web` service calls the `simple-backend` service, and we ultimately see the response message `Hello from simple-backend-1`. If we repeat this call a few more times, we get responses from `simple-backend-1` and `simple-backend-2`:

```
$ for in in {1..10}; do \
curl -s -H "Host: simple-web.istioinaction.io" localhost \
| jq ".upstream_calls[0].body"; printf "\n"; done

"Hello from simple-backend-1"
"Hello from simple-backend-1"
"Hello from simple-backend-2"
"Hello from simple-backend-2"
"Hello from simple-backend-2"
"Hello from simple-backend-1"
"Hello from simple-backend-2"
"Hello from simple-backend-1"
"Hello from simple-backend-1"
"Hello from simple-backend-2"
```

Notice that the calls between `simple-web` and `simple-backend` are effectively load-balanced to the different `simple-backend` endpoints. We are seeing client-side load balancing between the `simple-web` and `simple-backend` services because the service proxy deployed with `simple-web` knows about all of the `simple-backend` endpoints and is using the default algorithm to determine which endpoints get requests. We configured our `DestinationRule` resource to use `ROUND_ROBIN` load balancing, but by default, Istio service proxy uses a `ROUND_ROBIN` load-balancing strategy anyway. How can client-side load balancing contribute to a service's resilience?

Let's look at a somewhat realistic scenario using a load generator and changing the latency of the `simple-backend` service. Then we can use Istio's load-balancing strategies to help pick an appropriate configuration.

6.2.2   *Setting up our scenario*

In a realistic setting, services take time to process requests. The amount of time can vary for several reasons:

- Request size
- Processing complexity

- Database usage
- Calling other services that take time

Reasons outside the service may also contribute to the response time:

- Unexpected, stop-the-world garbage collections
- Resource contention (CPU, network, and so on)
- Network congestion

To mimic this for our example service, we will introduce delays and variance into our response times. Let's call our service again and observe the initially configured differences in overall service response times:

```
$ time curl -s -o /dev/null -H \
  "Host: simple-web.istioinaction.io" localhost
real    0m0.189s
user    0m0.003s
sys     0m0.013s

$ time curl -s -o /dev/null -H \
  "Host: simple-web.istioinaction.io" localhost
real    0m0.179s
user    0m0.003s
sys     0m0.005s

$ time curl -s -o /dev/null -H \
  "Host: simple-web.istioinaction.io" localhost
real    0m0.186s
user    0m0.003s
sys     0m0.006s
```

Each time we call the service, the response times are different. Load balancing can be an effective strategy to reduce the effect of endpoints experiencing periodic or unexpected latency spikes. We will use a CLI load generation tool called Fortio (http://github.com/fortio/fortio) to exercise our services and observe differences in client-side load balancing. You can download Fortio for your platform from https://github.com/fortio/fortio/releases.

Getting Fortio for your platform

If you cannot find a distribution of Fortio for your platform, follow the instructions at https://github.com/fortio/fortio#installation to install it. If that doesn't work, you can still use Fortio to follow the next steps by running it within Kubernetes. You may not have the same experience outlined here, but it will work. For example, you can call Fortio by running it within Kubernetes with the following command:

```
kubectl -n default run fortio --image=fortio/fortio:1.6.8 \
--restart='Never' -- load -H "Host: simple-web.istioinaction.io" \
-jitter -t 60s -c 10 -qps 1000 \
http://istio-ingressgateway.istio-system/
```

Let's make sure Fortio can call our service:

```
$  fortio curl -H "Host: simple-web.istioinaction.io"  http://localhost/
```

You should see a response similar to when we called the service with `curl` directly.

6.2.3   *Testing various client-side load-balancing strategies*

Now that our Fortio load-testing client is ready to go, let's explore the use case. We will use Fortio to send 1,000 requests per second through 10 connections for 60 seconds. Fortio will track the latency numbers for each call and plot them on a histogram with a latency percentile breakdown. Before our test, we'll introduce a version of the `simple-backend-1` service that increases latency for up to one second. This will simulate one of the endpoints experiencing a long garbage-collection event or other application latency. We will vary our load-balancing strategy between round robin, random, and least connection and observe the differences.

Let's deploy the delayed `simple-backend-1` service:

```
$  kubectl apply -f ch6/simple-backend-delayed.yaml
```

By running Fortio in `server` mode, we can access a web dashboard where we can input the parameters of our test, execute the test, and visualize the results:

```
$  fortio server
```

Open your browser to the Fortio UI (http://localhost:8080/fortio) and fill in the following parameters, as shown in figure 6.5:

- Title: `roundrobin`
- URL: `http://localhost`
- QPS: `1000`

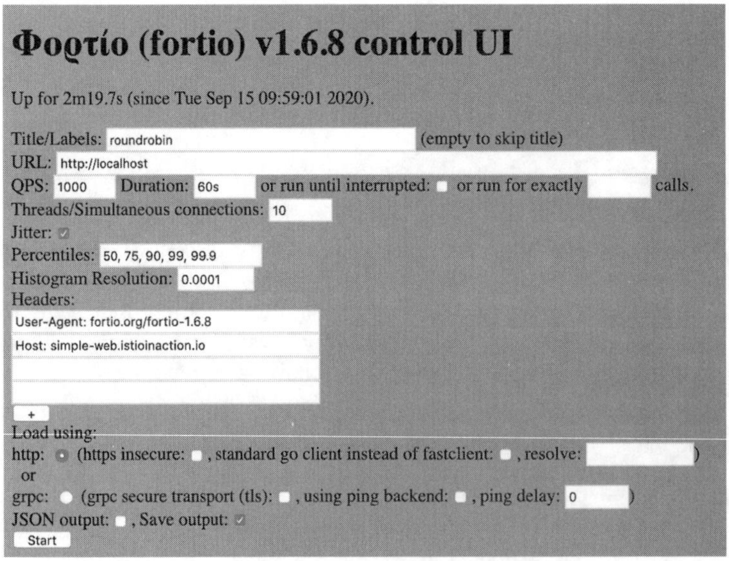

Figure 6.5 Fortio server UI for setting up our load test

- Duration: `60s`
- Threads: `10`
- Jitter: Checked
- Headers: `"Host: simple-web.istioinaction.io"`

Start running the test by clicking the Start button about halfway down the Fortio web page (see figure 6.6), and wait for the test to complete. When it does, it saves a results file to your file system with a name similar to 2020-09-15-101555_roundrobin.json. It also displays a results graph like that shown in figure 6.7.

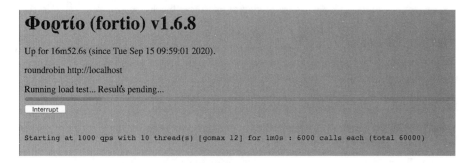

Figure 6.6 Fortio load test is in progress for 60s

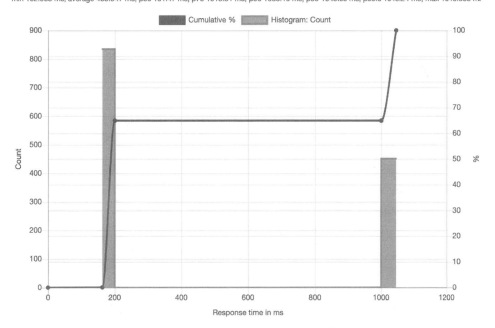

Figure 6.7 Results for load-testing round-robin client-side load balancing

For this round-robin load-balancing strategy, the resulting latencies are as follows:

- 50%: 191.47 ms
- 75%: 1013.31 ms
- 90%: 1033.15 ms
- 99%: 1045.05 ms
- 99.9%: 1046.24 ms

Now, let's change the load-balancing algorithm to RANDOM and try the same load test again:

```
$  kubectl apply -f ch6/simple-backend-dr-random.yaml
destinationrule.networking.istio.io/simple-backend-dr configured
```

Now, go back to the Fortio load-testing page (click the Back button or the Top link). Fill in the information as before, but change the title to random:

- Title: random
- URL: http://localhost
- QPS: 1000
- Duration: 60s
- Threads: 10
- Jitter: Checked
- Headers: "Host: simple-web.istioinaction.io"

Click the Start button, and wait for the results. For this random load-balancing strategy, the resulting latencies are as follows (see figure 6.8):

- 50%: 189.53 ms
- 75%: 1007.72 ms
- 90%: 1029.68 ms
- 99%: 1042.85 ms
- 99.9%: 1044.17 ms

Finally, do the same for least-connection load balancing:

```
$  kubectl apply -f ch6/simple-backend-dr-least-conn.yaml
destinationrule.networking.istio.io/simple-backend-dr configured
```

Use these load-testing settings:

- Title: leastconn
- URL: http://localhost
- QPS: 1000
- Duration: 60s
- Threads: 10
- Jitter: Checked
- Headers: "Host: simple-web.istioinaction.io"

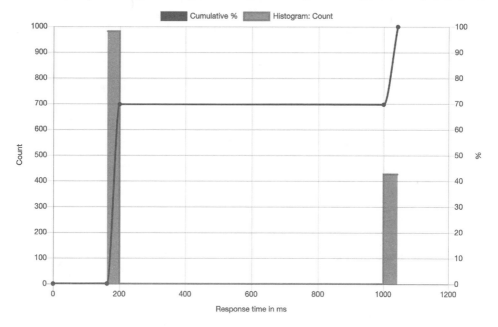

Figure 6.8 **Results for load-testing random client-side load balancing**

Click the Start button. For this least-connection load-balancing strategy, the latencies are as follows (see figure 6.9):

- 50%: 184.79 ms
- 75%: 195.63 ms
- 90%: 1036.89 ms
- 99%: 1124.00 ms
- 99.9%: 1132.71 ms

6.2.4 Understanding the different load-balancing algorithms

The load-testing result diagrams in figures 6.7, 6.8, and 6.9 show several things. First, the different load balancers produce different results under realistic service latency behavior. Second, their results differ in both the histogram and their percentiles. Finally, least connection performs better than both random and round robin. Let's see why.

Round robin and random are both simple load-balancing algorithms. They're simple to implement and simple to understand. Round robin (or next-in-loop) delivers requests to endpoints in a successive loop. Random uniformly picks an endpoint at random. With both, you would expect a similar distribution. The challenge with these strategies is that the endpoints in the load-balancer pool are not typically uniform,

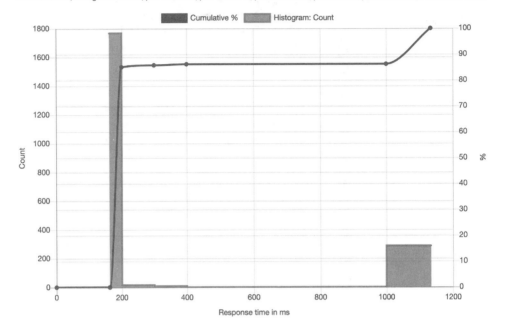

Figure 6.9   Results for load-testing least-connection client-side load balancing

even if they are backed by the same service and resources. As we simulated in our tests, any of these endpoints can experience garbage collection or resource contention that introduces high latency, and round robin and random do not take any runtime behavior into account.

The least-connection load balancer (in Envoy, it's implemented as *least request*) *does* take into account the latencies of the specific endpoints. When it sends requests out to endpoints, it monitors the queue depths, tracking active requests, and picks the endpoints with the fewest active requests in flight. Using this type of algorithm, we can avoid sending requests to endpoints that behave poorly and favor those that are responding more quickly.

Envoy least-request load balancing

Even though the Istio configuration refers to the least-request load balancing as `LEAST_CONN`, Envoy is tracking request depths for endpoints, not connections. The load balancer picks two random endpoints, checks which has the fewest active requests, and chooses the one with the fewest active requests. It does the same thing for successive load-balancing tries. This is known as the *power of two choices*: it has been shown to be a good trade-off (versus a full scan) when implementing a load balancer like this, and it achieves good results. See the Envoy documentation for more on this load balancer (http://mng.bz/enQJ).

At this point, we are finished with the Fortio web UI. Shut down the `fortio server` command by pressing Ctrl-C.

6.3 *Locality-aware load balancing*

One role of a control plane like Istio's is understanding the topology of services and how that topology may evolve. An advantage of understanding the overall topology of services in a service mesh is automatically making routing and load-balancing decisions based on heuristics like the locations of services and peer services.

Istio supports a type of load balancing that gives weights to routes and makes routing decisions based on where a particular workload is. For example, Istio can identify the region and availability zone in which a particular service is deployed and give priority to services that are closer. If the `simple-backend` service is deployed across multiple regions (us-west, us-east, europe-west), there are multiple options to call it. If `simple-web` is deployed in the us-west region, we want calls from `simple-web` to `simple-backend` to stay local to us-west (see figure 6.10). If we treat all endpoints equally, we will likely incur high latency as well as cost when we cross zones or regions.

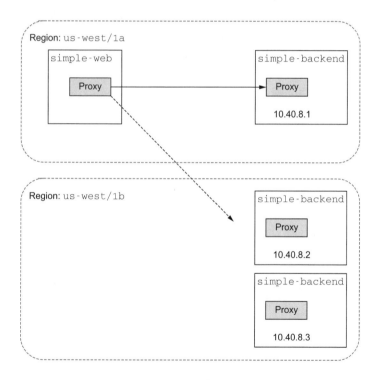

Figure 6.10 Prefer calling services in the same locality.

6.3.1 *Hands-on with locality load balancing*

Let's see locality load balancing in action. When deploying in Kubernetes, region and zone information can be added to labels on the Kubernetes nodes. For example, the labels `failure-domain.beta.kubernetes.io/region` and `failure-domain.beta .kubernetes.io/zone` allow us to specify the region and zone, respectively. Often these labels are automatically added by cloud providers like Google Cloud and Amazon Web Services (AWS). Istio picks up these node labels and enriches the Envoy load-balancing endpoints with the locality information.

> ### Kubernetes failure domain labels
>
> In previous versions of Kubernetes' API, `failure-domain.beta.kubernetes.io/region` and `failure-domain.beta.kubernetes.io/zone` were the labels used to identify the region and zone, respectively. In recent, generally available versions of the Kubernetes API, those labels have been replaced with `topology.kubernetes.io/region` and `topology.kubernetes.io/zone`. Be aware that cloud vendors still use the older `failure-domain` labels. Istio looks for both.

Since we're using Docker Desktop for this book, it's a little more difficult to demonstrate locality-aware routing using the out-of-the-box locality information that Istio pulls from the nodes. We could set up multiple nodes and label them with a desktop deployment of Kubernetes (using Kind or K3s, for example), but luckily for us, Istio provides an approach to explicitly set the locality of our workloads. We can label our Pod with `istio-locality` and give it an explicit region/zone. This will be sufficient to demonstrate locality-aware routing and load balancing. For example, our `simple-web` deployment could look like this:

```
apiVersion: apps/v1
kind: Deployment
metadata:
  labels:
    app: simple-web
  name: simple-web
spec:
  replicas: 1
  selector:
    matchLabels:
      app: simple-web
  template:
    metadata:
      labels:
        app: simple-web
        istio-locality: us-west1.us-west1-a    ◁─┐ Locality
    spec:                                          │ label
      serviceAccountName: simple-web
      containers:
      - image: nicholasjackson/fake-service:v0.14.1
        imagePullPolicy: IfNotPresent
        name: simple-web
        ports:
        - containerPort: 8080
          name: http
          protocol: TCP
        securityContext:
          privileged: false
```

When we deploy the `simple-backend` service, we'll annotate it with a couple of different localities. We will deploy `simple-backend-1` in the same locality as `simple-web`: `us-west1-a`. And will deploy `simple-backend-2` in `us-west1-b`. In this case, the localities are in the same region but in different zones. Istio's ability to load-balance across localities includes region, zone, and even a finer-grained subzone.

Let's deploy these services:

```
$ kubectl apply -f ch6/simple-service-locality.yaml

deployment.apps/simple-web configured
deployment.apps/simple-backend-1 configured
deployment.apps/simple-backend-2 configured
```

We have now deployed our services with locality information. Istio's locality-aware load balancing is enabled by default. If you wish to disable it, you can configure the `mesh-Config.localityLbSetting.enabled` setting to be `false`.

Locality aware load balancing is enabled by default

When a cluster's nodes are deployed into multiple availability zones, as simulated in our previous setup, you must consider that the default locality-aware load balancing may not be desirable. In our example, we never show fewer replicas of `simple-back-end` (the target service) than `simple-web` (the calling service) in any one locality. But you could end up with a deployment in your environment where there are fewer target-service instances than there are calling-service instances in a single locality. This could potentially overwhelm the target service and make the overall system load balancing less balanced than intended.

This great blog post by Karl Stoney at https://karlstoney.com/2020/10/01/locality -aware-routing gives more details. The bottom line is to tune load balancing given your specific load characteristics and topology.

With the locality information in place, we expect calls from `simple-web` in `us-west1 -a` to go to `simple-backend` services deployed in the same zone: `us-west1-a`. In our example, we expect all traffic from `simple-web` to go to `simple-backend-1`, which is in `us-west1-a`. Deployment of the `simple-backend-2` service is in `us-west1-b`, which is not in the same zone as `simple-web`, so we expect traffic to go to that endpoint only if the services in `us-west1-a` start to fail.

Let's call our Istio ingress gateway (configured in the previous section to accept traffic and route to `simple-web`):

```
$ for in in {1..10}; do \
curl -s -H "Host: simple-web.istioinaction.io" localhost \
| jq ".upstream_calls[0].body"; printf "\n"; done

"Hello from simple-backend-1"
"Hello from simple-backend-1"
"Hello from simple-backend-2"
```

```
"Hello from simple-backend-2"
"Hello from simple-backend-2"
"Hello from simple-backend-1"
"Hello from simple-backend-2"
"Hello from simple-backend-1"
"Hello from simple-backend-1"
"Hello from simple-backend-2"
```

What happened? The traffic has been load-balanced across all of the available endpoints that make up the simple-backend service. It appears that the locality information was not taken into account.

For locality-aware load balancing to work in Istio, we need to configure one last piece of the puzzle: health checking. Without health checking, Istio does not know which endpoints in the load-balancing pool are unhealthy and what heuristics to use to spill over into the next locality.

Outlier detection passively watches the behavior of endpoints and whether they appear healthy. It does so by tracking errors that an endpoint may return and marking them as unhealthy. We cover outlier detection in more detail in the following sections.

Let's add a passive health-checking configuration by configuring outlier detection for the simple-backend service:

```
apiVersion: networking.istio.io/v1beta1
kind: DestinationRule
metadata:
  name: simple-backend-dr
spec:
  host: simple-backend.istioinaction.svc.cluster.local
  trafficPolicy:
    connectionPool:
      http:
        http2MaxRequests: 10
        maxRequestsPerConnection: 10
    outlierDetection:
      consecutiveErrors: 1
      interval: 1m
      baseEjectionTime: 30s
```

Let's apply this destination rule. Run the following from the root folder in the book's source code:

```
$  kubectl apply -f ch6/simple-backend-dr-outlier.yaml
destinationrule.networking.istio.io/simple-backend-dr created
```

Now let's try calling the simple-web service through the Istio ingress gateway:

```
$  for in in {1..10}; do \
curl -s -H "Host: simple-web.istioinaction.io" localhost \
| jq ".upstream_calls[0].body"; printf "\n"; done

"Hello from simple-backend-1"
"Hello from simple-backend-1"
"Hello from simple-backend-1"
```

```
"Hello from simple-backend-1"
"Hello from simple-backend-1"
"Hello from simple-backend-1"
"Hello from simple-backend-1"
"Hello from simple-backend-1"
"Hello from simple-backend-1"
"Hello from simple-backend-1"
```

All the traffic went to the `simple-backend` service, which is in the same zone as `simple-web`. To see traffic spill over to another availability zone, let's put the `simple-backend-1` service into a state where it misbehaves. Whenever `simple-web` calls `simple-backend-1`, it will get an HTTP 500 error 100% of the time:

```
$ kubectl apply -f ch6/simple-service-locality-failure.yaml
deployment.apps/simple-backend-1 configured
```

Give the new Pod a few moments to come to the ready state.

When we call our service through the Istio ingress gateway, all traffic should go to the `simple-backend-2` service. This happens because `simple-backend-1`, which is in the same locality as `simple-web`, returns with an HTTP 500 error and is marked as unhealthy. When enough of the endpoints in the same locality as the `simple-web` service are unhealthy, load balancing will automatically spill over to the next-closest locality—in this case, the endpoints in the `simple-backend-2` deployment:

```
$ for in in {1..10}; do \
curl -s -H "Host: simple-web.istioinaction.io" localhost \
| jq ".upstream_calls[0].body"; printf "\n"; done

"Hello from simple-backend-2"
"Hello from simple-backend-2"
"Hello from simple-backend-2"
"Hello from simple-backend-2"
"Hello from simple-backend-2"
"Hello from simple-backend-2"
"Hello from simple-backend-2"
"Hello from simple-backend-2"
"Hello from simple-backend-2"
"Hello from simple-backend-2"
```

Now we get the locality-aware load-balancing outcome we expect when services in a particular locality do not behave well. Note that this locality-aware load balancing is within a single cluster; we will explore locality-aware load-balancing behavior across multiple clusters in chapter 12.

6.3.2 *More control over locality load balancing with weighted distribution*

In the previous section, we saw locality-aware load balancing in action. The last aspect of locality-aware load balancing to know about is that you can control some of how it works. By default, Istio's service proxy sends all traffic to services in the same locality and spills over only when there are failures or unhealthy endpoints. We can influence this behavior in scenarios where we may wish to load-balance some of the traffic across multiple locality zones, also known as *weighted distribution across localities* (see figure 6.11). We may wish to do this when we expect services in a particular locality to become overloaded because of peak or seasonal traffic.

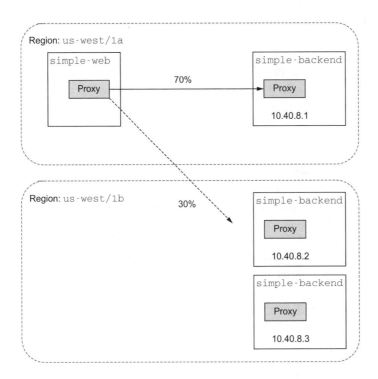

Figure 6.11 Defining locality weights more explicitly

In the previous examples, we introduced a misbehaving service. Let's restore our services so they all behave correctly and return HTTP 200 responses:

```
$  kubectl apply -f ch6/simple-service-locality.yaml
deployment.apps/simple-web unchanged
deployment.apps/simple-backend-1 configured
deployment.apps/simple-backend-2 unchanged
```

Let's say there is incoming load that the services in a certain zone or region won't be able to handle. We want to spill over to a neighboring locality so that 70% of traffic goes to the closest locality and 30% goes to the neighboring locality. Following our previous example, we will send 70% of the traffic destined for simple-backend service to us-west1-a and 30% to us-west1-b. This roughly translates to 70% of traffic to the simple-backend-1 service and 30% to simple-backend-2.

To accomplish this configuration, we specify our locality load-balancing preferences in a DestinationRule resource:

```
apiVersion: networking.istio.io/v1beta1
kind: DestinationRule
metadata:
  name: simple-backend-dr
spec:
  host: simple-backend.istioinaction.svc.cluster.local
  trafficPolicy:
    loadBalancer:                        ◁─┐ Adds the load-balancer
      localityLbSetting:                   │ configuration
        distribute:
        - from: us-west1/us-west1-a/*    ◁─┤ Origin zone
          to:
            "us-west1/us-west1-a/*": 70  ◁─┤ Destination zone
            "us-west1/us-west1-b/*": 30  ◁─┐ Destination
    connectionPool:                        │ zone
      http:
        http2MaxRequests: 10
        maxRequestsPerConnection: 10
    outlierDetection:
      consecutive5xxErrors: 1
      interval: 5s
      baseEjectionTime: 30s
      maxEjectionPercent: 100
```

Let's apply this so it takes effect:

```
$ kubectl apply -f ch6/simple-backend-dr-outlier-locality.yaml
destinationrule.networking.istio.io/simple-backend-dr configured
```

Now we call our service once again:

```
$ for in in {1..10}; do \
curl -s -H "Host: simple-web.istioinaction.io" localhost \
| jq ".upstream_calls[0].body"; printf "\n"; done

"Hello from simple-backend-1"
"Hello from simple-backend-1"
"Hello from simple-backend-1"
"Hello from simple-backend-1"
"Hello from simple-backend-2"
"Hello from simple-backend-1"
"Hello from simple-backend-1"
"Hello from simple-backend-1"
"Hello from simple-backend-2"
"Hello from simple-backend-1"
```

Some of the requests were load-balanced, mostly to the closest locality but with some wiggle room to spill over to the next-closest locality. Note that this is not exactly the same as controlling the traffic explicitly, as we did in chapter 5. With traffic routing, we can control the traffic between different subsets of our services, typically when there are different classes of service or versions of service within the overall group. In this case, we're weighting the traffic based on the deployed topology of the services, independent of subsets. These are not mutually exclusive concepts: they can be layered so that the fine-grained traffic control and routing that we saw in chapter 5 can be applied on top of the location-aware load balancing we explored in this section.

6.4 Transparent timeouts and retries

When building systems that rely on components distributed over the network, the biggest issues include latency and failures. We saw in earlier sections how we could use Istio to mitigate these challenges using load balancing and locality. What happens if these network calls take too long? Or what if we experience intermittent failures as a result of latency or due to other network factors? How can Istio help with these issues? Istio allows us to configure various types of timeouts and retries to overcome inherent network unreliability.

6.4.1 Timeouts

One of the most difficult scenarios to handle in a distributed environment is latency. When things slow down, resources may be held longer, services can back up, and the situation can potentially trigger cascading failures. To guard against these unexpected latent scenarios, we should implement timeouts on the connection, a request, or both.

An important point to note is how timeouts across service calls interact with each other. For example, if service A calls service B with a timeout of one second, but service B calls service C with a timeout of two seconds, which timeout will trip first? The most restrictive will time out first, so the timeout on the call from service B to service C may never be invoked. Generally, it makes sense to have larger timeouts at the edge (where traffic comes in) of an architecture and shorter (or more restrictive) timeouts for the layers deeper in the call graph. Let's see how Istio can be used to control policies around timeouts.

Let's reset our environment to a known state:

```
$  kubectl apply -f ch6/simple-web.yaml
$  kubectl apply -f ch6/simple-backend.yaml
$  kubectl delete destinationrule simple-backend-dr
```

If we call the services through the Istio ingress gateway and calculate how long each call takes, we can see they respond with HTTP 200 and are generally around 10 to 20 ms:

```
$  for in in {1..10}; do time curl -s \
-H "Host: simple-web.istioinaction.io" localhost \
| jq .code; printf "\n"; done

...

real    0m0.170s
user    0m0.025s
sys     0m0.007s

200

real    0m0.169s
user    0m0.024s
sys     0m0.007s
```

```
200
```

```
real     0m0.171s
user     0m0.025s
sys      0m0.007s
```

```
...
```

Let's deploy a version of the `simple-backend` service that inserts a one-second delay in processing for 50% of the calls to that instance:

```
$  kubectl apply -f ch6/simple-backend-delayed.yaml
deployment.apps/simple-backend-1 configured
```

When we make the calls again, some take one second or longer:

```
$  for in in {1..10}; do time curl -s \
-H "Host: simple-web.istioinaction.io" localhost \
| jq .code; printf "\n"; done
```

```
...
```

```
real     0m1.117s
user     0m0.025s
sys      0m0.007s
```

```
200
```

```
real     0m0.169s
user     0m0.024s
sys      0m0.007s
```

```
200
```

```
real     0m0.169s
user     0m0.024s
sys      0m0.007s
```

```
...
```

Maybe 1 second is okay, but what if the latency for `simple-backend` jumped to 5 seconds—or 100 seconds? Let's use Istio to enforce a timeout for calls to the `simple-backend` service.

We can specify per-request timeouts with the Istio `VirtualService` resource. For example, to specify a half-second timeout for calls to `simple-backend` from clients in the mesh, we can do something like this:

```
apiVersion: networking.istio.io/v1alpha3
kind: VirtualService
metadata:
  name: simple-backend-vs
spec:
  hosts:
  - simple-backend
  http:
  - route:
```

```
    - destination:
        host: simple-backend              Specifies the
    timeout: 0.5s                         timeout value
```

Let's apply this to our service mesh:

```
$  kubectl apply -f ch6/simple-backend-vs-timeout.yaml
```

When we call the services again, the maximum time is 0.5 second, but the calls fail with an HTTP 500 error:

```
$  for in in {1..10}; do time curl -s \
-H "Host: simple-web.istioinaction.io" localhost \
| jq .code; printf "\n"; done

. . .

real      0m0.174s
user      0m0.026s
sys       0m0.010s

500

real      0m0.518s
user      0m0.025s
sys       0m0.007s

500

real      0m0.517s
user      0m0.025s
sys       0m0.007s

. . .
```

In the next section, we discuss other options to remedy failures like timeouts.

6.4.2   Retries

When calling a service and experiencing intermittent network failures, we may want the application to retry the request. If we don't retry the request, we make our services susceptible to common and expected failures that could deliver a bad user experience. On the other hand, we have to balance out the fact that unbridled retries can contribute to degraded system health, including causing cascading failures. If a service is legitimately overloaded and misbehaving, retrying requests will only amplify the degraded situation. Let's take a look at the retry options provided by Istio.

Before we begin, let's set our example services back to some sane defaults:

```
$  kubectl apply -f ch6/simple-web.yaml
$  kubectl apply -f ch6/simple-backend.yaml
```

Istio has retries enabled by default and will retry up to two times. We need to understand the default behavior before we start fine-tuning it. To begin, let's disable the default retries for our example application by configuring `VirtualService` resources to set the maximum retries to 0:

```
$  istioctl install --set profile=demo \
 --set meshConfig.defaultHttpRetryPolicy.attempts=0
```

> ### Retry attempts in earlier Istio versions
> If you are using a version of Istio before 1.12.0, you will have to change the retry attempts in each `VirtualService`. You can use the following to do this for the examples:
>
> ```
> $  kubectl apply -f ch6/simple-service-disable-retry.yaml
> ```

Now let's deploy a version of the `simple-backend` service that has periodic (75%) failures. In this case, one of the three endpoints (`simple-backend-1`) returns HTTP 503 on 75% of its calls, as illustrated in figure 6.12:

```
$  kubectl apply -f ch6/simple-backend-periodic-failure-503.yaml
deployment.apps/simple-backend-1 configured
```

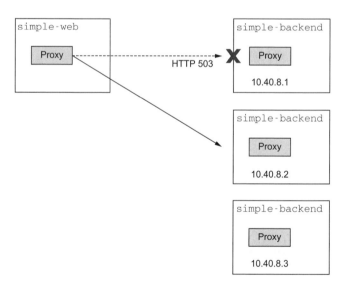

Figure 6.12 Service `simple-web` calling `simple-backend` with failures from `simple-backend-1`

If we call the service a number of times, we should see some failures:

```
$  for in in {1..10}; do curl -s \
-H "Host: simple-web.istioinaction.io" localhost \
| jq .code; printf "\n"; done
```

```
200
500                    <─┤  Expected failure
200
200
200
500                    <─┤  Expected failure
200
200
200
200
```

By default, Istio tries a call and, if it fails, tries two more times. This default retry only applies to certain situations. Typically, it is safe to retry a request in these default situations because they indicate that network connectivity could not be established, and the request could not have been sent on the first try:

- `connect-failure`
- `refused-stream`
- `unavailable` (gRPC status code 14)
- `cancelled` (gRPC status code 1)
- `retriable-status-codes` (defaults to HTTP 503 in Istio)

In the previous configurations, we disabled the default retry policy. Let's explicitly configure retry attempts to be 2 for calls to `simple-backend` with the following `VirtualService` resource:

```
apiVersion: networking.istio.io/v1alpha3
kind: VirtualService
metadata:
  name: simple-backend-vs
spec:
  hosts:
  - simple-backend
  http:
  - route:
    - destination:
        host: simple-backend
    retries:
      attempts: 2
```

```
$  kubectl apply -f ch6/simple-backend-enable-retry.yaml
virtualservice.networking.istio.io/simple-backend-vs configured
```

If we call our service again, we see no failures:

```
$  for in in {1..10}; do curl -s \
-H "Host: simple-web.istioinaction.io" localhost \
| jq .code; printf "\n"; done

200
200
200
200
200
```

```
200
200
200
200
200
```

Although there were failures (as we saw earlier), they are not bubbled up to the caller because we enabled Istio's retry policy to work around those errors. By default, HTTP 503 is one of the retriable status codes. The following `VirtualService` retry policy shows what parameters are configurable out of the box for retries:

```
apiVersion: networking.istio.io/v1alpha3
kind: VirtualService
metadata:
  name: simple-backend-vs
spec:
  hosts:
  - simple-backend
  http:
  - route:
    - destination:
        host: simple-backend
    retries:
      attempts: 2                                          Maximum retries
      retryOn: gateway-error,connect-failure,retriable-4xx   Errors to retry
      perTryTimeout: 300ms                                   Timeouts
      retryRemoteLocalities: true     Whether to retry endpoints
                                      in other localities
```

The various settings for retries give us some control over retry behavior (how many, how long, which endpoints to retry) and on which status codes to retry. As we mentioned previously, not all requests can or should be retried.

For example, if we deploy our `simple-backend` service to return HTTP 500 codes, the default retry behavior will not catch that:

```
$ kubectl apply -f ch6/simple-backend-periodic-failure-500.yaml
deployment.apps/simple-backend-1 configured
```

When we call our service again, those HTTP 500 failures bubble up:

```
$ for in in {1..10}; do curl -s \
-H "Host: simple-web.istioinaction.io" localhost \
| jq .code; printf "\n"; done

500
200
500
200
200
200
200
500
200
200
```

HTTP 500 is not among the status codes that are retried. Let's use a `VirtualService` retry policy that retries on all HTTP 500 codes (including `connect-failure` and `refused-stream`):

```
apiVersion: networking.istio.io/v1alpha3
kind: VirtualService
metadata:
  name: simple-backend-vs
spec:
  hosts:
  - simple-backend
  http:
  - route:
    - destination:
        host: simple-backend
    retries:
      attempts: 2
      retryOn: 5xx          ⟵──┐ Retries on
                               │ HTTP 5xx
```

Let's apply this `VirtualService`:

```
$  kubectl apply -f ch6/simple-backend-vs-retry-500.yaml

virtualservice.networking.istio.io/simple-backend-vs created
```

No HTTP 500 errors bubble up:

```
$  for in in {1..10}; do curl -s \
-H "Host: simple-web.istioinaction.io" localhost \
| jq .code; printf "\n"; done

200
200
200
200
200
200
200
200
200
200
```

For more about the available `retryOn` configurations, see the Envoy documentation at http://mng.bz/p2BP.

RETRIES IN TERMS OF TIMEOUTS

Each retry has its own `perTryTimeout`. One thing to note about this setting is that the `perTryTimeout` value multiplied by the total number of attempts must be less than the overall request timeout (described in the previous section). For example, an overall timeout of one second and a retry policy of three attempts with a per-retry timeout of 500 ms won't work. The overall request timeout will kick in before all of the retries get a chance. Also keep in mind there is a backoff delay between retries, which goes against the overall request timeout. We talk more about the backoff next.

HOW IT WORKS

When a request flows through the Istio service proxy, if it fails to be delivered upstream, it is marked as failed and retried up to the maximum `attempts` field defined in the `VirtualService` resource. This means with an `attempts` value of 2, the request will actually be delivered up to three times: once for the original request and twice for the retries. Between retries, Istio will "back off" the retry with a base of 25 ms. See figure 6.13 for an illustration of the retry and backoff behavior. This means for each successive retry, Istio backs off (waits) until (25 ms x attempt #) to stagger the retries. At the moment, this retry base is fixed; but as we discuss in the next section, we can make changes to parts of the Envoy API that are not exposed by Istio.

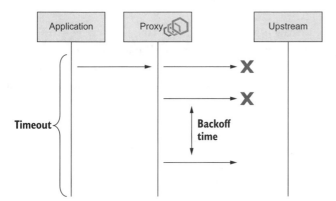

Figure 6.13 Request flow on retries when requests fail

As mentioned, Istio by default has retry `attempts` set to 2. You may wish to override this setting so that different layers of your system retry a different number of times. Naive retry settings (like the default) can lead to a significant retry "thundering herd" problem (see figure 6.14). For example, if a service chain is 5 calls deep and each step can retry a request 2 times, we could end up with 32 requests for each incoming request. If

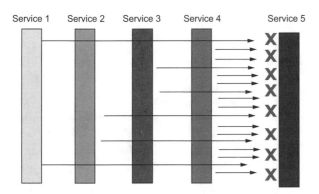

Figure 6.14 The "thundering herd" effect when retries compound each other

a resource at the end of the chain is overloaded, this extra load could overwhelm the target resource to the point that it falls over. An option to deal with this situation is to limit the retry attempts at the edges of your architecture to one or none and only retry deep into your call stack, with intermediate components not retrying. This may not work very well either. Another tactic is to put caps on total overall retries. We can do that with retry budgets; however, budgets are not yet exposed in the Istio API. There are workarounds for this issue in Istio, but they are outside the scope of this book.

Finally, retries are attempted against endpoints in their own locality by default. The `retryRemoteLocalities` setting affects this behavior: if we set it to `true`, Istio allows retries to spill over to other localities. This may come in handy before outlier detection determines that the locally preferred endpoints are misbehaving.

6.4.3 *Advanced retries*

In the previous section, we saw how Istio can help make our services resilient to intermittent network failures by using automatic retries. We also discussed parameters we can tune for retry use cases. Some of the retry capabilities take into account defaults that aren't easy to change, like the backoff retry time and the default retriable status codes. By default, the backoff time is 25 ms, and the retriable code is limited to HTTP 503. Even though the Istio API doesn't expose these configurations at the time of writing, we can use the Istio extension API to alter these values directly in the Envoy configuration. We use the `EnvoyFilter` API to do this:

```
apiVersion: networking.istio.io/v1alpha3
kind: EnvoyFilter
metadata:
  name: simple-backend-retry-status-codes
  namespace: istioinaction
spec:
  workloadSelector:
    labels:
      app: simple-web
  configPatches:
  - applyTo: HTTP_ROUTE
    match:
      context: SIDECAR_OUTBOUND
      routeConfiguration:
        vhost:
          name: "simple-backend.istioinaction.svc.cluster.local:80"
    patch:
      operation: MERGE
      value:
        route:                        Directly from the
          retry_policy:      ◁──┘     Envoy configuration
            retry_back_off:                        Increases the
              base_interval: 50ms      ◁──┘        base interval
            retriable_status_codes:    ◁─┐  Adds retriable
            - 408                           codes
            - 400
```

NOTE The `EnvoyFilter` API is a "break glass" solution. In general, Istio's API is an abstraction over the underlying data plane. The underlying Envoy API may change at any time between releases of Istio, so be sure to validate any Envoy filter you put into production. Do not assume any backward compatibility here. See chapter 14 for more about configuring Envoy's HTTP filters with the `EnvoyFilter` resource.

We use the Envoy API directly here to configure/override retry policy settings. Let's apply these configurations:

```
$ kubectl apply -f ch6/simple-backend-ef-retry-status-codes.yaml
envoyfilter.networking.istio.io/simple-backend-retry-status-codes configured
```

We also want to update our `retryOn` field to include `retriable-status-codes`:

```
apiVersion: networking.istio.io/v1alpha3
kind: VirtualService
metadata:
  name: simple-backend-vs
spec:
  hosts:
  - simple-backend
  http:
  - route:
    - destination:
        host: simple-backend
    retries:
      attempts: 2
      retryOn: 5xx,retriable-status-codes    ◁──┐  Includes the retriable
                                                  │  status codes
```

Let's apply this new retry configuration:

```
$ kubectl apply -f ch6/simple-backend-vs-retry-on.yaml
virtualservice.networking.istio.io/simple-backend-vs configured
```

Finally, let's update our `sample-backend` service to return HTTP 408 (timeout) and verify that we continue to get HTTP 200:

```
$ kubectl apply -f ch6/simple-backend-periodic-failure-408.yaml
deployment.apps/simple-backend-1 configured

$ for in in {1..10}; do curl -s \
-H "Host: simple-web.istioinaction.io" localhost \
| jq .code; printf "\n"; done

200
200
200
200
200
200
200
200
200
200
```

REQUEST HEDGING

This last treatment of retries centers around an advanced topic that is also not directly exposed in the Istio API. When a request reaches its threshold and times out, we can optionally configure Envoy under the covers to perform what's called *request hedging*. With request hedging, if a request times out, Envoy can send another request to a different host to "race" the original, timed-out request. In this case, if the raced request returns successfully, its response is sent to the original downstream caller. If the original request returns before the raced request returns, the original request is returned to the downstream caller.

To set up request hedging, we can use the following `EnvoyFilter` resource:

```
apiVersion: networking.istio.io/v1alpha3
kind: EnvoyFilter
metadata:
  name: simple-backend-retry-hedge
  namespace: istioinaction
spec:
  workloadSelector:
    labels:
      app: simple-web
  configPatches:
  - applyTo: VIRTUAL_HOST
    match:
      context: SIDECAR_OUTBOUND
      routeConfiguration:
        vhost:
          name: "simple-backend.istioinaction.svc.cluster.local:80"
    patch:
      operation: MERGE
      value:
        hedge_policy:
          hedge_on_per_try_timeout: true
```

As we've seen in this section, the topic of timeouts and retries is not that simple. Coming up with good timeouts and retry policies for services is challenging, especially considering how they can be chained together. Misconfigured timeouts and retries can amplify undesirable behaviors in a system architecture to the extent that they overload the system and cause cascading failures. One last piece of the puzzle for building resilient architectures is skipping retries altogether: instead of retrying, we fail fast. Instead of promoting more load, we can limit load for a time to allow upstream systems to recover. For that, we can employ circuit breaking.

6.5   *Circuit breaking with Istio*

We use circuit-breaking functionality to help guard against partial or cascading failures. We want to reduce traffic to unhealthy systems, so we don't continue to overload them and prevent them from recovering. For example, if the `simple-web` service calls out to the `simple-backend` service and `simple-backend` returns errors for successive calls, then instead of doing continuous retries and adding more stress to the system, we may want to halt any calls to `simple-backend`. This approach is similar in spirit to how a circuit breaker works in the electrical system for a house. If we experience shorts in the system or repeated faults, a circuit breaker is designed to open the circuit to protect the rest of the system. The circuit-breaker pattern forces our application to deal with the fact that network calls can and do fail and helps safeguard the overall system from cascading failures.

Istio doesn't have an explicit configuration called "circuit breaker," but it provides two controls for limiting load on backend services, especially those experiencing issues, to effectively enforce a circuit breaker. The first is to manage how many connections and outstanding requests are allowed to a specific service. We use this control to guard against services that slow down and thus back up the client, as illustrated in figure 6.15.

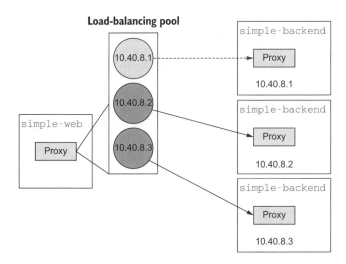

Figure 6.15   Circuit-breaking endpoints that don't behave correctly

If there are ten requests in flight to a particular service and that number keeps growing for the same amount of inbound load, it doesn't make sense to continue to send requests—sending more requests could overwhelm the upstream service. In Istio, we use the `connectionPool` settings in a destination rule to limit the number of connections and requests that can pile up when calling a service. If too many requests pile up, we can short-circuit them (fail fast) and return to the client.

The second control is to observe the health of endpoints in the load-balancing pool and evict misbehaving endpoints for a time. If certain hosts in a service pool are experiencing failures, we can skip sending traffic to them. If we exhaust all hosts, the circuit is effectively "open" for a while. Let's see how to implement each of these circuit-breaking controls with Istio.

6.5.1   *Guarding against slow services with connection-pool control*

To set up the examples here, let's first scale down the `simple-backend` service, so there is only a single Pod. We can take all of the `simple-backend-2` services down to a replica of `0`:

```
$  kubectl scale deploy/simple-backend-2 --replicas=0
deployment.apps/simple-backend-2 scaled
```

Next, let's deploy the version of `simple-backend` service that introduces a one-second delay in responses:

```
$  kubectl apply -f ch6/simple-backend-delayed.yaml
deployment.apps/simple-backend-1 configured
```

If there are any existing destination rules from previous sections, we delete them:

```
$  kubectl delete destinationrule --all
```

Now we can begin testing Istio's connection-limiting circuit breaking. Let's run a very simple load test with one connection (`-c 1`) sending one request per second (`-qps 1`). Also note that since the backend returns in approximately one second, we should have smooth traffic and 100% successful responses:

```
$  fortio load -H "Host: simple-web.istioinaction.io" \
-quiet -jitter -t 30s -c 1 -qps 1 http://localhost/

# target 50% 1.27611
# target 75% 1.41565
# target 90% 1.49938
# target 99% 1.54961
# target 99.9% 1.55464
Sockets used: 1 (for perfect keepalive, would be 1)
Jitter: true
Code 200 : 30 (100.0 %)
All done 30 calls (plus 1 warmup) 1056.564 ms avg, 0.9 qps
```

Let's introduce some connection and request limits and see what happens. We start with a very simple set of limits:

```
apiVersion: networking.istio.io/v1beta1
kind: DestinationRule
metadata:
  name: simple-backend-dr
spec:
  host: simple-backend.istioinaction.svc.cluster.local
  trafficPolicy:
    connectionPool:
      tcp:
        maxConnections: 1          ◁──┘ Total number
      http:                              of connections
        http1MaxPendingRequests: 1  ◁──┤ Queued requests          Requests per
        maxRequestsPerConnection: 1              ◁────────────┘   connection
        maxRetries: 1              ┌─ Maximum concurrent
        http2MaxRequests: 1    ◁──┘  requests to all hosts
```

Next, we apply this file:

```
$ kubectl apply -f ch6/simple-backend-dr-conn-limit.yaml
destinationrule.networking.istio.io/simple-backend-dr created
```

Let's run the same load test. We set maxConnections, http1MaxPendingRequests, and http2MaxRequests to a value of 1. We also set maxRetries and maxRequestsPer-Connection, but we won't dig into those here; we covered maxRetries in a previous section, and maxRequestsPerConnection is 1 for these HTTP 1.1 examples. Here's what these settings mean:

- maxConnections—The threshold at which we report a connection overflow. The Istio proxy (Envoy) uses connections to service requests up to an upper bound defined in this setting. In reality, we can expect the maximum number of connections to be one per endpoint in the load-balancing pool plus the value of this setting. Any time we go over this value, Envoy will report it in its metrics.
- http1MaxPendingRequests—The allowable number of requests that are pending and don't have a connection to use.
- http2MaxRequests—This setting is unfortunately misnamed in Istio. Under the covers, it controls the maximum number of parallel requests across all endpoints/hosts in a cluster regardless of HTTP2 or HTTP1.1 (see https://github.com/istio/istio/issues/27473).

Let's run our test again and verify that for these settings, when we send one request per second over one connection, things work fine:

```
$ fortio load -H "Host: simple-web.istioinaction.io" \
-quiet -jitter -t 30s -c 1 -qps 1 http://localhost/

...
Sockets used: 1 (for perfect keepalive, would be 1)
Jitter: true
Code 200 : 30 (100.0 %)
All done 30 calls (plus 1 warmup) 1027.857 ms avg, 1.0 qps
```

What would happen if we increased the number of connections and requests per second to two? From our load-testing tool, we'd basically start sending one request per second from two connections. On the Istio proxy side, we would be over our connection limit, and outgoing requests would begin to queue up. If we bumped up against either the maximum number of requests (one) or maximum number of pending requests (one), we might trip the circuit breaker. Let's try it:

```
$ fortio load -H "Host: simple-web.istioinaction.io" \
-quiet -jitter -t 30s -c 2 -qps 2 http://localhost/

...
Sockets used: 27 (for perfect keepalive, would be 2)
Jitter: true
Code 200 : 31 (55.4 %)
Code 500 : 25 (44.6 %)
All done 56 calls (plus 2 warmup) 895.900 ms avg, 1.8 qps
```

Requests were returned as failed (HTTP 5xx). How do we know for sure that they were affected by circuit breaking and not upstream failures? To determine this information, we need to enable more statistics collection in the Istio service proxy. By default, Istio's service proxy (Envoy) keeps a large number of statistics for each cluster, but Istio trims these down so as not to overwhelm the collection agents (such as Prometheus) with a large cardinality of statistics. Let's tell Istio to enable statistics collection for the `simple-web` service since that ends up calling the `simple-backend` service in our service graph.

To extend the statistics exposed by Istio, especially upstream circuit-breaking statistics, we use the annotation `sidecar.istio.io/statsInclusionPrefixes` in our `simple-web` Kubernetes deployment:

```
template:
  metadata:
    annotations:
      sidecar.istio.io/statsInclusionPrefixes:
      ➥"cluster.outbound|80||simple-backend.istioinaction.svc.cluster.local"
    labels:
      app: simple-web
```

Here we add additional statistics that follow the `cluster.<name>` format. You can see the entire deployment description and even deploy it by applying the simple-web-stats-incl.yaml file:

```
$ kubectl apply -f ch6/simple-web-stats-incl.yaml
deployment.apps/simple-web configured
```

Let's make sure we're starting from a known state with regard to statistics by resetting all the statistics for the Istio proxy in the `simple-web` service:

```
$ kubectl exec -it deploy/simple-web -c istio-proxy \
-- curl -X POST localhost:15000/reset_counters

OK
```

When we generate load again, we see similar results and can inspect the statistics to determine whether circuit breaking kicked in:

```
$ fortio load -H "Host: simple-web.istioinaction.io" \
-quiet -jitter -t 30s -c 2 -qps 2 http://localhost/

...
Sockets used: 25 (for perfect keepalive, would be 2)
Jitter: true
Code 200 : 31 (57.4 %)
Code 500 : 23 (42.6 %)
All done 54 calls (plus 2 warmup) 1020.465 ms avg, 1.7 qps
```

In this case, 23 calls failed. We believe that they failed because of our circuit-breaking settings, but we can verify that by looking at the statistics from the Istio proxy. Let's run the following query:

```
$ kubectl exec -it deploy/simple-web -c istio-proxy \
-- curl localhost:15000/stats | grep simple-backend | grep overflow

<omitted>.upstream_cx_overflow: 59
<omitted>.upstream_cx_pool_overflow: 0
<omitted>.upstream_rq_pending_overflow: 23
<omitted>.upstream_rq_retry_overflow: 0
```

We've omitted the cluster name here for readability. The statistics we're most interested in are upstream_cx_overflow and upstream_rq_pending_overflow, which indicate that enough connections and requests went over our specified thresholds (either too many requests in parallel or too many queued up) to trip the circuit breaker. There were 23 such requests, which exactly matches how many did not complete successfully in our load test. Note that no errors bubble up because of the connection overflow, but it's important to know that when connections overflow, more pressure is put on the existing connections. This results in the pending queue growing, which eventually trips the circuit breaker. The fail-fast behavior comes from those pending or parallel requests exceeding the circuit-breaking thresholds.

What if we increase our http2MaxRequests field to account for more requests happening in parallel? Let's raise that value to 2, reset our counters, and re-run our load test:

```
$ kubectl patch destinationrule simple-backend-dr --type merge \
--patch \
'{"spec": {"trafficPolicy": {"connectionPool": {
  "http": {"http2MaxRequests": 2}}}}}'

$ kubectl exec -it deploy/simple-web -c istio-proxy \
-- curl -X POST localhost:15000/reset_counters

$ fortio load -H "Host: simple-web.istioinaction.io" \
-quiet -jitter -t 30s -c 2 -qps 2 http://localhost/

...
Sockets used: 4 (for perfect keepalive, would be 2)
Jitter: true
Code 200 : 32 (94.1 %)
Code 500 : 2 (5.9 %)
All done 34 calls (plus 2 warmup) 1786.089 ms avg, 1.1 qps
```

Fewer requests were blocked by circuit breaking:

```
$ kubectl exec -it deploy/simple-web -c istio-proxy \
-- curl localhost:15000/stats | grep simple-backend | grep overflow

<omitted>.upstream_cx_overflow: 32
<omitted>.upstream_cx_pool_overflow: 0
<omitted>.upstream_rq_pending_overflow: 2
<omitted>.upstream_rq_retry_overflow: 0
```

What likely happened is that some requests tripped the pending queue circuit breaker. Let's increase the pending queue depth to 2 and re-run:

```
$ kubectl patch destinationrule simple-backend-dr --type merge \
--patch \
```

```
'{"spec": {"trafficPolicy": {"connectionPool": {
  "http": {"http1MaxPendingRequests": 2}}}}}'
$  kubectl exec -it deploy/simple-web -c istio-proxy \
-- curl -X POST localhost:15000/reset_counters

$  fortio load -H "Host: simple-web.istioinaction.io" \
-quiet -jitter -t 30s -c 2 -qps 2 http://localhost/

...
Sockets used: 2 (for perfect keepalive, would be 2)
Jitter: true
Code 200 : 33 (100.0 %)
All done 33 calls (plus 2 warmup) 1859.655 ms avg, 1.1 qps
```

With these limits, we successfully complete our load test.

When circuit breaking occurs, we can use statistics to determine what happened. But what about at runtime? In our example, simple-web calls simple-backend; but if the request fails because of circuit breaking, how does simple-web know that and discern the issue from an application or network failure?

When a request fails for tripping a circuit-breaking threshold, Istio's service proxy adds an x-envoy-overloaded header. One way to test this is to set the connection limits back to their most stringent settings (1 for connections, pending requests, and maximum requests) and run the load test again. If we also issue a single curl command while the load test is running, there's a high chance it will fail because of circuit breaking. When using curl, we can see the actual response from the simple service implementations:

```
curl -v -H "Host: simple-web.istioinaction.io"  http://localhost/

{
  "name": "simple-web",
  "uri": "/",
  "type": "HTTP",
  "ip_addresses": [
    "10.1.0.101"
  ],
  "start_time": "2020-09-22T20:01:44.949194",
  "end_time": "2020-09-22T20:01:44.951374",
  "duration": "2.179963ms",
  "body": "Hello from simple-web!!!",
  "upstream_calls": [
    {
      "uri": "http://simple-backend:80/",
      "headers": {
        "Content-Length": "81",
        "Content-Type": "text/plain",
        "Date": "Tue, 22 Sep 2020 20:01:44 GMT",
        "Server": "envoy",
        "x-envoy-overloaded": "true"          ◁──┐ Header
      },                                          │ indication
      "code": 503,
      "error": "Error processing
```

```
        upstream request: http://simple-backend:80//,
          expected code 200, got 503"
    }
  ],
  "code": 500
}
```

In general, you should write application code in such a way that the network can fail. If your application code watches for this header, it can make decisions about things like fallback strategies for responding to its calling client.

6.5.2 *Guarding against unhealthy services with outlier detection*

In the previous section, we saw how Istio can limit requests to services that are misbehaving when they introduce unexpected latency. In this section, we explore Istio's approach to removing certain hosts of a service that are misbehaving. Istio uses Envoy's outlier-detection functionality for this. We saw outlier detection in section 6.3.1, and we'll take a closer look here.

To get started, let's set everything back to a known-working state:

```
$ kubectl apply -f ch6/simple-backend.yaml
$ kubectl delete destinationrule --all
```

Note that we are staying with the simple-web deployment that has extended statistics about the simple-backend cluster. If you're not sure whether you're in that state (from section 6.5.1), you can be sure by deploying that version of simple-web:

```
$ kubectl apply -f ch6/simple-web-stats-incl.yaml
```

To explore the behavior, we also disable Istio's default retry mechanisms. Retry and outlier detection go well together, but we'll try to isolate the outlier-detection functionality for these examples (we add back retry at the end to see how they complement each other). See section 6.4.2 to disable retries for the entire mesh, although we will include the command here for a better experience. We will also need to remote any VirtualService resources that may have retry settings in them already:

```
$ istioctl install --set profile=demo \
 --set meshConfig.defaultHttpRetryPolicy.attempts=0

$ kubectl delete vs simple-backend-vs
```

Finally, before we run our tests, let's introduce failure from the simple-backend service. In this case, we'll fail with HTTP 500 on 75% of the calls to the simple-backend-1 endpoint:

```
$ kubectl apply -f ch6/simple-backend-periodic-failure-500.yaml
```

Now let's run our load test. We turned off retry and introduced periodic failures, so we expect some of the requests from the load test to fail:

```
$ fortio load -H "Host: simple-web.istioinaction.io" \
-allow-initial-errors -quiet -jitter -t 30s -c 10 -qps 20 http://localhost/
```

```
...
Sockets used: 197 (for perfect keepalive, would be 10)
Jitter: true
Code 200 : 412 (68.7 %)
Code 500 : 188 (31.3 %)
All done 600 calls (plus 10 warmup) 189.855 ms avg, 19.9 qps
```

Some calls did indeed fail. We expected that because we made `simple-backend-1`
endpoints return failures. If we are sending requests to a service that is failing regu-
larly, and the other endpoints that make up the service do not, maybe it's overloaded
or somehow degraded, and we should stop sending traffic to it for a while. Let's configure outlier detection to do exactly that:

```
apiVersion: networking.istio.io/v1beta1
kind: DestinationRule
metadata:
  name: simple-backend-dr
spec:
  host: simple-backend.istioinaction.svc.cluster.local
  trafficPolicy:
    outlierDetection:
      consecutive5xxErrors: 1
      interval: 5s
      baseEjectionTime: 5s
      maxEjectionPercent: 100
```

In this destination rule, we configure `consecutive5xxErrors` with a value of 1, which
means outlier detection will trip after only one bad request (see figure 6.16). This
might be good for our example, but you may want to target something more realistic
for your environment. The `interval` setting specifies how often the Istio service
proxy checks on the hosts and decides whether to eject an endpoint based on the
`consecutive5xxErrors` setting. If a service endpoint is ejected, it is ejected for

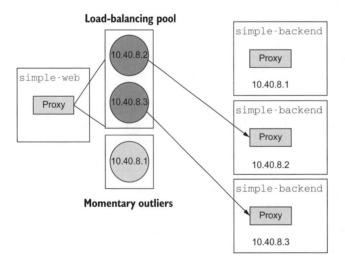

Figure 6.16   If endpoints
are misbehaving, eject
them for a time.

n * baseEjectionTime, where n is the number of times that particular endpoint has been ejected. After the time has elapsed, the endpoint is added back to the load-balancing pool. Finally, we can control how many of the hosts in the load-balancing pool are eligible for ejection. In this particular configuration, we're willing to eject 100% of the hosts. This is analogous to a circuit being tripped open: no requests will pass through when all the hosts are misbehaving.

Let's enable outlier detection and re-run our tests:

```
$ kubectl apply -f ch6/simple-backend-dr-outlier-5s.yaml
destinationrule.networking.istio.io/simple-backend-dr created

$ fortio load -H "Host: simple-web.istioinaction.io" \
-allow-initial-errors -quiet -jitter -t 30s -c 10 -qps 20 http://localhost/

...
Sockets used: 22 (for perfect keepalive, would be 10)
Jitter: true
Code 200 : 589 (98.2 %)
Code 500 : 11 (1.8 %)
All done 600 calls (plus 10 warmup) 250.173 ms avg, 19.7 qps
```

Our error rate is reduced dramatically because the misbehaving endpoint was ejected for a time. However, we still have 11 failed calls. To prove that these errors were caused by the misbehaving endpoints, we can check the statistics:

```
$ kubectl exec -it deploy/simple-web -c istio-proxy -- \
curl localhost:15000/stats | grep simple-backend | grep outlier

<omitted>.outlier_detection.ejections_active: 0
<omitted>.outlier_detection.ejections_consecutive_5xx: 3
<omitted>.outlier_detection.ejections_detected_consecutive_5xx: 3
<omitted>.outlier_detection.ejections_detected_
  consecutive_gateway_failure: 0
<omitted>.outlier_detection.ejections_detected_
  consecutive_local_origin_failure: 0
<omitted>.outlier_detection.ejections_detected_failure_percentage: 0
<omitted>.outlier_detection.ejections_detected_
  local_origin_failure_percentage: 0
<omitted>.outlier_detection.ejections_detected_
  local_origin_success_rate: 0
<omitted>.outlier_detection.ejections_detected_success_rate: 0
<omitted>.outlier_detection.ejections_enforced_consecutive_5xx: 3
<omitted>.outlier_detection.ejections_enforced_
  consecutive_gateway_failure: 0
<omitted>.outlier_detection.ejections_enforced_
  consecutive_local_origin_failure: 0
<omitted>.outlier_detection.ejections_enforced_failure_percentage: 0
<omitted>.outlier_detection.ejections_enforced_
  local_origin_failure_percentage: 0
<omitted>.outlier_detection.ejections_enforced_
  local_origin_success_rate: 0
<omitted>.outlier_detection.ejections_enforced_success_rate: 0
<omitted>.outlier_detection.ejections_enforced_total: 3
```

```
<omitted>.outlier_detection.ejections_overflow: 0
<omitted>.outlier_detection.ejections_success_rate: 0
<omitted>.outlier_detection.ejections_total: 3
```

The `simple-backend-1` host was ejected three times; and during the previous run, 11 calls failed. During the five-second `interval` setting, requests hit this misbehaving host, and it wasn't until the outlier-detection check happened (after five seconds) that some of those requests hit the misbehaving host—hence the errors.

What can we do to work around those last few errors? We can add default retry settings (or explicitly set them in each `VirtualService`):

```
$ istioctl install --set profile=demo \
  --set meshConfig.defaultHttpRetryPolicy.attempts=2
```

Try the load test once again, and you should see no errors.

Prior to this chapter, we've seen how we can use Istio's functionality and APIs to change the behavior of the network from the edge using the ingress gateway to intra-cluster communication. However, as we established at the beginning of this chapter, manual intervention to react to unexpected network failures may be nearly impossible in large-scale, constantly changing systems.

In this chapter, we dug deep into Istio's various client-side resilience features that allow services to transparently recover from intermittent network issues or topology changes. In the next chapters, we'll layer onto these capabilities by exploring how to observe network behaviors.

Summary

- Load-balancing is configured with `DestinationRule` resources. The supported algorithms are as follows:
  - `ROUND_ROBIN` delivers requests to endpoints in succession (or "next-in-loop") and is the default algorithm.
  - `RANDOM` routes traffic to endpoints at random.
  - `LEAST_CONN` routes traffic to endpoints with the fewest active requests in flight.
- Istio uses the zone and region information of nodes in combination with the health of endpoints (for which `outlierDetection` must be configured) to route traffic to workloads within the same zone (when possible, and spill over to next localities when not).
- Using destination rules, we can configure clients to do a weighted distribution across localities.
- Retries and timeouts are configured in `VirtualService` resources.
- `EnvoyFilter` resources can be used to implement capabilities of Envoy that are not exposed by the Istio API. We showcased that with request hedging.
- Circuit breaking is configured in `DestinationRule` resources, which allows upstream services time to recover before additional traffic is sent their way.

Observability: Understanding the behavior of your services

7

This chapter covers

- Collecting basic request-level metrics
- Understanding Istio's standard service-to-service metrics
- Using Prometheus to scrape workload and control-plane metrics
- Adding new metrics in Istio to track in Prometheus

Recently, you may have heard the term *observability* start to creep into the vocabulary of software engineers, operations, and site-reliability teams. These teams have to deal with the near-exponential increase in complexity when operationalizing a microservices-style architecture on cloud infrastructure. When we start to deploy our application as tens or hundreds of services (or more) per application, we increase the number of moving pieces, reliance on the network for things to succeed, and the number of things that can and do go wrong.

As our systems go down this path and become bigger, there is a higher probability that at least some part of the system is always running in a degraded state. Not only must we build our applications to be more reliable and resilient, but we also must improve our tooling and instrumentations to be able to understand what's really happening when they are running. If we can confidently comprehend what's happening with our services and infrastructure at run time, we can learn to detect failures and dive deep into debugging when we observe something unexpected. This effort will help us improve our mean time to recovery (MTTR), an important measure of high-performing teams and their impact on the business.

In this chapter, we look at some of the fundamentals of observability and how Istio helps lay the foundation for metrics collection at the network level to support observability. In the next chapter, which builds on this one, we will see how to use some of this information to visually understand our network call graphs.

7.1   What is observability?

Observability is a characteristic of a system that is measured by the level to which you can understand and reason about a system's internal state just by looking at its external signals and characteristics. Observability is important to implement controls for a system in which we can change its run-time behavior. This definition is based on the study of control theory first introduced in the 1960 paper from "On the General Theory of Control Systems" by Rudolf E. Kálmán. In more practical terms, we value stability in our systems, and we need to understand when things are going well in order to discern when things are going wrong and implement the right levels of automated and manual control to maintain this dynamic.

Figure 7.1 illustrates that Istio's data plane is in a position to affect the behavior of a request through the system. Istio can help implement controls like traffic shifting, resilience, policy enforcement, and more; but to know what controls to engage and when, we need to understand what's happening in the system. Since most of Istio's control capabilities are implemented at the network level for application requests, we shouldn't be surprised to find that Istio's ability to collect metrics to inform our observations is also at this level. This does not mean that using Istio to help with observability

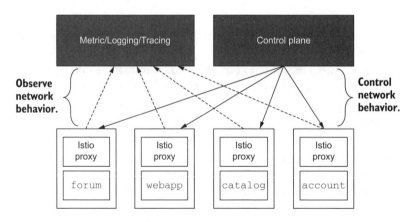

Figure 7.1   Istio is in a position to implement controls and observations.

is the only thing you need to get observability into your system. Observability is a characteristic of a system involving various levels, not an off-the-shelf solution, and it must incorporate a combination of application instrumentation, network instrumentation, signal collection infrastructure, and databases as well as a way to sift through the vast amount of data to piece together a picture when unpredictable things happen. Istio helps with one part of observability: application-level network instrumentation.

7.1.1 Observability vs. monitoring

The term *observability* has brought a level of confusion to the market in terms of a practice with which you may already be familiar: monitoring. *Monitoring* is the practice of collecting metrics, logs, traces, and so on, aggregating them, and matching them against predefined criteria of system states that we should carefully watch. When we find that one of our metrics has crossed a threshold and may be heading toward a known bad state, we take action to remedy the system. For example, operations teams can collect information about disk usage for a particular database installation. If those metrics show the disk usage approaching its capacity, we can fire an alert to trigger some kind of remediation like adding more storage to the disks.

Monitoring is a subset of observability. With monitoring, we are specifically collecting and aggregating metrics to watch for known undesirable states and then alert on them. On the other hand, observability supposes that our systems are highly unpredictable, and we cannot know all of the possible failure modes in advance. We need to collect much more data—even high-cardinality data like user IDs, request IDs, source IPs, and so on, where the entire set could be exponentially large—and use tools to quickly explore and ask questions about the data. For example, suppose a particular user—say, user John Doe, with user ID 400000021—tries to pay for the items in their cart and experiences a 10-second delay choosing a payment option. All the predefined metric thresholds (disk usage, queue depth, machine health, and so on) may be at acceptable levels, but John Doe is highly irritated at this user experience. If we have designed with observability in mind, we can sift through the many layers of services and determine the exact path a request may have taken through the system.

7.1.2 How Istio helps with observability

Istio is in a unique position to help build an observable system because Istio's data-plane proxy, Envoy, sits in the network request path between services. Through the Envoy service proxy, Istio can capture important metrics related to request handling and service interaction, such as the number of requests per second, how long requests are taking (broken out into percentiles), how many failed requests we've experienced, and so on. Istio can also help dynamically add new metrics to a system to capture new information we hadn't thought about ahead of time.

Another aspect of understanding a distributed system is tracing requests through the system to understand what services and components are involved in a request flow and how long each node in that graph takes to process the request. We cover distributed tracing in the next chapter.

Finally, Istio comes with some out-of-the-box sample tools like Prometheus, Grafana, and Kiali, which can help you visualize and explore the state of the service mesh and the services it knows about. We will *not* be using the sample out-of-the-box Prometheus, Grafana, or Kiali tools—they are add-ons that we installed in chapter 2 and are intended to be used for demo purposes. In this chapter and the next, we use a more realistic setup.

Let's delete the sample tools that we installed in chapter 2. From the root of the Istio distribution that you downloaded in chapter 2, run the following:

```
$  cd istio-1.13.0
$  kubectl delete -f samples/addons/
```

7.2   *Exploring Istio metrics*

Istio's data plane handles requests, and Istio's control plane configures the data plane to handle requests. Both keep a very deep set of metrics that give insight into what's going on at run time in terms of the application network and the operation of the mesh. Let's dig into what metrics are available for the data plane and control plane.

7.2.1   *Metrics in the data plane*

Envoy can keep a large set of connection, request, and run-time metrics that we can use to form a picture of a service's network and communication health. First, let's deploy a subset of our example application and explore its components to understand where those metrics come from and how to access them. We'll explore Istio's capabilities for building an observable system by collecting metrics around application networking and bringing those back to an area we can explore and visualize.

Let's assume that we have Istio deployed (see chapter 2 to do that) but that we don't have any other application components deployed. If you are continuing from previous chapters, you may have to clean up any left-behind deployments, services, gateways, and virtual services:

```
$  kubectl config set-context $(kubectl config current-context) \
 --namespace=istioinaction
$  kubectl delete virtualservice,deployment,service,\
destinationrule,gateway --all
```

To deploy the application for this section, run the following command from the root of the book's source code:

```
$  kubectl apply -f services/catalog/kubernetes/catalog.yaml
$  kubectl apply -f services/webapp/kubernetes/webapp.yaml
$  kubectl apply -f services/webapp/istio/webapp-catalog-gw-vs.yaml
```

Now we can run the following command to verify that we can reach our services and that they return correctly:

```
$  curl -H "Host: webapp.istioinaction.io" http://localhost/api/catalog
```

The first things we discover are the metrics kept by a service's sidecar proxy. If we list the Pods that we have deployed and that have a sidecar proxy deployed alongside, we see both the webapp and catalog services :

```
$  kubectl get pod
NAME                         READY   STATUS    RESTARTS    AGE
webapp-67bd5dfd77-g7gcf      2/2     Running   0           20m
catalog-c89594fb9-hm47h      2/2     Running   0           20m
```

Let's execute a query to view the statistics from the webapp Pod:

```
$  kubectl exec -it deploy/webapp -c istio-proxy \
-- curl localhost:15000/stats
```

> ### Querying Envoy admin endpoints without using curl
>
> Why might you query Envoy's admin endpoints without curl? For security reasons Istio provides a set of distroless images (http://mng.bz/KB2n) that contain the bare minimum dependencies to run pilot-agent. Not surprisingly, curl doesn't make the cut.
>
> Querying the endpoints is important when debugging the envoy proxy, so a minimalistic command-line interface has been added to pilot-agent to query the endpoints. For example, you can still query the statistics as follows:
>
> ```
> $  kubectl exec -it deploy/webapp -c istio-proxy \
>     -- pilot-agent request GET stats
> ```
>
> You can learn more about the other Envoy admin endpoints by querying the help endpoint:
>
> ```
> pilot-agent request GET help
> ```
>
> We will keep using curl to query the endpoints, but be aware that this option exists in case you use distroless images.

Wow! That's a lot of information kept by the sidecar proxy. In fact, the proxy keeps even more information, but much of it has been trimmed out by default. What we see here is mostly information about the proxy connected to the control plane, how many cluster or listener updates have taken place, and other high-level statistics. We also see some request- and response-level metrics, but they're buried in the output. Look for something like this:

```
reporter=.=destination;.;source_workload=.=istio-ingressgateway;.;
source_workload_namespace=.=istio-system;.;source_principal=.
=spiffe://cluster.local/ns/istio-system/sa/istio
-ingressgateway-service-account;.;source_app=.=istio-ingressgateway;.
;source_version=.=unknown;.;source_canonical_service=.
=istio-ingressgateway;.;source_canonical_revision=.=
latest;.;destination_workload=.=webapp;.
;destination_workload_namespace=.=istioinaction;.;destination_principal=.
=spiffe://cluster.local/ns/istioinaction/sa/webapp;.
;destination_app=.=webapp;.;
```

```
destination_version=.=unknown;.;destination_service=.
=webapp.istioinaction.svc.cluster.local;.;destination_service_name=.
=webapp;.;destination_service_namespace=.=istioinaction;.;
destination_canonical_service=.=webapp;
  .;destination_canonical_revision=.
=latest;.;request_protocol=.=http;.;response_flags=.=-;.
;connection_security_policy=.=mutual_tls;.;response_code=.=200;.
;grpc_response_status=.=;.;destination_cluster=.=Kubernetes;.
;source_cluster=.=Kubernetes;.;istio_requests_total: 2
```

The most important part of this line is the last bit: `istio_requests_total`. If you read through the rest of it, you can see that this is a metric for requests coming from the ingress gateway to the `webapp` service with a request total of 2. If you don't see these metrics, try calling the service a few times.

The following histograms are the standard Istio metrics kept for each proxy for both inbound and outbound calls. They provide a wealth of information without having to tune or do anything for your metrics collection:

- `istio_requests_total`
- `istio_request_bytes`
- `istio_response_bytes`
- `istio_request_duration`
- `istio_request_duration_milliseconds`

See the Istio documentation at https://istio.io/latest/docs/reference/config/metrics for more about the standard Istio metrics.

CONFIGURING PROXIES TO REPORT MORE ENVOY STATISTICS

Sometimes we need to see more information than the standard Istio metrics to troubleshoot the behavior of the network. In earlier chapters, we showed a sneak preview of enabling these other metrics, but let's take a closer look.

When a call from an application goes through its client-side proxy, the proxy makes routing decisions and routes to an upstream cluster. An upstream cluster is the actual service that is called along with any settings associated with calling the service (load balancing, security, circuit-breaking settings, and so on). In this example, the `webapp` service routes to the `catalog` service. Let's enable more information for the calls to the upstream `catalog` service.

How do we do this? We have the option to configure this as a mesh-wide setting during the Istio installation by specifying the default proxy configuration, as follows:

```
apiVersion: install.istio.io/v1alpha1
kind: IstioOperator
metadata:
  name: control-plane
spec:
  profile: demo
  meshConfig:
    defaultConfig:        ◁──┐ Defines the default proxy
      proxyStatsMatcher:      configuration for all services   ┐ Customizes the
                                          ◁─────────────────────┘ reported metrics
```

```
inclusionPrefixes:                                          ◁─┐  Metrics matching the prefix
- "cluster.outbound|80||catalog.istioinaction"                │  will be reported alongside
                                                              │  the default ones.
```

NOTE To learn more about proxy configuration possibilities, check out the API reference documentation at http://mng.bz/9K08.

Increasing the collected metrics in the entire mesh can overload your metrics-collection system and for that reason should be done very carefully. A better approach is to specify the included metrics as an annotation on a per-workload basis. For example, to get the metrics for the webapp deployment, we can add the same configuration to the proxy.istio.io/config annotation:

```
metadata:
 annotations:                             │ Proxy configurations for
   proxy.istio.io/config: |-      ◁───────┘ the webapp replicas
     proxyStatsMatcher:
       inclusionPrefixes:
       - "cluster.outbound|80||catalog.istioinaction"
```

Let's apply the annotated webapp deployment:

```
$ kubectl apply -f ch7/webapp-deployment-stats-inclusion.yaml
```

Now make a few more calls through the service chain:

```
$ curl -H "Host: webapp.istioinaction.io" http://localhost/api/catalog
```

And grab the statistics again—but this time, let's grep for only the catalog service entries:

```
$ kubectl exec -it deploy/webapp -c istio-proxy \
-- curl localhost:15000/stats | grep catalog
```

The output is massive for this command, so we've omitted it; however, let's cover a few key metrics. Note that your output may look slightly different, as we've trimmed the fully qualified domain name (FQDN) from the listing. In this case, we omitted istio-inaction.svc.cluster.local, which will appear in your listing.

These metrics indicate whether circuit breaking is in effect for connections or requests going to this upstream cluster:

```
cluster.outbound|80||catalog.circuit_breakers.default.cx_open: 0
cluster.outbound|80||catalog.circuit_breakers.default.cx_pool_open: 0
cluster.outbound|80||catalog.circuit_breakers.default.rq_open: 0
cluster.outbound|80||catalog.circuit_breakers.default.rq_pending_open: 0
cluster.outbound|80||catalog.circuit_breakers.default.rq_retry_open: 0
```

Envoy has a notion of *internal origin* versus *external origin* when identifying traffic. *Internal* is typically what we recognize as traffic from within the mesh, and *external* is traffic originating outside the mesh (traffic coming into an ingress gateway). With the cluster_name.internal.* metrics, we can see how many successful requests have come from an internal origin or within the mesh:

```
cluster.outbound|80||catalog.internal.upstream_rq_200: 2
cluster.outbound|80||catalog.internal.upstream_rq_2xx: 2
```

The `cluster_name.ssl.*` metrics are very useful to determine whether the traffic is going to the upstream cluster over TLS and any other details (cipher, curve, and so on) associated with the connections:

```
cluster.outbound|80||catalog.ssl.ciphers.ECDHE-RSA-AES256-GCM-SHA384: 1
cluster.outbound|80||catalog.ssl.connection_error: 0
cluster.outbound|80||catalog.ssl.curves.X25519: 1
cluster.outbound|80||catalog.ssl.fail_verify_cert_hash: 0
cluster.outbound|80||catalog.ssl.fail_verify_error: 0
cluster.outbound|80||catalog.ssl.fail_verify_no_cert: 0
cluster.outbound|80||catalog.ssl.fail_verify_san: 0
cluster.outbound|80||catalog.ssl.handshake: 1
```

Finally, `upstream_cx` and `upstream_rq` give more fidelity about what's happening on the network. As the names indicate, they are metrics about upstream connections and requests:

```
cluster.outbound|80||catalog.upstream_cx_active: 1
cluster.outbound|80||catalog.upstream_cx_close_notify: 0
cluster.outbound|80||catalog.upstream_cx_connect_attempts_exceeded: 0
cluster.outbound|80||catalog.upstream_cx_connect_fail: 0
cluster.outbound|80||catalog.upstream_cx_connect_timeout: 0
cluster.outbound|80||catalog.upstream_cx_destroy: 0
cluster.outbound|80||catalog.upstream_cx_destroy_local: 0
cluster.outbound|80||catalog.upstream_cx_destroy_local_with_active_rq: 0
cluster.outbound|80||catalog.upstream_cx_destroy_remote: 0
cluster.outbound|80||catalog.upstream_cx_destroy_remote_with_active_rq: 0
cluster.outbound|80||catalog.upstream_cx_destroy_with_active_rq: 0
cluster.outbound|80||catalog.upstream_cx_http1_total: 1
cluster.outbound|80||catalog.upstream_cx_http2_total: 0
cluster.outbound|80||catalog.upstream_cx_idle_timeout: 0
cluster.outbound|80||catalog.upstream_cx_max_requests: 0
cluster.outbound|80||catalog.upstream_cx_none_healthy: 0
cluster.outbound|80||catalog.upstream_cx_overflow: 0
cluster.outbound|80||catalog.upstream_cx_pool_overflow: 0
cluster.outbound|80||catalog.upstream_cx_protocol_error: 0
cluster.outbound|80||catalog.upstream_cx_rx_bytes_buffered: 1386
cluster.outbound|80||catalog.upstream_cx_rx_bytes_total: 2773
cluster.outbound|80||catalog.upstream_cx_total: 1
cluster.outbound|80||catalog.upstream_cx_tx_bytes_buffered: 0
cluster.outbound|80||catalog.upstream_cx_tx_bytes_total: 2746
cluster.outbound|80||catalog.upstream_rq_200: 2
cluster.outbound|80||catalog.upstream_rq_2xx: 2
cluster.outbound|80||catalog.upstream_rq_active: 0
cluster.outbound|80||catalog.upstream_rq_cancelled: 0
cluster.outbound|80||catalog.upstream_rq_completed: 2
cluster.outbound|80||catalog.upstream_rq_maintenance_mode: 0
cluster.outbound|80||catalog.upstream_rq_max_duration_reached: 0
cluster.outbound|80||catalog.upstream_rq_pending_active: 0
cluster.outbound|80||catalog.upstream_rq_pending_failure_eject: 0
cluster.outbound|80||catalog.upstream_rq_pending_overflow: 0
```

```
cluster.outbound|80||catalog.upstream_rq_pending_total: 1
cluster.outbound|80||catalog.upstream_rq_per_try_timeout: 0
cluster.outbound|80||catalog.upstream_rq_retry: 0
cluster.outbound|80||catalog.upstream_rq_retry_backoff_exponential: 0
cluster.outbound|80||catalog.upstream_rq_retry_backoff_ratelimited: 0
cluster.outbound|80||catalog.upstream_rq_retry_limit_exceeded: 0
cluster.outbound|80||catalog.upstream_rq_retry_overflow: 0
cluster.outbound|80||catalog.upstream_rq_retry_success: 0
cluster.outbound|80||catalog.upstream_rq_rx_reset: 0
cluster.outbound|80||catalog.upstream_rq_timeout: 0
cluster.outbound|80||catalog.upstream_rq_total: 2
cluster.outbound|80||catalog.upstream_rq_tx_reset: 0
```

You can learn more about these metrics, and any of the others for upstream clusters, in the Envoy documentation (http://mng.bz/jyg9).

Let's try another query to list information about all of the backend clusters and their respective endpoints that the proxy knows about:

```
$  kubectl exec -it deploy/webapp -c istio-proxy \
-- curl localhost:15000/clusters
```

Wow! The proxy knows about a lot of upstream services. Let's grep for only the metrics related to the catalog service:

```
$  kubectl exec -it deploy/webapp -c istio-proxy \
-- curl localhost:15000/clusters | grep catalog

outbound|80||catalog::default_priority::max_connections::4294967295
outbound|80||catalog::default_priority::max_pending_requests::4294967295
outbound|80||catalog::default_priority::max_requests::4294967295
outbound|80||catalog::default_priority::max_retries::4294967295
outbound|80||catalog::high_priority::max_connections::1024
outbound|80||catalog::high_priority::max_pending_requests::1024
outbound|80||catalog::high_priority::max_requests::1024
outbound|80||catalog::high_priority::max_retries::3
outbound|80||catalog::added_via_api::true
outbound|80||catalog::10.1.0.71:3000::cx_active::1
outbound|80||catalog::10.1.0.71:3000::cx_connect_fail::0
outbound|80||catalog::10.1.0.71:3000::cx_total::1
outbound|80||catalog::10.1.0.71:3000::rq_active::0
outbound|80||catalog::10.1.0.71:3000::rq_error::0
outbound|80||catalog::10.1.0.71:3000::rq_success::1
outbound|80||catalog::10.1.0.71:3000::rq_timeout::0
outbound|80||catalog::10.1.0.71:3000::rq_total::1
outbound|80||catalog::10.1.0.71:3000::hostname::
outbound|80||catalog::10.1.0.71:3000::health_flags::healthy
outbound|80||catalog::10.1.0.71:3000::weight::1
outbound|80||catalog::10.1.0.71:3000::region::
outbound|80||catalog::10.1.0.71:3000::zone::
outbound|80||catalog::10.1.0.71:3000::sub_zone::
outbound|80||catalog::10.1.0.71:3000::canary::false
outbound|80||catalog::10.1.0.71:3000::priority::0
outbound|80||catalog::10.1.0.71:3000::success_rate::-1.0
outbound|80||catalog::10.1.0.71:3000::local_origin_success_rate::-1.0
```

In this output, we see more information about a particular upstream cluster, including what endpoints exist for it (10.1.0.71, in this case); what region, zone, and subzone the endpoint lives in; and any active request or errors for this upstream endpoint. The previous set of statistics provided data for the cluster as a whole. With this set of statistics, we see detailed information about each endpoint.

The proxies do a good job of collecting metrics, but we don't want to have to go to each service instance and each proxy to retrieve them. The Istio service proxy can be scraped by a metric-collection system such as Prometheus or Datadog. We explore how to set up Prometheus in upcoming sections. Before that, let's see what metrics are available in the control plane.

7.2.2   *Metrics in the control plane*

The control plane istiod keeps a wealth of information about how it performs, such as how many times it has synchronized configuration with the various data-plane proxies, how long configuration synchronization takes, and other information such as bad configurations, certificate issuance/rotation, and much more. We will cover these metrics in greater detail when we look at tuning control-plane performance in chapter 11.

To view the control-plane metrics, run the following command:

```
kubectl exec -it -n istio-system deploy/istiod -- curl localhost:15014/metrics
```

This returns a large number of metrics. Let's explore some of the interesting ones.

Here we can see when the root certificate used to sign workload certificate requests (CSRs) expires as well as how many CSR requests and issued certificates have come into the control plane:

```
citadel_server_root_cert_expiry_timestamp 1.933249372e+09
citadel_server_csr_count 55
citadel_server_success_cert_issuance_count 55
```

We can also see run-time information about the version of the control plane. In this case, we are running Istio 1.13.0 in the control plane:

```
istio_build{component="pilot",tag="1.13.0"} 1
```

This section shows a distribution about how long it takes for configuration to be pushed and synchronized with the data-plane proxies. In this case, 1,101 out of 1,102 configuration convergence events happened in less than one-tenth of a second, as indicated by le="0.1", while one of them took longer (le stands for "less than or equal to"):

```
pilot_proxy_convergence_time_bucket{le="0.1"} 1101
pilot_proxy_convergence_time_bucket{le="0.5"} 1102
pilot_proxy_convergence_time_bucket{le="1"} 1102
pilot_proxy_convergence_time_bucket{le="3"} 1102
pilot_proxy_convergence_time_bucket{le="5"} 1102
pilot_proxy_convergence_time_bucket{le="10"} 1102
```

1,101 updates were distributed to proxies in less than 0.1 milliseconds.

One request took longer and fell in the range from 0.1 to 0.5.

```
pilot_proxy_convergence_time_bucket{le="20"} 1102
pilot_proxy_convergence_time_bucket{le="30"} 1102
pilot_proxy_convergence_time_bucket{le="+Inf"} 1102
pilot_proxy_convergence_time_sum 11.862998399999995
pilot_proxy_convergence_time_count 1102
```

This section shows how many services are known to the control plane, how many VirtualService resources have been configured by users, and how many proxies are connected:

```
# HELP pilot_services Total services known to pilot.
# TYPE pilot_services gauge
pilot_services 14
# HELP pilot_virt_services Total virtual services known to pilot.
# TYPE pilot_virt_services gauge
pilot_virt_services 1
# HELP pilot_vservice_dup_domain Virtual services with dup domains.
# TYPE pilot_vservice_dup_domain gauge
pilot_vservice_dup_domain 0
# HELP pilot_xds Number of endpoints connected to this pilot using XDS.
# TYPE pilot_xds gauge
pilot_xds{version="1.13.0"} 4
```

This last section shows the number of updates for any particular part of the xDS API. In chapter 3, we covered how to dynamically update the Envoy configuration for areas such as cluster discovery (CDS), endpoint discovery (EDS), listener and route discovery (LDS/RDS), and secret discovery (SDS):

```
pilot_xds_pushes{type="cds"} 756
pilot_xds_pushes{type="eds"} 1077
pilot_xds_pushes{type="lds"} 671
pilot_xds_pushes{type="rds"} 538
pilot_xds_pushes{type="sds"} 55
```

We cover more control-plane metrics when we explore performance tuning of the Istio control plane in chapter 11.

At this point, we have demonstrated how much detail the data plane and control plane report about what's going on under the covers. Exposing this detail is crucial for building an observable system. Although the service-mesh components we explored expose this information, how does an operator or user of the mesh consume these metrics? It's not practical to expect to log in to each data-plane or control-plane component to get these metrics, so let's examine how we can use metrics-collection and time-series database systems to automate this process and display the data in a useable fashion.

7.3 *Scraping Istio metrics with Prometheus*

Prometheus is a metrics-collection engine and set of related monitoring and alerting tools that originated at SoundCloud and was loosely based on Google's internal monitoring system, Borgmon (in a way similar to how Kubernetes was based on Borg). Prometheus is slightly different from other telemetry or metrics-collection systems in that it "pulls" metrics from its targets rather than expects agents to "push" metrics to it. With Prometheus, we expect our applications or the Istio service proxy to expose an endpoint with the latest metrics from which Prometheus can then pull or scrape the information.

In this book, we won't discuss whether pull or push metric collection is better, but we'll acknowledge that both exist and that an organization may choose one over the other or both. The podcast with Brian Brazil at https://thenewstack.io/exploring -prometheus-use-cases-brian-brazil tells more about Prometheus's approach to pull-based metrics and how it differs from push-based systems.

We can quickly spin up a Prometheus server and begin scraping metrics even if we have other Prometheus servers already scraping from the metrics endpoints on individual targets (Pods, in this case). In fact, this is how Prometheus can be configured to be highly available: we can run multiple Prometheus servers scraping the same targets (see figure 7.2).

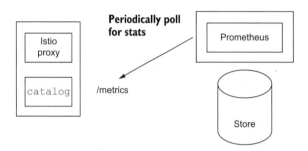

Figure 7.2   **Prometheus scraping Istio service proxy for metrics**

One of the benefits of using Prometheus is that using a simple HTTP client or web browser, we can examine our metrics endpoints. Let's use a curl command to scrape an HTTP endpoint that exposes our Istio service proxy metrics in Prometheus format.

First, we list our Pods and pick any of the services running. For this example, we use the webapp Pod:

```
$  kubectl get pod
NAME                          READY    STATUS     RESTARTS    AGE
webapp-76b86b49fd-gj589       2/2      Running    0           22h
catalog-68666d4988-sglvz      2/2      Running    0           22h
```

Next, we issue a curl command to port 15090, where the service proxy exposes the Prometheus metrics:

```
$  kubectl exec -it deploy/webapp -c istio-proxy \
-- curl localhost:15090/stats/prometheus


...
envoy_cluster_assignment_stale{cluster_name="
  outbound|80||catalog.istioinaction.svc.cluster.local"} 0
envoy_cluster_assignment_stale{cluster_name="xds-grpc"} 0
```

```
envoy_cluster_assignment_timeout_received{cluster_name="
   outbound|80||catalog.istioinaction.svc.cluster.local"} 0
envoy_cluster_assignment_timeout_received{cluster_name="xds-grpc"} 0

envoy_cluster_bind_errors{cluster_name="
   outbound|80||catalog.istioinaction.svc.cluster.local"} 0
envoy_cluster_bind_errors{cluster_name="xds-grpc"} 0

envoy_cluster_client_ssl_socket_factory_downstream_
   context_secrets_not_ready{cluster_name="
      outbound|80||catalog.istioinaction.svc.cluster.local"} 0

envoy_cluster_client_ssl_socket_factory_ssl_context_
   update_by_sds{cluster_name="
      outbound|80||catalog.istioinaction.svc.cluster.local"} 2

envoy_cluster_client_ssl_socket_factory_upstream_
   context_secrets_not_ready{cluster_name="
      outbound|80||catalog.istioinaction.svc.cluster.local"} 0

envoy_cluster_default_total_match_count{
      cluster_name="
         outbound|80||catalog.istioinaction.svc.cluster.local"} 0
envoy_cluster_default_total_match_count{cluster_name="xds-grpc"} 1

envoy_cluster_http1_dropped_headers_with_underscores{
      cluster_name="
         outbound|80||catalog.istioinaction.svc.cluster.local"} 0
...
```

We see a list of metrics formatted the way Prometheus expects. All of our applications that have the Istio service proxy injected automatically expose these Prometheus metrics. All we have to do is set up a Prometheus server to scrape them.

7.3.1 Setting up Prometheus and Grafana

As we mentioned earlier in the chapter, we removed the sample Prometheus and Grafana that ship with Istio, as they're intended only for demo usage. In this section, we explore a more production-like setup. If you didn't remove the sample add-ons earlier in the chapter, navigate to the root of the Istio distribution that we downloaded in chapter 2 and run this command:

```
$  cd istio-1.13.0
$  kubectl delete -f samples/addons/
```

We will set up a realistic observability system called kube-prometheus that uses Prometheus and many other components (https://github.com/prometheus-operator/kube-prometheus). This project tries to curate and pre-integrate a realistic, highly available deployment of Prometheus with the Prometheus operator, Grafana, and a lot of ancillary pieces like Alertmanager, node exporters, adapters for the Kube API, and others. See the kube-prometheus docs for more. In this chapter, we cover connecting to Prometheus; in chapter 8, we discuss integrating with Grafana.

To install kube-prometheus, we use the kube-prometheus-stack Helm chart (http://mng.bz/W7PX). Note that, for this section, we slightly trim the number of components, so we don't overwhelm our local installation of Docker Desktop.

To install the chart, we initially have to add the Helm repository containing it and do a `helm repo update`:

```
$  helm repo add prometheus-community \
https://prometheus-community.github.io/helm-charts

$  helm repo update
```

After doing so, we can run the Helm installer. Notice that we are disabling some components of kube-prometheus while keeping the overall spirit of the realistic deployment. To do this, we pass in a values.yaml file that explicitly controls what is installed. Feel free to review this file to understand it a bit more:

```
$  kubectl create ns prometheus
$  helm install prom prometheus-community/kube-prometheus-stack \
--version 13.13.1 -n prometheus -f ch7/prom-values.yaml
```

At this point, we should have successfully installed Prometheus and Grafana. To verify the components that were installed to support observability for us, let's check the Pods in the `prometheus` namespace :

```
$  kubectl get po -n prometheus

NAME                                                        READY STATUS   AGE
prom-grafana-5ff645dfcc-qp57d                               2/2   Running  21s
prom-kube-prometheus-stack-operator-5498b9f476-j6hjc        1/1   Running  21s
prometheus-prom-kube-prometheus-stack-prometheus-0          2/2   Running  17s
```

A newly deployed Prometheus does not know how to scrape the Istio workloads. Let's see how to configure Prometheus to scrape the Istio data-plane and control-plane metrics.

7.3.2 Configuring the Prometheus Operator to scrape the Istio control plane and workloads

To configure Prometheus to collect metrics from Istio, we will use the Prometheus Operator custom resources `ServiceMonitor` and `PodMonitor`. These CRs are described in good detail in the design doc on the Prometheus Operator repo (http://mng.bz/8lpg). Here's how we can set up a `ServiceMonitor` resource to scrape the Istio control-plane components:

```
apiVersion: monitoring.coreos.com/v1
kind: ServiceMonitor
metadata:
  name: istio-component-monitor
  namespace: prometheus
  labels:
    monitoring: istio-components
    release: prom
```

```
spec:
  jobLabel: istio
  targetLabels: [app]
  selector:
    matchExpressions:
    - {key: istio, operator: In, values: [pilot]}
  namespaceSelector:
    any: true
  endpoints:
  - port: http-monitoring
    interval: 15s
```

Let's apply this `ServiceMonitor` to begin scraping the control plane. From the root directory of the book's source code, run the following:

```
$ kubectl apply -f ch7/service-monitor-cp.yaml
```

At this point, we start to see important telemetry about the control plane, such as the number of sidecars attached to the control plane, configuration conflicts, the amount of churn in the mesh, and basic memory/CPU usage of the control plane in Prometheus. Let's port-forward Prometheus's simple query dashboard and see what exists:

```
$ kubectl -n prometheus port-forward \
statefulset/prometheus-prom-kube-prometheus-stack-prometheus 9090
```

Navigate to http://localhost:9090 and begin typing `pilot_xds` (one of the control-plane metrics) in the expression field, as shown in figure 7.3, to see various control-plane metrics. Note, it may take a few minutes for the metric names to propagate to Prometheus.

Figure 7.3   Querying Istio control-plane metrics from Prometheus

Meanwhile, to enable scraping for the data plane, we use a `PodMonitor` resource that configures the Prometheus Operator to scrape metrics from every Pod containing the `istio-proxy` container:

```
apiVersion: monitoring.coreos.com/v1
kind: PodMonitor
```

```
metadata:
  name: envoy-stats-monitor
  namespace: prometheus
  labels:
    monitoring: istio-proxies
    release: prom
spec:
  selector:
    matchExpressions:
    - {key: istio-prometheus-ignore, operator: DoesNotExist}
  namespaceSelector:
    any: true
  jobLabel: envoy-stats
  podMetricsEndpoints:
  - path: /stats/prometheus
    interval: 15s
    relabelings:
    - action: keep
      sourceLabels: [__meta_kubernetes_pod_container_name]
      regex: "istio-proxy"
    - action: keep
      sourceLabels: [
        __meta_kubernetes_pod_annotationpresent_prometheus_io_scrape]
    - sourceLabels: [
      __address__, __meta_kubernetes_pod_annotation_prometheus_io_port]
      action: replace
      regex: ([^:]+)(?::\d+)?;(\d+)
      replacement: $1:$2
      targetLabel: __address__
    - action: labeldrop
      regex: "__meta_kubernetes_pod_label_(.+)"
    - sourceLabels: [__meta_kubernetes_namespace]
      action: replace
      targetLabel: namespace
    - sourceLabels: [__meta_kubernetes_pod_name]
      action: replace
      targetLabel: pod_name
```

Just as we did for the `ServiceMonitor`, let's apply this `PodMonitor` to begin scraping the data-plane proxies. From the root directory of the book's source code, run the following:

```
$ kubectl apply -f ch7/pod-monitor-dp.yaml
```

Let's also generate some load for the data plane, so metrics will start to trickle into Prometheus:

```
$ for i in {1..100}; do curl http://localhost/api/catalog -H \
"Host: webapp.istioinaction.io"; sleep .5s; done
```

We can revisit the Prometheus query window and try to find a data-plane metric like `istio_requests_total`, as shown in figure 7.4. We see that metrics from the Istio data plane and control plane are being scraped into Prometheus. In the next chapter, we'll look at how to graph these metrics using a dashboard tool like Grafana.

Figure 7.4   Querying Istio data-plane metrics from Prometheus

7.4   *Customizing Istio's standard metrics*

Early in the chapter, we introduced some of Istio's standard metrics that are enabled by default for service-to-service communication. Table 7.1 lists the standard metrics and their types.

Table 7.1   Istio standard metrics

Metric	Description
`istio_requests_total`	COUNTER that increments for each request that comes through
`istio_request_duration_milliseconds`	DISTRIBUTION of request durations
`istio_request_bytes`	DISTRIBUTION that measures request body sizes
`istio_response_bytes`	DISTRIBUTION that measures response body sizes
`istio_request_messages_total`	(gRPC) COUNTER incremented for messages from a client
`istio_response_messages_total`	(gRPC) COUNTER incremented for messages sent from a server

Please see the Istio docs (https://istio.io/latest/docs/reference/config/metrics) for the most current list of metrics.

Istio uses a couple of plugins to the Envoy proxy sidecar to control how metrics are displayed, customized, and created. We explore this plugin in detail in this section. But before we get to that, we need to understand three main concepts:

- Metric
- Dimension
- Attribute

A *metric* is a counter, gauge, or histogram/distribution of telemetry between service calls (inbound/outbound). For example, the `istio_requests_total` metric counts the total number of requests to a service (inbound) or originating from (outbound) a service. We see two entries for the `istio_requests_total` metric if a service has both inbound and outbound requests. *Inbound* or *outbound* is an example of a *dimension* for a metric. When we query the statistics on Istio's proxy, we will see separate statistics for metric and dimension combinations. This will become clear when we look at an example.

Direction is not the only dimension, however. A metric can contain many dimensions, such as the following default dimensions for `istio_requests_total`:

```
# TYPE istio_requests_total counter
istio_requests_total{
  response_code="200",          ◁─┤ Request details
  reporter="destination",         ◁─────────────┐
  source_workload="istio-ingressgateway",        │ Point of view
  source_workload_namespace="istio-system",      │ of metric
  source_app="istio-ingressgateway",    ◁─┤ Caller
  source_version="unknown",
  source_cluster="Kubernetes",
  destination_workload="webapp",
  destination_workload_namespace="istioinaction",
  destination_app="webapp",                    ◁─┤ Target of call
  destination_version="unknown",
  destination_service="webapp.istioinaction.svc.cluster.local",
  destination_service_name="webapp",
  destination_service_namespace="istioinaction",
  destination_cluster="Kubernetes",
  request_protocol="http",
  response_flags="-",
  grpc_response_status="",
  connection_security_policy="mutual_tls",
  source_canonical_service="istio-ingressgateway",
  destination_canonical_service="webapp",
  source_canonical_revision="latest",
  destination_canonical_revision="latest"
} 6                                      ◁─┤ Number of calls
```

If any of these dimensions are different, we'll see a new entry for this metric. For example, if there are any HTTP 500 response codes, we'll see this in a different line (some dimensions are left out for brevity):

```
istio_requests_total{
    response_code="200",   ◁─┤ HTTP 200 calls
    reporter="destination",
    source_workload="istio-ingressgateway",
    source_workload_namespace="istio-system",
    destination_workload="webapp",
    destination_workload_namespace="istioinaction",
    request_protocol="http",
    connection_security_policy="mutual_tls",    │ Number of HTTP
  } 5                                      ◁─────┘ 200 calls
```

```
istio_requests_total{
    response_code="500",      <——| HTTP 500 calls
    reporter="destination",
    source_workload="istio-ingressgateway",
    source_workload_namespace="istio-system",
    destination_workload="webapp",
    destination_workload_namespace="istioinaction",
    request_protocol="http",
    connection_security_policy="mutual_tls",  | Number of HTTP
  } 3                                         <——| 500 calls
```

We see two different entries for istio_requests_total if the dimensions differ. In this case, the response_code dimension is different between the two metrics.

The dimensions to populate and report for a particular metric can be specified at configuration time. Where do the values for a particular dimension come from? From attributes that are run-time values kept by the Envoy proxy. For example, some of the default out-of-the-box attributes for requests are listed in table 7.2.

Table 7.2   Out-of-the-box Envoy request attributes

Attribute	Description
request.path	The path portion of the URL
request.url_path	The path portion of the URL without the query string
request.host	The host portion of the URL
request.scheme	The scheme portion of the URL (such as "http")
request.method	Request method (such as "GET")
request.headers	All request headers indexed by the lowercased header name
request.referer	Referrer request header
request.useragent	User agent request header
request.time	Time of the first byte received
request.id	Request ID corresponding to the x-request-id header value
request.protocol	Request protocol

These are just the request attributes available in Envoy. There are also other attributes:

- Response attributes
- Connection attributes
- Upstream attributes
- Metadata/filter state attributes
- Wasm attributes

See the Envoy documentation (http://mng.bz/Exdr) for more details about which attributes are available out of the box from Envoy.

Another set of attributes comes from Istio's peer-metadata filter (built into the Istio proxy) and is available for both `upstream_peer` and `downstream_peer` in a service invocation. The attributes listed in table 7.3 are available.

Table 7.3   Istio specific attributes contributed by the metadata exchange filter

Attribute	Description
name	Name of the Pod
namespace	Namespace the Pod runs in
labels	Workload labels
owner	Workload owner
workload_name	Workload name
platform_metadata	Platform metadata with prefixed keys
istio_version	Version identifier for the proxy
mesh_id	Unique identifier for the mesh
cluster_id	Identifier for the cluster to which this workload belongs
app_containers	List of short names for the application containers

To use any of these attributes, prefix them with `upstream_peer` or `downstream_peer` for the respective upstream (outgoing from proxy) or downstream (incoming to the proxy) metrics. For example, to refer to the Istio proxy version of a caller to a service, you use `downstream_peer.istio_version`. To refer to the cluster of an upstream service, you use `upstream_peer.cluster_id`.

Attributes are used to define the value of a dimension. Let's see how we can customize an existing metric's dimensions using attributes.

7.4.1   Configuring existing metrics

By default, Istio metrics are configured in the `stats` proxy plugin using an `Envoy-Filter` resource that's installed when you first install Istio. For example, the following Envoy filters are available out of the box on a default installation:

```
$ kubectl get envoyfilter -n istio-system
```

```
NAME                     AGE
stats-filter-1.11        45h
stats-filter-1.12        45h
stats-filter-1.13        45h
tcp-stats-filter-1.11    45h
tcp-stats-filter-1.12    45h
tcp-stats-filter-1.13    45h
```

If you look at `stats-filter-1.13`, you should see something like the following:

Listing 7.1 Default `stats-filter` configuration

```
- applyTo: HTTP_FILTER
  match:
    context: SIDECAR_OUTBOUND
    listener:
      filterChain:
        filter:
          name: envoy.filters.network.http_connection_manager
          subFilter:
            name: envoy.filters.http.router
    proxy:
      proxyVersion: ^1\.13.*
  patch:
    operation: INSERT_BEFORE
    value:
      name: istio.stats       <──┤ Filter name
      typed_config:
        '@type': type.googleapis.com/udpa.type.v1.TypedStruct
        type_url: type.googleapis.com/
          envoy.extensions.filters.http.wasm.v3.Wasm
        value:
          config:          <──┤ Filter configuration
            configuration:
              '@type': type.googleapis.com/google.protobuf.StringValue
              value: |
                {
                  "debug": "false",
                  "stat_prefix": "istio"
                }
            root_id: stats_outbound
            vm_config:
              code:
                local:
                  inline_string: envoy.wasm.stats
              runtime: envoy.wasm.runtime.null
              vm_id: stats_outbound
```

This Envoy filter directly configures a filter called `istio.stats`, which is a Web-Assembly (Wasm) plugin that implements the statistics functionality. This Wasm filter is actually compiled directly into the Envoy codebase and runs against a `NULL` VM, so it's not run in a Wasm VM. To run it in a Wasm VM, you must pass the `--set values .telemetry.v2.prometheus.wasmEnabled=true` flag to installation with `istioctl` or the respective `IstioOperator` configuration. We will dig more into Wasm in chapter 14.

ADDING DIMENSIONS TO EXISTING METRICS

Let's say we want to add two new dimensions to the `istio_requests_total` metric. Maybe, for upgrade-tracking reasons, we want to check what versions of proxies exist on the upstream call for which `meshId`. Let's add `upstream_proxy_version` and `source_mesh_id` dimensions (we could also remove existing dimensions that we don't want to track or that create more information than we want):

```
apiVersion: install.istio.io/v1alpha1
kind: IstioOperator
```

```
spec:
  profile: demo
  values:
    telemetry:
      v2:
        prometheus:
          configOverride:
            inboundSidecar:
              metrics:
              - name: requests_total              New dimensions
                dimensions:                   ◁┘  added
                  upstream_proxy_version: upstream_peer.istio_version
                  source_mesh_id: node.metadata['MESH_ID']
                tags_to_remove:      ◁──┐ List of tags to
                - request_protocol         │ be removed
            outboundSidecar:
              metrics:
              - name: requests_total
                dimensions:
                  upstream_proxy_version: upstream_peer.istio_version
                  source_mesh_id: node.metadata['MESH_ID']
                tags_to_remove:
                - request_protocol
            gateway:
              metrics:
              - name: requests_total
                dimensions:
                  upstream_proxy_version: upstream_peer.istio_version
                  source_mesh_id: node.metadata['MESH_ID']
                tags_to_remove:
                - request_protocol
```

In this configuration, we are specifically configuring the `requests_total` metric (notice that we don't prefix it with `istio_`—that happens automatically) to have two new dimensions that come from attributes. We also remove the `request_protocol` dimension. Let's update the Istio installation with those changes:

```
$  istioctl install -f ch7/metrics/istio-operator-new-dimensions.yaml -y
```

What happens behind the scenes?

After we update the Istio installation with the `IstioOperator` configuration containing the new dimensions, behind the scenes, `istioctl` updates the Envoy filter `stats-filter-1.13`, which, as we mentioned earlier, configures the Istio metrics.

You can verify that using the following command:

```
kubectl get envoyfilter -n istio-system stats-filter-{stat-postfix}
-o yaml
```

Before we can see this dimension in our metrics, we need to let Istio's proxy know about it. To do this, we have to annotate our deployment Pod spec with the `sidecar.istio.io/extraStatTags` annotation. Note that this annotation needs to go on the `spec.template.metadata` Pod template, not on the deployment metadata itself:

```
spec:
  replicas: 1
  selector:
    matchLabels:
      app: webapp
  template:
    metadata:
      annotations:
        proxy.istio.io/config: |-
          extraStatTags:
          - "upstream_proxy_version"
          - "source_mesh_id"
      labels:
        app: webapp
```

Let's apply this change:

```
$ kubectl -n istioinaction apply -f \
ch7/metrics/webapp-deployment-extrastats.yaml
```

Now let's call our services and check the metrics:

```
$ curl -H "Host: webapp.istioinaction.io" \
http://localhost/api/catalog
```

We can check the metrics directly on the proxy for the `webapp` service like this:

```
$ kubectl -n istioinaction exec -it deploy/webapp -c istio-proxy \
-- curl localhost:15000/stats/prometheus | grep istio_requests_total
```

You should see something similar to the following (you may see two entries: one for inbound traffic and one for outbound traffic):

```
istio_requests_total{
    response_code="200",
    reporter="destination",
    source_workload="istio-ingressgateway",
    source_workload_namespace="istio-system",
    destination_workload="webapp",
    destination_workload_namespace="istioinaction",
    request_protocol="http",
    upstream_proxy_version="{1.13.0}",         ⟵┐ Upstream
                                                 ┘ proxy
    source_mesh_id="cluster.local"    ⟵─┤ Mesh ID
  } 5
```

Some of the output has been trimmed. Also note that the `request_protocol` dimension is not in the list of dimensions, because we removed it in the previous configuration (understandably, you'd still find this dimension in the previously generated metrics).

> ### Using the new Telemetry API
>
> Istio introduced a new Telemetry API in Istio 1.12, which gives the user more flexibility and control over how metrics are configured. In this section, we used the `Istio-Operator` to install new metric configurations, but this approach configures the metrics globally. If we want to limit the metric configuration to just a single namespace or a single workload, we can use the new Telemetry API.
>
> At the time of writing (Istio 1.13), the Telemetry API is in `alpha` form, which means it's subject to changes. We cover bits and pieces of the Telemetry API in chapter 4 for access logging and chapter 8 for tracing. For this chapter, we point you to any new information in the Istio docs at https://istio.io/latest/docs/reference/config/telemetry/#Telemetry. We also offer an example of how to do the equivalent metric configuration:
>
> ```
> $  kubectl apply -f ch7/metrics/v2/add-dimensions-telemetry.yaml
> ```

7.4.2   Creating new metrics

We've seen how to customize the dimensions of *existing* standard metrics like `istio_requests_total`, but what if we want to create our own metric? To do so, we can configure the `stats` plugin with new metric definitions. Here's an example:

```
apiVersion: install.istio.io/v1alpha1
kind: IstioOperator
spec:
  profile: demo
  values:
    telemetry:
      v2:
        prometheus:
          configOverride:
            inboundSidecar:
              definitions:
              - name: get_calls
                type: COUNTER
                value: "(request.method.startsWith('GET') ? 1 : 0)"
            outboundSidecar:
              definitions:
              - name: get_calls
                type: COUNTER
                value: "(request.method.startsWith('GET') ? 1 : 0)"
            gateway:
              definitions:
              - name: get_calls
                type: COUNTER
                value: "(request.method.startsWith('GET') ? 1 : 0)"
```

Here we create a new metric called `istio_get_calls`, but note that we define it with a name of `get_calls`. As mentioned previously, the `istio_` prefix is added automatically. We define this metric as a `COUNTER`, but `GAUGE` and `HISTOGRAM` are options as well. The value of the metric is a string that is a Common Expression Language (CEL; https://opensource.google/projects/cel) expression that must return an integer for type COUNTER. The CEL expression operates on attributes, and in this case, we are counting the number of requests that are HTTP GET requests.

Let's apply this configuration to create a new metric called istio_get_calls:

```
$ istioctl install -f ch7/metrics/istio-operator-new-metric.yaml -y
```

In the previous section, we had to explicitly tell the Istio proxy about our new dimensions. When we create new metrics, we need to tell Istio to expose them on the proxy with the sidecar.istio.io/statsInclusionPrefixes annotation on the webapp deployment Pod spec:

```
spec:
  replicas: 1
  selector:
    matchLabels:
      app: webapp
  template:
    metadata:
      annotations:
        proxy.istio.io/config: |-
          proxyStatsMatcher:
            inclusionPrefixes:
            - "istio_get_calls"
      labels:
        app: webapp
```

Let's apply this new configuration:

```
$ kubectl -n istioinaction apply -f \
ch7/metrics/webapp-deployment-new-metric.yaml
```

Now we can put some traffic through our example services:

```
$ curl -H "Host: webapp.istioinaction.io" \
http://localhost/api/catalog
```

And if we check the metrics on the Istio proxy, we see our new metric:

```
$ kubectl -n istioinaction exec -it deploy/webapp -c istio-proxy \
-- curl localhost:15000/stats/prometheus | grep istio_get_calls

# TYPE istio_get_calls counter
istio_get_calls{} 2
```

We do not have any dimensions specified for this metric. You can follow the steps in the previous section to customize the dimensions you wish to see. In this case, we are trying to count the number of GET requests across any requests in the system—a contrived example to illustrate the power of creating new metrics. What if you want to count the number of requests for all GET requests to the /items endpoint on the catalog service? The Istio stats plugin is powerful enough to do it. We can get finer grained by creating new dimensions and new *attributes*. Let's take a look in the next section.

7.4.3   Grouping calls with new attributes

We can create new attributes based on existing attributes to be finer-grained or domain specific. For example, we can create a new attribute called `istio_operationId`, which combines `request.path_url` and `request.method` to try to track the number of `GET` calls to the `/items` API on the catalog service. To do this, we use the Istio attribute-gen proxy plugin, which is another Wasm extension used to customize the behavior of the proxy's metrics. The `attribute-gen` plugin complements the `stats` plugin, which we used in the previous section. The `attribute-gen` plugin layers in before the `stats` plugin so that any attributes it creates can be used in `stats`.

Let's see how to configure the `attribute-gen` plugin using an `EnvoyFilter` resource:

```
{
  "attributes": [
    {
                                                            Attribute
      "output_attribute": "istio_operationId",      ◁──┘ name
      "match": [
        {                                    Attribute
          "value": "getitems",      ◁──┘ values
          "condition": "request.url_path == '/items'
            && request.method == 'GET'"
        },
        {
          "value": "createitem",
          "condition": "request.url_path == '/items'
            && request.method == 'POST'"
        },
        {
          "value": "deleteitem",
          "condition": "request.url_path == '/items'
            && request.method == 'DELETE'"
        }
      ]
    }
  ]
}
```

You can see the full `EnvoyFilter` resource in the ch7/metrics/attribute-gen.yaml file.

This configuration combines a couple of different out-of-the-box attributes to create a new attribute called `istio_operationId`, which can identify certain classes of calls. In this case, we are trying to identify and count calls to a particular API, `/items`. We add this `attribute-gen` plugin to the outbound calls from the `webapp` service to track calls to `/items` on the `catalog` service:

```
$ kubectl apply -f ch7/metrics/attribute-gen.yaml
```

We also create a new dimension called `upstream_operation` that uses this attribute in the `istio_requests_total` metric to identify the API calls to `catalog`. Let's update our `stats` plugin configuration to the following:

```
configOverride:
  outboundSidecar:
    metrics:
    - name: requests_total
      dimensions:
        upstream_operation: istio_operationId       ⟵─┘ New
                                                        dimension
```

Now we apply this new configuration:

```
$ istioctl install -y -f ch7/metrics/istio-operator-new-attribute.yaml
```

When we use new dimensions, we also need to add them to the `extraStats` annotation in our service. Let's apply that:

```
$ kubectl apply -f ch7/metrics/webapp-deployment-extrastats-new-attr.yaml
```

At this point, if we put traffic through our services and query the metrics, we see the new dimension in our `istio_requests_total` metric with the new `upstream_operation` dimension:

```
$ curl -H "Host: webapp.istioinaction.io" \
http://localhost/api/catalog
```

We can check the metrics directly on the proxy for the `webapp` service like this:

```
$ kubectl -n istioinaction exec -it deploy/webapp -c istio-proxy \
-- curl localhost:15000/stats/prometheus | grep istio_requests_total
```

You should see something similar to the following for the `istio_requests_total` metric for the outgoing calls (trimmed for brevity):

```
istio_requests_total{
    response_code="200",
    reporter="destination",
    source_workload="istio-ingressgateway",
    source_workload_namespace="istio-system",
    destination_workload="webapp",
    destination_workload_namespace="istioinaction",
    request_protocol="http",
    upstream_proxy_version="1.9.2",
    source_mesh_id="cluster.local",                    New
    upstream_operation="getitems"     ⟵─┘             dimension
  } 1
```

The new dimension is added—and with that, we are at the end of the chapter. You should know that the more our applications communicate over the network, the more things can go wrong. Having a consistent view into what's happening between services, regardless of who wrote the application or what language was used, is almost a prerequisite to running a microservice-style architecture. Istio makes metrics collection between services easier by observing things like success rate, failure rate, number of retries, latency, and so on, without the developer having to explicitly code this into their applications. This does not mean app- or business-level metrics are not needed—they most definitely are, but Istio can simplify collecting *golden-signal* networking metrics. (The Google SRE book [https://sre.google/sre-book/monitoring-distributed-systems] refers to the following as the golden-signal metrics: latency, throughput, errors, and saturation.)

In this chapter, we've covered how to scrape metrics from the Istio service proxy (Envoy proxy) and the control plane, how to extend the metrics that are exposed, and how to aggregate the metrics into a time-series system like Prometheus. From there, we can visualize the metrics using Grafana or Kiali, as we'll see in the next chapter.

Summary

- Monitoring is the process of collecting and aggregating metrics to watch for known undesirable states so that corrective measures can be taken.
- Istio collects the metrics used for monitoring when intercepting requests in the sidecar proxy. Because the proxy acts at layer 7 (the application-networking layer), it has access to a great deal of information such as status codes, HTTP methods, and headers that can be used in metrics.
- One of the key metrics is `istio_requests_total`, which counts requests and answers questions such as how many requests ended with status code 200.
- The metrics exposed by the proxies set the foundation to build an observable system.
- Metrics-collection systems collect and aggregate the exposed metrics from the proxies.
- By default, Istio configures the proxies to expose only a limited set of statistics. You can configure the proxies to report more mesh-wide using the `meshConfig.defaultConfig` or on a per-workload basis using the annotation `proxy.istio.io/config`.
- The control plane also exposes metrics for its performance. The most important is the histogram `pilot_proxy_convergence_time`, which measures the time taken to distribute changes to the proxies.
- We can customize the metrics available in Istio using the `IstioOperator` and use them in services by setting the `extraStats` value in the annotation `proxy.istio.io/config` that defines the proxy configuration. This level of control gives the operator (end user) flexibility over what telemetry gets scraped and how to present it in dashboards.

Observability: Visualizing network behavior with Grafana, Jaeger, and Kiali

This chapter covers
- Using Grafana to observe metrics visually
- Distributed tracing instrumentation with Jaeger
- Visualizing the network call graph with Kiali

In this chapter, we build on the foundation we established in the previous chapter, and we use some tools to visualize data from the service mesh. We saw how Istio's data-plane and control-plane components expose a lot of very useful operational metrics and how we can scrape those into a time-series system like Prometheus. In this chapter, we use tools like Grafana and Kiali to visualize those metrics to better understand the behavior of the services in the mesh as well as the mesh itself. We also dig into visualizing the network call graph with distributed tracing tools.

8.1 Using Grafana to visualize Istio service and control-plane metrics

In the previous chapter, we removed the sample Prometheus and Grafana add-ons that come with a demo installation of Istio. Instead, we installed kube-prometheus (https://github.com/prometheus-operator/kube-prometheus), which is a more realistic set of observability tools.

To double-check that you've got the `kube-prometheus` stack installed correctly, check what's in the `prometheus` namespace:

```
$ kubectl get po -n prometheus
```

```
NAME                                                   READY  STATUS   AGE
prom-grafana-5ff645dfcc-qp57d                          2/2    Running  21s
prom-kube-prometheus-stack-operator-5498b9f476-j6hjc   1/1    Running  21s
prometheus-prom-kube-prometheus-stack-prometheus-0     2/2    Running  17s
```

If you don't have this namespace or the installation doesn't look right, see chapter 7 to install the `kube-prometheus` stack. The list of Pods in the `prometheus` namespace includes a Pod named `prom-grafana-xxx`: this is the deployment of Grafana that we use in this chapter.

Let's verify that we can access and log in to the Grafana dashboards. We port-forward the Grafana Pod on port 3000 to our local machine:

```
$ kubectl -n prometheus port-forward svc/prom-grafana 3000:80
```

Log in with the following credentials:

```
Username: admin
Password: prom-operator
```

You should now see the Grafana home page, shown in figure 8.1. If you're familiar with Grafana, you can poke around and see what dashboards are available out of the box. Otherwise, don't worry about it; in the next section, we walk through installing and using the Istio dashboards so we can visualize metrics from our service mesh.

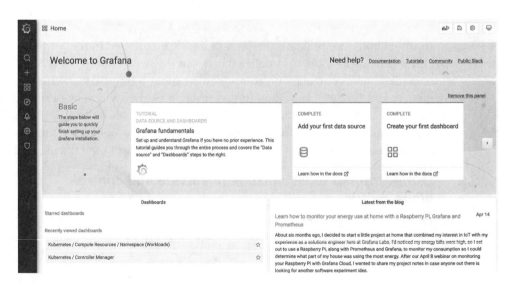

Figure 8.1   Grafana home screen

8.1.1 Setting up Istio's Grafana dashboards

Istio has some preconfigured Grafana dashboards that are a good place to start visualizing Istio's metrics. Unfortunately, they are no longer part of the official distribution, so you have to download them directly from the Istio source code on GitHub. We have included them in the source code in ch8/dashboards for use in this part of the book. You can also find them published with other community dashboards at https://grafana.com/orgs/istio/dashboards. Navigate to the ch8 directory of the book's source code, and run the following command:

```
$  cd ch8/

$  kubectl -n prometheus create cm istio-dashboards \
--from-file=pilot-dashboard.json=dashboards/pilot-dashboard.json \
--from-file=istio-workload-dashboard.json=dashboards/\
istio-workload-dashboard.json \
--from-file=istio-service-dashboard.json=dashboards/\
istio-service-dashboard.json \
--from-file=istio-performance-dashboard.json=dashboards/\
istio-performance-dashboard.json \
--from-file=istio-mesh-dashboard.json=dashboards/\
istio-mesh-dashboard.json \
--from-file=istio-extension-dashboard.json=dashboards/\
istio-extension-dashboard.json
```

This creates a `configmap` resource with the dashboard JSON source, which we can import to Grafana. Finally, we need to label this `configmap` resource so that our Grafana picks it up:

```
$  kubectl label -n prometheus cm istio-dashboards grafana_dashboard=1
```

Wait a few moments, and then click the Home menu item in the top-left corner of the Grafana dashboard (see figure 8.2), which takes you to a screen of available Grafana dashboards. The list includes Istio dashboards for things like the control plane, workloads, and services (if you don't see the dashboards, you may have to refresh the page).

Figure 8.2   Click the Home link to see available dashboards (you may have to refresh).

8.1.2   Viewing control-plane metrics

To view graphs of the control-plane metrics, click Istio Control Plane Dashboard, as shown in figure 8.3. In the previous chapter, we set up the `ServiceMonitor` resource to scrape the control plane. After a few minutes, metrics begin to appear in the control-plane graph (see figure 8.4).

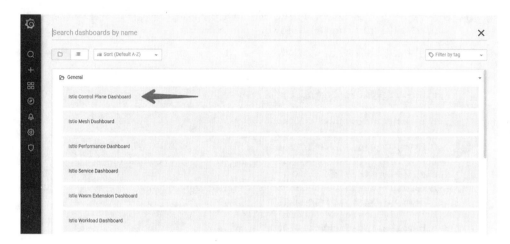

Figure 8.3   Select Istio Control Plane Dashboard.

Figure 8.4   The control-plane dashboard with metrics graphed

You should see information like graphs of CPU, memory, and goroutines, as well as vital data about any control-plane errors, configuration sync issues, active data-plane connections, and more. Click around to see what information you can glean from the control plane. Try clicking the details of one of the graphs and the Explore option to view the raw queries used to generate the graph as shown in figure 8.4. For example, if you check the for Pilot Push Time graph, you will find that it's visualizing the `pilot_proxy_convergence_time` metric; as we learned in the previous chapter, this metric measures the time taken to distribute changes to the proxies.

8.1.3 Viewing data-plane metrics

To review the metrics for specific services that come from the data plane, click Istio Service Dashboard in the list of dashboards. You can select a specific service like `webapp.istioinaction` (see figure 8.5).

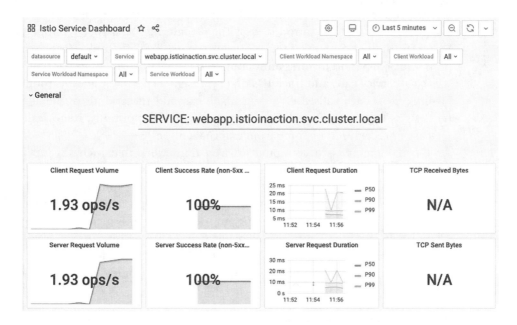

Figure 8.5 The service dashboard for the `webapp` service with metrics graphed

These graphs are populated with the Istio standard metrics. You can tweak and tune them or add new graphs for different metrics. See chapter 7 for how to enable custom metrics or specific Envoy metrics.

8.2 Distributed tracing

As we build more applications as microservices, we are creating a network of distributed components that work together to achieve a business objective, as illustrated in figure 8.6. When things start to go wrong on the request path, it's critical to understand what's

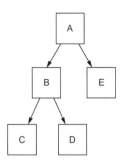

Figure 8.6   Services often take multiple hops to service a request. We need the ability to see what hops were involved for a given request and how long each hop took.

happening so we can diagnose it quickly and fix it. In the previous sections, we've seen how Istio can help collect metrics and telemetry related to networking on behalf of the application. In this section, we look at a concept called *distributed tracing* and how it can help diagnose misbehaving requests as it traverses a web of microservices.

In a monolith, if things start to misbehave, we can jump in and start debugging with familiar tools at our disposal. We have debuggers, runtime profilers, and memory analysis tools to find areas where parts of the code introduce latency or trigger faults that cause an application feature to misbehave. With an application made up of distributed parts, we need a new set of tools to accomplish the same things.

Distributed tracing gives us insights into the components of a distributed system involved in serving a request. It was introduced by the Google Dapper paper ("Dapper, a Large-Scale Distributed Systems Tracing Infrastructure," 2010, https://research.google/pubs/pub36356) and involves annotating requests with correlation IDs that represent service-to-service calls and trace IDs that represent a specific request through a graph of service-to-service calls. Istio's data plane can add these kinds of metadata to the requests as they pass through the data plane (and, importantly, remove them when they are unrecognized or come from external entities).

OpenTelemetry is a community-driven framework that includes OpenTracing, which is a specification that captures concepts and APIs related to distributed tracing. Distributed tracing, in part, relies on developers instrumenting their code and annotating requests as they are processed by the application and make new requests to other systems. A tracing engine helps put together the full picture of a request flow, which can be used to identify misbehaving areas of our architecture.

With Istio, we can provide the bulk of the heavy lifting developers would otherwise have to implement themselves and provide distributed tracing as part of the service mesh.

8.2.1   *How does distributed tracing work?*

At its simplest form, distributed tracing with OpenTracing consists of applications creating Spans, sharing those Spans with an OpenTracing engine, and propagating a trace context to any of the services it subsequently calls. A Span is a collection of data representing a *unit of work* within a service or component. This data includes things like the start time of the operation, the end time, the operation name, and a set of tags and logs.

In turn, those upstream services do the same thing: create a Span capturing its part of the request, send that to the OpenTracing engine, and further propagate the trace context to other services. Using these Spans and the trace context, the distributed-tracing engine can construct a Trace, which is a causal relationship between services that show direction, timing, and other debugging information. Spans have their own ID and a Trace ID. These IDs are used for correlation and are expected to be propagated between services. See figure 8.7 for an illustration.

OpenTracing implementations include systems like these:

- Jaeger
- Zipkin
- Lightstep
- Instana

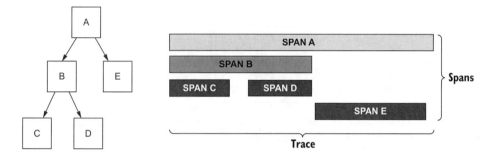

Figure 8.7   With distributed tracing, we can collect Spans **for each network hop, capture them in an overall** Trace, **and use them to debug issues in our call graph.**

Istio can handle sending the Spans to the distributed tracing engine, so you don't need language-specific libraries and application-specific configuration to do this. When a request traverses the Istio service proxy, a new trace is started if there isn't one in progress, and the start and end times for the request are captured as part of the Span. Istio appends HTTP headers, commonly known as the Zipkin tracing headers, to the request that can be used to correlate subsequent Span objects to the overall Trace. If a request comes into a service and the Istio proxy recognizes the distributed-tracing headers, the proxy treats it as an in-progress trace and does not try to generate a new one. The following Zipkin tracing headers are used by Istio and the distributed-tracing functionality:

- x-request-id
- x-b3-traceid
- x-b3-spanid
- x-b3-parentspanid
- x-b3-sampled
- x-b3-flags
- x-ot-span-context

For the distributed-tracing functionality provided by Istio to work across the entire request call graph, each application needs to propagate these headers to any outgoing calls it makes (see figure 8.8). The reason is that Istio cannot know which outgoing calls were a result of which incoming requests. To correctly correlate upstream calls with calls that came into the service, the application must assume responsibility for propagating these headers. Many times, out-of-the-box RPC frameworks integrate with or directly support OpenTracing and can automatically propagate these headers for you. Either way, the application must ensure that these headers are propagated.

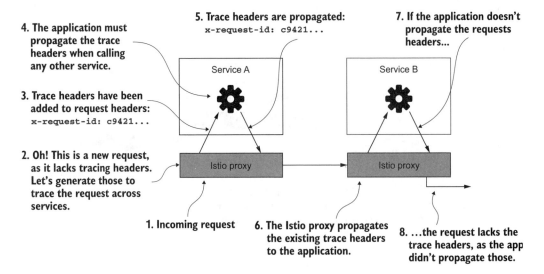

Figure 8.8   The application must propagate the tracing headers. Otherwise, we lose the full span of the request.

8.2.2   *Installing a distributed tracing system*

In section 7.1.2, we removed the default sample apps to give a more realistic deployment of the various components. Jaeger is a bit more complex and requires a database. For that reason, in this book, we stick with the sample Jaeger all-in-one deployment. This deployment also creates a zipkin Kubernetes service that allows us to plug directly in with some of the defaults Istio expects. See section 8.2.5 for more on customization of the distributed tracing functionality. Also, refer to the Jaeger documentation for full production deployment steps (http://mng.bz/GGdN).

Let's install the sample Jaeger all-in-one deployment from the Istio samples directory:

```
$ kubectl apply -f istio-1.13.0/samples/addons/jaeger.yaml

deployment.apps/jaeger created
service/tracing created
service/zipkin created
service/jaeger-collector created
```

The following Pods are in `istio-system`:

```
$ kubectl get pod -n istio-system
```

```
NAME                                   READY   STATUS    RESTARTS   AGE
istio-egressgateway-96cf6b468-9n65h    1/1     Running   0          11d
istio-ingressgateway-57b94d999-6llwn   1/1     Running   0          26h
istiod-58c5fdd87b-lr4jf                1/1     Running   0          11d
jaeger-7f78b6fb65-cr7n6                1/1     Running   0          34s
```

Finally, let's check the services that were installed. We see a `zipkin` service. Jaeger is compatible with the Zipkin format (http://mng.bz/zQrZ), and this is how we will configure Istio in the next section:

```
$ kubectl get svc -n istio-system
```

```
istio-egressgateway    ClusterIP      10.104.124.38    <none>
istio-ingressgateway   LoadBalancer   10.111.91.191    localhost
istiod                 ClusterIP      10.103.244.151   <none>
jaeger-collector       ClusterIP      10.96.251.47     <none>
tracing                ClusterIP      10.102.201.5     <none>
zipkin                 ClusterIP      10.107.57.119    <none>
```

If your output looks similar to this, you should be good to go. Next, we need to configure the data plane to send traces to the new Jaeger service.

8.2.3 *Configuring Istio to perform distributed tracing*

We can configure Istio for distributed tracing multiple levels: global mesh, namespace, or specific workload. We will cover global and workload tracing configurations in this chapter.

> **NOTE** Istio 1.12 introduced a more granular API for logging, metrics, and tracing called the Telemetry API (https://istio.io/latest/docs/tasks/observability/telemetry). At the time of writing, this API is considered Alpha and has had issues working correctly. We do not cover the Telemetry API in this chapter; however, we will try to keep the source code repo up to date with appropriate examples.

CONFIGURING TRACING AT INSTALLATION

Istio supports distributed tracing backends including Zipkin, Datadog, Jaeger (Zipkin compatible), and others. Here's a sample configuration using an `IstioOperator` resource when installing Istio, which would configure various distributed tracing backends:

```
apiVersion: install.istio.io/v1alpha1
kind: IstioOperator
metadata:
  namespace: istio-system
spec:
  meshConfig:
    defaultConfig:
```

```
tracing:
  lightstep: {}
  zipkin: {}
  datadog: {}
  stackdriver: {}
```

If we want to use Jaeger, for example, which is Zipkin compatible, we configure something like this:

```
apiVersion: install.istio.io/v1alpha1
kind: IstioOperator
metadata:
  namespace: istio-system
spec:
  meshConfig:
    defaultConfig:
      tracing:
        zipkin:
          address: zipkin.istio-system:9411
```

Then we run this command from `istioctl` or with the Istio operator to do the installation with this configuration:

```
$ istioctl install -y -f ch8/install-istio-tracing-zipkin.yaml
```

We configure the global mesh configuration object with the correct tracing settings. We can also do that directly in the `MeshConfigconfigmap` that is installed with Istio if we didn't configure tracing on installation.

CONFIGURING TRACING USING MESHCONFIG

If you have already installed Istio and did not configure a tracing backend, or if you want to update the configuration, you can see Istio's mesh-wide defaults in the `Mesh-Config` object in the `istioconfigmap` in the `istio-system` namespace:

```
$ kubectl get cm istio -n istio-system -o yaml
```

```
apiVersion: v1
data:
  mesh: |-
    defaultConfig:
      discoveryAddress: istiod.istio-system.svc:15012
      proxyMetadata: {}
      tracing:
        zipkin:
          address: zipkin.istio-system:9411
    enablePrometheusMerge: true
    rootNamespace: istio-system
    trustDomain: cluster.local
  meshNetworks: 'networks: {}'
```

You can update any of the configurations for the mesh-wide defaults in the `default-Config.tracing` section of the configuration.

CONFIGURING TRACING PER WORKLOAD

It's often desirable to have the granularity to configure tracing parameters on individual workloads. We can do that with annotations on the Deployment resources of a workload. Here's an example:

```
apiVersion: apps/v1
kind: Deployment
...
spec:
  template:
    metadata:
      annotations:
        proxy.istio.io/config: |
          tracing:
            zipkin:
              address: zipkin.istio-system:9411
```

This configures the tracing system for the one specific workload specified by this deployment.

EXAMINING THE DEFAULT TRACING HEADERS

At this point, we have configured the distributed tracing engine and Istio to send traces to the correct location. Let's try a few tests to make sure we see what we expect from Istio regarding generation of the Zipkin headers for tracing.

To demonstrate Istio automatically injecting the OpenTracing headers and correlation IDs, we'll try to use Istio's ingress gateway to call an external httpbin service and call an endpoint that displays the request headers. Let's deploy an Istio Virtual-Service resource that does this routing:

```
$ kubectl apply -n istioinaction \
-f ch8/tracing/thin-httpbin-virtualservice.yaml
```

Now, let's call the Istio ingress gateway on localhost and watch how it forwards to an external service, which should return the headers used originally in the request:

```
$  curl -H "Host: httpbin.istioinaction.io" http://localhost/headers
{
  "headers": {
    "Accept": "*/*",
    "Content-Length": "0",
    "Host": "httpbin.istioinaction.io",
    "User-Agent": "curl/7.54.0",
    "X-Amzn-Trace-Id": "Root=1-607f16c8-4ea437616d5505ac516bbfe1",
    "X-B3-Sampled": "1",
    "X-B3-Spanid": "17ed6f800f125ecb",
    "X-B3-Traceid": "05516f0b84c9de6817ed6f800f125ecb",
    "X-Envoy-Attempt-Count": "1",
    "X-Envoy-Decorator-Operation": "httpbin.org:80/*",
    "X-Envoy-Internal": "true",
    "X-Envoy-Peer-Metadata": "<omitted>",
    "X-Envoy-Peer-Metadata-Id": "<omitted>"
  }
}
```

When we called our Istio ingress gateway, we were routed to an external URL, http://httpbin.org, which is a simple HTTP testing service. When we GET the /headers endpoint, it returns the request headers we used with the request. We can clearly see that the x-b3-* Zipkin headers were automatically appended to our request. These Zipkin headers are used to create Spans and are sent to Jaeger.

8.2.4   Viewing distributed tracing data

When spans are sent to Jaeger (or any OpenTracing engine), we need a way to query and view the Traces and their associated spans. Using the out-of-the-box Jaeger UI, we can do just that. To view the UI, let's port-forward it locally:

```
$  istioctl dashboard jaeger --browser=false

http://localhost:16686
skipping opening a browser
```

This is a shortcut for port-forwarding the Jaeger UI to localhost. Now, if we navigate to http://localhost:16686, we see the Jaeger UI. Press Ctrl-C to exit the istioctl dashboard command (when you're ready to shut down the connection).

Click the Services dropdown and select istio-ingressgateway, as shown in figure 8.9. At bottom left, click Find Traces. If you don't see any traces, try sending some traffic through the istio-ingressgateway:

```
$ curl -H "Host: webapp.istioinaction.io" http://localhost/api/catalog
```

Figure 8.9   Choose the istio-ingressgateway service to see the requests that have come into the cluster.

Click back to the UI, and try Find Traces again. You should see a new trace for each attempt you made to call the sample services, as shown in figure 8.10.

You still may not see any traces (or far fewer than you expect). If that is the case, skip to the next section, where we discuss the trace-collection aperture. However, when we installed Istio in chapter 2, we installed the demo profile, which should set trace sampling to 100%. The next section discusses how to control this sampling rate.

Figure 8.10   Clicking into a specific trace shows more granular detail like the specific spans that make up the trace.

> ### Propagating trace context and headers
>
> For the sample applications to work correctly, they must propagate the Zipkin trace headers:
>
> - `x-request-id`
> - `x-b3-traceid`
> - `x-b3-spanid`
> - `x-b3-parentspanid`
> - `x-b3-sampled`
> - `x-b3-flags`
> - `x-ot-span-context`
>
> This means that when the application code takes the request and begins processing it, it should save these headers and their values and insert them into any outgoing requests the application must make. This cannot be done automatically by the proxy.

8.2.5 *Trace sampling, force traces, and custom tags*

Distributed tracing and span collection can impose a hefty performance penalty on your system, so you may opt to restrict how frequently you collect distributed traces when your services are running correctly. Earlier in the book, we installed Istio using the demo profile, which sets the sampling for distributed tracing to 100%. You can control the sampling of traces by configuring the percentage of traces to collect in the system.

TUNING THE TRACE SAMPLING FOR THE MESH

Just as we configured the backend distributed tracing at install time, at run time, or per workload, we can do the same thing with the sampling rate. Let's edit the istio-configmap in the istio-system namespace and edit the MeshConfig to look like this for the tracing configuration:

```
$  kubectl edit -n istio-system cm istio

apiVersion: v1
data:
  mesh: |-
    accessLogFile: /dev/stdout
    defaultConfig:
      discoveryAddress: istiod.istio-system.svc:15012
      proxyMetadata: {}
      tracing:
        sampling: 10
        zipkin:
          address: zipkin.istio-system:9411
```

This changes the sampling rate to 10% globally for all the workloads in the service mesh.

Instead of global configuration, we can also configure this per workload in annotations. Here we edit the annotations for a deployment's Pod template to include the tracing configuration:

```
apiVersion: apps/v1
kind: Deployment
...
spec:
  template:
    metadata:
      annotations:
        proxy.istio.io/config: |
          tracing:
            sampling: 10
            zipkin:
              address: zipkin.istio-system:9411
```

For example, we can apply this deployment like this:

```
$  kubectl apply -f ch8/webapp-deployment-zipkin.yaml
```

FORCE-TRACING FROM THE CLIENT

In production, it makes a lot of sense to keep the sampling rate of traces to a minimum and then enable it per workload when there are issues. Sometimes you will need to enable tracing for specific traces. You can configure Istio to force tracing for specific requests.

For example, in an application, we can add the x-envoy-force-trace header to a request to trigger Istio to capture the spans and traces for a particular call graph generated by the request. Let's try it in our sample application:

```
$ curl -H "x-envoy-force-trace: true" \
-H "Host: webapp.istioinaction.io" http://localhost/api/catalog
```

Every time we send in this x-envoy-force-trace header, we trigger tracing for that request and the entire call graph of that request. We can build tools on top of Istio, like API gateways and diagnostics services, that can inject this header when we want to know more about a particular request. Building these types of tools is outside the scope of this book.

CUSTOMIZING THE TAGS IN A TRACE

Adding tags to a span is a way for an application to attach additional metadata to a trace. A *tag* is just a key-value pair with custom, application or organization-specific information that is added to spans that are sent to the backend distributed tracing engine. At the time of writing, you can configure three different types of custom tags:

- Explicitly specifying a value
- Pulling a value from environment variables
- Pulling a value from request headers

For example, to add a custom tag to our spans in the webapp service, we can annotate the Deployment resource of that workload with the following:

```
apiVersion: apps/v1
kind: Deployment
...
spec:
  template:
    metadata:
      annotations:
        proxy.istio.io/config: |
          tracing:
            sampling: 100
            customTags:
              custom_tag:
                literal:
                  value: "Test Tag"
            zipkin:
              address: zipkin.istio-system:9411
```

We can apply this deployment of the webapp service like this:

```
$ kubectl apply \
-f ch8/webapp-deployment-zipkin-tag.yaml \
-n istioinaction
```

Sending traffic through the ingress gateway generates some of the traces we expect in the Jaeger UI:

```
$ curl -H "Host: webapp.istioinaction.io" \
http://localhost/api/catalog
```

Go to the Jaeger UI, find a recent trace, and click it. Then, click the span representing the webapp service, as shown in figure 8.11.

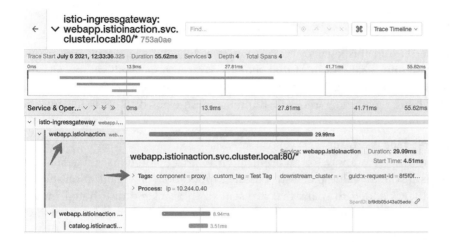

Figure 8.11
Clicking into a specific trace shows the specific spans that make up the trace.

Once you expand the span, you'll see a Tags entry, as shown in figure 8.12. Custom tags can be used for reporting, filtering, and otherwise exploring the tracing data. See the Istio documentation (https://istio.io/latest/docs/tasks/observability/distributed-tracing/) for more details on customizing the tags included in a span or trace.

Figure 8.12
Clicking into a specific span shows more granular detail, such as tags.

CUSTOMIZING THE BACKEND DISTRIBUTED TRACING ENGINE

In this last section on distributed tracing, we explore how to configure the backend settings for connecting with the distributed tracing engine. As mentioned earlier, Istio released a new Alpha API for Telemetry including tracing in Istio 1.12, so you can expect the user experience to improve in the tracing configuration area. What we cover here in this section is a bit advanced and may not be applicable for your use case.

In the examples so far, we've configured Istio with the hostname and port of the tracing engine backend; but what if you need to tune more configurations? For example, with Zipkin compatibility from Jaeger, we need to send the traces to a specific endpoint on the Jaeger collector. By default, that is configured in Istio's proxy via static settings.

Let's look at the default tracing configuration for Zipkin-based tracing engines (note that you need the `jq` tool to perform this command):

```
$ istioctl pc bootstrap -n istioinaction deploy/webapp \
-o json | jq .bootstrap.tracing
{
  "http": {
    "name": "envoy.tracers.zipkin",
    "typedConfig": {
      "@type": "type.googleapis.com/envoy.config.trace.v3.ZipkinConfig",
      "collectorCluster": "zipkin",
      "collectorEndpoint": "/api/v2/spans",
      "traceId128bit": true,
      "sharedSpanContext": false,
      "collectorEndpointVersion": "HTTP_JSON"
    }
  }
}
```

We configure the tracing engine to be based on Zipkin, to send to the `/api/v2/spans` endpoint, and to treat this as a JSON endpoint. If we need to override these settings or tune them in any way, we must be able to override the static definitions built into Istio when using Zipkin as the tracing engine. We can do that with a custom bootstrap configuration. To do this, we specify the snippet of the configuration that we want to tune in a Kubernetes `configmap`:

```
apiVersion: v1
kind: ConfigMap
metadata:
  name: istio-custom-zipkin
data:
  custom_bootstrap.json: |
    {
      "tracing": {
        "http": {
          "name": "envoy.tracers.zipkin",
          "typedConfig": {
            "@type": "type.googleapis.com/
              envoy.config.trace.v3.ZipkinConfig",
            "collectorCluster": "zipkin",
```

```
                    "collectorEndpoint": "/zipkin/api/v1/spans",
                    "traceId128bit": "true",
                    "collectorEndpointVersion": "HTTP_JSON"
                }
            }
        }
    }
```

We can apply this `configmap` to the same namespace where the workload resides that we want to configure with this bootstrap configuration override:

```
$  kubectl apply -f ch8/istio-custom-bootstrap.yaml \
-n istioinaction
```

Next, we need to add an annotation to the Pod template of the `Deployment` resource to refer to this `configmap`:

```
apiVersion: apps/v1
kind: Deployment
metadata:
  labels:
    app: webapp
  name: webapp
spec:
  replicas: 1
  selector:
    matchLabels:
      app: webapp
  template:
    metadata:
      annotations:
        sidecar.istio.io/bootstrapOverride: "istio-custom-zipkin"
```

Let's apply this deployment to use our custom Zipkin configuration:

```
$  kubectl apply -f ch8/webapp-deployment-custom-boot.yaml \
-n istioinaction
```

If we check the bootstrap configuration for tracing, we see our changes:

```
$  istioctl pc bootstrap -n istioinaction deploy/webapp \
-o json | jq .bootstrap.tracing

{
  "http": {
    "name": "envoy.tracers.zipkin",
    "typedConfig": {
      "@type": "type.googleapis.com/envoy.config.trace.v3.ZipkinConfig",
      "collectorCluster": "zipkin",
      "collectorEndpoint": "/zipkin/api/v1/spans",
      "traceId128bit": true,
      "collectorEndpointVersion": "HTTP_JSON"
    }
  }
}
```

WARNING Using custom bootstrap files to configure some of the static settings of the Istio proxy is an advanced scenario. The custom bootstrap configuration is tied to the version of the Envoy proxy being used under the covers, and there is no guarantee of backward compatibility. Any misconfiguration could take down your service. Please proceed with caution and thoroughly test out your changes before applying to any live services.

The above bootstrap configuration will break the tracing of the webapp service. Before proceeding any further let's set the service to a working configuration without the bootstrap config:

```
kubectl apply -f services/webapp/kubernetes/webapp.yaml
```

8.3 *Visualization with Kiali*

Istio can be used with a powerful visualization dashboard from an open source project named Kiali (www.kiali.io) that can assist in understanding the service mesh at run time. Kiali pulls a lot of the metrics from Prometheus and the underlying platform and establishes a run-time graph of the components in the mesh to give you a visual overview of what services are communicating with others. You can also interact with the graph and dig into areas that could be problems to learn more about what's happening. Kiali is different from Grafana in that it focuses on building a directed graph of how the services interact with each other with live-updating metrics. Grafana is great at dashboards with gauges, counters, charts, and more but does not present an interactive drawing or map of the services in the cluster. In this section, we look at the capabilities of the Kiali dashboard.

8.3.1 *Installing Kiali*

Just like for Prometheus and Grafana, Istio ships with a sample version of Kiali out of the box; but for realistic deployments, the Istio and Kiali teams recommend using the Kiali Operator (https://github.com/kiali/kiali-operator). That is the approach we'll take for this section. For more details on installing Kiali, see the official install guide at https://v1-41.kiali.io/docs/installation/installation-guide/. We start by installing the Kiali Operator:

```
$  kubectl create ns kiali-operator
$  helm install \
      --set cr.create=true \
      --set cr.namespace=istio-system \
      --namespace kiali-operator \
      --repo https://kiali.org/helm-charts \
      --version 1.40.1 \
      kiali-operator \
      kiali-operator
```

NOTE Kiali visualizes the Istio metrics stored in Prometheus. Therefore, Prometheus is a hard dependency that must be installed and configured before Kiali is installed. In chapter 7, we installed Prometheus, and the subsequent installation of Kiali will depend on that.

Let's check that it's up and running:

```
$ kubectl get po -n kiali-operator

NAME                                READY   STATUS    RESTARTS   AGE
kiali-operator-67f4977465-rq2b8     1/1     Running   0          42s
```

Next, we will create an instance of Kiali in the `istio-system` namespace. This will be the actual application with a web dashboard that we can use to visualize the call graph of services in the Istio service mesh. Let's define the Kiali instance to connect to the Prometheus and Jaeger instances we deployed in the previous sections:

```
apiVersion: kiali.io/v1alpha1
kind: Kiali
metadata:
  namespace: istio-system
  name: kiali
spec:
  istio_namespace: "istio-system"
  istio_component_namespaces:
    prometheus: prometheus
  auth:                           ┐  Allows anonymous
    strategy: anonymous    ◄──────┘  access
  deployment:
    accessible_namespaces:
    - '**'
  external_services:         ┐  Configuration of Prometheus
    prometheus:        ◄─────┘  running in the cluster
      cache_duration: 10                        Configuration of Jaeger
      cache_enabled: true                       running in the cluster
      cache_expiration: 300
      url: "http://prom-kube-prometheus-stack-prometheus.prometheus:9090"
    tracing:                                                    ◄────────
      enabled: true
      in_cluster_url: "http://tracing.istio-system:16685/jaeger"
      use_grpc: true
```

Kiali uses the telemetry signals that Prometheus scrapes from the Istio control plane and data plane and the traces sent to Jaeger. In chapter 7, we installed Prometheus, but for Kiali, we need to configure it to use our specific Prometheus. In the configuration, we show how to configure Kiali to connect to Prometheus and Jaeger. You may be wondering how to secure the connection between them. Neither Prometheus nor Jaeger comes with any out-of-the-box security strategies—they recommend running a reverse proxy in front. From Kiali, we can use TLS and basic authentication to connect to Prometheus. This is left as an exercise for the reader.

Let's create the Kiali instance:

```
$ kubectl apply -f ch8/kiali.yaml
```

After a few moments, the Kiali instances are available in the `istio-system` namespace:

```
$ kubectl get po -n istio-system
```

```
NAME                                      READY  STATUS   RESTARTS  AGE
istio-egressgateway-96cf6b468-9n65h       1/1    Running  0         10d
istio-ingressgateway-57b94d999-6llwn      1/1    Running  0         15h
istiod-58c5fdd87b-lr4jf                   1/1    Running  0         10d
jaeger-7f78b6fb65-cr7n6                   1/1    Running  0         10d
kiali-6cfd9945c7-lchjj                    1/1    Running  0         102s
```

We port-forward to the Kiali deployment, so we can view the dashboard locally:

```
$ kubectl -n istio-system port-forward deploy/kiali 20001
```

The Kiali console is now accessible from http://localhost:20001. In this installation, we configured Kiali to have an anonymous authentication strategy, so you should not be prompted for any credentials to log in (see figure 8.13).

Figure 8.13 Overview dashboard of the service mesh using Kiali

> **NOTE** We are installing this Kiali dashboard with anonymous authentication, but there are various ways to configure Kiali. For example, in the blog post at https://www.solo.io/blog/securing-kiali-in-istio-1-7, we dig deeply into using OpenID Connect (OIDC); but we definitely recommend checking the official documentation for Kiali installations and authentication strategies: https://kiali.io/docs/.

The overview dashboard shows the different namespaces and how many applications are running in each. You also have a visual indication of the overall health of the applications running in the respective namespaces. If you click the green checkmark circle link next to Applications in the Istioinaction box in the overview dashboard in figure 8.13, you're taken to an overview of all the applications in that namespace (figure 8.14). If you have any issues with the applications, you are given more information about what's happening with the traffic. Click the Graph tab in the menu on the left in figure 8.13 to go to a directed graph showing the traffic flow in the service mesh.

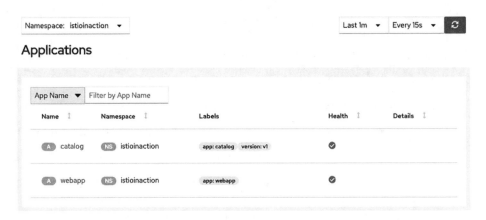

Figure 8.14   Information about application health in a particular Kubernetes namespace

To get some meaningful reporting in the Kiali dashboard, let's make a few calls to the application:

```
$  for i in {1..20}; do curl http://localhost/api/catalog -H \
"Host: webapp.istioinaction.io"; sleep .5s;  done
```

After a few moments, you should start to see the graph shown in figure 8.15. From the graph, we can observe the following about the mesh:

- Traversal and flow of traffic
- Number of bytes, requests, and so on

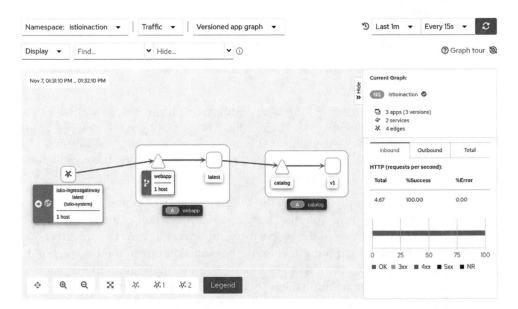

Figure 8.15   Simple visual graph of the services in our namespace and how they're connected to each other

- Multiple traffic flows for multiple versions (such as canary release or weighted routing)
- Requests/second; percentage of total traffic for multiple versions
- Application health based on network traffic
- HTTP/TCP traffic
- Networking failures, which can be quickly identified

If we select one of the workloads, we see the traffic and traces related to it.

CORRELATION OF TRACES, METRICS, AND LOGS

Kiali is gradually evolving into the one dashboard that answers all service mesh observability questions. One of the Kiali features—correlating traces, metrics, and logs—is just a promise of the possibilities to come.

To view the correlation between telemetry data, drill into one of the workloads by clicking the Workloads menu item at left in the overview dashboard in figure 8.13, and then select a workload from the list. The menu items in the Workload view reveal the following (see, for example, figure 8.16):

- *Overview*—Pods of the service, Istio configuration applied to it, and a graph of the upstreams and downstreams
- *Traffic*—Success rate of inbound and outbound traffic

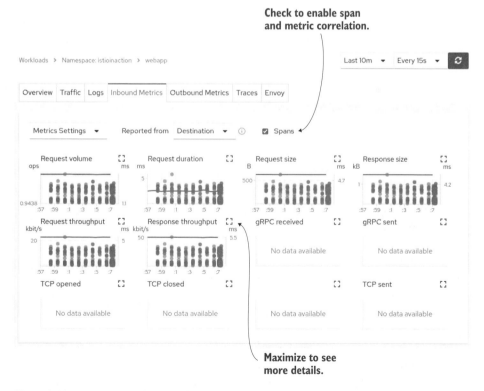

Figure 8.16   The Inbound Metrics tab shows the correlation of metrics and traces.

- *Logs*—Application logs, Envoy access logs, and spans correlated together
- *Inbound Metrics and Outbound Metrics* —Correlated with spans
- *Traces*—The traces reported by Jaeger
- *Envoy*—The Envoy configuration applied to the workload, such as clusters, listeners, and routes

When correlated, the telemetry immensely simplifies the debugging process, as you don't have to switch between different windows and check (or quadruple check) if the time is the same between all graphs. In the dashboard, if there is a spike in request duration, you have the traces correlated to it, which could reveal that those requests were being served by a new version of an application or by a degraded service. Feel free to explore the dashboard while sending in traffic.

Understanding Kiali workload vs. application

In Kiali, you'll notice a distinction between a *workload* and an *application*. For our example application, they're effectively the same, but the big distinction between the two is this:

- A *workload* is a running binary that can be deployed as a set of identical running replicas. For example, in Kubernetes, this would be the Pods part of a deployment. A service A deployment with three replicas would be a workload.
- An *application* is a grouping of workloads and associated constructs like services and configuration. In Kubernetes, this would be a service A along with a service B and maybe a database. Each would be its own workload, and together they would make up a Kiali application.

As we'll see in chapter 10, Kiali is useful for service mesh operators, too, as it can validate the following Istio resources:

- `VirtualService` pointing to non-existent `Gateway`
- Routing to destinations that do not exist
- More than one `VirtualService` for the same host
- Service subsets not found

Many others are documented in Kiali validations: https://kiali.io/docs/features/validations.

8.3.2   *Conclusion*

In this chapter, we built on the foundation we set in chapter 7 to show how to graph the metrics collected by Prometheus. Prometheus scrapes metrics from both the data and control planes and makes them available to tools like Grafana. We used Grafana and the out-of-the-box Istio dashboards to watch what was happening at the service level as well as the control-plane level.

We then explored distributed tracing, which is a powerful way to understand where there may be latencies in a multi-hop service-call graph. Distributed tracing allows developers to annotate their requests with metadata to correlate requests; Istio can automatically detect that metadata and send those spans to a backend tracing engine.

Finally, we saw how we can use the Kiali tool to visually represent the traffic flow between services in a graph and then dig into the configuration that enables this traffic flow. In the next chapter, we look at how to secure this traffic.

Summary

- Grafana can be used to visualize Istio metrics, including using out-of-the-box dashboards for the Istio control plane and data plane.
- Distributed tracing gives us insights into the components involved in serving a request. To do so, it annotates requests with trace headers at the service proxy.
- Applications need to propagate trace headers in order to get a full view of a request.
- A *trace* is a collection of *spans* that can be used to debug latency and request hops in a distributed system.
- Istio can be configured to route tracing headers using `defaultConfig` during Istio installation, which applies to the entire mesh; or the same configuration can be applied on a per-workload basis using the annotation `proxy.istio.io/ config`.
- The Kiali Operator can be configured to read metrics from Prometheus and traces from Jaeger.
- Kiali has quite a few Istio-specific debugging dashboards, including a networking graph and metric correlation to aid debugging.

Securing microservice communication

In chapter 4, we covered admitting traffic into the mesh, including some ways to secure that traffic. Here, we take a closer look at transparently improving the security posture of a services-based architecture by using the capabilities of the service mesh.

Istio is *secure by default*. In this chapter, we see what that means, how it works, how service-to-service and end-user authentication are implemented, and the access control we have over services in the service mesh. Before getting to the features, we give a brief refresher of security topics; see appendix C for more detailed information about how security works in Istio.

9.1 The need for application-networking security

Application security comprises all activities that contribute to protecting application data that is of critical value and should not be compromised, stolen, or otherwise accessed by an unauthorized user. To protect user data, we need the following:

- Authentication and authorization of the user before allowing access to a resource
- Encryption of data in transit to prevent it from being eavesdropped on while it's passing through multiple networking devices to reach the client requesting the data

NOTE *Authentication* is the process by which a client or server proves its identity using something it knows (a password), something it has (a device, a certificate), or something it is (a unique trait such as a fingerprint). *Authorization* is the process of allowing or denying an already authenticated user to perform an operation such as creating, reading, updating, or deleting a resource.

9.1.1 *Service-to-service authentication*

To be secure, a service should authenticate any services it interacts with. In other words, it should trust the other service only after it presents a verifiable document of identity. Usually, this document is validated with the trusted third party that issued the document. In this chapter, we show how Istio provides an automated way to issue the identity of services using the Secure Production Identity Framework for Everyone (SPIFFE) framework. The issued identity is used for services to mutually authenticate.

9.1.2 *End-user authentication*

Authentication of end users is key for applications that store private user data. There are multiple mature end-user authentication protocols; however, most of those revolve around redirecting a user to an authentication server where, on successful login, they are given a credential (stored as an HTTP cookie, or a JSON Web Token [JWT], and so on) that contains user information. Users present this credential to services for authentication. Services validate the credential with the authentication server that issued it before permitting any sort of access.

9.1.3 *Authorization*

Authorization occurs after a caller is authenticated. The caller identifies to the server "who" they are, and then the server checks "what" operations this identity is allowed to perform and accordingly admits or rejects it. For example, in web applications, authorization typically takes the form of checking whether a user is allowed to create, read, update, or delete a resource. Istio builds on service authentication and its identity model to provide fine-grained authorization capabilities between services or between end users and services.

9.1.4 *Comparison of security in monoliths and microservices*

Both microservices and monoliths need to implement end-user and service-to-service authentication and authorization. However, microservices have a lot more interconnections and requests flying around the network that need to be secured. In contrast,

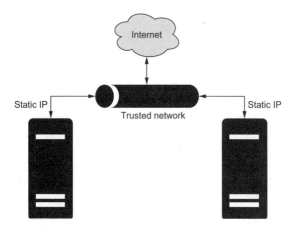

Figure 9.1   Monolithic application running on-premises with static IPs

monoliths have fewer connections and typically are run on more static infrastructure like virtual or physical machines. Being run in static infrastructure makes IP addresses a good source of identity, and for that reason, they are commonly used in certificates for authentication (as well as network firewall rules). Figure 9.1 shows a static infrastructure where IPs are a good source of trust.

On the other hand, microservices easily grow into hundreds and thousands of services, which makes operating the services in a static environment untenable. For this reason, teams utilize dynamic environments such as cloud computing and container orchestration, where services are scheduled into numerous servers and are short-lived. This makes traditional methods such as using IP addresses a nonreliable source of identity. To make things worse, the services are not necessarily run within the same network and can span different cloud providers and even run on-premises, as shown in figure 9.2.

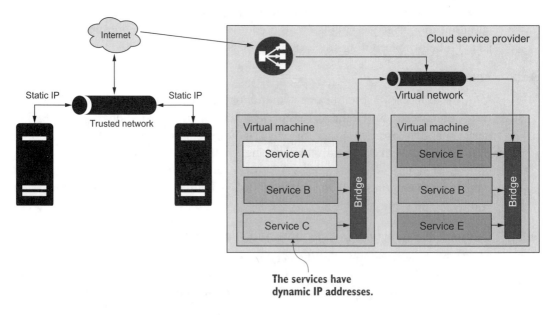

Figure 9.2   Microservices running on the cloud and on-premises with many interconnections

To resolve these challenges and provide identity in highly dynamic and heterogeneous environments, Istio uses the SPIFFE specification. SPIFFE is a set of open source standards for providing identity to workloads in highly dynamic and heterogeneous environments. See appendix C for a more detailed treatment of SPIFFE and how it underpins the identity assumptions in Istio.

9.1.5 How Istio implements SPIFFE

SPIFFE identity is an RFC 3986 compliant URI composed in the format spiffe://*trust-domain/path*, where

- The *trust-domain* represents the issuer of identities, such as an individual or organization.
- The *path* uniquely identifies a workload within the trust domain.

The details on how the path identifies the workload are left open-ended and can be decided by the implementer of the SPIFFE specification. Istio populates this path using the service account under which a particular workload runs. This SPIFFE identity is encoded in an X.509 certificate, also known as a SPIFFE Verifiable Identity Document (SVID), which Istio's control plane mints for workloads. These certificates are then used to secure the transport for service-to-service communication by encrypting data in transit. Again, in appendix C, we go into much more detail about how all this works. In this chapter, we focus on improving our security posture with Istio's functionality.

9.1.6 Istio security in a nutshell

To understand Istio security, let's change to the perspective of the service mesh operator who configures the service proxies using custom resources defined by Istio:

- The `PeerAuthentication` resource configures the proxy to authenticate service-to-service traffic. On successful authentication, the proxy extracts the information encoded in the peer's certificate and makes it available to authorize the request.
- The `RequestAuthentication` resource configures the proxy to authenticate end-user credentials against the servers that issued them. On successful authentication, it also extracts the information encoded in the credential and makes it available for authorizing the request.
- The `AuthorizationPolicy` resource configures the proxy to authorize or reject requests by making decisions based on the data extracted by the previous two resources.

Figure 9.3 shows how the `PeerAuthentication` and `RequestAuthentication` resources configure the proxy to authenticate a request, at which point the data encoded into the credentials (SVID or JWT) is extracted and stored as filter metadata. The *filter metadata* represents the *connection identity*. `AuthorizationPolicy` resources decide whether to allow or reject a request based on its connection identity.

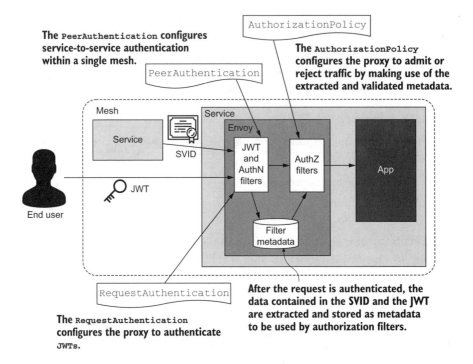

The `PeerAuthentication` **configures service-to-service authentication within a single mesh.**

The `AuthorizationPolicy` **configures the proxy to admit or reject traffic by making use of the extracted and validated metadata.**

The `RequestAuthentication` **configures the proxy to authenticate JWTs.**

After the request is authenticated, the data contained in the SVID and the JWT are extracted and stored as metadata to be used by authorization filters.

Figure 9.3   **The resources that configure the service proxy to authenticate and authorize a request**

This is Istio security in a nutshell. Next, let's put the resources into action and learn about their intricacies.

9.2   *Auto mTLS*

Traffic between services that have the sidecar proxy injected is encrypted and mutually authenticated by default. Having an automated process that issues and rotates certificates is very important because, historically, the process was error-prone when managed by humans. This caused needless and costly outages that would have been avoided using an automated process such as that implemented by Istio.

Figure 9.4 shows how services use the certificates issued by the control plane to mutually authenticate and

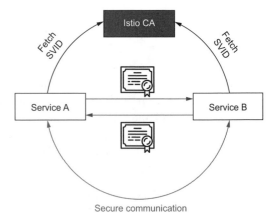

Figure 9.4   **Workloads mutually authenticate using SVID certificates issued by the Istio certificate authority.**

encrypt traffic—thus being secure by default. Actually, when we say "secure by default," we mean *almost* secure by default, as work is still required on our side to make the mesh more secure.

First we need to configure the service mesh to allow only mutually authenticated traffic. You may wonder why this isn't the default on installation. It's a design decision to simplify the adoption of the mesh—in larger enterprises where different teams manage their own services, an orchestrated effort of months and years might be required until all services were migrated into the mesh.

Second, having the services authenticated enables us to adhere to the principle of least privilege, create policies for each service, and allow only the minimum access needed for its functions. This is very important because when a certificate representing the identity of a service ends up in the wrong hands, the damage is scoped only to the few services the identity was permitted to access.

9.2.1 Setting up the environment

Execute the following commands to clean up your environment, so we start from the same clean slate:

```
$ kubectl config set-context $(kubectl config current-context) \
  --namespace=istioinaction
$ kubectl delete virtualservice,deployment,service,\
destinationrule,gateway --all
```

To demonstrate the capabilities of mutual TLS, we'll set up three services, as shown in figure 9.5. The webapp and catalog services are already familiar. We added the sleep service, which represents a legacy workload, meaning it lacks a sidecar proxy and thus cannot mutually authenticate.

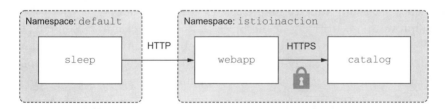

Figure 9.5   The three workloads we'll set up

To install the services, execute these commands:

Listing 9.1   Installing all services

```
$ kubectl label namespace istioinaction istio-injection=enabled
$ kubectl apply -f services/catalog/kubernetes/catalog.yaml
$ kubectl apply -f services/webapp/kubernetes/webapp.yaml
$ kubectl apply -f services/webapp/istio/webapp-catalog-gw-vs.yaml
$ kubectl apply -f ch9/sleep.yaml -n default
```

Verify that the services are correctly set up by executing a clear-text request from the legacy `sleep` workload to the `webapp` workload:

```
$  kubectl -n default exec deploy/sleep -c sleep -- \
     curl -s webapp.istioinaction/api/catalog \
     -o /dev/null -w "%{http_code}"

200
```

The successful response shows that the services are set up correctly and that the `webapp` service accepted a clear-text request from the `sleep` service. By default, Istio permits clear-text requests so that teams can gradually adopt the service mesh without causing outages until all workloads are migrated into the mesh. However, clear-text traffic can be prohibited using a `PeerAuthentication` resource.

9.2.2   *Understanding Istio's PeerAuthentication resource*

The `PeerAuthentication` resource enables configuration of workloads to either strictly require mTLS or be permissive and accept clear-text traffic, using the `STRICT` or `PERMISSIVE` authentication mode, respectively. The mutual authentication mode can be configured in different scopes:

- *Mesh-wide* `PeerAuthentication` policies apply to all workloads of the service mesh.
- *Namespace-wide* `PeerAuthentication` policies apply to all workloads in a name-space.
- *Workload-specific* `PeerAuthentication` policies apply to all workloads that match the selector specified in the policy.

Let's introduce all of the scopes with practical examples.

DENYING ALL NON-AUTHENTICATED TRAFFIC USING A MESH-WIDE POLICY

To improve the security of our mesh, we can prohibit clear-text traffic by creating a mesh-wide policy that enforces the `STRICT` mutually authentication mode. A mesh-wide `PeerAuthentication` policy must fulfill two conditions: it must be applied in the Istio installation namespace, and it must be named `"default"`.

> **NOTE** Naming mesh-wide resources "default" is not a requirement but rather a convention so that only one mesh-wide `PeerAuthentication` resource is created.

If you've followed the instructions in the book, then you have installed Istio in the `istio-system` namespace. Thus the following `PeerAuthentication` definition fulfills both conditions and applies to the entire mesh:

```
apiVersion: "security.istio.io/v1beta1"
kind: "PeerAuthentication"
metadata:                          Mesh-wide policies must
  name: "default"          ◁──┘    be named "default".
  namespace: "istio-system"   ◁─────────────  Istio installation
                                              namespace
```

```
spec:
  mtls:
    mode: STRICT        <----| Mutual TLS mode
```

Apply it to the cluster:

```
$  kubectl apply -f ch9/meshwide-strict-peer-authn.yaml
```

Next, verify that clear-text requests from the sleep service are no longer permitted:

```
$  kubectl -n default exec deploy/sleep -c sleep -- \
     curl -s webapp.istioinaction/api/catalog

command terminated with exit code 56
```

This verifies that the clear-text request was rejected. Having a STRICT mutual authentication requirement is a good default, but such a drastic change is not feasible for ongoing projects as coordination between multiple teams is needed to migrate workloads. A better approach is to gradually increase the restrictions we put in place and allow a timeframe in which teams can migrate their services to become part of the service mesh. The PERMISSIVE mutual authentication does just that: it permits workloads to accept both encrypted and clear-text requests.

PERMITTING NON-MUTUALLY AUTHENTICATED TRAFFIC

Using a namespace-wide policy, we can override the mesh-wide policy and apply more specific PeerAuthentication requirements for workloads in a namespace. The following PeerAuthentication resource allows workloads in the istioinaction namespace to accept clear-text traffic from legacy workloads that are not part of the mesh, such as the sleep service:

```
apiVersion: "security.istio.io/v1beta1"
kind: "PeerAuthentication"
metadata:                                       Uses the "default" naming
  name: "default"      <---------------------   convention so that only one
                                                namespace-wide resource exists
  namespace: "istioinaction"   <---|  Specifies the namespace
spec:                                |  to apply the policy
  mtls:
    mode: PERMISSIVE   <---|  PERMISSIVE allows
                           |  HTTP traffic.
```

But let's not do that. We can definitely do better and allow unauthenticated traffic only from the sleep workload to the webapp and still keep STRICT mutual authentication requirements for the catalog workload. This will keep the attack surface area smaller when the security of our network is compromised.

APPLYING WORKLOAD-SPECIFIC PEERAUTHENTICATION POLICIES

To target only webapp, we update the earlier PeerAuthentication policy to specify the workload selector; thus it applies only to workloads that match the selector. Additionally, we change the name from "default" to webapp. This doesn't change the functionality, but we follow the convention of giving the name "default" only to PeerAuthentication policies that apply to the entire namespace:

```
apiVersion: "security.istio.io/v1beta1"
kind: "PeerAuthentication"
metadata:
  name: "webapp"
  namespace: "istioinaction"
spec:
  selector:
    matchLabels:               Workloads matching the label use
      app: "webapp"     <──┘   the PERMISSIVE mode of mTLS.
  mtls:
    mode: PERMISSIVE
```

This way, the permissive mutual authentication policy applies only to the webapp workload, and it doesn't apply to the catalog workload because it doesn't match the selector. Apply the policy to the cluster by executing this command:

```
$  kubectl apply -f ch9/workload-permissive-peer-authn.yaml
```

And verify that clear-text requests are accepted by webapp:

```
$  kubectl -n default exec deploy/sleep -c sleep -- \
     curl -s webapp.istioinaction/api/catalog

[
  {
    "id": 1,
    "color": "amber",
    "department": "Eyewear",
    "name": "Elinor Glasses",
    "price": "282.00"
  },
  <omitted>
]
```

This returns a successful response! Using the mesh-wide policy, we applied strict defaults. But for some services (the laggards), we use workload-specific policies to allow non-mutually authenticated traffic until those are migrated into the mesh (see figure 9.6).

> **NOTE** By now we have a good understanding of how Istio works, but let's hit this point once more: istiod listens to the creation of the PeerAuthentication resource, transforms the resource into an Envoy-specific configuration, and applies it to the service proxies using the listener discovery service (LDS). The configured policies are evaluated for every incoming request.

TWO ADDITIONAL MUTUAL AUTHENTICATION MODES

Most of the time, you will use either STRICT or PERMISSIVE mode. But there are two additional modes:

- UNSET—Inherit the PeerAuthentication policy of the parent.
- DISABLE—Do not tunnel the traffic; send it directly to the service.

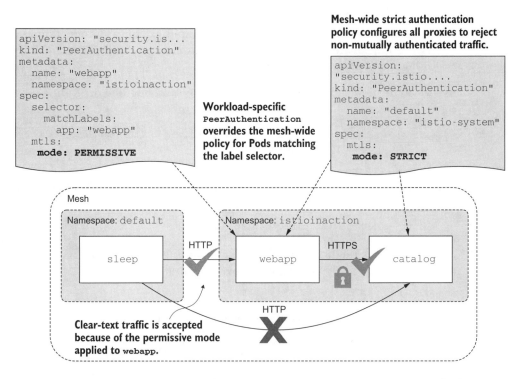

```
apiVersion: "security.is...
kind: "PeerAuthentication"
metadata:
  name: "webapp"
  namespace: "istioinaction"
spec:
  selector:
    matchLabels:
      app: "webapp"
  mtls:
    mode: PERMISSIVE
```

Workload-specific PeerAuthentication overrides the mesh-wide policy for Pods matching the label selector.

Mesh-wide strict authentication policy configures all proxies to reject non-mutually authenticated traffic.

```
apiVersion:
"security.istio....
kind: "PeerAuthentication"
metadata:
  name: "default"
  namespace: "istio-system"
spec:
  mtls:
    mode: STRICT
```

Clear-text traffic is accepted because of the permissive mode applied to webapp.

Figure 9.6 webapp **accepts HTTP traffic. The** catalog **service requires mutual authentication.**

With that, we have put the PeerAuthentication resource to use. It allows us to specify the type of traffic to tunnel to the workload, such as mutually authenticated traffic, clear-text traffic, or forward requests directly to the application without going to the proxy. In the next section, let's verify that the traffic is encrypted when using mutual TLS.

EAVESDROPPING ON SERVICE-TO-SERVICE TRAFFIC USING TCPDUMP

The Istio proxy comes with the tcpdump command-line utility preinstalled. This utility captures and analyzes network traffic going through our network interfaces. For security purposes, it requires privileged permissions; and by default, those are turned off. To turn on privileged permissions, update the Istio installation by setting the property values.global.proxy.privileged=true using istioctl:

```
$ istioctl install -y --set profile=demo \
    --set values.global.proxy.privileged=true
```

Once we've updated Istio to inject privileged sidecar proxies, we need to re-create the webapp workloads in order for the changes to be configured with auto-injection when the new Pod replaces the deleted one:

```
$ kubectl delete po -l app=webapp -n istioinaction
```

TIP Elevated permissions on the service proxy provide a vector of attack for malicious users. *Do not* install Istio with elevated proxies in production clusters. To quickly debug one service, you can change the fields manually by editing the deployment: `kubectl edit`.

As soon as the new `webapp` Pods are ready, we can sniff out the Pod traffic by executing the following `tcpdump` command:

```
$ kubectl -n istioinaction exec deploy/webapp -c istio-proxy \
    -- sudo tcpdump -l --immediate-mode -vv -s 0 \
    '(((ip[2:2] - ((ip[0]&0xf)<<2)) - ((tcp[12]&0xf0)>>2)) != 0)'
```

Open a second terminal to trigger a request from the `sleep` workload to the `webapp`:

```
$ kubectl -n default exec deploy/sleep -c sleep -- \
    curl -s webapp.istioinaction/api/catalog
```

Now, if we check the first terminal, which is sniffing out traffic, we see that the information is in clear text, as shown in the example output in figure 9.7.

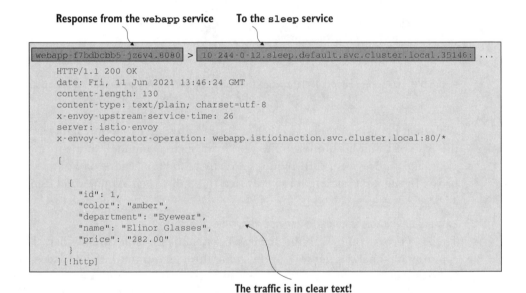

The traffic is in clear text!

Figure 9.7   Output of terminal 1. The sniffed traffic is in clear text.

Malicious users can easily exploit clear-text traffic to get to end-user data by intercepting it in any intermediary networking devices. You should always aim to have only encrypted traffic between workloads, as is the case from the `webapp` to the `catalog` workload where traffic is mutually authenticated and encrypted. Figure 9.8 shows this traffic.

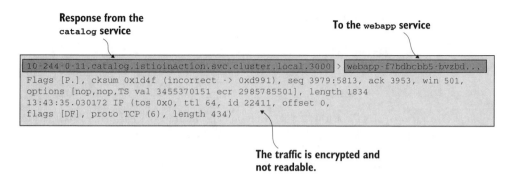

Response from the catalog service

To the webapp service

```
10-244-0-11.catalog.istioinaction.svc.cluster.local.3000 > webapp-f7bdbcbb5-bvzbd...
Flags [P.], cksum 0x1d4f (incorrect -> 0xd991), seq 3979:5813, ack 3953, win 501,
options [nop,nop,TS val 3455370151 ecr 2985785501], length 1834
13:43:35.030172 IP (tos 0x0, ttl 64, id 22411, offset 0,
flags [DF], proto TCP (6), length 434)
```

The traffic is encrypted and not readable.

Figure 9.8   Mutually authenticated traffic is encrypted and cannot be sniffed.

This verifies that the traffic between mutually authenticated workloads is encrypted in transit. Furthermore, it showcases how insecure it is to have legacy services in the service mesh, as data to and from it is in clear text and can be sniffed out (by unsuspecting observers) while it is in transit through multiple networking devices.

VERIFYING THAT WORKLOAD IDENTITIES ARE TIED TO THE WORKLOAD SERVICE ACCOUNT

Before we end the mutual-authentication section, let's check that the issued certificates are valid SVID documents and have the SPIFFE ID encoded in them, and that the ID matches the workload service account. Use the `openssl` command utility to check out the contents of the X.509 certificate of the `catalog` workload:

```
$ kubectl -n istioinaction exec deploy/webapp -c istio-proxy \
    -- openssl s_client -showcerts \
    -connect catalog.istioinaction.svc.cluster.local:80 \
    -CAfile /var/run/secrets/istio/root-cert.pem | \
    openssl x509 -in /dev/stdin -text -noout
```

With this convoluted command, we query the certificate of the `catalog` service and print it in a human-readable format. The certificate contains the SPIFFE ID, which is set to the workload's service account:

```
# shortened for brevity
X509v3 Subject Alternative Name: critical
    URI:spiffe://cluster.local/ns/istioinaction/sa/catalog
```

Using the `openssl verify` utility, let's make sure the contents of the X.509 SVID are valid by checking its signature against the certificate authority (CA) root certificate, which is mounted to the `istio-proxy` container in the following path: /var/run/secrets/istio/root-cert.pem. Get a shell into the running Pod by executing this command:

```
$ kubectl -n istioinaction exec -it \
    deploy/webapp -c istio-proxy -- /bin/bash
```

Next, verify the certificate:

```
$ openssl verify -CAfile /var/run/secrets/istio/root-cert.pem \
    <(openssl s_client -connect \
    catalog.istioinaction.svc.cluster.local:80 -showcerts 2>/dev/null)

/dev/fd/63: OK
```

On successful validation, an OK message is displayed in the command output. This informs us that the Istio CA signed the certificate, and the data in it is to be trusted.

NOTE   Remember, to exit from the remote shell type exit.

Now that we have verified all the components that facilitate peer-to-peer authentication, we are assured that the issued identities are verifiable and that traffic is secure. Having verifiable identities is the precursor to being able to control access. In other words, since we know the identity of a workload, we can define the operations it is allowed to perform. In the following sections, we look at authorization policies.

9.3   *Authorizing service-to-service traffic*

Authorization is the process that defines whether an authenticated subject is allowed to perform an operation, such as accessing, editing, or deleting a resource. Policies are formed in conjunction with the authenticated subject (the "who") and authorization (the "what") and define who can do what.

Istio provides the AuthorizationPolicy resource, which is a declarative API to define mesh-wide, namespace, or workload-specific access policies in a service mesh. Figure 9.9 shows how access policies limit the scope or blast radius of access if a particular identity is compromised.

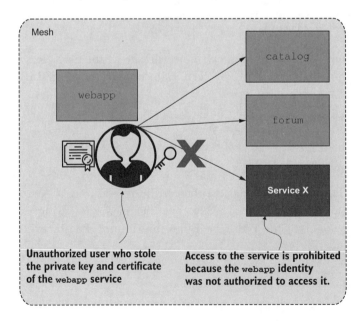

Figure 9.9   Authorization reduces the attack scope to only what the stolen identity was authorized to access.

Before diving into authorization policies, it's useful to understand how authorization is implemented in Istio. Let's quickly explore the fundamentals in the next section.

9.3.1 *Understanding authorization in Istio*

The service proxy deployed with each service is the authorization or enforcement engine, because it contains all the policies for determining whether a request should be denied or allowed. Thus access control in Istio is extremely efficient, as decisions are made directly in the proxy. Proxies are configured with the `AuthorizationPolicy` resource, which defines the policies. A sample `AuthorizationPolicy` definition is shown next:

```
apiVersion: "security.istio.io/v1beta1"
kind: "AuthorizationPolicy"
metadata:
  name: "allow-catalog-requests-in-web-app"
  namespace: istioinaction
spec:
  selector:
    matchLabels:
      app: webapp
  action: ALLOW
  rules:
  - to:
    - operation:
        paths: ["/api/catalog*"]
```

When `istiod` sees that a new `AuthorizationPolicy` has been applied to the cluster, it processes and updates the data-plane proxies with the resource, just like other Istio resources. Don't worry about understanding each part of the configuration just yet; we explore it in detail in the following sections.

PROPERTIES OF AN AUTHORIZATION POLICY

The `AuthorizationPolicy` resource specification provides three fields to configure and define a policy:

- The `selector` field defines the subset of workloads to which the policy applies.
- The `action` field specifies whether this is an `ALLOW`, `DENY`, or `CUSTOM` policy. The action will be applied only if one of the rules matches the request.
- The `rules` field defines a list of rules that identify a request for which the policy will be activated.

The `rules` property is more complex and warrants a deeper investigation.

UNDERSTANDING AUTHORIZATION POLICY RULES

Authorization policy rules specify the *source* of the connection and (optionally) the *operation* that, when matched, activates the rule. Authorization policy enforcement is activated only if one of the rules matches the source and the operation. In that case only, the policy is activated, and the connection is either allowed or denied according to the `action` property.

The fields of a single rule are as follows:

- The `from` field specifies the source of the request, which can be one of the following types:
  - `principals`—A list of source identities (SPIFFE ID, as seen in the mTLS examples). A negated property, `notPrincipals`, applies when the request is not from a set of principals. Services must mutually authenticate for this to work.
  - `namespaces`—A list of namespaces that match the source namespace. The source namespace is retrieved from the SVID of the peer. For that reason, `mTLS` must be enabled for this to work.
  - `ipBlocks`—A list of single IP addresses or ranges using classless inter-domain routing (CIDRs) that match the source IP address.
- The `to` field specifies the operations of the request, such as the host or method of the request.
- The `when` field specifies a list of conditions that need to be met after the rule has matched.

NOTE Istio documents all the properties of `AuthorizationPolicy` at https://istio.io/latest/docs/reference/config/security/authorization-policy.

If these properties sound a bit complex, don't worry. We clarify them in the following few examples.

9.3.2 *Setting up the workspace*

We'll continue with the same state from the earlier sections. However, if you've made modifications and want a fresh start, execute the following commands to reset and restore the expected state:

```
$ kubectl config set-context $(kubectl config current-context) \
 --namespace=istioinaction                                          Resets the
$ kubectl delete virtualservice,deployment,service,\               environment
destinationrule,gateway --all

$ kubectl apply -f services/catalog/kubernetes/catalog.yaml
$ kubectl apply -f services/webapp/kubernetes/webapp.yaml          Installs
$ kubectl apply -f services/webapp/istio/webapp-catalog-gw-vs.yaml apps
$ kubectl apply -f ch9/sleep.yaml -n default

$ kubectl apply -f ch9/meshwide-strict-peer-authn.yaml        Applies PeerAuthentication
$ kubectl apply -f ch9/workload-permissive-peer-authn.yaml    resources
```

Let's summarize the state of the environment that we have running (see figure 9.7):

- The `sleep` workload is deployed in the `default` namespace and used to trigger clear-text HTTP requests.
- The `webapp` workload is deployed in the `istioinaction` namespace and accepts unauthenticated requests from workloads in the `default` namespace.

- The catalog workload is deployed in the istioinaction namespace and accepts requests only from authenticated workloads in the same namespace.

9.3.3 *Behavior changes when a policy is applied to a workload*

Before we go into the details, there is one "gotcha" that you should know up front, as it's easy to get bitten by (and waste many hours of debugging!): if one or more ALLOW authorization policies are applied to a workload, access to that workload is denied by default for all traffic. In order for traffic to be accepted, at least one ALLOW policy must match it.

Let's illustrate with an example. The following AuthorizationPolicy resource allows requests to webapp containing the HTTP path /api/catalog*:

```
apiVersion: "security.istio.io/v1beta1"
kind: "AuthorizationPolicy"
metadata:
  name: "allow-catalog-requests-in-web-app"
  namespace: istioinaction
spec:
  selector:
    matchLabels:
      app: webapp          <──┘ Selector for
  rules:                         workloads
  - to:
    - operation:
        paths: ["/api/catalog*"]  <──┘ Matches requests with
  action: ALLOW                         the path /api/catalog
                          <──┐
                             │ If a match,
                             │ ALLOW.
```

Due to its simplicity, instead of applying this authorization policy to the cluster, let's mentally examine the outcomes for the following two requests:

```
$  kubectl -n default exec deploy/sleep -c sleep -- \
     curl -sSL webapp.istioinaction/api/catalog    <──┐
```
The request is allowed, as the authorization policy matches the path, and the action allows the request.

```
$  kubectl -n default exec deploy/sleep -c sleep -- \
     curl -sSL webapp.istioinaction/hello/world    <──┐
```
The request is denied, because no authorization policy explicitly allows the request.

The first scenario is plain and simple: a policy allowed the request because the path matched. However, the second scenario may raise some eyebrows—why was the request rejected when a policy neither allowed nor rejected it? This is the *deny-by-default* behavior that applies only when ALLOW policies are applied to a workload. In other words, if a workload has ALLOW policies, one has to match for traffic to be allowed.

To simplify the thought process and not have to ask yourself for every service whether a call will be allowed and whether an ALLOW policy is applied, it's recommended to add a deny catch-all policy that is activated whenever no other policy applies to incoming traffic. Thus you only have to think about the traffic you want to admit, and create policies for it.

Figure 9.10 shows how the `deny` catch-all policy changes our thought process to "We deny requests if not explicitly specified otherwise." Thus we only have to ensure that we allow traffic.

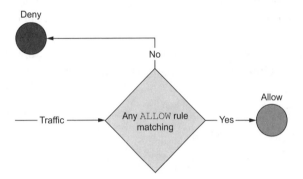

Figure 9.10   Denying traffic by default allows us to only think about what we want to admit.

9.3.4   *Denying all requests by default with a catch-all policy*

To increase security and simplify our thought process, let's define a mesh-wide policy that denies all requests that do not explicitly specify an `ALLOW` policy. In other words, we define a catch-all `deny-all` policy:

```
apiVersion: security.istio.io/v1beta1
kind: AuthorizationPolicy
metadata:
 name: deny-all
 namespace: istio-system                        Policies in the Istio
spec: {}                                         installation namespace target
                                                 all workloads in the mesh.
             Policies with an empty
             specification deny
             every request.
```

Let's apply the deny-all policy to the cluster:

```
$  kubectl apply -f ch9/policy-deny-all-mesh.yaml
```

Wait for a short time until the proxies receive the new configuration and trigger a request from the `sleep` service. Because no policy allows the request, it is denied by the catch-all `deny-all` policy:

```
$  kubectl -n default exec deploy/sleep -c sleep -- \
     curl -sSL webapp.istioinaction/api/catalog

RBAC: access denied
```

The output shows that the deny-all authorization policy has kicked into effect and denied the request.

Catch-all authorization policies

Just as the lack of any rule is an indicator that no requests are allowed, the opposite, the presence of an empty rule means all requests are allowed. For an example, the following allows all requests by default:

```
apiVersion: security.istio.io/v1beta1
kind: AuthorizationPolicy
metadata:
  name: allow-all
  namespace: istio-system
spec:
  rules:
  - {}
```

9.3.5 Allowing requests originating from a single namespace

Frequently, you will want to allow traffic for all services originating from a namespace. This can be done using the source.namespace property. The following example allows HTTP GET traffic from a single namespace:

```
apiVersion: "security.istio.io/v1beta1"
kind: "AuthorizationPolicy"
metadata:
  name: "webapp-allow-view-default-ns"      ⟵── Workloads in
  namespace: istioinaction                       istioinaction
spec:
  rules:                    Source originating from
  - from:        ⟵──       the default namespace
    - source:
        namespaces: ["default"]
    to:                            ⟵──┐  Only for the HTTP
    - operation:                       │  GET method
        methods: ["GET"]
```

Here, we configure workloads in the istioinaction namespace to admit traffic originating from workloads in the default namespace for HTTP GET traffic. So if we apply this resource, traffic from the sleep service will be served by webapp, right?

Nope—in our case, that won't work! The sleep service is a legacy workload; it doesn't have a sidecar, and as such, it lacks identity. Thus the webapp proxy cannot validate whether the request is from a workload in the default namespace.

To solve this, we can do one of the following:

- Inject a service proxy into the sleep service.
- Allow non-authenticated requests in webapp.

The recommended approach is to inject the service proxy into the sleep service. Doing so bootstraps the identity and performs mutual authentication with other workloads, enabling them to verify the source of the request and the namespace. But for demonstration purposes, let's suppose the first approach is not possible (the entire team is on holiday) and we are forced to take the second (less secure) approach: allowing non-authenticated requests.

9.3.6 *Allowing requests from non-authenticated legacy workloads*

To allow requests from non-authenticated workloads, we need to drop the `from` field:

```
apiVersion: "security.istio.io/v1beta1"
kind: "AuthorizationPolicy"
metadata:
 name: "webapp-allow-unauthenticated-view"
 namespace: istioinaction
spec:
  selector:
    matchLabels:
      app: webapp
  rules:
  - to:
    - operation:
        methods: ["GET"]
```

To apply this policy only to `webapp`, we add the selector `app: webapp`. This way, the `catalog` service still requires mutual authentication.

Apply the policy to the cluster by executing this command:

```
$  kubectl apply -f ch9/allow-unauthenticated-view-default-ns.yaml
```

Retrying the request from the `sleep` service to `webapp`, we get the following error response:

```
$  kubectl -n default exec deploy/sleep -c sleep -- \
      curl -sSL webapp.istioinaction/api/catalog

error calling Catalog service
```

This is an application error, not an Istio error. `webapp` received the request from the `sleep` service, but the mesh-wide `deny-all` policy denied the subsequent request to the `catalog` service. Remember why we added this `deny-all` policy? We only want to think about admitting traffic; we didn't add an `ALLOW` policy for requests to the `catalog` service, and the request was rejected. Let's fix this in the next section.

9.3.7 *Allowing requests from a single service account*

A simple way to authenticate that traffic is from the `webapp` service is to use the service account injected into it. The service account information is encoded into the SVID, and during mutual authentication, that data is validated and stored in filter metadata. The following policy configures the `catalog` service to use the filter metadata and, based on it, admit traffic only from workloads with the `webapp` service account:

```
apiVersion: "security.istio.io/v1beta1"
kind: "AuthorizationPolicy"
metadata:
 name: "catalog-viewer"
```

```
  namespace: istioinaction
spec:
 selector:
  matchLabels:
    app: catalog
 rules:
 - from:
   - source:
       principals: ["cluster.local/ns/istioinaction/sa/webapp"]
   to:
   - operation:
       methods: ["GET"]
```

**Allows requests with
the identity of webapp**

Apply the policy to the cluster by executing this command:

```
$   kubectl apply -f ch9/catalog-viewer-policy.yaml
```

Now, if we try once more, our request successfully reaches the `catalog` workload:

```
$   kubectl -n default exec deploy/sleep -c sleep -- \
      curl -sSL webapp.istioinaction/api/catalog

[
  {
    "id": 0,
    "color": "teal",
    "department": "Clothing",
    "name": "Small Metal Shoes",
    "price": "232.00"
  }
  <omitted>
]
```

But more importantly, we have strict authorization policies in place so that if the identity of a workload is stolen, the damage will be limited to the smallest scope possible.

9.3.8 *Conditional matching of policies*

Often, a policy applies only when a condition is met, such as allowing all operations when a user is an administrator. This can be achieved using the `when` property of an authorization policy, such as this example:

```
apiVersion: "security.istio.io/v1beta1"
kind: "AuthorizationPolicy"
metadata:
  name: "allow-mesh-all-ops-admin"
  namespace: istio-system
spec:
  rules:
    - from:
      - source:
          requestPrincipals: ["auth@istioinaction.io/*"]
      when:
      - key: request.auth.claims[group]
        values: ["admin"]
```

**Specifies the
Istio attribute**

**Specifies a list of values
that must match**

This policy allows requests only if two conditions are met: first, that the token was issued by the request principal auth@istioinaction.io/*; and second, that the JWT contains the group claim with the value of admin.

Alternatively, we can use the notValues property to define all the values for which this policy should not apply. A full list of Istio attributes that can be used in conditions can be found at https://istio.io/latest/docs/reference/config/security/conditions.

Principals vs. request principals

In the documentation for defining a source (http://mng.bz/NxYD), the from clause provides two options for identifying the subject of a request: principals and requestPrincipals. The difference between them is that principals is the peer from an mTLS connection configured by PeerAuthentication, and requestPrincipals is for end-user RequestAuthentication and comes from a JWT. We cover RequestAuthentication in subsequent sections.

9.3.9   *Understanding value-match expressions*

In the earlier examples, we saw that values do not always have to match exactly. Istio supports simple match expressions to make rules more versatile:

- *Exact matching* of values. For example, GET matches only the exact value.
- *Prefix matching* of values. For example, /api/catalog* matches all values starting with that prefix, such as /api/catalog/1.
- *Suffix matching* of values. For example, *.istioinaction.io matches all of its subdomains, such as login.istioinaction.io.
- *Presence matching*, which matches all values and is denoted with *. This specifies that a field must be present, but the value is not important and can be anything.

UNDERSTANDING HOW POLICY RULES ARE EVALUATED

To understand policy rules, let's break down a more complex rule concretely to what requests it applies to:

```
apiVersion: "security.istio.io/v1beta1"
kind: "AuthorizationPolicy"
metadata:
  name: "allow-mesh-all-ops-admin"
  namespace: istio-system
spec:
  rules:                    First
    - from:          <──┘   rule
      - source:
          principals: ["cluster.local/ns/istioinaction/sa/webapp"]
      - source:
          namespaces: ["default"]
      to:
```

```
  - operation:
      methods: ["GET"]
      paths: ["/users*"]
  - operation:
      methods: ["POST"]
      paths: ["/data"]
  when:
  - key: request.auth.claims[group]
    values: ["beta-tester", "admin", "developer"]
- to:                              <─────────────┐   Second
  - operation:                                   │   rule
      paths: ["*.html", "*.js", "*.png"]
```

For this authorization policy to apply to a request, either the first rule *or* the second rule needs to match. Let's dive deeper into the cases when the first rule will match:

```
- from:    <───┤ Sources
  - source:
      principals: ["cluster.local/ns/istioinaction/sa/webapp"]
  - source:
      namespaces: ["default"]
  to:                    <───┤ Operations
  - operation:
      methods: ["GET"]
      paths: ["/users*"]
  - operation:
      methods: ["POST"]
      paths: ["/data"]
  when:        <─────────────────┤ Conditions
  - key: request.auth.claims[group]
    values: ["beta-tester", "admin", "developer"]
```

For this rule to match a request, we need matches in all three properties: one source defined in the sources list needs to match with one operation defined in the operations list, and all of the conditions need to match. In other words, one source defined in from is AND-ed with one of the operations defined in to, and both are AND-ed with all the conditions specified in when.

Let's take a closer look at the operations to understand how one operation matches:

```
to:
  - operation:       <───┤ First operation
      methods: ["GET"]              Two properties that need to match
      paths: ["/users*"]           for the first operation to match
  - operation:       <───┤ Second operation
      methods: ["POST"]            Two properties that need to match
      paths: ["/data"]            for the second operation to match
```

For this rule to have an operation match, either the first *or* the second operation needs to match. For an operation to match, all of its properties need to match, meaning the properties are AND-ed together. Meanwhile, for the when property, all conditions need to match because they are AND-ed together.

9.3.10 Understanding the order in which authorization policies are evaluated

The complexity of policies arise when many are applied to a workload, and it is difficult to understand the order. Many solutions use a priority field to define the order. Istio uses a different approach for evaluating policies:

1   CUSTOM policies are evaluated first. We will show an example of CUSTOM policies later, when we integrate with an external authorization server.
2   DENY policies are evaluated next. If no DENY policy is matched . . .
3   ALLOW policies are evaluated. If one matches, the request is allowed. Otherwise. . .
4   According to the presence or absence of a catch-all policy, we have two outcomes:
   a   When a catch-all policy is present, it determines whether the request is approved.
   b   When a catch-all policy is absent, the request is:
      – Allowed if there are no ALLOW policies, or it's
      – Rejected when there are ALLOW policies but none matches.

Because the behavior changes based on conditions, some visual folks find it easier to understand using a flow diagram like that in figure 9.11. The flow is slightly complex, but it becomes much simpler when you define a catch-all DENY policy. If no CUSTOM and DENY policies reject the request, you only need to make sure to have an ALLOW policy to allow it.

This completes our discussion of authentication and authorization for workload-to-workload requests. In the next section, we look at end-user authentication and authorization capabilities.

9.4   End-user authentication and authorization

We mentioned briefly that end-user authentication and authorization are supported by Istio when using JWT. Before diving into the details of how authentication and authorization of requests work, let's have a brief refresher on JWTs. If you already have basic knowledge of this topic, you can skip to the next section.

9.4.1 What is a JSON web token?

A JWT is a compact claims representation used to authenticate a client to a server. JWTs consist of the following three parts:

- *Header*—Composed of the type and the hashing algorithm
- *Payload*—Contains the user claims
- *Signature*—Used to verify the authenticity of the JWT

Those three parts—the header, payload, and signature—are separated by dots (.) and Base64 URL encoded, which makes a JWT perfect for use in HTTP requests.

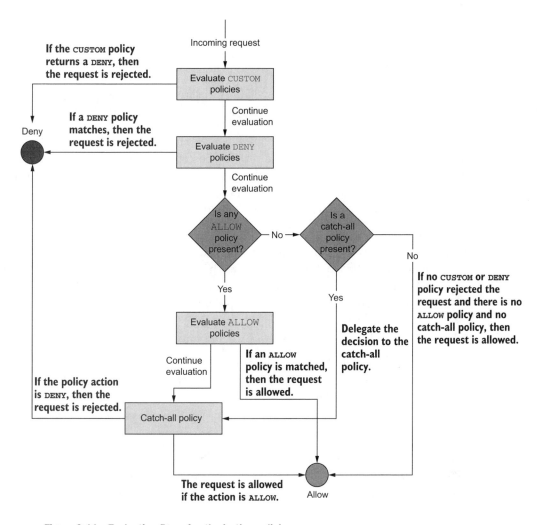

Figure 9.11 Evaluation flow of authorization policies

Let's check out the contents of a token located in ch9/enduser/user.jwt and decode its payload using the jwt-cli utility (https://github.com/mike-engel/jwt-cli):

```
$  cat ./ch9/enduser/user.jwt | jwt decode -

Token header
------------
{
  "typ": "JWT",
  "alg": "RS256",
  "kid": "CU-ADJJEbH9bXl0tpsQWYuo4EwlkxFUHbeJ4ckkakCM"
}
```

```
Token claims
------------
{                                Expiration
  "exp": 4743986578,        ◁── time
  "group": "user",          ◁── "group" claim
  "iat": 1590386578,            ◁── Issue time    Token
  "iss": "testing@secure.istio.io",               issuer    Subject or principal
  "sub": "9b792b56-7dfa-4e4b-a83f-e20679115d79"   ◁──       of the token
}                                                        ◁──
```

This data represents the claims of the subject. The claims enable the service to determine the identity and authorization of a client. For example, this token belongs to a subject in the user group. The service can use this information to decide the level of access for this subject. For claims to be trusted, the token needs to be verifiable.

HOW IS A JWT ISSUED AND VALIDATED?

The JWT is issued by an authentication server that contains a private key for signing the token and a public key for validating it. The public key is known as a JSON Web Key Set (JWKS) and is exposed at a well-known HTTP endpoint. At this well-known HTTP endpoint, a service can retrieve the public key to validate tokens issued by the authentication server.

There are multiple solutions to set up an authentication server:

1 It can be implemented in the application backend framework.
2 It can be implemented as a service on its own, such as OpenIAM (openiam .com) or Keycloak (keycloak.org).
3 It can be implemented as an Identity-as-a-Service solution, such as Auth0 (auth0.com), Okta (okta.com), and so on.

Figure 9.12 visualizes how the server uses the JWKS to validate a token. The JWKS contains the public key that is used to decrypt the signature which is then compared to the hash of the token data. If those match, the token claims can be trusted.

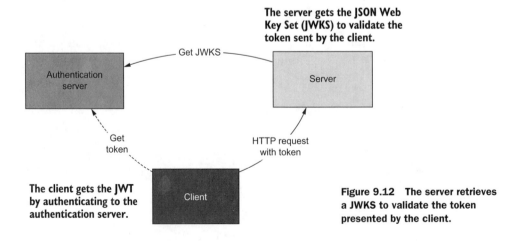

Figure 9.12   The server retrieves a JWKS to validate the token presented by the client.

9.4.2 *End-user authentication and authorization at the ingress gateway*

Istio workloads can be configured to authenticate and authorize end-user requests with JWTs. *End user* means the user that was authenticated by an identity provider and received a token issued to represent its identity and claims.

Although end-user authorization can be done at any workload level, this function is typically performed at the Istio ingress gateway. This improves performance, as invalid requests are rejected early on. Additionally, it enables Istio to redact the JWT from the request so that subsequent services cannot accidentally leak it or malicious users perform replay attacks with it.

SETTING UP THE WORKSPACE

Let's remove all the resources created so far and start from a fresh environment:

```
$ kubectl config set-context $(kubectl config current-context) \
 --namespace=istioinaction
$ kubectl delete virtualservice,deployment,service,\
destinationrule,gateway,peerauthentication,authorizationpolicy --all
$ kubectl delete peerauthentication,authorizationpolicy \
-n istio-system --all
```

Now, let's set up the sample workloads:

```
$ kubectl apply -f services/catalog/kubernetes/catalog.yaml
$ kubectl apply -f services/webapp/kubernetes/webapp.yaml
```

Before setting up authentication and authorization, we need to admit traffic into Istio's ingress gateway using a `Gateway` resource, as discussed in chapter 4. Additionally, a `VirtualService` resource is needed to route the traffic to the webapp service. Those resources can be applied by executing this command:

```
$ kubectl apply -f ch9/enduser/ingress-gw-for-webapp.yaml
```

```
gateway.networking.istio.io/webapp-gateway created
virtualservice.networking.istio.io/webapp-virtualservice created
```

Now the workspace is prepared to begin exploring the `RequestAuthentication` resource.

9.4.3 *Validating JWTs with RequestAuthentication*

The main purpose of the `RequestAuthentication` resource is to validate JWTs, extract the claims of valid tokens, and store those claims in filter metadata, which is used by authorization policies to take actions based on the data. Filter metadata is a set of key-value pairs available in the service proxy while processing the request between filters. As an Istio user, this is mostly an implementation detail. For example, if a request with the claim `group: admin` is validated, this value is stored as filter metadata, which is used by authorization policies to allow or deny the request.

There can be three different outcomes based on the end-user requests:

- Requests with valid tokens are admitted into the cluster, and their claims are made available to policies in the form of filter metadata.

- Requests with invalid tokens are rejected.
- Requests without tokens are admitted into the cluster but lack a request identity, meaning that no claims are stored in filter metadata.

The difference between a request with a JWT and a request without is that the former has been validated by the RequestAuthentication filter and has the JWT claims stored in its connection filter metadata; in contrast, requests without JWTs lack claims in their connection filter metadata. An important implicit detail here is that Request-Authentication resources by themselves do not enforce authorizations. You still need an AuthorizationPolicy for that.

In the next section, we create a RequestAuthentication resource and showcase all the previously mentioned cases with practical examples.

CREATING A REQUESTAUTHENTICATION RESOURCE

The following RequestAuthentication resource applies to Istio's ingress gateway. It configures the ingress gateway to validate tokens issued from auth@istioinaction.io:

```
apiVersion: "security.istio.io/v1beta1"
kind: "RequestAuthentication"
metadata:
 name: "jwt-token-request-authn"        Applied in this
 namespace: istio-system          ◁──┘  namespace
spec:
  selector:
    matchLabels:
      app: istio-ingressgateway
 jwtRules:                                        Expected issuer:
 - issuer: "auth@istioinaction.io"      ◁──┘      auth@istioinaction.io
   jwks: |                                    ◁──┐ Verifiable with
     { "keys": [{"e":"AQAB","kid":"##REDACTED##",  a specific JWKS
       ➡"kty":"RSA","n":"##REDACTED##"}]}
```

Apply the resource to the cluster by executing this command:

```
$ kubectl apply -f ch9/enduser/jwt-token-request-authn.yaml
```

With the request authentication resource created, let's verify the three types of requests and their expected outcomes.

REQUESTS WITH TOKENS FROM VALID ISSUERS ARE ACCEPTED

Let's make a request with a valid JWT, which is stored in the file ch9/enduser/user.jwt:

```
$  USER_TOKEN=$(< ch9/enduser/user.jwt); \
   curl -H "Host: webapp.istioinaction.io" \
        -H "Authorization: Bearer $USER_TOKEN" \
        -sSl -o /dev/null -w "%{http_code}" localhost/api/catalog

200
```

Great! The response code shows that the authentication was successful. And as no authorization policies were applied to the workload, it was allowed by default.

REQUESTS WITH TOKENS FROM INVALID ISSUERS ARE REJECTED

For demonstration purposes, let's make a request with a token issued by old-auth@istioinaction.io, located in the file ch9/enduser/not-configured-issuer.jwt:

```
$  WRONG_ISSUER=$(< ch9/enduser/not-configured-issuer.jwt); \
   curl -H "Host: webapp.istioinaction.io" \
        -H "Authorization: Bearer $WRONG_ISSUER" \
        -sSl localhost/api/catalog
```

```
Jwt issuer is not configured
```

This fails as expected. The error message clarifies that the JWT we used could not be authenticated by any of the `RequestAuthentication` resources applied to the workload.

REQUESTS WITHOUT TOKENS ARE ADMITTED INTO THE CLUSTER

For this case, let's execute a `curl` request without a token:

```
$  curl -H "Host: webapp.istioinaction.io" \
     -sSl -o /dev/null -w "%{http_code}" localhost/api/catalog
```

```
200
```

The response code shows that the request was admitted into the cluster. This is confusing, as you'd expect requests without tokens to be rejected. But in practice, there are many scenarios in which requests do not have tokens, such as serving the frontend of an application. For this reason, rejecting requests without tokens requires a little extra work that we'll show next.

DENYING REQUESTS WITHOUT JWTs

To deny requests without a JWT, we need to create an `AuthorizationPolicy` resource that explicitly denies them:

```
apiVersion: security.istio.io/v1beta1
kind: AuthorizationPolicy
metadata:
 name: app-gw-requires-jwt
 namespace: istio-system
spec:
 selector:
   matchLabels:
     app: istio-ingressgateway
 action: DENY
 rules:
 - from:
   - source:
       notRequestPrincipals: ["*"]        ◄──┘ Matches all sources where the request
   to:                                          principal doesn't contain any value
   - operation:
       hosts: ["webapp.istioinaction.io"]  ◄──┘ The rule applies only for
                                                 this particular host.
```

This policy matches all requests from sources that lack the `requestPrincipals` property and then denies them (as specified by the `action` property). You might be surprised where `requestPrincipals` is initialized: it is composed of the issuer and subject JWT claims (concatenated in the format *iss/sub*). The claims are authenticated by the `RequestAuthentication` resource and then made available as connection metadata to be used by other filters, such as the `AuthorizationPolicy` filter.

Apply the resource to the cluster as follows:

```
$ kubectl apply -f ch9/enduser/app-gw-requires-jwt.yaml
```

And now, trigger a request without a token and verify that it fails authorization because it lacks a request principal:

```
$ curl -H "Host: webapp.istioinaction.io" \
    -sSl -o /dev/null -w "%{http_code}" localhost/api/catalog
```

```
403
```

Great! We prohibited requests without tokens, and as such, we have ensured that only authenticated end users have full access to the endpoints exposed by webapp. Thus we have denied unauthenticated requests. Another frequent requirement for real-world apps is to allow different levels of access for different users.

DIFFERENT LEVELS OF ACCESS BASED ON JWT CLAIMS

In this example, we allow regular users to read data from the API but prohibit writing any new data or changing existing data. Meanwhile, we'll allow administrators full access. For the example requests used in this section, the "regular" user token is found in the file ch9/enduser/user.jwt, and the "admin" user token is found in the file ch9/enduser/admin.jwt. The tokens have different claims: the regular user has the claim `group: user`, and the admin has the claim `group: admin`.

Let's set up an `AuthorizationPolicy` resource to allow regular users to read data when they are targeting webapp:

```
apiVersion: security.istio.io/v1beta1
kind: AuthorizationPolicy
metadata:
 name: allow-all-with-jwt-to-webapp
 namespace: istio-system
spec:
 selector:
   matchLabels:
     app: istio-ingressgateway
 action: ALLOW
 rules:
 - from:
   - source:
       requestPrincipals: ["auth@istioinaction.io/*"]   <──┐ Represents the end-user
   to:                                                      │ request principal
   - operation:
       hosts: ["webapp.istioinaction.io"]
       methods: ["GET"]
```

And with the `AuthorizationPolicy` resource, we allow all operations to an admin user:

```
apiVersion: "security.istio.io/v1beta1"
kind: "AuthorizationPolicy"
metadata:
  name: "allow-mesh-all-ops-admin"
  namespace: istio-system
spec:
  rules:
    - from:
      - source:
          requestPrincipals: ["auth@istioinaction.io/*"]
      when:
      - key: request.auth.claims[group]          Allows only requests
        values: ["admin"]              ◁─────────  containing this claim
```

NOTE In this example, we omitted to explicitly set the value of `action` to `ALLOW` as that's the default value.

Apply these resources to the cluster:

```
$ kubectl apply -f \
      ch9/enduser/allow-all-with-jwt-to-webapp.yaml
$ kubectl apply -f ch9/enduser/allow-mesh-all-ops-admin.yaml
```

Now, let's verify that the regular user can read data:

```
$  USER_TOKEN=$(< ch9/enduser/user.jwt);
   curl -H "Host: webapp.istioinaction.io" \
     -H "Authorization: Bearer $USER_TOKEN" \
     -sSl -o /dev/null -w "%{http_code}" localhost/api/catalog
```

```
200
```

But writing is not allowed for a regular user:

```
$  USER_TOKEN=$(< ch9/enduser/user.jwt);
   curl -H "Host: webapp.istioinaction.io" \
     -H "Authorization: Bearer $USER_TOKEN" \
     -XPOST localhost/api/catalog \
     --data '{"id": 2, "name": "Shoes", "price": "84.00"}'
```

```
RBAC: access denied
```

Next, let's verify that for the administrator, writing is allowed:

```
$  ADMIN_TOKEN=$(< ch9/enduser/admin.jwt);
   curl -H "Host: webapp.istioinaction.io" \
     -H "Authorization: Bearer $ADMIN_TOKEN" \
     -XPOST -sSl -w "%{http_code}" localhost/api/catalog/items \
     --data '{"id": 2, "name": "Shoes", "price": "84.00"}'
```

```
200
```

The response shows that the request with the claim `group: admin` was admitted into the cluster, and thus administrators are allowed to create new items in the catalog.

9.5   *Integrating with custom external authorization services*

We've seen how Istio's authentication mechanism built on SPIFFE provides a foundation on which service authorizations can be built. Istio uses Envoy's out-of-the-box role-based access control (RBAC) capabilities to implement authorization—but what if we need a more sophisticated or custom mechanism for authorization? We can configure Istio's service proxy to call out to a different authorization service to determine whether to allow a request.

In figure 9.13, a request that comes into the service proxy pauses while the proxy calls out to an external authorization (ExtAuthz) service. This ExtAuthz service can live in the mesh, as a sidecar to the application, or even outside of the mesh. ExtAuthz needs to implement Envoy's CheckRequest API (http://mng.bz/DxRE). Examples of external authorization services that implement this API include the following:

- Open Policy Agent (https://www.openpolicyagent.org/docs/latest/envoy-tutorial-istio)
- Signal Sciences (www.signalsciences.com/blog/integrations-envoy-proxy-support)
- Gloo Edge Ext Auth (https://docs.solo.io/gloo-edge/latest/guides/security/auth/extauth)
- Istio sample Ext Authz (https://github.com/istio/istio/tree/release-1.9/samples/extauthz)

The ExtAuthz service returns an "allow" or "deny" message that the proxy then uses to enforce authorizations.

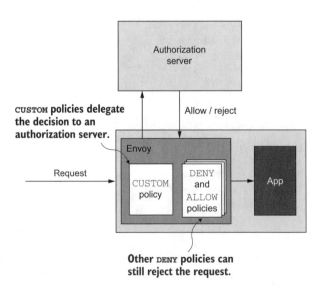

Figure 9.13   Using CUSTOM policies to get requests authorized by an external server

> **ExtAuthz performance tradeoffs**
>
> The call out to the `ExtAuthz` service happens in the request path, so you should be prepared for a latency hit when using this approach. Istio's built-in authorizations should be sufficient and flexible, but if you need full control, you have to evaluate the trade-off in performance of calling out to an external authorization service. As mentioned in the previous paragraphs, it's possible to deploy an `ExtAuthz` service as a sidecar to your application to minimize network overhead. See the Istio documentation (https://istio.io/latest/docs/tasks/security/authorization/authz-custom) for more information.

9.5.1 Hands-on with external authorization

To get started with a custom authorization policy and external authorization, let's delete all of the existing authentication and authorization policies:

```
$ kubectl delete authorizationpolicy,peerauthentication,\
requestauthentication --all -n istio-system
```

We are deleting these policies so we can see how the custom authorization works by itself. Just as we layered in authentication and authorization throughout the chapter, we can do the same with custom authorization.

Let's deploy a sample external authorization service that comes from the Istio samples. Navigate to your Istio distribution, and run the following:

```
$ kubectl apply \
    -f istio-1.13.0/samples/extauthz/ext-authz.yaml \
    -n istioinaction
```

If you list the Pods in the `istioinaction` namespace, you should see our new ext-authz service:

```
$ kubectl get pod -n istioinaction
```

```
NAME                         READY   STATUS    RESTARTS   AGE
webapp-f7bdbcbb5-cpng5       2/2     Running   0          5d14h
catalog-68666d4988-pb498     2/2     Running   0          5d14h
ext-authz-6c85b4d8d-drh4x    2/2     Running   0          52s
```

A Kubernetes service called `ext-authz` was also created. We use this service name to configure Istio's `ExtAuthz` capabilities:

```
$ kubectl get svc -n istioinaction
```

```
NAME        TYPE        CLUSTER-IP      PORT(S)             AGE
webapp      ClusterIP   10.99.80.174    80/TCP              5d14h
catalog     ClusterIP   10.99.216.206   80/TCP              5d14h
ext-authz   ClusterIP   10.106.20.54    8000/TCP,9000/TCP   94s
```

The `ext-authz` service we created is very simple and only checks whether an incoming request contains the `x-ext-authz` header for a value of `allow`. If the header is included in the request, the request is allowed; if it's not included, the request is denied. You can write your own external authorization service to evaluate other properties of the request or use one of the existing services mentioned previously.

9.5.2   *Configuring Istio for ExtAuthz*

We need to configure Istio to know about this new ExtAuthz service. To do this, we need to configure extensionProviders in the main Istio meshconfig configuration. This configuration lives in the istioconfigmap in the istio-system namespace. Let's edit this configmap and add the following appropriate configuration for our new ExtAuthz service:

```
$ kubectl edit -n istio-system cm istio
```

Add the following snippet to the configmap:

```
    extensionProviders:
  - name: "sample-ext-authz-http"
    envoyExtAuthzHttp:
      service: "ext-authz.istioinaction.svc.cluster.local"
      port: "8000"
      includeHeadersInCheck: ["x-ext-authz"]
```

You should now have something similar to the following:

```
apiVersion: v1
data:
  mesh: |-
    extensionProviders:
    - name: "sample-ext-authz-http"
      envoyExtAuthzHttp:
        service: "ext-authz.istioinaction.svc.cluster.local"
        port: "8000"
        includeHeadersInCheck: ["x-ext-authz"]
    accessLogFile: /dev/stdout
    defaultConfig:
      discoveryAddress: istiod.istio-system.svc:15012
      proxyMetadata: {}
      tracing:
        zipkin:
          address: zipkin.istio-system:9411
    enablePrometheusMerge: true
    rootNamespace: istio-system
    trustDomain: cluster.local
  meshNetworks: 'networks: {}'
```

We've configured Istio to be aware of a new extension called sample-ext-authz-http, an HTTP implementation of the envoyExtAuthz service. This service is defined to live at ext-authz.istioinaction.svc.cluster.local, which lines up with the Kubernetes service we saw in the previous section. We can configure what headers to pass along to the ExtAuthz service: in this configuration, we pass along the x-ext-authz header. In our example `ExtAuthz` service, this header is used to determine an authorization result. The last step in using this `ExtAuthz` functionality is to configure an `AuthorizationPolicy` resource to use it. Let's see how that works.

9.5.3 Using a custom AuthorizationPolicy resource

In the previous sections, we created `AuthorizationPolicy` resources with an `action` of `DENY` or `ALLOW`. In this section, we create an `AuthorizationPolicy` with an `action` of `CUSTOM` and then specify exactly what `ExtAuthz` service to use:

```
apiVersion: security.istio.io/v1beta1
kind: AuthorizationPolicy
metadata:
  name: ext-authz
  namespace: istioinaction
spec:
  selector:
    matchLabels:
      app: webapp
    action: CUSTOM          <──┘ Uses a custom action
    provider:
      name: sample-ext-authz-http   <──┘ Must match the meshconfig name
    rules:
    - to:
      - operation:
          paths: ["/"]      <──┘ Path on which to apply authz
```

This `AuthorizationPolicy` resource is applied to the webapp workload in the istio-inaction namespace that delegates to an `ExtAuthz` service named sample-ext-authz-http. Note that the name specified in the `provider` section must match the name given in the Istio `configmap` that we configured earlier:

```
$ kubectl apply -f ch9/custom-authorization-policy.yaml
```

In the previous section, we deployed a `sleep` service in the default namespace that is not part of the mesh. Please refer back to the beginning of this chapter to see how to deploy sleep. If we call our webapp service from the `sleep` service in the default namespace, it does not pass the external authorization checks using our sample Ext-Authz service:

```
$ kubectl -n default exec -it deploy/sleep -- \
    curl webapp.istioinaction/api/catalog

denied by ext_authz for not found header `x-ext-authz: allow` in the request
```

The example `ExtAuthz` service is simple enough that it only checks for the x-ext-authz header to be present with a value of `allow`. Let's add this header to our call and verify that it passes the authorization checks:

```
$ kubectl -n default exec -it deploy/sleep -- \
    curl -H "x-ext-authz: allow" webapp.istioinaction/api/catalog
```

```
[
  {
    "id": 1,
    "color": "amber",
    "department": "Eyewear",
    "name": "Elinor Glasses",
    "price": "282.00"
  },
  <omitted>
]
```

Now the call should succeed! If it does not, go back and check that you've applied the configurations in this section correctly. Also double-check that you've removed any other `AuthorizationPolicy` or `PeerAuthentication` policies that may be blocking the request.

In the next chapter, we'll dive deeper into how to troubleshoot the data-plane component of the service mesh, how to gain visibility using envoy access logs, and much more.

Summary

- `PeerAuthentication` is used for defining peer-to-peer authentication, and applying strict authentication requirements ensures that traffic is encrypted and cannot be eavesdropped on.
- The `PERMISSIVE` policy allows an Istio workload to accept both encrypted traffic and clear-text traffic and can be used to slowly migrate without downtime.
- `AuthorizationPolicy` is used for authorizing service-to-service and end-user requests based on the set of verifiable metadata extracted from either the workload identity certificate or the end-user JWT.
- `RequestAuthentication` is used for authenticating end-user requests containing JWTs.
- We can integrate external authorization services using the `CUSTOM` action of authorization policies.

Part 3

Istio day-2 operations

This part of the book discusses troubleshooting issues and day-2 operations. Chapters 10 and 11 show you how to troubleshoot issues in the data plane and maintain the stability and performance of the control plane.

Troubleshooting the data plane

This chapter covers
- Troubleshooting a misconfigured workload
- Detecting and preventing misconfigurations using `istioctl` and Kiali
- Using `istioctl` to investigate the service proxy configuration
- Making sense of Envoy logs
- Using telemetry to gain insights into apps

When communicating over the network, many things can go wrong, as we've demonstrated throughout this book. A major reason why Istio exists is to help shine a light on network communication when things go wrong and put in place remediation capabilities like timeouts, retries, and circuit breaking so that applications can automatically respond to network issues. The service proxy gives us a very detailed view of what's happening on the network, but what happens when the proxy itself behaves unexpectedly?

Figure 10.1 shows the components that participate in serving a request:

- istiod, which ensures that the data plane is synchronized to the desired state
- The ingress gateway that admits traffic into the cluster
- The service proxy that provides access control and handles traffic from downstream to the local application
- The application itself, which serves the request and may request another service that continues the chain to another upstream service, and so on

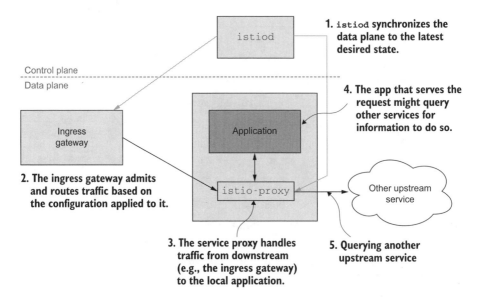

Figure 10.1   Components that participate in routing a request

Thus, unexpected issues can be related to any of the components in this chain. Debugging every component could take a lot of time, which we don't have when apps are impacting the entire cluster or system. In this chapter, we use the tools at our disposal to troubleshoot an erroneous scenario by examining the proxy and its associated configuration.

10.1 *The most common mistake: A misconfigured data plane*

Istio exposes a human-readable format to configure the services proxies in the form of custom resource definitions such as VirtualService, DestinationRule, and so on. These resources are translated into the Envoy configuration and applied to the data plane. After we apply new resources, if the behavior of the data plane doesn't match our expectations, the most common cause is that we misconfigured it.

To showcase how to troubleshoot the data plane when it's misconfigured, we'll set up the following example: we'll use a `Gateway` resource to allow traffic through the Istio ingress gateway and a `VirtualService` resource to route 20% of the requests to the subset `version-v1` and the other 80% of the requests to the subset `version-v2`, as shown in figure 10.2. For more information on traffic routing and splitting, see chapter 5.

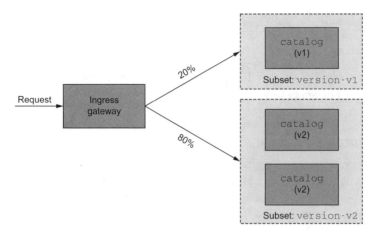

Figure 10.2 The ingress gateway is configured to route requests to non-existent subsets.

You may think "So far, so good"—but no. Without a `DestinationRule` resource, the ingress gateway has no cluster definitions for subsets `version-v1` and `version-v2`, and thus all requests will fail. This is a good issue to troubleshoot!

First, let's assume that we have Istio deployed (see chapter 2), but we don't have any other application components deployed. If you are continuing from previous chapters, you may have to clean up any left-behind deployments, services, gateways, and virtual services, as follows:

```
$ kubectl config set-context $(kubectl config current-context) \
  --namespace=istioinaction
$ kubectl delete virtualservice,deployment,service,\
destinationrule,gateway,authorizationpolicy,peerauthentication --all
$ kubectl delete authorizationpolicy,peerauthentication --all -n istio-system
```

To deploy the application for the purposes of this section, let's run the following command from the root of the book's source code:

```
$ kubectl apply -f services/catalog/kubernetes/catalog.yaml
$ kubectl apply -f ch10/catalog-deployment-v2.yaml
$ kubectl apply -f ch10/catalog-gateway.yaml
$ kubectl apply -f ch10/catalog-virtualservice-subsets-v1-v2.yaml
```

This starts the `catalog` workload in the cluster and creates a `Gateway` resource to configure the ingress gateway to admit HTTP traffic. Finally, it creates a `VirtualService` resource to route traffic to the `catalog` workload.

With the resources created, open a new terminal and execute a continuously running command to generate traffic to the `catalog` workloads:

```
$ for i in {1..100}; do curl http://localhost/items \
-H "Host: catalog.istioinaction.io" \
-w "\nStatus Code %{http_code}\n"; sleep .5s; done

Status Code 503
```

In the output, we see that due to the missing subsets, the response code is 503: "Service Unavailable." This gives us enough content to showcase how to troubleshoot the data plane when workloads are misconfigured.

10.2 Identifying data-plane issues

In day-to-day operations, you will most commonly deal with data-plane issues. Diving directly into debugging the data plane can become a habit, but it's critical to quickly rule out control-plane issues. Considering that the primary function of the control plane is to synchronize the data plane to the latest configuration, the first step is to verify that the control plane and data plane are in sync.

10.2.1 How to verify that the data plane is up to date

The data-plane configuration is eventually consistent by design. This means changes to the environment (services, endpoints, health) or changes to the configuration are not immediately reflected in the data plane until proper synchronization has occurred with the control plane. For example, as we've seen in previous chapters, the control plane sends each individual endpoint IP address for a particular service to the data plane (roughly equal to the IP address of each Pod in a service). If any one of those endpoints becomes unhealthy, it takes a while for Kubernetes to recognize that and mark the Pod as unhealthy. At some point, the control plane also recognizes the issue and removes the endpoint from the data plane. Thus the data plane is back to the latest configuration, and the proxy configuration is consistent again. Figure 10.3 visualizes the events that take place to update the data plane.

> **NOTE** For larger clusters, where the number of workloads and events increases, the period needed for the data plane to be synchronized increases proportionally. We'll explore how to improve performance in larger clusters in chapter 11.

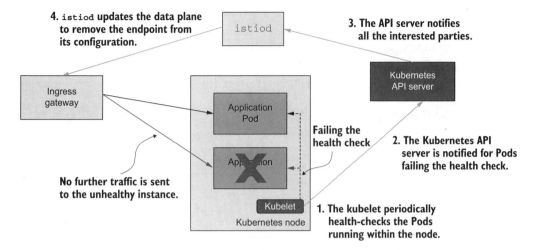

Figure 10.3 Series of events until the configuration of a data-plane component is updated after a workload becomes unhealthy

Let's check whether the data plane is synchronized with the latest configuration, using the istioctl proxy-status command:

```
$ istioctl proxy-status
```

```
NAME                                       CDS      LDS      RDS
catalog.<...>.istioinaction                SYNCED   SYNCED   SYNCED
catalog.<...>.istioinaction                SYNCED   SYNCED   SYNCED
catalog.<...>.istioinaction                SYNCED   SYNCED   SYNCED
istio-egressgateway.<...>.istio-system     SYNCED   SYNCED   NOT SENT
istio-ingressgateway.<...>.istio-system    SYNCED   SYNCED   SYNCED
```

The output lists all workloads and their synchronization state for every xDS API. The status for EDS is redacted from the output to improve readability (see chapter 3 for more details on Envoy xDS).

- SYNCED—Envoy has acknowledged the last configuration sent by the control plane.
- NOT SENT—The control plane hasn't sent anything to Envoy. This is usually because the control plane has nothing to send. Such is the case of the route discovery service (RDS) for istio-egressgateway, shown in the previous snippet.
- STALE—The istiod control plane has sent an update, but it wasn't acknowledged. This indicates one of the following: the control plane is overloaded; lack or drop of connectivity between Envoy and the control plane; or a bug on Istio.

However, our output shows that there are no stale workloads that didn't receive the configuration. Thus we are assured that the issue is unlikely to be in the control plane, and we should investigate the data-plane components.

The most common issues with the data-plane components are due to workload misconfiguration. Using Kiali, we can perform a quick validation of the configuration.

10.2.2 *Discovering misconfigurations with Kiali*

In chapter 8, we briefly mentioned that Kiali can discover misconfigured services. Now let's see those capabilities in action. Open the Kiali dashboard, shown in figure 10.4:

```
$ istioctl dashboard kiali
http://localhost:20001/kiali
```

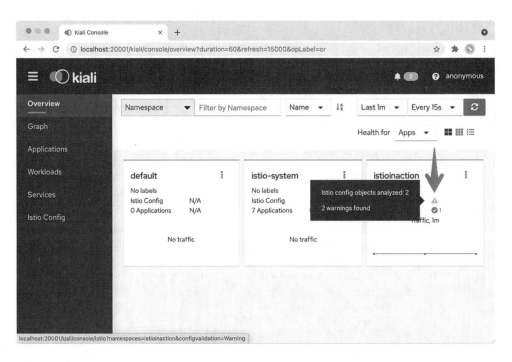

Figure 10.4   The Kiali Overview dashboard shows one error in the `istioinaction` namespace.

The dashboard shows a warning in the `istioinaction` namespace. Clicking it redirects you to the Istio Config view (see figure 10.5), which lists all Istio configurations applied in the selected namespace. Misconfigured Istio configurations are accompanied by notifications, as is the case for the `catalog-v1-v2 VirtualService` resource. Clicking the warning icon shown in figure 10.5 redirects you to the YAML view of the virtual service, where the misconfigured sections are highlighted in the embedded editor (see figure 10.6).

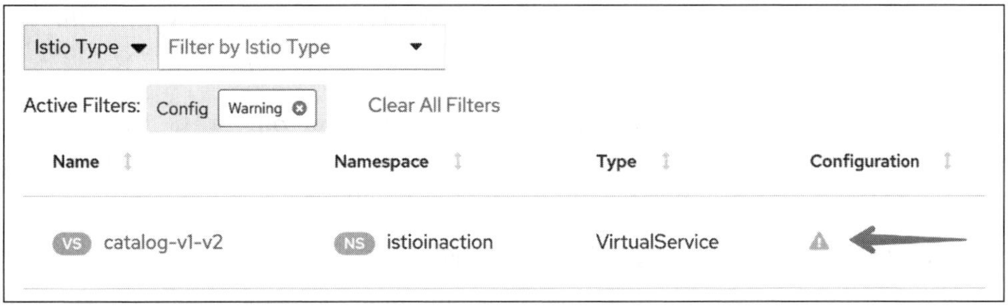

Figure 10.5 The `catalog` virtual service has warnings.

Figure 10.6 Kiali Istio configuration YAML view displaying a warning message

Hovering over the warning icon shows the warning message "KIA1107 Subset not found." For more information about this warning, check out the Kiali validations page of the Kiali docs at http://mng.bz/2jzX; this page provides a description, severity, and resolution for the identified errors. As an example, here is the Resolution section for the KIA1107 warning:

> *Fix the routes that points to a non existing subsets. It might be fixing a typo in the subset's name or defining the missing subset in a* `DestinationRule`.

This description helps us identify and fix the issue, as it correctly points out what is misconfigured. In this case, the subsets are missing, and we should create a `DestinationRule` resource to define them.

The Kiali validations are helpful and should be one of the first stops when your workloads are not behaving according to your expectations. The next step is to use `istioctl`, which provides another set of validations.

10.2.3 *Discovering misconfigurations with istioctl*

To automatically troubleshoot misconfigured workloads, two of the most useful `istioctl` commands are `istioctl analyze` and `istioctl describe`. Let's explore them.

ANALYZING ISTIO CONFIGURATIONS WITH ISTIOCTL

The `istioctl analyze` command is a powerful diagnostic tool that analyzes Istio configurations. It can be run on clusters that are already experiencing issues or can validate configurations before they are applied to clusters to prevent misconfiguring resources in the first place.

The `analyze` command runs a set of analyzers, each of which is specialized to detect a certain set of issues. It is easily extendable, which ensures that it evolves alongside Istio.

Let's analyze the `istioinaction` namespace and see the issues that are detected:

```
$  istioctl analyze -n istioinaction

Error [IST0101] (VirtualService catalog-v1-v2.istioinaction)
➥Referenced host+subset in destinationrule not found:
➥"catalog.istioinaction.svc.cluster.local+version-v1"
Error [IST0101] (VirtualService catalog-v1-v2.istioinaction)
➥Referenced host+subset in destinationrule not found:
➥"catalog.istioinaction.svc.cluster.local+version-v2"
Error: Analyzers found issues when analyzing namespace: istioinaction.

See https://istio.io/v1.13/docs/reference/config/analysis
➥for more information about causes and resolutions.
```

The output shows that the subsets are not found. In addition to the error message `Referenced host+subset in destinationrule not found`, it provides the error code IST0101, with which we can find more details about the issue in Istio's documentation (https://istio.io/latest/docs/reference/config/analysis).

DETECTING WORKLOAD-SPECIFIC MISCONFIGURATIONS

The `describe` subcommand is used to describe the workload-specific configuration. It analyzes the Istio configuration that affects one workload directly or indirectly and prints a summary. This summary answers questions about the workload such as

- Is it part of the service mesh?
- What virtual services and destination rules apply to it?
- Does it require mutually authenticated traffic?

Pick the name of any of the `catalog` workloads, and execute the following `describe` command:

```
$ istioctl x describe pod catalog-68666d4988-vqhmb

Pod: catalog-68666d4988-q6w42
   Pod Ports: 3000 (catalog), 15090 (istio-proxy)
--------------------
Service: catalog
   Port: http 80/HTTP targets pod port 3000

Exposed on Ingress Gateway http://13.91.21.16
VirtualService: catalog-v1-v2
  WARNING: No destinations match pod subsets (checked 1 HTTP routes)

    Warning: Route to subset version-v1 but NO DESTINATION RULE defining
    subsets!

    Warning: Route to subset version-v2 but NO DESTINATION RULE defining
    subsets!
```

The output shows the warning message `Route to subset version-v1 but NO DES-TINATION RULE defining subsets`. That means the routing is configured for non-existent subsets. For completeness, let's show how the `istioctl describe` output would look like if the workload was correctly configured:

```
Pod: catalog-68666d4988-q6w42
   Pod Ports: 3000 (catalog), 15090 (istio-proxy)
--------------------
Service: catalog
   Port: http 80/HTTP targets pod port 3000
DestinationRule: catalog for "catalog.istioinaction.svc.cluster.local"
   Matching subsets: version-v1                        Matching
      (Non-matching subsets version-v2)         Non-matching  subset
   No Traffic Policy                             subsets

Exposed on Ingress Gateway http://13.91.21.16    Virtual service that routes
VirtualService: catalog-v1-v2                     traffic to this Pod
   Weight 20%
```

Both the `analyze` and `describe` subcommands are helpful to identify common errors in configurations and are usually enough to suggest fixes. For issues that do not surface with these commands or do not give enough guidance for how to fix them, you will need to dig deeper! That's what we do in the next section.

10.3 *Discovering misconfigurations manually from the Envoy config*

Whenever the automated analyzers fall short, we need to investigate the entire Envoy configuration manually. We can retrieve the Envoy configuration that is applied on a workload using the Envoy administration interface or `istioctl`.

10.3.1 *Envoy administration interface*

The Envoy administration interface exposes the Envoy configuration and other capabilities to modify aspects of the proxy, such as increasing the logging level. This interface is accessible for every service proxy on port 15000. Using `istioctl`, we can port-forward it to our localhost:

```
$ istioctl dashboard envoy deploy/catalog -n istioinaction

http://localhost:15000
```

A new browser window opens, listing all the options exposed by the admin dashboard. Figure 10.7 shows a subset.

Command	Description
certs	print certs on machine
clusters	upstream cluster status
config_dump ←	dump current Envoy configs (experimental)
contention	dump current Envoy mutex contention stats (if enabled)

Figure 10.7   A subset of the options in the Envoy administration dashboard

We can use `config_dump` to print the currently loaded Envoy configuration in the proxy. Be warned before clicking it: it contains an immense amount of data. To see just how much, let's count the number of lines:

```
$  curl -s localhost:15000/config_dump | wc -l
    13934
```

Wow! This output is so large that it's basically not human-readable. For this reason, `istioctl` provides tools to filter the output into smaller chunks, which aids readability and comprehension.

> **NOTE** You can find out more about the Administration interface in the official Envoy docs: https://www.envoyproxy.io/docs/envoy/v1.20.1/operations/admin

10.3.2 *Querying proxy configurations using istioctl*

The `istioctl proxy-config` command enables us to retrieve and filter the proxy configuration of a workload based on the Envoy xDS APIs, where each subcommand is appropriately named:

- `cluster`—Retrieves the cluster configuration
- `endpoint`—Retrieves the endpoint configuration
- `listener`—Retrieves the listener configuration
- `route`—Retrieves the route configuration
- `secret`—Retrieves the secret configuration

Understanding what configuration to query is simpler when you understand Envoy's underlying API. We explored this API in chapter 3, but let's have a brief Envoy API refresher.

THE INTERACTION OF ENVOY APIS TO ROUTE A REQUEST

Figure 10.8 shows the Envoy APIs that configure the routing of a request. These APIs have the following effects on the proxy:

- Envoy *listeners* define a networking configuration such as an IP address and port that allows downstream traffic into the proxy.
- An HTTP *filter* chain is created for the admitted connections. The most important filter in the chain is the router filter, which performs the advanced routing tasks.
- Envoy *routes* are sets of rules that match the virtual hosts to clusters. Routes are processed in the listed order. The first to match is used to route traffic to clusters of workloads. Routes can be configured statically, but in Istio, RDS is used to dynamically configure them.
- In Envoy *clusters*, each cluster has a group of endpoints to similar workloads. Subsets are used to further divide workloads within a cluster, which enables fine-grained traffic management.
- Envoy endpoints represent the IP addresses of the workloads that serve the requests.

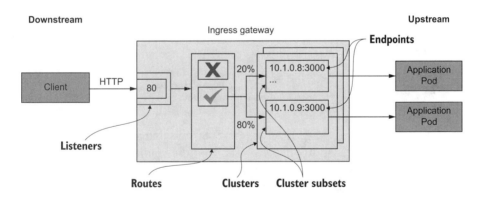

Figure 10.8   Interaction of Envoy APIs to route a request

In the next section, we query and manually validate the listeners, routes, clusters, and endpoints configurations for the ingress gateway. This lets us verify if it's configured properly to route traffic to the `catalog` workloads.

QUERYING THE ENVOY LISTENER CONFIGURATION

Begin by ensuring that traffic reaching the ingress gateway on localhost port 80 is admitted into the cluster. As mentioned earlier, admitting traffic is the responsibility of Envoy listeners, which are configured in Istio using the Gateway resource. Let's query the listener configuration of the gateway and verify that traffic is admitted in port 80:

```
$ istioctl proxy-config listeners \
    deploy/istio-ingressgateway -n istio-system

ADDRESS PORT  MATCH DESTINATION
0.0.0.0 8080  ALL   Route: http.8080        ◁─────  Requests on port 8080 are
0.0.0.0 15021 ALL   Inline Route: /healthz/ready*    configured to route according
0.0.0.0 15090 ALL   Inline Route: /stats/prometheus*  to the route http.8080.
```

In the printed summary, we see that

- A listener is configured on port 8080.
- The traffic is routed according to the route named http.8080 for that listener.

You may be surprised that route http.8080 is configured to listen on port 8080 and not port 80. Be assured that port 8080 is the correct port: traffic from port 80 to 8080 is forwarded by the Kubernetes service named istio-ingressgateway, which can be seen when we print the service definition, as shown next. Additionally, the ingress gateway listens on port 8080 since that's not a restricted port:

```
$ kubectl -n istio-system get svc istio-ingressgateway -o yaml \
| grep "ports:" -A 10
  ports:
  - name: status-port
    nodePort: 30618
    port: 15021
    protocol: TCP
    targetPort: 15021
  - name: http2
    nodePort: 32589
    port: 80           ◁─────  Traffic in port 80 targets
    protocol: TCP              Pods on port 8080.
    targetPort: 8080   ◁─────
```

We have verified that traffic reaches port 8080 and that a listener exists to admit it into the ingress gateway. Additionally, we saw that the routing for this listener is done by route http.8080, which is our next checkpoint.

QUERYING THE ENVOY ROUTE CONFIGURATION

The Envoy route configuration defines the set of rules that determine the cluster where traffic is routed. Istio configures Envoy routes using the VirtualService resource. Meanwhile, clusters are either auto-discovered or defined using the DestinationRule resource.

To find out to which clusters traffic is routed to for the http.8080 route, let's query its configuration:

```
$ istioctl pc routes deploy/istio-ingressgateway \
    -n istio-system --name http.8080
```

```
NOTE: This output only contains routes loaded via RDS.
NAME         DOMAINS                    MATCH      VIRTUAL SERVICE
http.8080    catalog.istioinaction.io   /*         catalog.istioinaction
```

The summary shows that traffic for the host `catalog.istioinaction.io` whose URL matches the path prefix `/*` is routed to the catalog `VirtualService`, located in the catalog service in the `istioinaction` namespace. Details about the clusters behind the `catalog.istioinaction` virtual service are shown when the route configuration is printed in JSON format:

```
$  istioctl pc routes deploy/istio-ingressgateway -n istio-system \
      --name http.8080 -o json
```

```
<omitted>
"routes": [
  {
    "match": {
      "prefix": "/"        ◁─┐ Route rule that
    },                          └─ has to match
    "route": {
      "weightedClusters": {      ┌ Clusters to which traffic is routed
        "clusters": [       ◁─┘ when the rule is matched
          {
            "name": "outbound|80|version-
    v2|catalog.istioinaction.svc.cluster.local",
            "weight": 80
          },
          {
            "name": "outbound|80|version-
    v1|catalog.istioinaction.svc.cluster.local",
            "weight": 20
          }
        ]
    },
<omitted>
}
```

The output shows that two clusters are receiving the traffic when the route is matched:

- `outbound|80|version-v1|catalog.istioinaction.svc.cluster.local`
- `outbound|80|version-v2|catalog.istioinaction.svc.cluster.local`

Let's investigate the meaning of each pipe-separated section and investigate how workloads are assigned as members to these clusters.

QUERYING THE ENVOY CLUSTER CONFIGURATION

The Envoy cluster configuration defines the backend services to which requests can be routed. Clusters load-balance across instances or endpoints. These endpoints, typically IP addresses, represent individual workload instances that serve end-user traffic.

Using `istioctl`, we can query the clusters that the ingress gateway is aware of; however, there are many clusters, as one is configured for every backend routable service. We can only print clusters using the following `istioctl proxy-config clusters` flags:

Figure 10.9   Components forming the cluster name

direction, fqdn, port, and subset. The information for all the flags is contained within the cluster name we retrieved earlier, as shown in figure 10.9.

Let's query one of the clusters: for example, the cluster of the subset version-v1 for which the ingress gateway is configured. We can specify all the cluster properties (as shown in figure 10.9) in the query:

```
$  istioctl proxy-config clusters \
     deploy/istio-ingressgateway.istio-system \
     --fqdn catalog.istioinaction.svc.cluster.local  \
     --port 80 \
     --subset version-v1
```

```
SERVICE FQDN    PORT    SUBSET    DIRECTION    TYPE    DESTINATION RULE
```

There is no cluster for the subset version-v1—or even version-v2, for that matter! Without clusters for these subsets, requests fail because the virtual service is routing to clusters that do not exist.

Clearly, this is a case of misconfiguration, and we can fix it by creating a destination rule that defines the clusters for these subsets. A destination rule for these clusters is defined in the file catalog-destinationrule-v1-v2.yaml located in the chapter 10 directory. But before applying it to the cluster, let's use the istioctl analyze subcommand to validate that this configuration would fix the service mesh errors identified way back in section 10.2.3:

```
istioctl analyze ch10/catalog-destinationrule-v1-v2.yaml \
    -n istioinaction
```

```
✓ No validation issues found when analyzing
  ➥ch10/catalog-destinationrule-v1-v2.yaml.
```

The output shows no validation errors in the cluster when simulating the impact of applying the resource. This means applying the destination rule fixes the cluster configuration. Let's do that:

```
$  kubectl apply -f ch10/catalog-destinationrule-v1-v2.yaml
```

```
destinationrule.networking.istio.io/catalog created
```

Querying the clusters again, we should see the newly defined subsets for version-v1 and version-v2:

```
$  istioctl pc clusters deploy/istio-ingressgateway -n istio-system \
     --fqdn catalog.istioinaction.svc.cluster.local --port 80
```

```
SERVICE FQDN           PORT  SUBSET       DIRECTION  TYPE  DESTINATION RULE
catalog.<...>.local 80       -            outbound   EDS   catalog.<...>
catalog.<...>.local 80       version-v1   outbound   EDS   catalog.<...>
catalog.<...>.local 80       version-v2   outbound   EDS   catalog.<...>
```

Voilà! Now that the `DestinationRule` resource defines the clusters for subsets `version-v1` and `version-v2`, traffic can be routed to the members of those clusters.

Recall that a cluster is a set of endpoints (or IP addresses). Let's dig into how endpoints are retrieved.

HOW CLUSTERS ARE CONFIGURED

The Envoy proxy provides multiple approaches to discover the endpoints of a cluster. The option in use can be discovered by printing the cluster `version-v1` in JSON format using `istioctl` (the following output is truncated to show the `edsClusterConfig` section):

```
$ istioctl pc clusters deploy/istio-ingressgateway -n istio-system \
--fqdn catalog.istioinaction.svc.cluster.local --port 80 \
--subset version-v1 -o json

# Output is truncated
"name": "outbound|80|version-v1|catalog.istioinaction.svc.cluster.local",
"type": "EDS",
"edsClusterConfig": {
    "edsConfig": {
        "ads": {},
        "resourceApiVersion": "V3"
    },
    "serviceName":
      "outbound|80|version-v1|catalog.istioinaction.svc.cluster.local"
},
```

The output shows that `edsClusterConfig` is configured to use the Aggregated Discovery Service (ADS) to query the endpoints. The service name `outbound|80|version-v1|catalog.istioinaction.svc.cluster.local` is used as a filter for the endpoints to query from ADS.

QUERYING ENVOY CLUSTER ENDPOINTS

Now that we know the Envoy proxy is configured to query ADS with the service name, we can use this information to manually query the endpoints for this cluster in the ingress gateway using the `istioctl proxy-config` endpoints command:

```
$ istioctl pc endpoints deploy/istio-ingressgateway -n istio-system \
--cluster "outbound|80|version-v1|catalog.istioinaction.svc.cluster.local"

ENDPOINT           STATUS    OUTLIER CHECK   CLUSTER
10.1.0.60:3000     HEALTHY   OK              outbound|80|version-v1|catalog...
```

The output lists the endpoint of the only workload that's behind this cluster. Let's query the Pod with this IP address and verify that there is an actual workload behind it:

```
$ kubectl get pods -n istioinaction \
    --field-selector status.podIP=10.1.0.60
```

```
NAME                       READY   STATUS    RESTARTS   AGE
catalog-5b56677c4c-v7hkj   2/2     Running   0          3h47m
```

And there it is! We've completed the entire chain of Envoy API resources that configure the service proxy to route traffic to a workload. It's a long path, but after going through it a couple of times, you will be able to internalize it.

This concludes our discussion of discovering misconfigured workloads. In the next section, we investigate how service proxies help us debug application issues.

10.3.3 *Troubleshooting application issues*

For a microservice-based application, the logs and metrics generated by service proxies are helpful to troubleshoot many issues such as discovering services that are causing a performance bottleneck, identifying frequently failing endpoints, detecting performance degradation, etc. In chapter 6, we saw how to work around those application resilience issues. In this section, we use the Envoy access logs and metrics to troubleshoot some of these issues. But first, let's update our services to have an issue that we can troubleshoot.

SETTING UP AN INTERMITTENTLY SLOW WORKLOAD THAT TIMES OUT

The `catalog` workloads can be configured to intermittently return slow responses using the following command:

```
$  CATALOG_POD=$(kubectl get pods -l version=v2 -n istioinaction -o \
     jsonpath={.items..metadata.name} | cut -d ' ' -f1) \

$ kubectl -n istioinaction exec -c catalog $CATALOG_POD  \
  -- curl -s -X POST -H "Content-Type: application/json" \
  -d '{"active": true, "type": "latency", "volatile": true}' \
  localhost:3000/blowup

blowups=[object Object]
```

Let's configure the `catalog-v1-v2` virtual service to time out when requests take more than half a second to be served:

```
$  kubectl patch vs catalog-v1-v2 -n istioinaction --type json \
     -p '[{"op": "add", "path": "/spec/http/0/timeout", "value": "0.5s"}]'
```

Those changes are represented visually in figure 10.10.

Let's generate continuous traffic to the `catalog` workloads in a separate terminal. Doing so produces logs and telemetry that we need in subsequent sections:

```
$  for i in {1..9999}; do curl http://localhost/items \
-H "Host: catalog.istioinaction.io" \
-w "\nStatus Code %{http_code}\n"; sleep 1s;  done
```

In the continuously triggered requests, we see that some are routed to the slow workload; as a result, they end with a timeout. The output is as follows:

```
upstream request timeout
Status Code 504
```

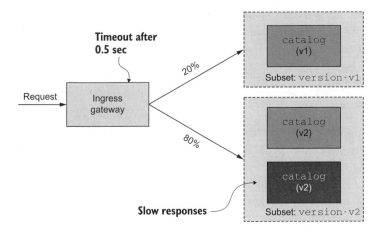

Figure 10.10 Two changes: requests time out after half a second, and a workload is intermittently slow.

Status code 504, "Gateway Timeout," is a piece of information we can use to query the Envoy access logs.

UNDERSTANDING ENVOY ACCESS LOGS

Envoy access logs record all requests processed by the Envoy proxy, which aids in debugging and troubleshooting. By default, Istio configures the proxies to use the TEXT format for the logs, which is concise but difficult to read:

```
$ kubectl -n istio-system logs deploy/istio-ingressgateway \
  | grep 504

# output is truncated to a single failing request
[2020-08-22T16:20:20.049Z] "GET /items HTTP/1.1" 504 UT "-" "-" 0 24
501 - "192.168.65.3" "curl/7.64.1" "6f780bed-9996-9c95-a899-a5e293cd9fe4"
"catalog.istioinaction.io" "10.1.0.68:3000"
outbound|80|version-v2|catalog.istioinaction.svc.cluster.local
10.1.0.69:34488 10.1.0.69:8080 192.168.65.3:55962 - -
```

That's a lot of recorded information for every request (which is helpful for debugging), but it's very difficult to make sense of the current format. In particular, new users may scratch their heads and wonder what each value means. Fortunately, we can configure the service proxies to use the JSON format, which is easier to read.

Enabling access logging mesh-wide

The service proxy access logs are configurable. By default, only Istio's demo installation profile prints access logs to standard output. If you use any of the other profiles or deviate from the installation as shown in chapter 2, you need to set the following meshConfig.accessLogFile="/dev/stdout" property during Istio installation:

```
$ istioctl install --set meshConfig.accessLogFile="/dev/stdout"
```

Note that this enables access logging for the entire mesh. To enable access logging for one particular workload, you can use the Telemetry API, as shown in chapter 7.

CHANGING THE ENVOY ACCESS LOG FORMAT

Using `istioctl`, we can update the Istio installation to print access logs in JSON format. The benefit of this format is that values are associated with keys so we know their meaning:

```
$ istioctl install --set profile=demo \
    --set meshConfig.accessLogEncoding="JSON"
```

This update is applied to the entire mesh, which tremendously increases the amount of logging for every workload proxy. On larger clusters, this is discouraged, as it causes strain on the logging infrastructure.

After the Istio installation is updated, we can query the access logs again. And this time, because the output is JSON, we can pipe it to `jq` to improve readability:

```
$ kubectl -n istio-system logs deploy/istio-ingressgateway \
| grep 504 | tail -n 1 | jq
{
  "user_agent":"curl/7.64.1",
  "Response_code":"504",
  "response_flags":"UT",                        ◁─────────  Envoy
  "start_time":"2020-08-22T16:35:27.125Z",                  response flag
  "method":"GET",
  "request_id":"e65a3ea0-60dd-9f9c-8ef5-42611138ba07",
  "upstream_host":"10.1.0.68:3000",      ◁──  Upstream host receiving
  "x_forwarded_for":"192.168.65.3",          the request
  "requested_server_name":"-",
  "bytes_received":"0",
  "istio_policy_status":"-",
  "bytes_sent":"24",
  "upstream_cluster":
    "outbound|80|version-v2|catalog.istioinaction.svc.cluster.local",
  "downstream_remote_address":"192.168.65.3:41260",
  "authority":"catalog.istioinaction.io",
  "path":"/items",
  "protocol":"HTTP/1.1",
  "upstream_service_time":"-",
  "upstream_local_address":"10.1.0.69:48016",
  "duration":"503",                      ◁──────  Exceeds the
  "upstream_transport_failure_reason":"-",        duration of 500 ms
  "route_name":"-",
  "downstream_local_address":"10.1.0.69:8080"
}
```

Now, reading and understanding the access logs is much easier. Two things stand out:

- The `response_flags` value is `UT`, which stands for "upstream request timeout."
- The `upstream_host` value represents the actual IP address of the workload that handled the request.

Envoy response flags

Envoy provides more details for connection failures using response flags. For example, the response flag UT means "the upstream was very slow according to the timeout configuration." Having the response flag UT associated with this request is important as it enables us to distinguish that the timeout decision was made by the proxy and not by the application. Some of the response flags you will see most often are as follows:

- UH—No healthy upstream (the cluster has no workloads)
- NR—No route configured
- UC—Upstream connection termination
- DC—Downstream connection termination

The entire list can be found in the Envoy documentation at http://mng.bz/PWaP.

The upstream_host helps isolate which application is intermittently slow. What's left is to search the Pod with that IP address and then debug what has gone awry with it. However, we won't stop after showing one way to find the host that's malfunctioning. There are multiple ways to get to the same conclusion, and we will explore all of them.

Let's store the slow catalog name in the variable SLOW_POD to use it later, in section 10.3.4:

```
$ SLOW_POD_IP=$(kubectl -n istio-system logs deploy/istio-ingressgateway \
| grep 504 | tail -n 1 | jq -r .upstream_host | cut -d ":" -f1)
$ SLOW_POD=$(kubectl get pods -n istioinaction \
    --field-selector status.podIP=$SLOW_POD_IP \
    -o jsonpath={.items..metadata.name})
```

In this case, we were able to find the slow Pod that's causing issues. When access logs don't provide enough information, we can increase the level of logging for Envoy proxies to get more detailed logs.

INCREASING THE LOGGING LEVEL FOR THE INGRESS GATEWAY

istioctl provides tools to read and change the logging levels of the Envoy proxy. The current logging level can be printed as shown here:

```
$ istioctl proxy-config log \
    deploy/istio-ingressgateway -n istio-system

active loggers:
  connection: warning
  conn_handler: warning       Connection scope logs information
  filter: warning             related to the network layer.
  http: warning               HTTP scope logs information related
  http2: warning              to the application layer, such as
  jwt: warning                HTTP headers, path, and so on.
  pool: warning
  router: warning             Routing scope logs details
  stats: warning              such as to which cluster
# output is truncated         the request is routed to.
```

From the output, let's elaborate on the meaning of `connection: warning`. The key `connection` represents the logging scope. Meanwhile, the value `warning` represents the logging level for this scope, which means only logs with a logging level of `warning` are printed for connection-related logs.

Other possible logging levels are `none`, `error`, `warning`, `info`, and `debug`. Being able to specify different logging levels for different scopes enables us to precisely increase the logging level for the area of our interest without drowning in the logs generated by Envoy.

In our case, we can find helpful logs in those scopes:

- `connection`—Logs related to layer 4 (transport); TCP connection details
- `http`—Logs related to layer 7 (application); HTTP details
- `router`—Logs related to the routing of HTTP requests
- `pool`—Logs related to how a connection pool acquires or drops a connection's upstream host

Let's increase the logging level for `connection`, `http`, and `router` loggers to get more insight into our proxy behavior:

```
$ istioctl proxy-config log deploy/istio-ingressgateway \
  -n istio-system \
  --level http:debug,router:debug,connection:debug,pool:debug
```

Now, let's print the logs of the ingress gateway. For simplicity, we redirect the output into a temporary file:

```
$ kubectl logs -n istio-system deploy/istio-ingressgateway \
> /tmp/ingress-logs.txt
```

Open the logs stored in the temporary file with your favorite editor, and search for the HTTP 504 response code in the output. You'll find a section similar to this:

```
2020-08-29T13:59:47.678259Z    debug    envoy http
[C198][S86652966017378412] encoding headers via codec (end_stream=false):
':status', '504'
'content-length', '24'
'content-type', 'text/plain'
'date', 'Sat, 29 Aug 2020 13:59:47 GMT'
'server', 'istio-envoy'
```

After finding the connection ID (which in this case is `C198`), we can query all the logs relevant to that connection:

```
2020-08-29T13:59:47.178478Z    debug    envoy http          Creates a new
[C198] new stream                                           connection stream
2020-08-29T13:59:47.178714Z    debug    envoy http
[C198][S86652966017378412] request headers complete (end_stream=true):
':authority', 'catalog.istioinaction.io'
':path', '/items'

2020-08-29T13:59:47.178739Z    debug    envoy http
[C198][S86652966017378412] request end stream
```

```
2020-08-29T13:59:47.178926Z    debug     envoy router
[C198][S86652966017378412] cluster
'outbound|80|version-v2|catalog.istioinaction.svc.cluster.local'
match for URL '/items'                    ◁──────────┐  Matches the cluster
2020-08-29T13:59:47.179003Z    debug     envoy router │  to route traffic to
[C198][S86652966017378412] router decoding headers:
':authority', 'catalog.istioinaction.io'
':path', '/items'
':method', 'GET'
':scheme', 'https'
```

A new stream is created for the connection. The stream ID S86652966017378412 is added to the subsequent logs. Following logs with this stream ID, we see that the router-scoped log prints the cluster that matched the routing rules: outbound|80|version-v2|catalog.istioinaction.svc.cluster.local.

After we decide which cluster to route the request to, a new upstream connection is created to one of the instances of that cluster, as shown in the following logs:

```
2020-08-29T13:59:47.179215Z    debug     envoy connection
[C199] connecting to 10.1.0.15:3000       ◁──────────┐  A new connection was
2020-08-29T13:59:47.179392Z    debug     envoy connection │  created to the upstream.
[C199] connection in progress
2020-08-29T13:59:47.179818Z    debug     envoy connection
[C199] connected
2020-08-29T13:59:47.180484Z    debug     envoy connection
[C199] handshake complete
2020-08-29T13:59:47.180548Z    debug     envoy router
[C198][S86652966017378412] pool ready
2020-08-29T13:59:47.67788Z     debug     envoy router  │  The timeout for the
[C198][S86652966017378412] upstream timeout ◁──┘  connection was exceeded.
2020-08-29T13:59:47.677983Z    debug     envoy router
[C198][S86652966017378412] resetting pool request
2020-08-29T14:52:37.036988Z    debug     envoy pool  │  The client
[C199] client disconnected, failure reason:  ◁──┘  disconnected.
2020-08-29T14:52:37.037060Z    debug     envoy http
[C198][S17065302543775437839] Sending local reply with details
➥upstream_response_timeout
2020-08-29T13:59:47.678259Z    debug     envoy http
[C198][S86652966017378412] encoding headers via
➥codec (end_stream=false):    ◁──────┐  A response with 504 was
':status', '504'                      │  sent to the downstream.
'content-length', '24'
'content-type', 'text/plain'
'date', 'Sat, 29 Aug 2020 13:59:47 GMT'
'server', 'istio-envoy'

2020-08-29T13:59:47.717360Z    debug     envoy connection
[C198] remote close                        ◁──────────┐  The connection to the
2020-08-29T13:59:47.717419Z    debug     envoy connection │  downstream was closed.
[C198] closing socket: 0                   ◁──────────┘
```

Two important findings are first, that the IP address of the upstream that responds slowly matches the IP address retrieved from the access logs, which further solidifies that only one instance is misbehaving instance; and second, that the client (proxy) terminated the connection to the upstream, as indicated by the log `[C199]` `client` `disconnected`. This matches our expectation that the client (proxy) is terminating the requests because the upstream instance is exceeding the timeout configuration.

Envoy loggers provide deep insights into how the proxy is behaving. In the next section, we investigate the network traffic on the server side.

10.3.4 *Inspect network traffic with ksniff*

We can validate that the proxy terminates the connection by inspecting the network traffic of the affected Pod. By now, this is not really necessary because we verified it using the Envoy logs. But the goal is to give you practice with the following network inspection tools:

- Ksniff—A `kubectl` plugin that uses tcpdump to capture the network traffic of a Pod and redirects it to Wireshark
- Wireshark—A network packet analyzing tool

Using both in conjunction provides a smooth debugging experience.

INSTALLING KREW, KSNIFF, AND WIRESHARK

To install ksniff, we need Krew, the `kubectl` plugin manager. The installation procedure for Krew is documented at https://krew.sigs.k8s.io/docs/user-guide/setup/install. With that done, the ksniff installation is as simple as installing a package:

```
$ kubectl krew install sniff
```

The last required tool is Wireshark. Follow the installation guide for your system at www.wireshark.org/download.html. After installing Wireshark, verify that it is accessible from the command line (that's how ksniff activates it):

```
$ wireshark -v

Wireshark 3.2.5 (v3.2.5-0-ged20ddea8138)
```

With the tools installed, we are ready to proceed.

INSPECTING NETWORK TRAFFIC ON THE LOCALHOST INTERFACE

To inspect network traffic of the malfunctioning Pod, execute the following command:

```
$ kubectl sniff -n istioinaction $SLOW_POD -i lo
```
⟵ **$SLOW_POD was set in the section "Changing the Envoy access log format."**

On a successful connection, ksniff uses tcpdump to capture network traffic from the localhost network interface and redirects the output to your local Wireshark instance for visualization. If you still have the script for generating traffic, sufficient traffic will be captured in a short period. If not, execute the command in a separate terminal window:

```
$ for i in {1..100}; do curl http://localhost/items \
-H "Host: catalog.istioinaction.io" \
-w "\nStatus Code %{http_code}\n"; sleep .5s;  done
```

After a couple of seconds, stop capturing traffic by clicking the stop icon on the main toolbar (see figure 10.11).

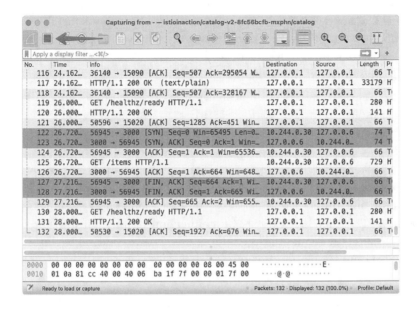

Figure 10.11 Stop capturing additional network packets.

To get a better overview, let's only show packets of the HTTP protocol of the GET method that have the path /items. This can be done using the Wireshark display filter with the query http contains "GET /items", as shown in figure 10.12.

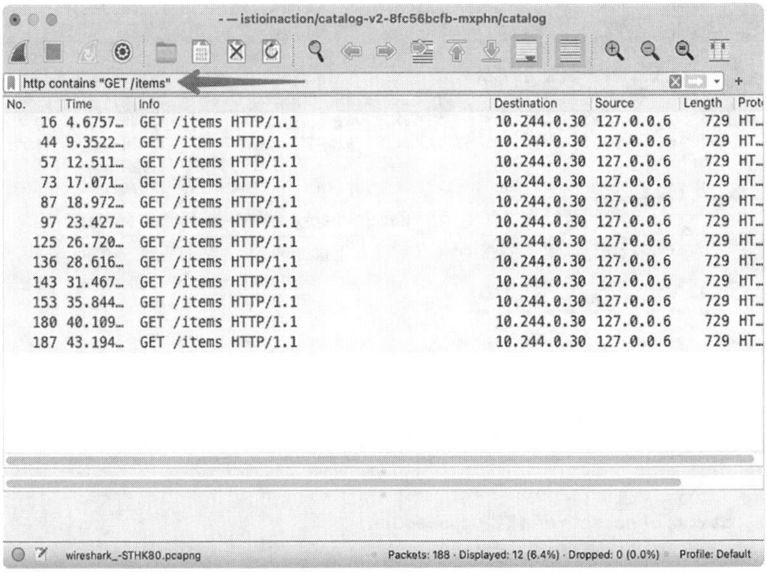

Figure 10.12   Filtering to show only HTTP "GET /items" requests

This reduces the output to only requests we are interested in. We can get more details about the start of a TCP connection up to when it was canceled by following its TCP stream. To do so, right-click the first row, select the Follow menu item, and then select TCP Stream. The Follow TCP Stream window opens, which shows the TCP stream in an easy-to-understand format. Feel free to close this window, as the filtered output in the main Wireshark window will suffice.

Figure 10.13 shows the TCP stream:

- *Point 1*—The TCP three-way handshake was performed to set up a TCP connection, as indicated by the TCP flags [SYN], [SYN, ACK], and [ACK].
- *Point 2*—After the connection is set up, we see that it is reused for multiple requests from the client, and all of those are successfully served.
- *Point 3*—Another request comes in from the client, which is acknowledged by the server, but the response takes longer than half a second. This can be seen from the time difference from packet number 133 to packet number 137.
- *Point 4*—The client initiates a TCP connection termination by sending a FIN flag. Because the request takes too long, this is acknowledged by the server side, and the connection is terminated.

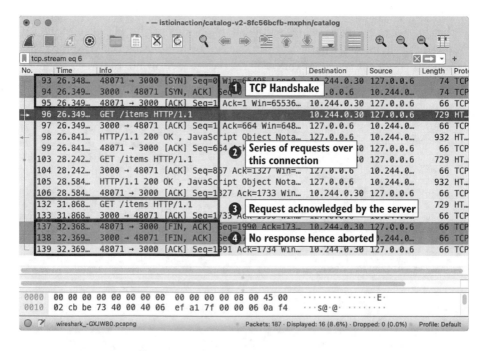

Figure 10.13   Stream of packets of a TCP connection

> **TCP control flags**
>
> TCP control flags indicate a particular state for a connection. The flags we see here are as follows:
>
> - Synchronization (SYN) is used to establish a new connection.
> - Acknowledgment (ACK) is used to acknowledge that a packet was successfully received.
> - Finish (FIN) is used to request connection termination.
>
> Knowledge of the TCP control flags simplifies inspecting the network traffic.

Inspecting the network traffic verified both of our earlier observations: the client initiates the connection termination, and the server is slow about responding to requests. In the next section, we investigate the success rate of the server to get an idea of whether this is a rare issue or a frequent one that requires immediate attention.

10.4 Understanding your application using Envoy telemetry

In chapter 7, section 7.2.1, we covered the metrics stored in Envoy proxies. With those metrics, we can find out the error rate of our services. The simplest way to get a quick overview is to use Grafana and the dashboards that come preinstalled with the Grafana addon.

10.4.1 Finding the rate of failing requests in Grafana

We'll continue with the same state we left earlier in this chapter. We can generate traffic as we did previously with the following command:

```
$ for i in {1..100}; do curl http://localhost/items \
-H "Host: catalog.istioinaction.io" \
-w "\nStatus Code %{http_code}\n"; sleep .5s;  done
```

Now, let's open the Grafana dashboard:

```
$ kubectl -n prometheus port-forward svc/prom-grafana 3000:80
```

Log in with the following credentials:

```
Username: admin
Password: prom-operator
```

Navigate to the Istio Service Dashboard, filter for the service `catalog.istioinaction.svc.cluster.local` and open the General panel. Here, check the diagram titled Client Success Rate (Non-5xx Responses). You should see a success rate similar to what we have shown in the figure 10.14. If you don't see the Istio Service Dashboard, refer back to chapter 7 to install Prometheus and Grafana and refer to chapter 8 to configure the dashboards.

Figure 10.14 The client success rate shows that approximately 30% of requests are failing.

When we compare to the server success rate (see figure 10.15), we see a difference. The server is reporting a success rate of 100% because the Envoy proxy marks the response code for downstream terminated requests with the value 0, which is not a 5xx response and hence doesn't count toward the failure rate. Meanwhile, the client marks the request with the correct status code of 504 ("Gateway timeout"); hence it's counted toward the failed requests (see figure 10.16).

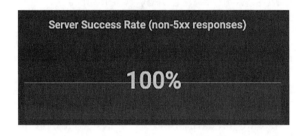

Figure 10.15 The server is not aware of any issues.

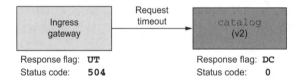

Figure 10.16 Differences in response flags and response codes as set by the client and server

With that clarified, we know that the correct rate is reported by the client. A failure rate of 20 to 30% requires immediate attention! But Grafana shows us the success rate of all workloads behind the `catalog` service. To identify the single instance that has issues, we need more detailed output.

10.4.2 *Querying the affected Pods using Prometheus*

Whenever the Grafana dashboard doesn't provide enough details, we can query Prometheus directly. For example, let's query and find out the failure rate for every Pod, which will help us isolate the unhealthy application.

Open the Prometheus dashboard:

```
$ kubectl -n prometheus port-forward \
svc/prom-kube-prometheus-stack-prometheus 9090
```

Now, let's query metrics that fulfill these criteria:

- Requests reported by the destination
- Requests whose destination service is the `catalog` service
- Requests with the response flag `DC` (downstream connection termination)

```
sort_desc(sum(irate(
    istio_requests_total{                          Filters to only metrics
        reporter="destination",          ◁──┘      reported by the destination
        destination_service=~"catalog.istioinaction.svc.cluster.local",   ◁──────
        response_flags="DC"}[5m]))        ◁───────────────
by (response_code, kubernetes_pod_name, version))                  Filters to only
                                                                  metrics when catalog
                      Filters to metrics that ended up with        is the destination
                      downstream connection termination
```

After executing this query, navigate to the Graph view, where the failure rate is represented visually (see figure 10.17). The graph shows that only one workload is reporting failures. This is important information, as it reduces the doubt that the deployment `version-v2` is faulty. But it doesn't entirely exclude the possibility—that would require further investigation.

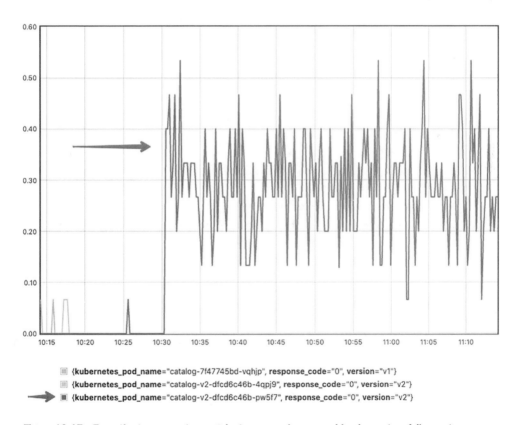

Figure 10.17 From the two `version-v2` instances, only one workload reports a failure rate.

NOTE Instead of deleting the Pod, we recommend just removing its label, so it doesn't match the Kubernetes service label selector (in our example, we need to remove the `app: catalog` label from the Pod). This will remove the Pod IP address from the Kubernetes service endpoints, a change that `istiod` propagates to the data plane.

If the Istio standard metrics do not provide the needed information, you can add custom metrics as shown in chapter 7, section 7.4. Additionally, you can use the Prometheus client libraries to instrument your application to your liking.

This concludes our exploration of the common tools used to troubleshoot the data plane. You should now have confidence and a clear starting point when facing various data-plane issues that previously might have seemed like black boxes. With the proper tools and a deeper understanding of how Istio works, debugging data-plane issues gets much easier (but it's never a piece of cake).

In the next chapter, we find out how to troubleshoot issues that occur in the control plane. We address how to improve control-plane performance, so it scales as the count of workloads is increased in the service mesh.

Summary

- Using `istioctl` commands, we gain insights into the service mesh and the service proxy:
  - `proxy-status` provides an overview of the data-plane synchronization state.
  - `analyze` analyzes the service mesh configuration.
  - `describe` gets a summary and validates a service proxy configuration.
  - `proxy-config` queries and modifies the service proxy configuration.

- We can use `istioctl analyze` to validate a configuration before applying it to the cluster.

- We can use Kiali and its validation capabilities to detect common configuration mistakes.

- To gain perspective on failures, use Prometheus and the collected metrics.

- We can capture the network traffic of affected Pods using ksniff.

- We can increase the logging level of the Envoy proxy using the command `istioctl proxy-config log`.

Performance-tuning
the control plane

This chapter covers

- Understanding the factors of control-plane performance
- How to monitor performance
- What are the key performance metrics
- Understanding how to optimize performance

In the previous chapter on troubleshooting the data plane, we took a deep dive into the debugging tools available to diagnose issues with proxy configuration and proxy behavior. Understanding the service proxy configuration simplifies troubleshooting when behaviors do not match our expectations.

In this chapter, we focus on optimizing control-plane performance. We investigate how the control plane configures the service proxies, the factors that slow down this process, how to monitor it, and the knobs we can turn to improve performance.

11.1 The control plane's primary goal

In previous chapters, we've said that the control plane is the brains of the service mesh and that it exposes an API for service-mesh operators. This API can be used

295

to manipulate the behavior of the mesh and configure the service proxies deployed alongside each workload instance. What we omitted for brevity is that service mesh operators—that is, us—making requests to this API is not the only way the mesh's behavior and configuration are affected. More generally, the control plane abstracts away details of the run-time environment such as what services exist (service discovery), which services are healthy, autoscaling events, and so on.

Istio's control plane listens to events from Kubernetes and updates the configuration to reflect the new desired state. This is an ongoing process to maintain a correctly behaving mesh, and it's important that this state reconciliation process happens in a timely fashion. Whenever the control plane fails to do so, it causes unexpected consequences because workloads are configured for a state that has already changed.

A common phenomenon that crops up when performance degrades is known as *phantom workloads*: services are configured to route traffic to endpoints that are already long gone, and hence the requests fail. The phantom workloads concept is illustrated in figure 11.1:

1 A workload that is becoming unhealthy triggers an event.
2 A delayed update causes services to have a stale configuration.
3 Because of the outdated configuration, the service routes traffic to the non-existent workload.

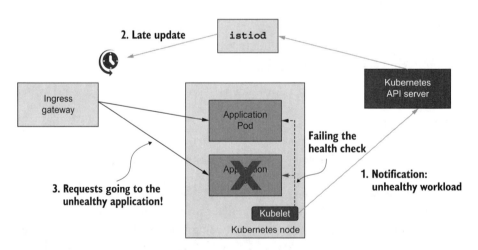

Figure 11.1 Routing traffic to phantom workloads due to an outdated configuration

Due to the eventually consistent nature of the data plane, having a stale configuration for a short time won't cause too many negative consequences, as other protective mechanisms can be employed. For example, by default, if a request fails for networking reasons, it will be retried twice, and potentially it will be served by other healthy endpoints.

Another remediation is outlier detection, which ejects endpoints from the cluster when requests to it fail. However, when the delay exceeds just a few seconds, it can begin to negatively affect end users, which we must avoid—and that's what this chapter is dedicated to.

11.1.1 *Understanding the steps of data-plane synchronization*

Synchronizing the data plane to the desired state is a multistep process: the control plane receives an event from Kubernetes. The event is converted into an Envoy configuration and pushed to the service proxies of the data plane. Understanding the process under the hood will guide your decision-making when fine-tuning and optimizing control-plane performance.

Figure 11.2 shows the sequence of steps to synchronize the data plane for an incoming change:

1 An incoming event triggers the synchronization process.
2 The `DiscoveryServer` component of `istiod` listens for these events. To improve performance, it delays adding the event to the push queue for a defined time to batch and merge subsequent events for that period. This is known as *debouncing* and ensures that time-consuming tasks do not fire too often.
3 After the delay period expires, the `DiscoveryServer` adds the merged events to the push queue, which maintains a list of pushes waiting to be processed.
4 The `istiod` server throttles (limits) the number of push requests that are processed concurrently, which ensures that faster progress is made on the items being processed and prevents CPU time from being wasted on context switching between the tasks.
5 The items that are processed are converted to Envoy configuration and pushed to the workloads.

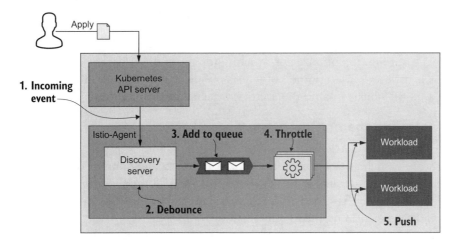

Figure 11.2   The sequence of actions to push the latest configuration to workloads

In these steps, we see how `istiod` protects itself from becoming overloaded by using the two practices of *debouncing* and *throttling*, which, as we see later, can be configured to improve performance.

11.1.2 Factors that determine performance

With a good understanding of the synchronization process, we can elaborate on the factors that affect the performance of the control plane (see figure 11.3):

- *The rate of changes*—A higher rate of changes requires more processing to keep the data plane synchronized.
- *Allocated resources*—If the demand exceeds the resources allocated to `istiod`, work has to be queued, which results in a slower distribution of updates.
- *Number of workloads to update*—More processing power and network bandwidth are required to distribute updates to more workloads.
- *Configuration size*—The distribution of larger Envoy configurations requires more processing power and more network bandwidth.

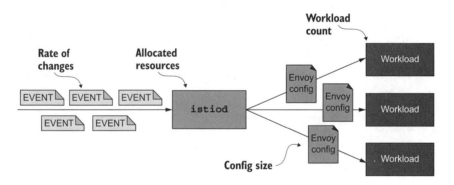

Figure 11.3   The properties that affect control-plane performance

We'll cover how to optimize performance for any of these factors. But before we do so, let's learn how to determine bottlenecks using the Grafana dashboards (as set up in chapter 8), which visualize the metrics collected by Prometheus for `istiod`.

11.2   Monitoring the control plane

`istiod` exposes metrics that measure the duration and frequency of key performance indicators, such as resource utilization, load due to incoming or outgoing traffic, the rate of errors, and much more. These metrics help illuminate how the control plane is performing, what is about to break, and how to troubleshoot something that may already be performing incorrectly.

The exposed metrics are described in the official Istio documentation (http://mng.bz/y44q), but the number of metrics is overwhelming. Here we will identify the key ones to pay attention to, and we'll organize the metrics as they loosely fit into the *four golden signals*.

11.2.1 *The four golden signals of the control plane*

The four golden signals, as defined by Google's *Site Reliability Engineering* book (https://sre.google/sre-book/table-of-contents), are the four key metrics to monitor to understand the external view of how a service is performing. If a particular service is falling outside its service-level objectives (SLOs), the golden metrics provide insights into the cause. The four signals are *latency, saturation, errors,* and *traffic*.

To get a quick view of the metrics in the control plane, we can query them using the following command:

```
kubectl exec -it -n istio-system deploy/istiod -- curl localhost:15014/metrics
```

We examine these metrics in the rest of the chapter through the Grafana dashboards.

LATENCY: THE TIME NEEDED TO UPDATE THE DATA PLANE

The latency signal provides an external view into how the service is performing in the eyes of end users. An increase in latency shows that the service is less performant. However, it doesn't guide us to what is causing the degradation. For that, other signals need to be investigated.

For Istio's control plane, latency is measured by how quickly the control plane distributes updates to the data plane. The key metric that measures latency is `pilot_proxy_convergence_time`. But to understand the step in the synchronization process where most of the time has been spent, there are two supporting metrics: `pilot_proxy_queue_time` and `pilot_xds_push_time`. Figure 11.4 shows the sections of the synchronization process that these metrics cover:

1 `pilot_proxy_convergence_time` measures the entire process's duration from the time a proxy push request lands in the queue until it is distributed to the workloads.

2 `pilot_proxy_queue_time` measures the time the push requests wait in the queue until they are processed by a worker. If a considerable amount of time is spent in the push queue, we might scale `istiod` vertically and increase the concurrent processing power.

3 `pilot_xds_push_time` measures the time required to push the Envoy configuration to workloads. An increase shows that network bandwidth is overloaded by the amount of data being transferred. We see in later sections how sidecars can considerably improve this situation by reducing the size of configuration updates and frequency of changes per proxy.

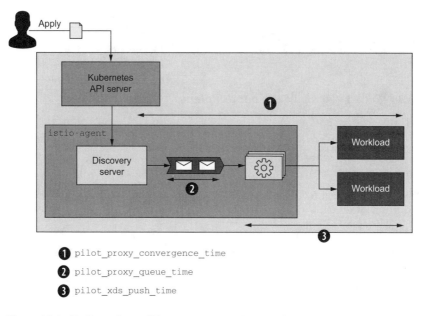

1. `pilot_proxy_convergence_time`
2. `pilot_proxy_queue_time`
3. `pilot_xds_push_time`

Figure 11.4   Portions of overall latency as covered by metrics

`pilot_proxy_convergence_time` is visualized in the Grafana dashboard and located in the Istio Control Plane Dashboard in the section Pilot Push Information with the title Proxy Push Time (see figure 11.5).

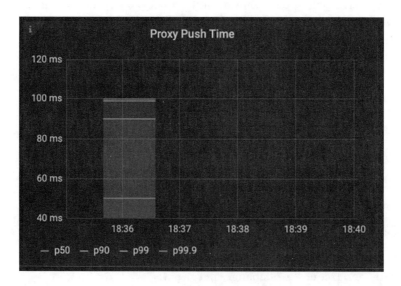

Figure 11.5   The graph shows that 99.9% of the pushes take less than 100 ms to be distributed to workloads, which is ideal!

TIP Update the Istio dashboards to display the latency metrics `pilot_proxy _queue_time` and `pilot_xds_push_time`.

As additional workloads are onboarded into the mesh, the latency for these various metrics gradually increases. That's expected, and you should not worry about slight increases. But we need to define acceptable thresholds and trigger alerts when the latency increases beyond an acceptable limit.

We recommend thinking about thresholds with these baselines:

- *Warning* severity when latency exceeds 1 second for more than 10 seconds
- *Critical* severity when latency exceeds 2 seconds for more than 10 seconds

When notified by the first alert, there's no reason to panic; it's just a call to action that service latency has increased and performance needs optimization. If left unchecked, however, further degradation will affect end users.

An increase in latency is the best indicator that control-plane performance is degraded, but it doesn't provide further insights into the cause of the degradation. For that, we need to dig deeper into the other metrics.

SATURATION: HOW FULL IS THE CONTROL PLANE?

The saturation metrics show the capacity at which resources are being utilized. If utilization is over 90%, the service is saturated or about to become so. When `istiod` is saturated, the distribution updates slow down as push requests are queued for longer periods, waiting to be processed.

Saturation is usually caused by the most constrained resource, and because `istiod` is CPU intensive, usually the CPU becomes saturated first. The metrics that measure CPU utilization are

- `container_cpu_usage_seconds_total` measures CPU utilization as reported by the Kubernetes container.
- `process_cpu_seconds_total` measures CPU utilization as reported by the istiod instrumentation.

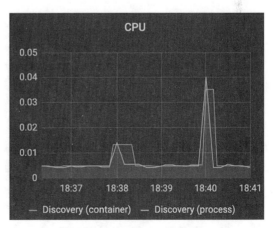

Figure 11.6 shows the graph that visualizes the CPU utilization metrics. It represents the most common pattern of CPU utilization for istiod, where much of the time is spent idle; when a service is deployed, compute requests spike as istiod is generating and pushing the Envoy configuration to every workload.

Figure 11.6 CPU utilization graph from the Istio Control Plane Dashboard in the section Resource Usage

When the control plane is saturated, it is running short on resources, and you should reconsider how much is allocated. If you've tried other approaches to optimize the behavior of the control plane, increasing resources may be the best option.

TRAFFIC: WHAT IS THE LOAD ON THE CONTROL PLANE?

The traffic metrics measure the load the system experiences. For example, for a web application, the load is defined by requests per second. Meanwhile, Istio's control plane is receiving incoming traffic (in the form of configuration changes) and has outgoing traffic (pushing changes to the data plane). We need to measure traffic in both directions to find the performance limiting factor; based on it, we can utilize different approaches to improve performance.

The metrics for incoming traffic are as follows:

- `pilot_inbound_updates` shows the count of configuration updates received per `istiod` instance.
- `pilot_push_triggers` is the total count of events that triggered a push. Push triggers can be one of the following types: `service`, `endpoint`, or `config`, where `config` represents any Istio custom resource such as `Gateway` or `Virtual-Service`.
- `pilot_services` measures the number of services known to the pilot. When more services are known to the pilot, more processing has to be done for incoming events to generate the Envoy configuration. As such, this metric plays a significant role in the load that `istiod` is put under due to incoming traffic.

The metrics for outgoing traffic are as follows:

- `pilot_xds_pushes` measures all types of pushes made by the control plane, such as `listener`, `route`, `cluster`, and `endpoint` updates. This metric is graphed in the Istio Control Plane Dashboard with the title Pilot Pushes (see figure 11.7).

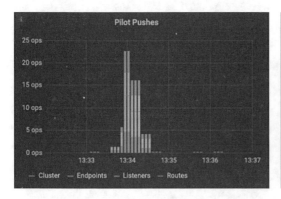 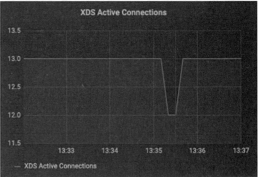

Figure 11.7   The Pilot Pushes graph shows the frequency of pushes. The XDS Active Connections graph shows the endpoints managed by a control plane.

- `pilot_xds` shows the total connections to workloads handled per pilot instance. This metric is graphed in the Istio Control Plane Dashboard with the title ADS Monitoring.
- `envoy_cluster_upstream_cx_tx_bytes_total` measures the configuration size that is transferred over the network.

The distinction between incoming and outgoing traffic clarifies the cause of saturation and the possible mitigation paths. When incoming traffic causes saturation, the performance bottleneck is due to the rate of changes, and the resolution is to increase the batching of events or scale up. If saturation correlates with outgoing traffic, the resolution is to scale out the control plane so that each pilot has fewer instances to manage, and to define `Sidecar` resources for every workload (demonstrated in later sections).

ERRORS: WHAT IS THE FAILURE RATE IN THE CONTROL PLANE?

Errors represent the failure rate of `istiod` and usually crop up when the service is saturated and its performance degrades. The most important error metrics are listed in table 11.1. They are visualized in the Istio Control Plane Dashboard with the title Pilot Errors.

Table 11.1 The most important error metrics

Metric	Description
`pilot_total_xds_rejects`	The count of rejected configuration pushes
`pilot_xds_eds_reject,` `pilot_xds_lds_reject,` `pilot_xds_rds_reject,` `pilot_xds_cds_reject`	The subsets of the *pilot_total_xds_rejects* metric, which are useful to reduce the scope of which API push was rejected
`pilot_xds_write_timeout`	The sum of errors and timeouts when initiating a push
`pilot_xds_push_context_errors`	The count of Istio Pilot errors while generating the Envoy configuration; usually bugs in Istio Pilot

That covers the most important metrics that provide insights into the control plane's state and how it is performing and help us uncover performance bottlenecks.

11.3 Tuning performance

Recall that the control-plane performance factors are the rate of changes in the cluster/environment, the resources allocated to it, the number of workloads it manages, and the configuration size pushed to those workloads. If any of those becomes a bottleneck, we have multiple ways to improve performance, as visualized in figure 11.8.

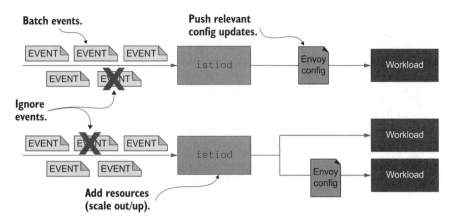

Figure 11.8   The options to improve control-plane performance

The knobs of control-plane performance are as follows:

- *Ignoring events* that are not relevant to the service mesh.
- *Batching events* for a longer period to reduce the number of pushes required to update the data plane.
- *Allocating additional resources* by
  - Scaling out the `istiod` deployment to reduce the load by splitting the number of workloads managed among pilot instances
  - Scaling up the `istiod` deployment to speed up the generation of the Envoy configuration and enable the processing of more push requests concurrently
- *Pushing only relevant updates* to workloads by defining a sidecar configuration that informs the control plane about the relevant configuration for a workload. This has two benefits:
  - Reduces the configuration size sent to a service proxy by sending only the minimal configuration needed for its processes
  - Reduces the number of proxies that are updated for a single event

To show how performance can be improved by these means, let's set up some services in our cluster and define a performance test.

11.3.1 Setting up the workspace

First, let's assume that we have Istio deployed but don't have any other application components deployed. If you are continuing from previous chapters, you may have to clean up any left-behind deployments, services, gateways, and virtual services:

```
$  kubectl config set-context $(kubectl config current-context) \
 --namespace=istioinaction
$  kubectl delete virtualservice,deployment,service,\
destinationrule,gateway --all
```

To give `istiod` some workloads to manage, let's create the `catalog` workloads and another 10 dummy workloads:

```
$ kubectl -n istioinaction apply -f services/catalog/kubernetes/catalog.yaml
$ kubectl -n istioinaction apply -f ch11/catalog-virtualservice.yaml
$ kubectl -n istioinaction apply -f ch11/catalog-gateway.yaml
$ kubectl -n istioinaction apply -f ch11/sleep-dummy-workloads.yaml
```

For the pilot, this is still too easy. Let's further aggravate the situation by bloating the Envoy configuration with some dummy services:

```
$ kubectl -n istioinaction apply -f ./ch11/resources-600.yaml
```

So now the single `istiod` instance manages 13 workloads, including ingress and egress gateways, and another 600 total services are known to it, which increases the amount of processing to generate the Envoy configuration and bloats the configuration that has to be pushed to the workloads.

11.3.2 *Measuring performance before optimizations*

We'll determine the control-plane performance with a test that generates load by creating services repeatedly and then measures both the number of pushes and the 99th percentile (P99) latency to distribute the configuration updates to the proxies.

> **Understanding P99**
>
> The P99, or *99th percentile*, measures the maximum latency of the fastest 99% of propagated updates. For example, a P99 latency of 80 ms tells us that 99% of requests were propagated faster than 80 ms! We don't exactly know where each of those requests falls, and the majority could be in the range of a few milliseconds. But we know that even the worst-performing request was served within 80 ms when considering only the fastest 99%.

Let's run the test with 10 repetitions and a delay of 2.5 seconds between repetitions to spread out the changes and avoid having them batched:

```
$ ./bin/performance-test.sh --reps 10 --delay 2.5

gateway.networking.istio.io/service-003c-0 created
service/service-003c-0 created
virtualservice.networking.istio.io/service-003c-0 created
<omitted>
==============                          | Push count to
Push count: 700                    <──┘ apply changes.      | Latency in the
Latency in the last minute: 0.49 ms              <──┘       | last minute
```

According to the test, with the current configuration to distribute the changes, 700 pushes were performed with a P99 latency of 0.49 ms. If we remove the delay between the services, we see that both the number of pushes and latency drop. That's because events are batched and served with less work (we explore how to configure batching in later sections). Keep in mind that the measurements will differ for you, and that's okay. The goal of this test is to make a "good enough" measurement that validates performance gains after we try out optimizations in subsequent sections.

REDUCING CONFIGURATION SIZE AND NUMBER OF PUSHES USING SIDECARS

In a microservice environment, it's common for one service to depend on other services. It's rare, however, for one service to require access to every other available service (or, at least, we avoid this situation). Out of the box, Istio cannot determine the access that each service needs, so by default, it configures every service proxy to know about every other workload in the mesh. You can imagine that this bloats the configuration of the proxies needlessly. For example, let's calculate the configuration size of the catalog workload:

```
$ CATALOG_POD=$(kubectl -n istioinaction get pod -l app=catalog \
    -o jsonpath={.items..metadata.name} | cut -d ' ' -f 1)

$ kubectl -n istioinaction exec -ti $CATALOG_POD -c catalog \
    -- curl -s localhost:15000/config_dump > /tmp/config_dump

$ du -sh /tmp/config_dump
2M      /tmp/config_dump
```

Right now, we have a configuration size of 2 MB. And that's a lot! Even for a medium cluster of 200 workloads, that adds up to 400 MB of Envoy configuration, which requires more compute power, network bandwidth, and memory as it is stored in every sidecar proxy.

THE SIDECAR RESOURCE

To resolve these concerns, we can use the Sidecar resource to fine-tune the configuration of inbound and outbound traffic for the sidecar proxies. To understand how it does this, let's take a closer look at an example Sidecar resource:

```
apiVersion: networking.istio.io/v1beta1
kind: Sidecar
metadata:
  name: default
  namespace: istioinaction
spec:
  workloadSelector:
    labels:
      app: foo
  egress:
  - hosts:
    - "./bar.istioinaction.svc.cluster.local"
    - "istio-system/*"
```

These fields are available for configuration:

- The workloadSelector field limits the workloads to which the sidecar configuration applies.
- The ingress field specifies the handling of inbound traffic to the application. If omitted, Istio configures the service proxy automatically by looking up the Pod definition.

- The egress field specifies the handling of the application's outbound traffic to an external service through the sidecar. If omitted, the configuration inherits the egress configuration from a more generic sidecar, if present; otherwise, it falls back on the default behavior of configuring access to all other services.
- The outboundTrafficPolicy field specifies the mode for handling outbound traffic. It can be set to either of the following:
  - REGISTRY_ONLY mode, which configures the workload to allow outbound traffic to only services it was configured for
  - ALLOW_ANY mode, which allows outbound traffic to any destination

When a Sidecar resource applies to a workload, the control plane uses the egress field to determine which services the workload requires access to. That enables Istio's control plane to discern relevant configuration and updates and send only those to the respective proxies. As a result, it avoids generating and distributing all the configurations on how to reach every other service, thus reducing CPU, memory, and network bandwidth consumption.

DEFINING BETTER DEFAULTS WITH A MESH-WIDE SIDECAR CONFIGURATION

The easiest way to reduce the Envoy configuration sent to every service proxy and improve control-plane performance is to define a mesh-wide sidecar configuration that permits egress traffic only to services in the istio-system namespace. Defining such a default configures all proxies in the mesh with the minimal configuration to connect only to the control plane and drops all configuration for connectivity to other services. This approach nudges service owners toward the correct path of defining more specific sidecar definitions for their workloads and explicitly stating all egress traffic their services require, thus ensuring that workloads receive minimal and relevant configuration needed for their processes.

With the following Sidecar definition, we configure all service sidecars in the mesh to connect only to the Istio services located in the istio-system namespace (and for Prometheus to scrape metrics):

```
apiVersion: networking.istio.io/v1beta1
kind: Sidecar
metadata:
  name: default
  namespace: istio-system
spec:
  egress:
  - hosts:
    - "istio-system/*"
    - "prometheus/*"
  outboundTrafficPolicy:
    mode: REGISTRY_ONLY
```

The sidecar in the istio-system namespace applies to the entire mesh.

Egress traffic is configured only for workloads in the istio-system namespace.

REGISTRY_ONLY mode allows outbound traffic only to services configured by the sidecar.

Let's apply it to the cluster:

```
$ kubectl apply -f ch11/sidecar-mesh-wide.yaml

sidecar.networking.istio.io/default created
```

Now, the control plane updates the current service proxies to have only the minimal configuration that enables connectivity to services in the `istio-system` namespace. If our hypothesis is correct, the Envoy configuration size for the `catalog` workload should be reduced considerably. Let's verify that:

```
$ kubectl -n istioinaction exec -ti $CATALOG_POD -c catalog \
    -- curl -s localhost:15000/config_dump > /tmp/config_dump

$ du -sh /tmp/config_dump
644K    /tmp/config_dump
```

That's a massive reduction of the configuration size, down to 600 KB from 2 MB. Furthermore, that's not the only benefit: from now on, the control plane will make fewer pushes as it determines which workloads need an update and which don't. Let's verify that using the performance test:

```
$ ./bin/performance-test.sh --reps 10 --delay 2.5

<omitted>
==============
Push count: 135
Latency in the last minute: 0.10 seconds
```

As expected, both the push count and latency have dropped. This increase in performance demonstrates the importance of defining a mesh-wide `Sidecar` resource. Doing so is beneficial to reduce the operational cost of the mesh, improve its performance, and ingrain good habits in the tenants of the platform to explicitly define egress traffic for their workloads.

For already existing clusters, to not cause service outages, you need to carefully check with users or tenants of the platform, so they first define the egress traffic of their workloads using more specific `Sidecar` resources. Then you can apply a default mesh-wide sidecar configuration. You should always test the changes in a pre-production environment.

Sidecar configuration scopes

Sidecar configurations, similar to `PeerAuthentication` resources, can be applied on different scopes:

- A *mesh-wide* sidecar applies to all workloads within the mesh and enables defining defaults, such as limiting egress traffic unless explicitly specified otherwise. To create a mesh-wide sidecar configuration, apply it in the Istio installation namespace (for us, `istio-system`). By convention, mesh-wide sidecars are named `default`.
- A *namespace-wide* sidecar configuration is more specific and overrides the mesh-wide configuration. To create a namespace-wide sidecar configuration, apply it in the desired namespace without defining the `workloadSelector` field. By convention, namespace-wide sidecars are named `default`.

- A *workload-specific* sidecar configuration targets specific workloads that match the `workloadSelector` property. Being the most specific, it overrides both mesh-wide and namespace-wide configurations.

At the time of this writing, multiple sidecar definitions of the same scope are not supported, and the expected behavior is not documented.

11.3.3 Ignoring events: Reducing the scope of discovery using discovery selectors

It may come as a surprise that the Istio control plane by default watches events for the creation of Pods, services, and other resources *in all namespaces*! In larger clusters, this can cause a strain in the control plane, which—to keep the data plane updated—processes and generates the Envoy configuration for every event.

To reduce this strain, in Istio 1.10, a new feature called *namespace discovery selectors* was added that allows you to fine-tune exactly what inbound events the control plane cares about. This functionality lets you specify exactly what namespaces to watch for workloads and endpoints. Using the namespace-selector approach, you can dynamically include namespaces and their respective workloads or exclude them from being processed by the mesh. You may wish to do this either when a particular cluster has a lot of workloads that may never be routed to by a workload in the mesh or when a particular cluster has workloads that churn constantly (like Spark jobs spinning up and down). In this case, you want the control plane to ignore the events generated for these workloads.

You can enable discovery selector functionality at startup with an `IstioOperator` file like the following:

```
apiVersion: install.istio.io/v1alpha1
kind: IstioOperator
metadata:
  namespace: istio-system
spec:
  meshConfig:                          Enables discovery
    discoverySelectors:      ◁┘        selectors
      - matchLabels:                        Specifies the
          istio-discovery: enabled   ◁┘     label to use
```

Here, we restrict the subset of namespaces that the control plane processes to only those with the label `istio-discovery: enabled`. If a namespace does not have this label, it is ignored.

If you have a cluster scenario where you want to include most of the namespaces and just exclude a small subset, you can use a label-match expression to specify which namespaces *not* to include. For example, you could use something like this:

```
apiVersion: install.istio.io/v1alpha1
kind: IstioOperator
metadata:
```

```
    namespace: istio-system
spec:
  meshConfig:
    discoverySelectors:
      - matchExpressions:
        - key: istio-exclude
          operator: NotIn
          values:
            - "true"
```

We can update our installation of Istio with the following to exclude certain name-spaces with the `istio-exclude: true` label without disrupting the existing behavior of scanning everything:

```
$ istioctl install -y -f ch11/istio-discovery-selector.yaml
```

Then we can create a new namespace with new workloads. Let's label this new name-space with the following:

```
$ kubectl label ns new-namespace istio-exclude=true
```

If we deploy a new workload into this namespace, the workloads in the `istioinaction` namespace will not see these endpoints. We leave this as an exercise for you to verify.

When we have reduced the scope of discovery to only relevant namespaces using `discoverySelectors` but the control plane is still saturated, our next option is to batch events and resolve them as a group, instead of resolving each event separately.

11.3.4 *Event-batching and push-throttling properties*

Events in the run-time environment that cause changes to the data-plane configura-tions are usually outside the operator's control. Events such as new services coming online, scaling up replicas, or services becoming unhealthy are all detected by the control plane and reconciled for the data-plane proxies. However, we have some con-trol when determining how long we *may* delay updates and batch those events. This has the benefit that the batched events are processed as a group and generate an Envoy configuration that is pushed to the data plane proxies as a single unit.

The sequence diagram in figure 11.9 shows how incoming events are delaying (debouncing) the action of pushing changes to the service proxy. If we increase the debounce period further, the last event (which is just falling out of the delay period) would be included in the batch as well, ensuring that all events are merged in one batch and pushed as a single request. On the other hand, delaying pushes by too much will cause the data-plane configuration to become stale, and we don't want that either, as discussed earlier in the chapter.

Meanwhile, going in the other direction and reducing the period ensures faster updates. However, doing so will produce many push requests that the control plane may not be able to distribute; those requests will be throttled in the push queue, lead-ing to an increase in latency.

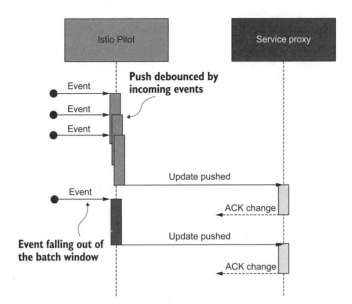

Figure 11.9 Sequence diagram of how events are merged and pushed

ENVIRONMENT VARIABLES THAT DEFINE THE BATCHING PERIOD AND PUSH THROTTLING

The environment variables that define the batching period are as follows:

- PILOT_DEBOUNCE_AFTER—Specifies the time to debounce, adding an event to the push queue. By default, it's set to 100 ms, meaning that when the control plane receives an event, it debounces the action of adding it to the push queue for 100 ms. Further events occurring in this period are merged with the former and debounce the action again. Whenever no events occur in this period, the resulting batch is added to the push queue and is ready for processing.
- PILOT_DEBOUNCE_MAX—Specifies the maximum time in which debouncing of events is allowed. When the time is passed, the currently merged events are added to the push queue. By default, this variable is set to 10 seconds.
- PILOT_ENABLE_EDS_DEBOUNCE—Specifies if endpoint updates comply with the debounce rules or have priority and land immediately in the push queue. By default, this variable is set to true, meaning endpoint updates are debounced as well.
- PILOT_PUSH_THROTTLE—Specifies push requests that istiod processes concurrently. By default, this variable is set to 100 concurrent pushes. If the CPU would be underutilized, you can set the throttle to a higher number for faster updates.

Some general guidance for using these configuration options:

- Increase event batching when the control plane is saturated and incoming traffic causes performance bottlenecks.
- Decrease event batching and increase concurrent pushes if the goal is to propagate updates faster. Doing so is recommended only when the control plane is *not* saturated.

- Reduce concurrent pushes when the control plane is saturated and outgoing traffic is the performance bottleneck.
- Increase concurrent pushes when the control plane is *not* saturated or you have scaled up and want faster updates.

INCREASING THE BATCHING PERIOD

To show the impact of batching, let's set `PILOT_DEBOUNCE_AFTER` to a ridiculously high value of 2.5 seconds. The adjective *ridiculous* is a good indicator that this shouldn't be done in production! It's meant only to demonstrate the batching of events:

```
$  istioctl install --set profile=demo \
     --set values.pilot.env.PILOT_DEBOUNCE_AFTER="2500ms"
```

Unless the limit is exceeded as defined by `PILOT_DEBOUNCE_MAX`, all events are merged and added to the push queue, which dramatically decreases the push count. Let's verify that by executing a performance test:

```
$  ./bin/performance-test.sh --reps 10 --delay 2.5

<omitted>
==============
Push count: 27
Latency in the last minute: 0.10 seconds
```

The push count is down to only 27 pushes! All the extra work of generating the Envoy configuration and pushing it to the workloads is avoided, and CPU utilization and network bandwidth consumption are reduced. Keep in mind that this example was just to illustrate the effect of debouncing events and not a general goal of configuring `istiod`. We recommended tuning the configuration for the Istio control plane based on your observed metrics and environment and doing so in small increments, which is safer than making a big change that could have an adverse effect on the performance of the control plane.

LATENCY METRICS DO NOT ACCOUNT FOR THE DEBOUNCE PERIOD!

After we increased the debounce period, the latency metric showed that the distribution of pushes took 10 ms, but that's not the case. Recall that the period measured by the latency metric starts from the point when the push request was added to the push queue (see figure 11.4). This means that while events were being debounced, updates were not delivered. And thus, the time of pushing updates increased, but this didn't appear in the latency metrics!

This increased latency caused by debouncing events for too long leads to stale configurations, just as low performance would. For this reason, make modest changes to the batching properties by slightly increasing or decreasing the values.

> **NOTE** The data plane is commonly affected by late endpoint updates. Setting the environment variable `PILOT_ENABLE_EDS_DEBOUNCE` to `false` ensures that endpoint updates are not delayed and skip the debouncing period.

ALLOCATING ADDITIONAL RESOURCES TO THE CONTROL PLANE

After defining a `Sidecar` resource, using discovery selectors, and configuring batching, the only other option to improve performance is to allocate additional resources to the control plane. When allocating additional resources, we can either *scale out* by adding more `istiod` instances or *scale up* by providing more resources to every instance.

The decision of whether to scale *out* or *up* depends on what's causing the performance bottleneck:

- *Scale out* when the outgoing traffic is the bottleneck. This occurs only when there are many workloads managed per `istiod` instance. Scaling out reduces the workload count that an `istiod` instance manages.
- *Scale up* when the incoming traffic is the bottleneck. This occurs when many resources (`Service`, `VirtualService`, `DestinationRule`, and so on) are processed to generate the Envoy configuration. Scaling up provides the `istiod` instances with more processing power.

The following command scales out `istiod` by setting the replica count to three instances and scales up the resources allocated to each `istiod` instance:

```
$  istioctl install --set profile=demo \
     --set values.pilot.resources.requests.cpu=2 \          Sets CPU requests to
                                                             two virtual cores
     --set values.pilot.resources.requests.memory=4Gi \
                                                             Sets memory
     --set values.pilot.replicaCount=3                       requests to 4 GB
                                        Number of replicas to
                                        scale the deployment to
```

By setting CPU and memory requests, we inform the kubelet (a Kubernetes component that runs containers on nodes) that it should reserve those resources for `istiod` instances. Meanwhile, increasing the replica count ensures that the deployment will have three replicas among which the management of workloads is split.

Autoscaling istiod deployment

Autoscaling is generally a good idea to optimize resource consumption, especially for burstable workloads like Istio's control plane. But as of now, this isn't effective for `istiod` because it initiates a 30-minute connection with the workloads, which is used to configure and update the proxies using the Aggregated Discovery Service (ADS).

So, newly spun up `istiod` replicas don't receive any load until the connections between the service proxies and the previous pilot expire. Because they don't receive any load, the new `istiod` replicas are scaled in. This produces a flapping behavior where the deployment repeatedly scales out and in, as shown in this figure:

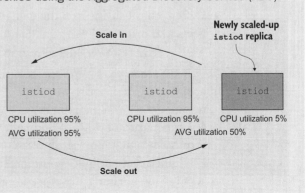

> **(continued)**
>
> Currently, the best way to configure autoscaling is for a gradual load increase—as in days, weeks, or even months. This reduces the human resource overhead to continually monitor performance and make decisions about scaling the deployment out or in.

The major takeaways of optimizing control-plane performance are as follows:

- Always define sidecar configurations for your workloads. This alone will provide you with the majority of benefits.
- Modify event batching only when the control plane is saturated and you already have a lot of resources allocated to it.
- Scale out when the bottleneck is outgoing traffic.
- Scale up when the bottleneck is incoming traffic.

11.4 *Performance tuning guidelines*

Before tuning performance, keep in mind that Istio is really performant. The Istio team tests every new release with the following parameters:

- 1,000 Kubernetes services that bloat the Envoy configuration
- 2,000 workloads that need to be synchronized
- 70,000 requests per second in the entire service mesh

This load consumes only one virtual core and 1.5 GB of memory for the single Istio Pilot instance, which synchronizes the entire mesh. (Performance is measured by Istio and published at http://mng.bz/g4xl.) Even a moderate allocation of resources, such as two vCPU and 2 GB with three replicas, will suffice for most production clusters.

> **NOTE** Performance is an important factor for Istio. Besides ensuring scalability for users of Istio, it benefits open source projects that are built on top of it, such as Knative, Kyma, and many others.

Here are some guidelines for control-plane performance tuning:

- *Ensure that this is a performance issue.* Answer questions such as
  - Is there connectivity from the data plane to the control plane?
  - Is it a platform issue? For example, on Kubernetes, is the API server healthy?
  - Are Sidecar resources defined to scope changes?
- *Identify the performance bottleneck.* Use the collected metrics for latency, saturation, and traffic to inform your tuning decisions. For example:
  - An increase in latency while the control plane is not saturated shows that resources are not utilized optimally. You can increase the concurrent push threshold so that more pushes are processed concurrently.
  - Low utilization but quick saturation under load shows that your changes are very bursty, meaning there are long periods without changes followed by a

spike of events for a short time. Increase the replica count of Istio Pilot or, if there is room for delaying updates, tweak the batching properties.

- *Make incremental changes.* After identifying the bottleneck, make incremental changes. For example, to resolve cases where the control plane is receiving a sequence of events for a longer time, it is tempting to double or even quadruple the debounce period, although doing so easily causes the data plane to become stale. Instead, make slight adjustments such as increasing or decreasing properties in the range of 10% to 30%. Then, monitor the benefits (or degradation) for a couple of days, and make informed decisions based on the new data.
- *Err on the safe side.* Istio Pilot is managing the network of the entire mesh; downtime easily causes outage. Always be gracious with the resources given to the control plane, never scale below two replicas, and err on the safe side.
- *Consider using burstable VMs.* Istio Pilot doesn't need CPU resources continuously and has burstable performance requirements.

Before finishing up, let's remove the `Sidecar` resource we created earlier, as it could cause unintended connectivity issues in future chapters:

```
$ kubectl delete -f ch11/sidecar-mesh-wide.yaml
```

In the next chapter, you learn how to scale Istio in your organization. We discuss using multiple gateways, adding support for non-Kubernetes workloads, using the existing certificate authority, and implementing control-plane availability patterns in your service mesh.

Summary

- The primary goal for the control plane is to keep the data plane synchronized to the desired state.
- The factors that affect Istio Pilot performance are the rate of changes, the resources allocated to the pilot, the workload count it manages, and the configuration size.
- The rate of changes received from the underlying platform is not in our control. But we can define how long to batch events and reduce the amount of work to update the data plane.
- Allocate resources to `istiod` graciously. The default production profile is a good starter.
- Always use the `Sidecar` custom resource to scope changes. Doing so ensures that
  - Fewer workloads are updated for an event.
  - The Envoy configuration size is reduced, as only relevant configuration is sent.
- Ignore events from namespaces that are not relevant to the mesh using discovery selectors.
- Use the Grafana Istio Control Plane Dashboard to decide how to tune the control plane.

Part 4

Istio in your organization

In the previous chapters, we saw how to configure and apply Istio's powerful capabilities for your service architectures. Chapters 12–14 deal with the reality of running Istio in your organization. How do you scale, troubleshoot, and tune Istio when running at scale? How do you include multiple clusters, VMs, and other constraints in your environments? Finally, we help answer how to customize and tailor the behavior of the service mesh for your particular use cases with technologies like WebAssembly (Wasm) and others.

Scaling Istio in
your organization

In the previous chapters, we have seen many of Istio's features and the capabilities they enable within a mesh on *a single cluster*. However, a service mesh is not bound to a single cluster; it can span many clusters and provide the same capabilities across all of them. In fact, a mesh's value increases when more workloads are part of it.

But when would we want a service mesh to span multiple clusters? What are the benefits of a multi-cluster service mesh compared to a single cluster? To answer those questions, let's revisit the fictitious ACME Inc., which moved to a cloud platform and experienced all the networking complexities added by microservice architectures.

12.1   *The benefits of a multi-cluster service mesh*

Early in its cloud migration efforts, ACME had the dilemma of how to size its clusters. The company started with a single large cluster but quickly changed that decision. ACME decided on multiple smaller clusters due to their benefits:

- *Improved isolation*—Ensures that mishaps of one team won't affect another
- *Failure boundary*—Draws a boundary around possible configurations or operations that could affect an entire cluster and reduces the impact on any other parts of the architecture if a cluster goes down
- *Regulatory and compliance*—Restricts services that access sensitive data from other parts of the architecture
- *Increased availability and performance*—Runs clusters in different regions for improved availability and routes traffic to the closest clusters to reduce latency
- *Multi- and hybrid clouds*—Enables running workloads in different environments, whether different cloud providers or hybrid clouds

During its initial evaluation, ACME considered the ability to expand service meshes across clusters and enable cross-cluster traffic management, observability, and security as the major drivers for opting into service meshes. To support the multi-cluster efforts, the company considered two approaches:

- *Multi-cluster service mesh*—A mesh that spans multiple clusters and configures workloads to route cross-cluster traffic. All of this is in accordance with the applied Istio configuration, such as `VirtualService`, `DestinationRule`, and `Sidecar` resources.
- *Mesh federation*, also known as *multi-mesh*—Exposes and enables the communication of workloads of two separate service meshes. This option is less automated and requires manual configuration on both meshes to configure service-to-service traffic. However, it's a good option when meshes are operated by different teams or have strict security isolation needs.

The option that we cover in this book is the multi-cluster service mesh. For mesh federation, you can see the Istio documentation at http://mng.bz/enMz.

12.2   *Overview of multi-cluster service meshes*

A multi-cluster service mesh connects services across clusters in a way that is fully transparent to the apps, meanwhile maintaining all of the service mesh's capabilities: fine-grained traffic management, resiliency, observability, and security for cross-cluster communication. Istio implements a multi-cluster service mesh by querying the services in all clusters and then using this queried information to configure service proxies on how to route service-to-service traffic across clusters.

Figure 12.1 shows what's required to join clusters into a single mesh:

- *Cross-cluster workload discovery*—The control planes must discover the workloads in the peer clusters in order to configure the service proxies (the API server of the clusters must be accessible to Istio's control plane in the opposite cluster).

- *Cross-cluster workload connectivity*—Workloads must have connectivity between each other. Awareness of a workload endpoint is not useful unless we can initiate a connection to it.
- *Common trust between clusters*—Cross-cluster workloads must mutually authenticate to enable the security features of Istio.

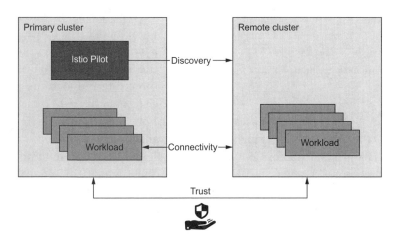

Figure 12.1   A multi-cluster service mesh requires cross-cluster discovery, connectivity, and common trust.

Fulfilling those criteria ensures that clusters are aware of the workloads running in other clusters, that workloads can connect to each other, and that workloads can authenticate and authorize using Istio policies. All of those are preconditions to setting up a multi-cluster service mesh.

> **Multi-cluster connectivity and security**
>
> As mentioned previously, for Istio to establish multi-cluster connectivity between the clusters, workloads can be discovered only by accessing the Kubernetes API in the peer clusters. For some organizations, this may be an undesirable security posture where each cluster has access to all other clusters' APIs. In this case, mesh federation is a better approach. Projects like Gloo Mesh (https://docs.solo.io/gloo-mesh/latest) can help with both automation and the security posture.

12.2.1 Istio multi-cluster deployment models

We distinguish between two types of clusters in multi-cluster service meshes:

- *Primary cluster*—The cluster in which Istio's control plane is installed
- *Remote cluster*—The cluster that is remote to the control-plane installation

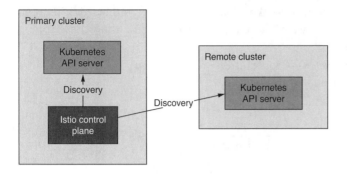

Figure 12.2   Primary-remote deployment model

Based on the availability we want to achieve, we have the following deployment models: primary-remote (shared control plane), primary-primary (replicated control plane), and external control plane.

The primary-remote deployment model (see figure 12.2) has a single control plane managing the mesh, and for that reason, it's often referred to as the *single control plane* or *shared control plane* deployment model. This model uses fewer resources; however, an outage in the primary cluster affects the entire mesh. As such, it has low availability.

The primary-primary deployment model (see figure 12.3) has multiple control planes, which ensures higher availability but has the trade-off of requiring more resources. This improves availability as outages are scoped to the clusters in which they occur. We refer to this model as the *replicated control plane* deployment model.

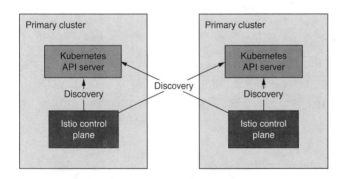

Figure 12.3   Primary-primary deployment model

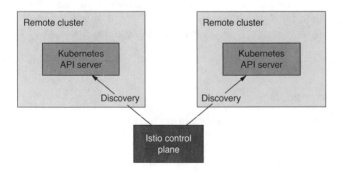

The external control plane (see figure 12.4) is a deployment model where all clusters are remote to the control plane. This deployment model enables cloud providers to provide Istio as a managed service.

Figure 12.4   The external control plane deployment model

12.2.2 *How workloads are discovered in multi-cluster deployments*

Istio's control plane needs to talk to the Kubernetes API server to gather relevant information to configure the service proxies, such as services and endpoints behind those services. Making requests to the Kubernetes API server is sort of a superpower, as you can look up resource details, query sensitive information, and update or delete resources to the degree of setting the cluster in a bad and irreversible state.

> **NOTE** Although we will cover securing access to a remote Kubernetes API using tokens and role-based access control (RBAC), an astute reader must consider the trade-offs of this approach. See the previous section for how mesh federation can mitigate this risk.

Kubernetes secures access to the API server using RBAC. Kubernetes RBAC is a broad topic—and out of the scope of this book—but we can highlight some of the concepts used to facilitate cross-cluster discovery:

- *Service accounts* provide identity to non-human clients such as machines or services.
- *Service account tokens* are automatically generated for every service account and represent its identity claim. Tokens are formatted as JSON Web Tokens and are injected by Kubernetes into Pods that can use the tokens to authenticate to the API server.
- *Roles and cluster roles* define the set of permissions for identity, such as a service account or a regular user.

Figure 12.5 visualizes the Kubernetes resources that provide authentication and authorization to `istiod`.

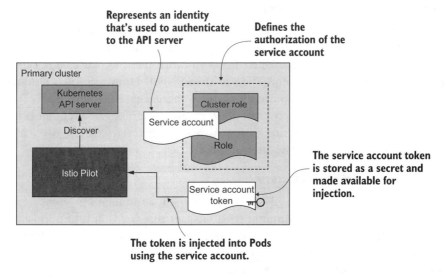

Figure 12.5 Resources that configure the identity and access of `istiod`

Cross-cluster workload discovery is technically the same. However, as shown in figure 12.6, we need to provide `istiod` with the service account token of the remote cluster (along with the certificates to initiate a secure connection to the API server, as we see when we get to the concrete examples). `istiod` uses the token to authenticate to remote clusters and discover workloads running in them.

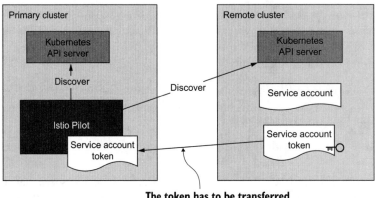

The token has to be transferred to the opposite cluster.

Figure 12.6   `istiod` **uses the service account credential to query the workload information of the second cluster.**

This may sound like an arduous process, but there is nothing to worry about. `istioctl` automates the process, as we see later in the chapter.

12.2.3 *Cross-cluster workload connectivity*

The other precondition is that workloads have cross-cluster connectivity. When clusters are in a flat network, such as sharing a single network (like Amazon VPC), or when their networks are connected using network peering, workloads can connect using IP addresses, and the condition is already met! However, when clusters are in different networks, we have to use special Istio ingress gateways that are located at the edge of the network and proxy cross-cluster traffic. Ingress gateways that bridge clusters in *multi-network* meshes are known as *east-west* gateways (see figure 12.7). We'll elaborate on east-west gateways later in this chapter.

12.2.4 *Common trust between clusters*

The last factor we need to resolve is that clusters in a multi-cluster service mesh must have *common trust*. Having common trust ensures that workloads of opposite clusters can mutually authenticate. There are two methods to achieve common trust between workloads of opposite clusters. The first uses what we call *plug-in CA certificates*: user-defined certificates issued from a common root CA. The second integrates an *external CA* that both clusters use to sign certificates.

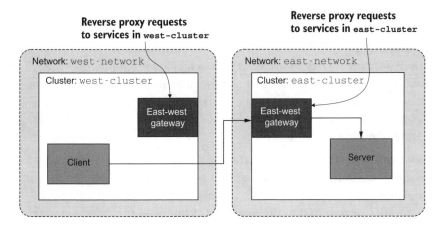

Figure 12.7   East-west gateways reverse proxy requests to the workloads in their respective clusters.

PLUG-IN CA CERTIFICATES

Using plug-in intermediate CA certificates is easy! Instead of letting Istio generate an intermediate CA, you specify the certificate to be used by providing it as a secret on the Istio installation namespace. You do so for both clusters and use intermediate CAs that were both signed by the common root CA. This approach is visualized in figure 12.8.

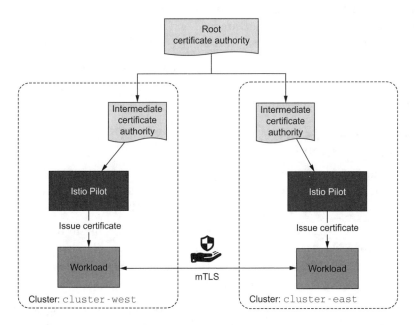

Figure 12.8   Using intermediate CA certificates that are signed by the same root

This method is favorable due to its simplicity; however, it poses a security risk if the intermediate CAs are exposed. Attackers can use them to sign certificates that are trusted until the exposure is detected and the intermediate CA's certificate is revoked. For this reason, organizations are reluctant to hand over intermediate CAs. The exposure risk can be reduced by only loading the intermediate CAs into memory and not persisting them as Kubernetes secrets into etcd (the datastore where Kubernetes resources such as secrets are stored). An even safer alternative is to integrate an external CA that signs the certificates.

EXTERNAL CERTIFICATE AUTHORITY INTEGRATION

In this solution, istiod acts as a registration authority that validates and approves certificate signing requests (CSRs) stored as Kubernetes CSRs. The Kubernetes CSRs that are approved are submitted to the external CA in one of the following ways:

- *Using cert-manager*—Only viable when our external CA is supported by cert-manager (see the supported external issuers: https://cert-manager.io/docs/configuration/external). If that's the case, then with cert-manager's istio-csr, we can listen for Kubernetes CSRs and submit them to the external CA for signing. This is discussed in more detail in Jetstack's blog post at www.jetstack.io/blog/cert-manager-istio-integration.
- *Custom development*—Create a Kubernetes controller that listens for approved Kubernetes CSRs and submits them to an external CA for signing. Istio's documentation on using custom CAs (http://mng.bz/p2JG) can be used as a starting point; however, the solution needs to be adapted to use an external CA instead of self-signing certificates with local keys. After the external CA signs the certificate, it is stored in the Kubernetes CSR, which istiod forwards to the workload using the Secret Discovery Service (SDS).

In this chapter, we set up common trust between clusters using plug-in CA certificates, because it's simpler and maintains focus on multi-cluster service meshes. We have now covered at a high level all the required conditions to set up a multi-cluster service mesh.

12.3 Overview of a multi-cluster, multi-network, multi-control-plane service mesh

We'll set up an infrastructure that mimics real-world enterprise services running in multiple clusters, deployed across different regions, and located in different networks. The infrastructure consists of the following (see figure 12.9):

- west-cluster—Kubernetes cluster with its private network in the *us-west region*. This is where we'll run the webapp service.
- east-cluster—Kubernetes cluster with its private network in the *us-east region*. This is where we'll run the catalog service.

Having the clusters in two different regions protects us from service outages when disasters occur in one of them. There is no technical reason for the webapp and catalog

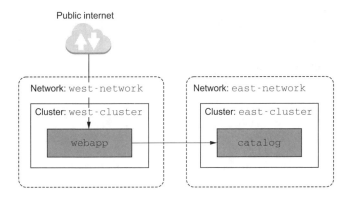

Public internet

Network: `west-network`
Cluster: `west-cluster`
webapp

Network: `east-network`
Cluster: `east-cluster`
catalog

Figure 12.9   Diagram of the multi-cluster service mesh

workloads to be in separate clusters—this is only for demonstration purposes. Whenever possible, workloads that are "chatty" should be in close proximity to reduce latency.

12.3.1 Choosing the multi-cluster deployment model

The multi-network infrastructure dictates that we need to use an east-west gateway to bridge the networks to achieve cross-cluster connectivity but leaves open the decision whether to use the replicated control-plane deployment model or a single control plane. The decision is driven by the business requirements. In ACME's case, its online store is highly popular: every minute of it being down would cost the business millions, for real! Hence high availability is a top priority, and we'll use the *primary-primary deployment model*, where the Istio control plane is deployed in each cluster. Putting it all together, we'll set up a multi-cluster, multi-network, multi-control-plane service mesh using an east-west gateway to bridge the networks and use the primary-primary deployment model. Let's get started!

12.3.2 Setting up the cloud infrastructure

For multi-clusters, local environments won't suffice; we have to use a cloud provider. In the examples that follow, we use Azure. However, you can follow along as soon as you set up two Kubernetes clusters in separate networks in any cloud provider.

CREATING CLUSTERS IN AZURE

The infrastructure consists of two Kubernetes clusters, each located on a different network (see figure 12.9). Their creation is automated with the following script. To execute the script, you need to install the Azure CLI (see http://mng.bz/OG1n) and sign in to get access to your subscription (see http://mng.bz/YgAN). After completing the prerequisites, execute the script to create the infrastructure:

```
$  sh ch12/scripts/create-clusters-in-azure.sh

== Creating clusters ==
Done
```

```
== Configuring access to the clusters for `kubectl` ==
Merged "west-cluster" as current context in ~/.kube/config
Merged "east-cluster" as current context in ~/.kube/config
```

This script creates the clusters and configures the kubectl command-line tool with two contexts: west-cluster and east-cluster. You can specify the context when executing kubectl commands:

```
$  kubectl --context="west-cluster" get pods -n kube-system
$  kubectl --context="east-cluster" get pods -n kube-system
```

Each command prints the list of running Pods in the respective cluster, confirming that the clusters are set up correctly. Let's create some aliases to save us keystrokes by not having to type the context all the time:

```
$  alias kwest='kubectl --context="west-cluster"'
$  alias keast='kubectl --context="east-cluster"'
```

With the aliases kwest and keast, the previous commands are reduced to

```
kwest get pods -n kube-system
keast get pods -n kube-system
```

Much neater! With the infrastructure created, the next step is to set up intermediate certificates and establish common trust between clusters.

12.3.3 *Configuring plug-in CA certificates*

In chapter 9, when we covered bootstrapping of workload identity—which is how workloads get a signed certificate that proves their identity—for simplicity we omitted the fact that Istio generates a CA to sign the certificates upon installation. This generated CA is stored as a secret named istio-ca-secret in the Istio installation namespace and is shared with istiod replicas. The default behavior can be overridden by plugging in our CA, which the Istio CA picks up instead of generating a new one. To do so, we have to store the CA certificates as a secret named cacerts in the installation namespace istio-system, containing the following data (see figure 12.10):

- ca-cert.pem—The intermediate CA's certificate.
- ca-key.pem—The intermediate CA's private key.
- root-cert.pem—The root CA's certificate that issued the intermediate CA. The root CA validates the certificates issued by any of its intermediate CAs, which is key for mutual trust across clusters.
- cert-chain.pem—The concatenation of the intermediate CA's certificate and the root CA certificate that forms the trust chain.

For your convenience, the intermediate CAs and the root CA are created in the directory ./ch12/certs. They are generated using the script ./ch12/scripts/generate-certificates.sh, which creates a root CA and uses it to sign two intermediate CA certificates. This results in two intermediate CAs that have common trust.

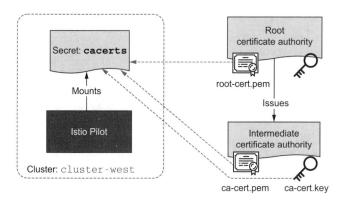

Figure 12.10 The `cacerts` secret is composed of the root CA's public key and the intermediate CA's public and private keys. The private key of the root CA is stored *securely* outside of the cluster.

APPLYING PLUG-IN CA CERTIFICATES

Configure the intermediate CAs in each cluster by creating the `istio-system` namespace and then applying the certificates as secrets named `cacerts`:

```
$  kwest create namespace istio-system
$  kwest create secret generic cacerts -n istio-system \
     --from-file=ch12/certs/west-cluster/ca-cert.pem \
     --from-file=ch12/certs/west-cluster/ca-key.pem \
     --from-file=ch12/certs/root-cert.pem \
     --from-file=ch12/certs/west-cluster/cert-chain.pem
```

Setting up certificates for the west-cluster

```
$  keast create namespace istio-system
$  keast create secret generic cacerts -n istio-system \
     --from-file=ch12/certs/east-cluster/ca-cert.pem \
     --from-file=ch12/certs/east-cluster/ca-key.pem \
     --from-file=ch12/certs/root-cert.pem \
     --from-file=ch12/certs/east-cluster/cert-chain.pem
```

Setting up certificates for the east-cluster

With the plug-in certificates configured, we can install the Istio control plane, which picks up the plug-in CA certificates (the user-defined intermediate certificates) to sign workload certificates.

12.3.4 *Installing the control planes in each cluster*

Before installing Istio's control plane, let's add network metadata for each cluster. Network metadata enables Istio to utilize the topology information and configure workloads based on it. Thus workloads can use locality information and prioritize routing traffic to workloads in close proximity. Another benefit when Istio understands the network topology is that it configures workloads to use east-west gateways when routing traffic to workloads in remote clusters that are in different networks.

LABELING NETWORKS FOR CROSS-CLUSTER CONNECTIVITY

The network topology can be configured within the Istio installation using the `Mesh-Network` configuration (http://mng.bz/GG6q). However, it's a legacy piece of configuration kept only for rare and advanced use cases. The simpler option is to label the Istio installation namespace with network topology information. For us, the Istio installation namespace is `istio-system`, and the network in the `west-cluster` is `west-network`. Thus we label the `istio-system` in the `west-cluster` with `topology.istio.io/network=west-network`:

```
$  kwest label namespace istio-system \
     topology.istio.io/network=west-network
```

And for the `east-cluster`, we set the network topology label to `east-network`:

```
$  keast label namespace istio-system \
     topology.istio.io/network=east-network
```

With these labels, Istio forms an understanding of the network topology and uses it to decide how to configure workloads.

INSTALLING THE CONTROL PLANES USING ISTIOOPERATOR RESOURCES

Because we have to make numerous modifications, we are going to use an Istio-Operator resource to define the Istio installations for the `west-cluster`:

```
apiVersion: install.istio.io/v1alpha1
metadata:
 name: istio-controlplane
 namespace: istio-system
kind: IstioOperator
spec:
  profile: demo
  components:                          Disables the
    egressGateways:              ◁──── egress gateway
    - name: istio-egressgateway
      enabled: false
 values:
   global:                         Name of
     meshID: usmesh          ◁──── the mesh
     multiCluster:                           Cluster identifier in the
       clusterName: west-cluster      ◁──── multi-cluster mesh
     network: west-network      ◁──  Network in which this
                                     installation is occurring
```

NOTE Kubernetes clusters can have many tenants and can span many teams. Istio provides the option of installing multiple meshes within a cluster, allowing teams to manage their mesh operations separately. The `meshID` property enables us to identify the mesh to which this installation belongs.

The previous definition is stored in the file ch12/controlplanes/cluster-west.yaml, and you can install Istio with that configuration using `istioctl`:

```
$  istioctl --context="west-cluster" install -y \
     -f ch12/controlplanes/cluster-west.yaml

✓ Istio core installed
✓ Istiod installed
```

```
✓ Ingress gateways installed
✓ Installation complete
```

After a successful installation of the west-cluster, you can install the replicated control plane in the east-cluster. The IstioOperator definition for the east-cluster differs from that of the west-cluster only in the cluster name and the network. And because we want both control planes to form the same mesh, we specify the same meshID that we used for the west-cluster installation:

```
apiVersion: install.istio.io/v1alpha1
metadata:
  name: istio-controlplane
  namespace: istio-system
kind: IstioOperator
spec:
  profile: demo
  components:
    egressGateways:
    - name: istio-egressgateway
      enabled: false
  values:
    global:
      meshID: usmesh
      multiCluster:
        clusterName: east-cluster
      network: east-network
```

Next, we install the control plane in the east-cluster:

```
$ istioctl --context="east-cluster" install -y \
    -f ch12/controlplanes/cluster-east.yaml
```

```
✓ Istio core installed
✓ Istiod installed
✓ Ingress gateways installed
✓ Installation complete
```

Before moving on, let's create aliases for the different cluster contexts in istioctl, as we did for kubectl earlier:

```
$ alias iwest='istioctl --context="west-cluster"'
$ alias ieast='istioctl --context="east-cluster"'
```

After installing the control planes on both clusters, we have two separate meshes—each running one istiod replica that discovers only local services—and a gateway for ingress traffic (see figure 12.11).

The meshes lack cross-cluster workload discovery and connectivity, which we set up in the following sections. But before proceeding, let's run some workloads in each cluster. The workloads will come in handy to verify that cross-cluster discovery and connectivity are set up correctly.

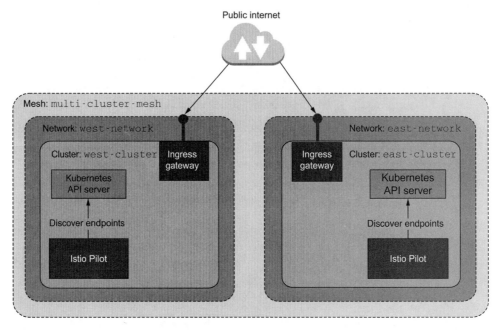

Figure 12.11   Current setup of the meshes

Running workloads on both clusters

With the control planes installed, let's run some workloads. In the west-cluster, we
deploy webapp:

```
$  kwest create ns istioinaction
$  kwest label namespace istioinaction istio-injection=enabled
$  kwest -n istioinaction apply -f ch12/webapp-deployment-svc.yaml
$  kwest -n istioinaction apply -f ch12/webapp-gw-vs.yaml
$  kwest -n istioinaction apply -f ch12/catalog-svc.yaml
```

> Stub catalog service
> to which webapp
> makes requests

In this listing, almost everything makes sense. For example, we create a namespace
and label it for auto-injection so that workloads get the sidecar proxies injected. Then
we deploy the webapp, including a service for it, and expose this service from the
ingress gateway by admitting traffic using a Gateway resource and routing traffic to it
with a VirtualService resource.

But why do we need a service for the catalog workload, considering that we want to
run it only in the east-cluster? The reason for adding this stub service is that in its
absence, the webapp container cannot resolve the fully qualified domain name
(FQDN) to any IP address, and thus the request would fail prior to reaching the point
where traffic leaves the application and is redirected to the proxy. By adding a stub
catalog service, the FQDN is resolved to the service cluster IP and traffic is initiated by
the application, which makes it possible for it to be redirected to the Envoy proxy
where the actual Envoy configuration exists and handles the cross-cluster routing. This

is an edge case that the Istio community plans to fix in upcoming versions when the DNS proxy is enhanced further, which is a topic we will examine in the next chapter.

Let's install the `catalog` service in the `east-cluster`:

```
$  keast create ns istioinaction
$  keast label namespace istioinaction istio-injection=enabled
$  keast -n istioinaction apply -f ch12/catalog.yaml
```

Suppose this is our starting point: two clusters, each with workloads that need to connect. But without cross-cluster workload discovery, the sidecar proxies are not configured for the workloads in opposite clusters. Thus our next step is enabling cross-cluster discovery.

12.3.5 *Enabling cross-cluster workload discovery*

For Istio to be authenticated for querying information from the remote cluster, it needs a service account that defines the identity and role bindings for its permissions. For this reason, Istio, upon installation, creates a service account (named `istio-reader-service-account`) with the minimal set of permissions that can be used by another control plane to authenticate itself and look up workload-related information such as services and endpoints. However, we need to make the service account token available to the opposite cluster, along with certificates to initiate a secure connection to the remote cluster.

CREATING THE SECRETS FOR REMOTE CLUSTER ACCESS

The `istioctl` utility has the `create-remote-secret` command, which by default creates the secret for remote cluster access using the default `istio-reader-service-account` service account. When creating the secret, it's important to specify the name of the cluster as specified during Istio installation in the `IstioOperator` (see the earlier listings for the `west-cluster` and the `east-cluster` in the section "Installing the control planes using IstioOperator resources"). Pay attention to how the cluster name is used as an identifier for the configuration to access the remote clusters:

```
$  ieast x create-remote-secret --name="east-cluster"

# This file is autogenerated, do not edit.
apiVersion: v1
kind: Secret
metadata:
  annotations:
    networking.istio.io/cluster: east-cluster
  labels:
    istio/multiCluster: "true"          ◁──┐ Secrets with this label set to true
  name: istio-remote-secret-east-cluster    │ are watched by Istio's control
  namespace: istio-system                    │ plane to register new clusters.
stringData:
  east-cluster: |
    apiVersion: v1
    kind: Config
    preferences: {}
    clusters:
```

```
- cluster:
    certificate-authority-data: <omitted>               ◁─────────┐
    server: https://east-clust-dkjqiu.hcp.eastus.azmk8s.io:443     │
  name: east-cluster
users:                                                      CA used to initiate a
- name: east-cluster                                        secure connection
  user:                        ┌── Token that represents the   to this cluster
    token: <omitted>      ◁────┘   identity of the service account
contexts:
- context:
    cluster: east-cluster
    user: east-cluster
  name: east-cluster
current-context: east-cluster
```

How kubectl talks to the Kubernetes API server

If you've checked how `kubectl` is configured to talk to the API server, the previous data will look familiar. It is formatted as a `kubeconfig` file and contains the following data:

- `clusters`—A list of clusters containing the cluster address and CA data to verify the connection presented by the API server
- `users`—A list that defines the users containing the token to authenticate to the API server
- `contexts`—A list of contexts, each grouping a user and a cluster, which simplifies switching clusters (not relevant for our use case)

This is all `kubectl` needs to initiate secure connections to the Kubernetes API server and authenticate to it. `istiod` uses the same approach to query remote clusters securely.

Instead of printing the secret, let's pipe it to the `kubectl` command and apply it to the `west-cluster`:

```
$  ieast x create-remote-secret --name="east-cluster" \
  | kwest apply -f -

secret/istio-remote-secret-east-cluster created
```

As soon as the secret is created, `istiod` picks it up and queries workloads in the newly added remote cluster. This is logged in `istiod`, as shown in its logs:

```
$ kwest logs deploy/istiod -n istio-system | grep 'Adding cluster'

2021-04-08T08:47:32.408052Z     info
➥Adding cluster_id=east-cluster from
➥secret=istio-system/istio-remote-secret-east-cluster
```

The logs verify that the cluster is initialized and that the `west-cluster` control plane can discover workloads in the `east-cluster`. For a primary-primary deployment, we need to do the opposite as well, configuring the `east-cluster` to query the `west-cluster`:

```
$  iwest x create-remote-secret --name="west-cluster" \
   | keast apply -f -

secret/istio-remote-secret-west-cluster created
```

Now the control planes can query the workloads on the opposite clusters. Does that mean we are done? Not yet! But we are one step closer. Next, we set up cross-cluster connectivity.

12.3.6 *Setting up cross-cluster connectivity*

In chapter 4, we discussed Istio's ingress gateway and saw that it's based on the Envoy proxy. It represents the ingress point for traffic originating in the public network and is directed to the organization's internal network. This type of traffic is often referred to as *north-south traffic*. In contrast, traffic between different internal networks—in our instance, the networks of the clusters—is known as *east-west traffic* (see figure 12.12).

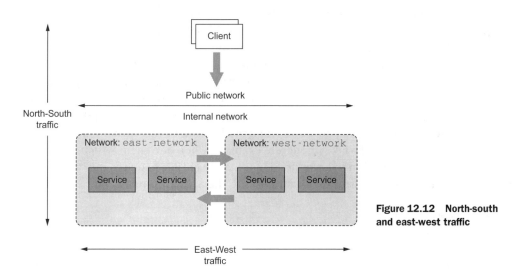

Figure 12.12   North-south and east-west traffic

To simplify east-west traffic, most cloud providers enable peering of virtual networks—provided the network address spaces do not overlap. Services in peered virtual networks initiate direct connections using IPv4 and IPv6 addresses. However, network peering is a cloud-specific feature. Whenever we want to connect clusters in different cloud providers or on-premises where network peering is not possible, the option Istio provides is an east-west gateway. The gateway must be exposed with a load balancer that's accessible to the workloads of the opposite clusters.

In this section, we set up cross-cluster connectivity and show how it works under the hood. It may seem complicated, but we believe understanding how this works is more important than just making it work. If things go wrong, you should have the knowledge and ability to troubleshoot and restore connectivity.

ISTIO'S EAST-WEST GATEWAY

The east-west gateway's goal, in addition to being an ingress point for cross-cluster east-west traffic, is to make this process transparent from the teams operating the services. To meet this goal, the gateway must

- Enable fine-grained traffic management across clusters
- Route encrypted traffic to enable mutual authentication between workloads

And service mesh operators shouldn't have to configure any additional resources! In other words, you shouldn't have to configure any additional Istio resources! This ensures that there is no difference when routing in-cluster or cross-cluster traffic. In both scenarios, workloads can target services in a fine-grained manner and can initiate mutually authenticated connections. (One nuance is what happens to load balancing when it crosses a cluster boundary. We explore that in the next section.) To understand how this is implemented, we need to introduce two of Istio's features—*SNI clusters* and *SNI auto passthrough*—and how they modify the gateway's behavior.

CONFIGURING EAST-WEST GATEWAYS WITH **SNI** CLUSTERS

East-west gateways are ingress gateways with additional configuration for *Server Name Indication (SNI) clusters* for every service. But what are SNI clusters? SNI clusters are just like regular Envoy clusters (see chapter 10, section 10.3.2, Querying the Envoy Cluster Configuration subsection), consisting of the direction, subset, port, and FQDN that group a set of similar workloads where traffic can be routed. However, SNI clusters have one key difference: they encode all Envoy cluster information in the SNI. This enables the east-west gateway to proxy encrypted traffic to the cluster specified by the client within the SNI. To take a concrete example, when one client—such as the webapp—initiates a connection to a workload in a remote cluster—such as the catalog workload—it encodes the cluster that it targets into the SNI, as shown in figure 12.13.

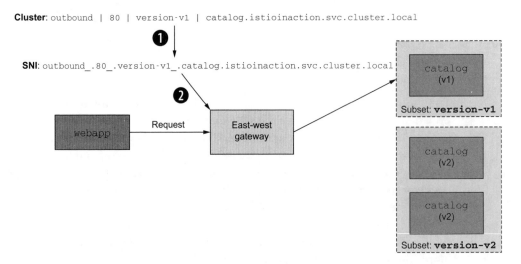

Figure 12.13 (1) Cluster information is encoded into the SNI. (2) The SNI contains the direction, port, version, and service name that dictates routing decisions.

Thus the client can make fine-grained routing decisions, and the gateway can read the cluster information from the SNI header and then proxy the traffic to the workload intended by the client. All this happens while maintaining a secure and mutually authenticated connection between the workloads.

Installing the east-west gateway with SNI clusters

For a gateway, the configuration of SNI clusters is an opt-in feature that can be enabled by setting the gateway router mode to `sni-dnat` using the environment variable `ISTIO_META_ROUTER_MODE`, as shown in the following `IstioOperator` definition:

```
apiVersion: install.istio.io/v1alpha1
kind: IstioOperator
metadata:
  name: istio-eastwestgateway        ◁─┐ The IstioOperator name should not
  namespace: istio-system              │ overlap the previous Istio installation.
spec:
  profile: empty           ◁─┐ The empty profile doesn't install
  components:                 │ additional Istio components.
    ingressGateways:
    - name: istio-eastwestgateway    ◁─┐ Name of
      label:                           │ the gateway
        istio: eastwestgateway
        app: istio-eastwestgateway
      enabled: true
      k8s:
        env:
          - name: ISTIO_META_ROUTER_MODE         │ The sni-dnat mode adds the SNI
            value: "sni-dnat"                     │ clusters required for proxying traffic.
          - name: ISTIO_META_REQUESTED_NETWORK_VIEW  │ Network in which the
            value: east-network                       │ gateway routes traffic
        service:
          ports:
            # redacted for brevity
  values:
    global:
      meshID: usmesh                    │ Mesh, cluster, and
      multiCluster:                     │ network identifying
        clusterName: east-cluster       │ information
      network: east-network
```

There is quite a lot to unravel in this definition:

- The name of the `IstioOperator` resource *must not* be the same as the resource initially used to install the control plane. If the same name is used, the previous installation will be overwritten.
- Setting `ISTIO_META_ROUTER_MODE` to `sni-dnat` configures SNI clusters automatically. When not specified, it falls back to the `standard` mode, which doesn't configure SNI clusters.
- `ISTIO_META_REQUESTED_NETWORK_VIEW` defines the network traffic is proxied to.

Install the east-west gateway using the previous `IstioOperator` definition, which is located in the file ch12/gateways/cluster-east-eastwest-gateway.yaml:

```
$  ieast install -y -f ch12/gateways/cluster-east-eastwest-gateway.yaml
```

✓ Ingress gateways installed
✓ Installation complete

With the east-west gateway installed and the router mode set to `sni-dnat` the next step is to expose the multi-cluster mTLS port through the east-west gateway using the SNI auto passthrough mode. Istio is clever and only then configures the gateway with the SNI clusters.

ROUTING CROSS-CLUSTER TRAFFIC USING SNI AUTO PASSTHROUGH

To understand SNI auto passthrough, let's recall that the *manual* SNI passthrough configures the ingress gateway to admit traffic based on the SNI header (see chapter 4, section 4.4.2). This shows that to route admitted traffic, service operators have to manually define a `VirtualService` resource (see figure 12.14). SNI auto passthrough, as the name suggests, doesn't require manually creating a `VirtualService` to route admitted traffic. It is done using the SNI clusters, which are configured automatically in the east-west gateway when its router mode is set to `sni-dnat` (figure 12.15).

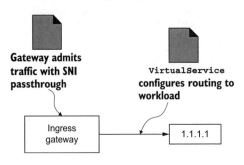

Figure 12.14   Traffic routing with SNI passthrough requires defining `VirtualService` resources.

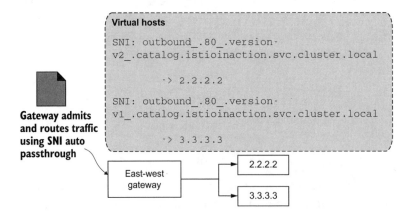

Figure 12.15   Traffic routing with SNI auto passthrough uses SNI clusters initialized in the `sni-dnat` router mode.

SNI auto passthrough mode is configured using the Istio `Gateway` resource. In the following definition, we use SNI auto passthrough for all traffic where the SNI header matches the expression `*.local`, which is the case for all Kubernetes services:

```
apiVersion: networking.istio.io/v1alpha3
kind: Gateway
metadata:
  name: cross-network-gateway
  namespace: istio-system
spec:
  selector:
    istio: eastwestgateway        <──┐  Configuration is applied
  servers:                            only to gateways
    - port:                           matching the selector.
        number: 15443        <──┐  In Istio, port 15443 is a
        name: tls                  special port designated for
        protocol: TLS              multi-cluster mTLS traffic.
      tls:
        mode: AUTO_PASSTHROUGH   <──┐  Resolves the destination
      hosts:                          using the SNI header and
        - "*.local"    <──┐          uses the SNI clusters
                           Admits traffic only for SNIs
                           matching the regex *.local
```

This resource is defined in the file ch12/gateways/expose-services.yaml. Applying it to the cluster exposes workloads of the east-cluster to the west-cluster:

```
$  keast apply -n istio-system -f ch12/gateways/expose-services.yaml

gateway.networking.istio.io/cross-network-gateway created
```

Before moving on, let's do the opposite as well: create an east-west gateway in the west-cluster and expose its services to the workloads in the east-cluster:

```
$  iwest install -y -f ch12/gateways/cluster-west-eastwest-gateway.yaml
$  kwest apply -n istio-system -f ch12/gateways/expose-services.yaml
```

Now, let's verify that SNI clusters are configured by querying the cluster proxy configuration of the east-west gateway and filtering the output to only lines containing the catalog text:

```
$  ieast pc clusters deploy/istio-eastwestgateway.istio-system  \
   | grep catalog | awk '{printf "CLUSTER: %s\n", $1}'
                                                            SNI cluster for the
                                                            catalog service
CLUSTER: catalog.istioinaction.svc.cluster.local
CLUSTER: outbound_.80_._.catalog.istioinaction.svc.cluster.local   <──┘
```

The output shows the SNI cluster is defined for the catalog workload! And as we configured the gateway with SNI auto passthrough, incoming traffic on the gateway uses the SNI clusters to route to the intended workloads. Istio's control plane listens for the creation of these resources and discovers that *now* a path exists to route cross-cluster traffic. Thus it updates all workloads with the newly discovered endpoints in the remote cluster.

VALIDATING CROSS-CLUSTER WORKLOAD DISCOVERY

Now, as the workloads in the east-cluster are exposed to the west-cluster, we expect that the Envoy clusters of the webapp have an endpoint to the catalog workload.

This endpoint should point to the east-west gateway's address, which proxies the request to the `catalog` workload in its network. To check this, let's get the address of the east-west gateway in the `east-cluster`:

```
$  keast -n istio-system get svc istio-eastwestgateway \
      -o jsonpath='{.status.loadBalancer.ingress[0].ip}'

40.114.190.251
```

Now, let's compare it to the address that the workloads in the `west-cluster` use when routing cross-cluster traffic:

```
$  iwest pc endpoints deploy/webapp.istioinaction | grep catalog
```

In figure 12.16 we show our output of the previous command.

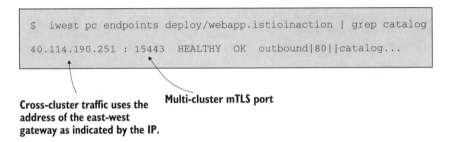

Cross-cluster traffic uses the address of the east-west gateway as indicated by the IP.

Multi-cluster mTLS port

Figure 12.16   The `catalog` endpoint refers to the east-west gateway multi-cluster port

If the endpoint of the `catalog` resource matches the address of the east-west gateway, then the workloads are discovered, and cross-cluster traffic is possible. Considering the proxy configuration, everything is set up correctly. Let's trigger a request manually and make this the final validation:

```
$  EXT_IP=$(kwest -n istio-system get svc istio-ingressgateway \
      -o jsonpath='{.status.loadBalancer.ingress[0].ip}')

$  curl http://$EXT_IP/api/catalog -H "Host: webapp.istioinaction.io"

[
  {
    "id": 0,
    "color": "teal",
    "department": "Clothing",
    "name": "Small Metal Shoes",
    "price": "232.00"
  }
]
```

Hooray! We see that when we triggered a request to the ingress gateway, it was routed to the webapp in the `west-cluster`. Then it was resolved to the `catalog` workload in the east-cluster, which in the end served the request. With that, we have validated that the multi-cluster, multi-network, multi-control plane service mesh is set up and workloads are discovered across clusters; they can initiate mutually authenticated connections using east-west gateways as a passthrough.

Let's recap what was required to set up a multi-cluster service mesh:

1 *Cross-cluster workload discovery* by providing each control plane with access to the peer cluster, using the kubeconfig containing the service account token and certificates. The process was facilitated using istioctl, and we only applied it to the opposite clusters.

2 *Cross-cluster workload connectivity* by configuring east-west gateways to route traffic between workloads in different clusters (that reside in different networks) and labeling each cluster with network information so that Istio knows the network workloads reside in.

3 *Configuring trust between clusters* by using a common root of trust that issues the intermediate certificates of the opposite clusters.

That's just a few steps, and they are mostly automated to set up multi-cluster service meshes. In the next section, let's verify some of the service-mesh behaviors across clusters.

12.3.7 *Load-balancing across clusters*

In chapter 6, we promised to explore cross-cluster, locality-aware load balancing. And now, with the multi-cluster service mesh at hand, we are ready to do so. To demonstrate this, we'll deploy two sample services, each of which is configured to return the name of the cluster in which the workload is running. Thus we can easily determine the locality of the workload that served the request.

Let's deploy the first service in the west-cluster:

```
$ kwest apply -f \                                      ◁──── Deploys a simple
ch12/locality-aware/west/simple-backend-deployment.yaml         backend deployment
                                                                in the west-cluster

$ kwest apply -f \
ch12/locality-aware/west/simple-backend-svc.yaml        ◁──── Kubernetes service for the
                                                                simple backend deployment

$ kwest apply -f \
ch12/locality-aware/west/simple-backend-gw.yaml         ◁──── Applies a Gateway
                                                                resource to admit traffic

$ kwest apply -f \
ch12/locality-aware/west/simple-backend-vs.yaml         ◁──── Applies a VirtualService resource
                                                                that routes traffic from the Gateway
                                                                to the simple backend workloads
```

As soon as the resources are created, we make a request to the service in the west-cluster and see that it returns the cluster name:

```
$ curl -s $EXT_IP -H "Host: simple-backend.istioinaction.io" | jq ".body"

"Hello from WEST"
```

Now we can deploy the service in the `east-cluster`:

```
$  keast apply -f ch12/locality-aware/east/simple-backend-deployment.yaml
$  keast apply -f ch12/locality-aware/east/simple-backend-svc.yaml
```

With the services running in both clusters, their endpoints are configured in the ingress gateway, and requests are load-balanced between them (see figure 12.17).

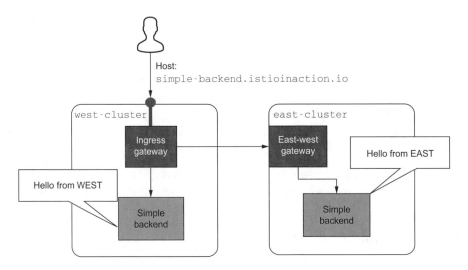

Figure 12.17   Cross-cluster load balancing

By default, Istio load-balances between workloads using the round-robin algorithm. Thus traffic is load-balanced equally:

```
$  for i in {1..10}; do curl --max-time 5 -s $EXT_IP \
    -H "Host: simple-backend.istioinaction.io" | jq .body; done

"Hello from EAST"
"Hello from WEST"
<...>
```

That's good! However, performance can be improved further using locality-aware load balancing so workloads prioritize routing traffic to workloads within their locality. We mentioned in previous chapters that cloud providers add the locality information into nodes as labels. Istio uses this information retrieved from the labels to configure the locality of workloads.

VERIFYING LOCALITY-AWARE ROUTING ACROSS CLUSTERS

Because we created the multi-cluster service mesh in Azure, the nodes are labeled with locality information from the cloud provider, as shown in this output:

```
$ kwest get nodes -o custom-columns="\
NAME:{.metadata.name},\
```

```
REGION:{.metadata.labels.topology\.kubernetes\.io/region},\
ZONE:{metadata.labels.topology\.kubernetes\.io/zone}"    ◁─── Formats the output to
                                                              show the node name,
NAME                                 REGION    ZONE          region, and zone
aks-nodepool1-31209271-vmss000003    westus    0
```

As expected, the node in the west-cluster is labeled with the westus region. Checking the east-cluster shows the eastus region. This information is picked up by istiod and propagated to the workloads when configuring the endpoints:

```
$ iwest pc endpoints deploy/istio-ingressgateway.istio-system \
    --cluster \
    'outbound|80||simple-backend.istioinaction.svc.cluster.local' \
    -o json

[{
   "name": "outbound|80||simple-backend.istioinaction.svc.cluster.local",
   "addedViaApi": true,
   "hostStatuses": [
        {
            "address": <omitted>,
            "stats": <omitted>,
            "healthStatus": {
                "edsHealthStatus": "HEALTHY"
            },
            "weight": 1,
            "locality": {
                "region": "westus",   │ Locality information of the
                "zone": "0"           │ workload in the west-cluster
            }
        },
        {
            "address": <omitted>,
            "stats": <omitted>,
            "healthStatus": {
                "edsHealthStatus": "HEALTHY"
            },
            "weight": 1,
            "locality": {
                "region": "eastus",   │ Locality information of the
                "zone": "0"           │ workload in the east-cluster
            }
        }
    ],
   "circuitBreakers": <omitted>
}]
```

The output shows that both endpoints have locality information. Recall from chapter 6 that in order for Istio to use locality information, passive health checking is required. Let's apply a destination rule that uses outlier detection to passively check the health of the endpoints:

```
$ kwest apply -f ch12/locality-aware/west/simple-backend-dr.yaml
```

After the configuration propagates, which usually takes a couple of seconds, we can verify that requests use the locality information and are routed within the same cluster:

```
$  for i in {1..10}; do curl --max-time 5 -s $EXT_IP \
      -H "Host: simple-backend.istioinaction.io" | jq .body; done

"Hello from WEST"
"Hello from WEST"
"Hello from WEST"
<...>
```

As expected, all requests are routed within the west-cluster, which is the closest to the ingress gateway that's routing the traffic. Because all the routing decisions are made in the Envoy proxy, we can conclude that the control plane must have modified its configuration, which explains the different behavior. Let's see how the configuration was modified by printing it again:

```
$  iwest pc endpoints deploy/istio-ingressgateway.istio-system \
      --cluster \
      'outbound|80||simple-backend.istioinaction.svc.cluster.local' \
      -o json

[{
  "name": "outbound|80||simple-backend.istioinaction.svc.cluster.local",
  "addedViaApi": true,
  "hostStatuses": [
      {
          <omitted>
          "weight": 1,
          "locality": {
              "region": "westus",
              "zone": "0"
          }
      },
      {
          <omitted>
          "weight": 1,
          "priority": 1,          ◁──── Priority of 1 for
          "locality": {                  the second host
              "region": "eastus",
              "zone": "0"
          }
      }
  ],
  "circuitBreakers": <omitted>
}]
```

Now we see the priority field that specifies the priority for traffic to be routed to this host. The highest priority is 0 (the default, when not specified)—that is why it's missing from the host in westus, which has the highest priority. A value of 1 has a lower priority, and so on. When hosts with the highest priority are unavailable, traffic is routed to those with a lower priority. Let's verify this.

VERIFYING CROSS-CLUSTER FAILOVER

To simulate that the simple backend deployment is failing, we can configure it to fail requests by setting the environment variable ERROR_RATE to 1. Let's do so for the workload in the west-cluster:

```
$  kwest -n istioinaction set env \
      deploy simple-backend-west ERROR_RATE='1'
```

After some time passes, outlier detection detects that the host is unhealthy and routes traffic to the workload in the east-cluster, which has the second-highest priority:

```
$  for i in {1..10}; do curl --max-time 5 -s $EXT_IP \
      -H "Host: simple-backend.istioinaction.io" | jq .body; done

"Hello from EAST"
"Hello from EAST"
"Hello from EAST"
<...>
```

This shows the cross-cluster failover in action: traffic was routed to the east-cluster because the workloads with the highest priority failed the passive health checks.

> **NOTE** As seen in this detailed walkthrough, cross-cluster traffic traverses the opposite cluster's east-west gateway and is treated as an SNI passthrough. This has implications for load balancing *once traffic reaches the remote cluster*. Since this call is an SNI/TCP connection and the gateway *does not terminate* the TLS connection, the east-west gateway can only forward the connection *as is* to the backend service. This opens a connection from the east-west gateway to the backend service *and does not have request-level load-balancing* capabilities. Thus, on failover or load balancing across multiple clusters, the load is balanced or failed over *from the client's point of view* but not necessarily balanced evenly across all instances on the remote cluster.

VERIFYING CROSS-CLUSTER ACCESS CONTROL USING AUTHORIZATION POLICIES

The last feature we will verify is access control across clusters. Recall that access control requires that traffic is mutually authenticated between workloads, producing reliable metadata that can be used to decide whether to admit or deny traffic. To demonstrate this, let's come up with a scenario. Suppose we want to admit traffic to the service *only* if its source is Istio's ingress gateway; otherwise, the traffic is denied. A policy to achieve that is defined and stored in the file ch12/security/only-ingress-policy.yaml. Apply it to the east-cluster:

```
$  keast apply -f ch12/security/allow-only-ingress-policy.yaml

authorizationpolicy.security.istio.io/allow-only-ingress created
```

Before executing any requests, let's clean up the service from the west-cluster so that only the instance in the east-cluster serves the traffic:

```
$ kwest delete deploy simple-backend-west -n istioinaction

deployment.apps "simple-backend-west" deleted
```

After the update is propagated, we can test the policy by triggering a request from a workload in the west-cluster. For that we will run a temporary Pod:

```
$ kubectl run -i --rm --restart=Never sleep --image=curlimages/curl \
--command -- curl -s simple-backend.istioinaction.svc.cluster.local

RBAC: access denied
```

As expected, the request was denied. Meanwhile, triggering a request to the ingress gateway and having the request routed from the gateway results in a successful response:

```
$ curl --max-time 5 -s $EXT_IP \
    -H "Host: simple-backend.istioinaction.io" | jq .body

"Hello from EAST"
```

We can see that the policy admitted the traffic originating from the ingress gateway. This shows that workloads were mutually authenticating across clusters, and policies could use the authenticated data encoded into the identity certificates for access control.

All our examples of load balancing, locality-aware routing, cross-cluster failover, mutually authenticated traffic, and access control demonstrate that workloads in multi-cluster service meshes can use all of Istio's capabilities regardless of the cluster in which they run. And they do so without requiring any additional configuration.

> **NOTE** Remember to clean up resources in the cloud provider. If you are using Azure, you can execute the script $ sh ch12/scripts/cleanup-azure-resources.sh.

Hopefully, this chapter has shown you how Istio can scale within your organization and incorporate multiple clusters into a single mesh and why this is important for many organizations. In the next chapter, we integrate virtual machines into the service mesh, which is a highly desirable feature for mature enterprises that have to operate legacy workloads.

Summary

- Istio supports three multi-cluster service mesh deployment models: single control plane (primary-remote), replicated control planes (primary-primary), and external control plane.
- We can establish common trust across clusters using plug-in CA certificates by installing intermediate certificates in the istio-system namespace.
- Cross-cluster workloads are discovered in replicated control-plane deployment models using service accounts as an identity in the remote cluster and making the service account token available to the opposite cluster as a secret.
- We can bridge the networks of multi-network service meshes using east-west gateways. The sni-dnat router mode configures SNI clusters to route cross-cluster traffic in a fine-grained manner.
- The east-west gateway can be configured to auto passthrough traffic and route based on the automatically configured SNI clusters.
- Istio's capabilities work across clusters in the same way they do within a cluster.

Incorporating virtual machine workloads into the mesh

This chapter covers

- Incorporating legacy workloads into Istio's service mesh
- Installing and configuring the `istio-agent` in VMs
- Provisioning identity for VMs
- Exposing cluster services to VMs, and vice versa
- Using the local DNS proxy to resolve FQDNs of cluster services

So far, we've covered the Istio service mesh from the perspective of containers and Kubernetes. In reality, however, workloads frequently run on virtual machines (VMs) or physical machines. Containers and Kubernetes are often used in an effort to modernize a technology stack, and this chapter shows how to bridge these two worlds at the application-networking layer with Istio. You may wonder why we don't simply modernize legacy workloads and run them in a Kubernetes cluster instead of integrating VMs into the mesh. We recommend that approach whenever it's possible, but in a few cases it's not—or at least, not when considering the cost:

- Enterprises may have to run the workloads on-premises—due to regulatory compliance—where they lack the expertise to set up and operate Kubernetes clusters.
- Containerizing applications is not that simple. Some apps may require rearchitecting; others might have dependencies that need to be updated but that conflict with other dependencies—dependency hell.
- Some have some unique dependencies on the VM they run on.

In this chapter, we show how any workload can become part of the mesh by installing and configuring the sidecar proxy. This approach provides interesting capabilities for enterprises that have legacy workloads and want to integrate them into the mesh in a resilient, secure, and highly available manner.

13.1 Istio's VM support

The integration of VMs into the mesh was supported from Istio's early days, but it required a ton of workarounds and automation external to the control plane. Istio's VM support graduated to beta in Istio 1.9.0 once some of the key features were implemented and the APIs settled on a suitable approach. Those key features are

- Sidecar proxy installation and configuration in a VM were simplified using `istioctl`.
- High availability of VMs was achieved by introducing two new Istio resources: `WorkloadGroup` and `WorkloadEntry`.
- DNS resolution of in-mesh services from VMs was made possible using a local DNS proxy, which is set up alongside Istio's sidecar.

Because there is a lot of information to juggle in this chapter, we begin by covering these new features at a high level. Then we put them into action with a concrete example by integrating a VM into the mesh.

13.1.1 Simplifying sidecar proxy installation and configuration in a VM

For the VM to become part of the mesh, we need to

- Install the sidecar proxy to manage network traffic
- Configure the proxy to connect to `istiod` and receive the mesh configuration
- Provide the VM with an identity token, used to authenticate to `istiod`

Figure 13.1 shows the prerequisites needed for any workload to become part of the mesh. The same steps are required for workloads running in Kubernetes as well:

- Install and configure the sidecar automatically with the webhook or using `istioctl`.
- Possess an identity token—Kubernetes injects it automatically into the Pod.

These conveniences do not extend to workloads external to Kubernetes. Thus VM owners must install and configure the proxy and provision a bootstrap token for workload identity—and only then can a workload become a part of the mesh.

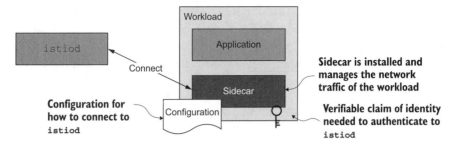

Figure 13.1 What it takes for a workload to become part of the mesh

A CLOSER LOOK AT PROVISIONING IDENTITY FOR VMS

Istio uses Kubernetes as the source of trust to provision the VM's identity. This works by generating a token in Kubernetes and transferring it to the machine. This token is picked up by the istio-agent installed in the machine and used to authenticate to istiod. Figures 13.2 and 13.3 show the differences between the way identity is provisioned for cluster workloads versus those in VMs.

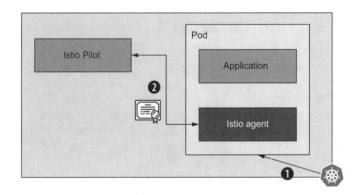

Figure 13.2 Workloads in the cluster (1) get the service account token injected into the Pod and (2) use the token to authenticate and retrieve an SVID.

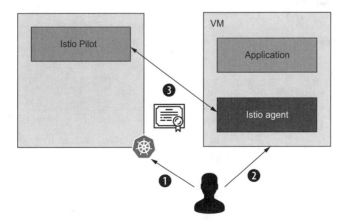

Figure 13.3 Because VMs are external, they require manual steps to (1) create a service account, (2) transfer the token to the VM, and (3) use the token to authenticate and receive an SVID.

The approaches are similar, with the sole difference that Kubernetes injects the token automatically into Pods. In contrast, for VMs, this has to be done by service mesh operators, which have to manually transfer the token securely to the VM. The istio-agent uses this token to authenticate to istiod and, as a result, istiod issues its identity in the form of a SPIFFE Verifiable Identity Document (SVID).

The drawback of this solution is that it requires service mesh operators to automate creating the tokens in Kubernetes and securely transferring them to VMs. This may not require a lot of effort, but if the organization follows a multi-cloud strategy, as most do, then it quickly adds up to a lot of effort.

Platform-assigned identity

There is work in progress in the Istio community to provide an automated solution to provision workload identity for machines in different cloud providers. This solution uses the platform-assigned identity of a VM as the source of trust, which is picked up by the istio-agent and used to authenticate to istiod. Understandably, Istio will expose an API to configure the validation of the token against the cloud provider. The entire process is visualized here:

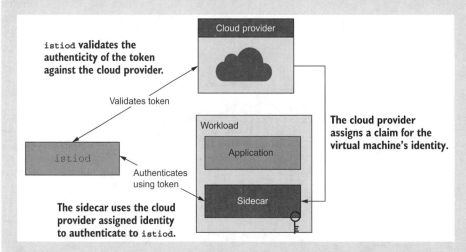

How the platform-assigned identity is used to authenticate workloads

This solution is still not developed, but you can find more about it in the design documentation for the identity provider at http://mng.bz/zQGa.

In our example that follows, we use Kubernetes as the source of trust to provision the identity of the machine. To keep the chapter snappy, we'll manually transfer the token to the VM.

13.1.2 *Virtual machine high availability*

To achieve high availability of VMs, Istio closely mimics the approach Kubernetes takes with its containerized workloads. Basically, Kubernetes achieves high availability with the following resources:

- Deployments, as higher-level resources, contain the configuration of how replicas should be created.
- Pods are the replicas created from that configuration. This ensures that nothing is unique about Pods, which can then be disposed of and replaced whenever they are not healthy (or scaled down when not needed), thus maintaining a highly available service.

The resources that Istio introduces for VMs closely align with the Kubernetes concepts of Deployments and Pods:

- The WorkloadGroup resource is similar to Kubernetes' Deployments as it defines the template for how the workloads it manages are configured. It specifies common properties such as the port in which the application is exposed, the labels assigned to the instances of the group, the service account that represents the workload's identity in the mesh, and how to probe the health of the application.
- The WorkloadEntry is similar to Kubernetes Pods. It represents a single VM that serves end-user traffic. In addition to the common properties defined by the WorkloadGroup, the WorkloadEntry possesses unique properties such as the address and health status of the instance it represents.

A WorkloadEntry can be created manually; however, the recommended approach is to use *workload auto-registration*, where newly provisioned workloads join the mesh automatically.

UNDERSTANDING WORKLOAD AUTO-REGISTRATION

During workload auto-registration, a workload connects to the control plane (using the configuration supplied to it) and authenticates itself as a member of a Workload-Group using the identity token. When this is done successfully, the control plane creates a WorkloadEntry to represent the VM in the mesh (see figure 13.4).

The representation of the VM in the mesh using a WorkloadEntry is important for many reasons. In particular, it can be selected by Kubernetes services or Istio Service-Entry resources using label selectors and used as the backend to route traffic to. Selecting workloads using Kubernetes services (that is, their fully qualified domain name [FQDN] in the cluster) and not their actual addresses makes it possible to dispose of workloads when they are not healthy or easily spin up new ones to meet increased demand without any knowledge or impact on the client side.

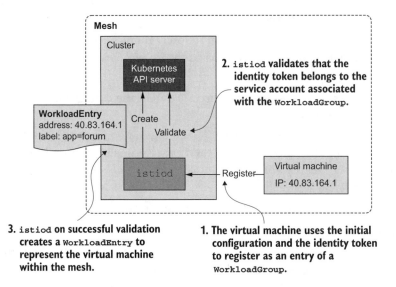

2. `istiod` **validates that the identity token belongs to the service account associated with the** `WorkloadGroup`.

3. `istiod` **on successful validation creates a** `WorkloadEntry` **to represent the virtual machine within the mesh.**

1. The virtual machine uses the initial configuration and the identity token to register as an entry of a `WorkloadGroup`.

Figure 13.4   **The workload auto-registration process**

Figure 13.5 illustrates how services can be used to target workload entries and Pods. You might want to do that to, for instance, reduce the risk when migrating from legacy workloads running in VMs to modernized workloads running in a Kubernetes cluster. This is done by running workloads in parallel and then using the traffic-shifting capabilities of the service mesh (as described in chapter 5) to gradually move all traffic from VMs to Pods, with the option of shifting traffic back to the VMs if there is an increase in errors.

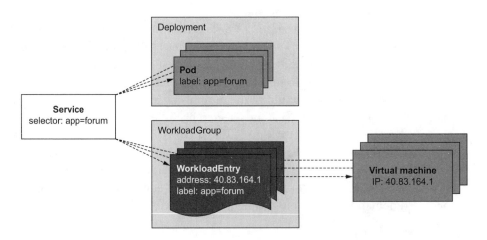

Figure 13.5   `WorkloadGroup` and `WorkloadEntry` **relation to Deployments and Pods**

Understanding the health checks performed by Istio

After becoming part of the service mesh, a workload needs to be ready to receive traffic and is probed by health checks. To maintain high availability of a service, we need two types of health checks (which are similar to how Kubernetes does health checking):

- *Readiness probes* check whether a workload is ready to receive traffic once it starts.
- *Liveness probes* check whether the application is healthy once it's running; if not, it should be restarted.

Liveness probes are not a service mesh concern! Ensuring the liveness of a workload is a platform feature where workloads are run. For example, Kubernetes, which is also a platform, performs liveness checks using the probes defined in the Deployment configuration. Similarly, when running workloads on VMs in the cloud, we need to use the features of the cloud to implement liveness probes and take corrective actions to heal the VM if the probe fails, such as provisioning a new instance.

To get you started, here are the docs for liveness checks and auto-healing for the three most popular cloud providers:

- Azure implements automatic instance repairs for VM scale sets: http://mng.bz/0wrx.
- Amazon Web Services implements health checks for auto-scale group instances: http://mng.bz/KB4K.
- Google Cloud Platform implements health checking and auto-healing for managed instance groups: http://mng.bz/9KNl.

How Istio performs readiness probes in VMs

The application's readiness to receive traffic is probed periodically by the `istio-agent`, according to the specification in the `WorkloadGroup` definition. The agent reports the application's health status to `istiod`, such as when the status switches from healthy to unhealthy or vice versa (see figure 13.6).

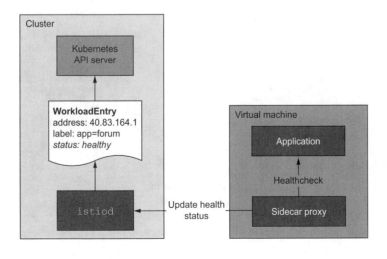

Figure 13.6 The sidecar proxy updates `istiod` with health information for the application.

The control plane uses the health status to determine whether traffic should be routed to a workload. For example, when the application is healthy, the data plane is configured with the endpoint of the VM that hosts the application. And the opposite is also true: the endpoint is removed from the data plane when the application is unhealthy.

As a service mesh operator, you have to configure the readiness checks of the application in the `WorkloadGroup` and create liveness checks in the infrastructure layer by following your cloud provider's recommended practices. We recommend using different configurations for liveness and readiness probes:

- Readiness probes performed by the `istio-agent` should be aggressive and prevent traffic from being routed to an instance that is returning errors.
- Liveness probes performed by the cloud provider should be more conservative and allow the VM time to recover.

Aim to avoid killing instances too hastily, which would terminate inflight requests without a grace period, causing end-user visible failures. A good rule of thumb is for *readiness probes to always fail before liveness probes.*

13.1.3 *DNS resolution of in-mesh services*

Because VMs are external to the Kubernetes cluster, they lack access to its internal DNS server. As a result, VMs cannot resolve the hostnames for cluster services. Providing a solution to this is the last milestone to integrate VMs into the service mesh.

You may wonder why we need DNS resolution in the first place. Doesn't the service proxy, deployed along with the application, possess the configuration to route traffic to all workloads? You're correct: the proxy has the configuration for how to route traffic! However, the issue lies in getting the traffic out of the application and to the proxy. A precondition for that to happen is for the hostname to be resolved. If it isn't, the traffic never leaves the application and cannot be redirected to the Envoy proxy. This issue is visualized in figure 13.7.

Previously, cluster hostnames were commonly resolved using a private DNS server configured with all Kubernetes services. The VMs were configured to use this as a

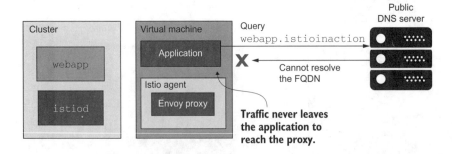

Figure 13.7   Outbound traffic never reaches the Envoy proxy because DNS resolution fails.

nameserver to which they sent DNS queries. Due to the dynamic nature of workloads in Kubernetes, the process of configuring the private DNS server had to be automated using a Kubernetes controller that listens for these changes and keeps the DNS server synchronized. `external-dns` (https://github.com/kubernetes-sigs/external-dns) is an open source solution that does exactly that.

However, that is a workaround and not an integrated solution that service mesh users would like. Later versions of Istio (1.8 and onward) introduced a local DNS proxy to the `istio-agent` sidecar, which is configured with all in-mesh services by `istiod` (see figure 13.8). The DNS proxy runs in Istio's sidecar alongside the Envoy proxy and handles DNS queries from the application, which are redirected to the DNS proxy using Iptable rules—the usual Istio traffic-capture approach. This differs slightly when using `istio-cni`.

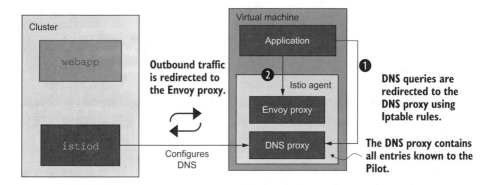

Figure 13.8   DNS queries are redirected to the DNS proxy for resolution, which is configured with the in-cluster services by `istiod`.

To keep the DNS proxy continuously updated, Istio introduced a new API called the Name Discovery Service (NDS). With the NDS, the control plane synchronizes the data plane with new DNS entries whenever a Kubernetes service or Istio `ServiceEntry` is added to the mesh. However, the DNS proxy is not limited to VMs. It enables a host of additional features, as described in the official Istio blog post at https://istio.io/latest/blog/2020/dns-proxy.

And with this, we conclude the discussion of the high-level concepts and their objectives. Next, let's put them into action by integrating a VM into the service mesh.

13.2   Setting up the infrastructure

Figure 13.9 shows the infrastructure we will set up to showcase mesh expansion. We will create a Kubernetes cluster and a VM, which will host our *cool-store* application:

- The `webapp` and `catalogs` services are deployed in the Kubernetes cluster.
- The `forum` service is deployed in a VM.

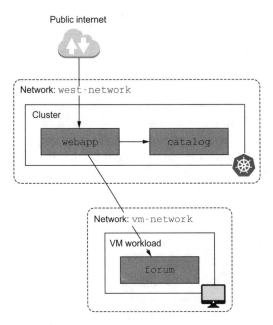

Figure 13.9 Virtual machine integration in the service mesh

It's noteworthy that the cluster and the VM are in different networks, which requires an east-west gateway to reverse-proxy traffic from the VM to the cluster services

13.2.1 Setting up the service mesh

In this chapter, we create the infrastructure in Azure. However, if you are using another cloud provider, you don't have to worry; as soon as you set up the infrastructure, all the other steps will work the same. Furthermore, because setting up this infrastructure could exceed the free tiers of cloud providers, we structured the chapter so that you can understand the process by just tagging along and not necessarily executing the steps.

We begin by creating a Kubernetes cluster:

```
$  sh ch13/scripts/create-cluster-in-azure.sh

== Create cluster ==
Cluster created

== Configure access to the cluster for kubectl ==
Merged "west-cluster" as current context in ~/.kube/config
```

With the cluster created and kubectl configured to access it, we are ready to deploy Istio to it. Because the cluster and the VM are in different networks, we need to label the Istio installation namespace with the network information:

```
$  kubectl create namespace istio-system

$  kubectl label namespace istio-system \
     topology.istio.io/network=west-network
```

Now we install the control plane and specify the west network:

```
$ istioctl install -y -f ch13/controlplane/cluster-in-west-network.yaml
```

After installing the control plane, we deploy the *cool-store* services:

```
$ kubectl create ns istioinaction
$ kubectl label namespace istioinaction \
    istio-injection=enabled
```
> **Creates and labels the namespace**

```
$ kubectl -n istioinaction apply \
    -f ch12/webapp-deployment-svc.yaml
$ kubectl -n istioinaction apply \
    -f ch12/webapp-gw-vs.yaml
```
> **Deploys the webapp and creates a service for it**

> **Deploys the catalog and creates a service for it**

```
$ kubectl -n istioinaction apply \
    -f ch12/catalog.yaml
```

We deploy and expose the workloads through Istio's ingress gateway. Let's trigger an HTTP request to verify the configuration:

```
$ EXT_IP=$(kubectl -n istio-system get svc istio-ingressgateway -o \
    jsonpath='{.status.loadBalancer.ingress[0].ip}')

$ curl -H "Host: webapp.istioinaction.io" \
    http://$EXT_IP/api/catalog/items/1

{
  "id": 1,
  "color": "amber",
  "department": "Eyewear",
  "name": "Elinor Glasses",
  "price": "282.00"
}
```

If your outcome differs, it's likely because you were too fast, and the workloads are not ready to receive traffic. Verify that the workloads are ready, and try again. On a successful response, we are ready to move to the next section.

13.2.2 *Provisioning the VM*

We are getting closer to the crux of this chapter: the VM. We will provision it in Azure in its own private network, with the following properties (yours doesn't have to be the same; but if it isn't, the scripts and commands shown here may not work for you):

- The operating system of the VM is Ubuntu 18.04. Istio releases binaries only for the Debian and Red Hat distributions. For any other distribution, you have to build the binaries for the `istio-agent` from the source code.
- It has a public IP address so the cluster can access it. Keep in mind that this is only for demonstration purposes. In real scenarios, you can peer the networks so that the VM and the cluster can connect through a private connection.

- It is accessible with a Secure Shell (SSH) connection. To configure the VM for remote access, we added SSH keys in the directory ch13/keys/ that scripts and commands use when creating the machine.
- The application port 8080 is exposed so that cluster services can reach the forum application listening on that port.

NOTE Keep in mind that your VM can have a different set of properties (the ones we listed are only for demonstration purposes in this chapter). For example, your VM may be in the cluster's private network and not have a publicly accessible IP address, and it will still work as long as you ensure that there is a connection between the VM and the control plane.

The following script creates a VM with these properties, exposes the application port, and configures it for remote access:

```
$ sh ch13/scripts/create-vm-in-azure.sh
```

It will take some time until the machine is up and running. Once it is running, verify that remote access is possible. A simple way to verify that is to list the files in the VM. Begin by retrieving the VM IP address:

```
$ VM_IP=$(az vm show -d --resource-group west-cluster-rg \
    --name forum-vm | jq .publicIps -r)
```

And then execute the command:

```
$ ssh -i ch13/keys/id_rsa azureuser@$VM_IP -- ls -la
```

If the command lists the directories, the VM is accessible, and remote shell connections are possible. Another useful validation that can spare us headaches is ensuring that we have opened the application port 8080 (our applications port) in the infrastructure layer so that workloads in the cluster can initiate TCP connections to it. We can do that using the Nmap utility. Nmap is an open source command-line tool used to explore networks (such as by scanning the open ports of a VM); it is available for the majority of operating systems from most package managers (apt, yum, Homebrew, and Chocolatey). After installing it, validate that port 8080 is accessible using the following command:

```
$ nmap -Pn -p 8080 $VM_IP
```

Our output is shown in figure 13.10. If your output matches, the port is accessible! If not, you need to configure the infrastructure to expose that port. Pay attention where the figure shows that the port state is closed, which means that currently no application is listening for packets on that port. That will change when we run the application later; for now, everything is ready for us to integrate the workload into the mesh.

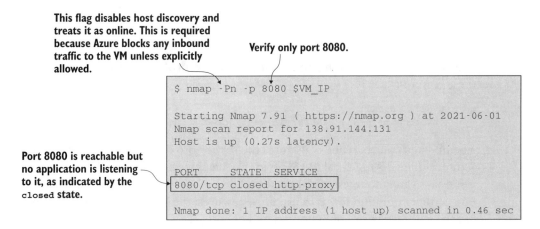

This flag disables host discovery and treats it as online. This is required because Azure blocks any inbound traffic to the VM unless explicitly allowed.

Verify only port 8080.

```
$ nmap -Pn -p 8080 $VM_IP

Starting Nmap 7.91 ( https://nmap.org ) at 2021-06-01
Nmap scan report for 138.91.144.131
Host is up (0.27s latency).

PORT      STATE  SERVICE
8080/tcp closed http-proxy

Nmap done: 1 IP address (1 host up) scanned in 0.46 sec
```

Port 8080 is reachable but no application is listening to it, as indicated by the `closed` state.

Figure 13.10   Using the Nmap utility to verify that port 8080 is accessible

13.3 Mesh expansion to VMs

The features to integrate a VM are in the beta phase[1] and not enabled by default. Hence we need to update the Istio installation using the following IstioOperator definition, which enables the following features: workload auto registration, health checks, capturing DNS queries, and redirecting those queries to the DNS proxy. These features, as covered earlier in this chapter, are required to integrate a VM into the mesh:

```
apiVersion: install.istio.io/v1alpha1
metadata:
  name: istio-controlplane
  namespace: istio-system
kind: IstioOperator
spec:
  profile: demo
  components:
    egressGateways:
    - name: istio-egressgateway
      enabled: false
  meshConfig:
    defaultConfig:
      proxyMetadata:
        ISTIO_META_DNS_CAPTURE: "true"      ⟵ DNS queries are captured and
  values:                                      redirected to the DNS proxy.
    pilot:
      env:                                                      Workloads can
        PILOT_ENABLE_WORKLOAD_ENTRY_AUTOREGISTRATION: true  ⟵ auto-register to
        PILOT_ENABLE_WORKLOAD_ENTRY_HEALTHCHECKS: true  ⟵  the control plane.
    global:                                                Workloads in VMs
      meshID: usmesh                                       are health-checked.
```

---

[1] To learn more about Istio's feature phases, check the documentation at https://istio.io/latest/docs/releases/feature-stages/.

```
multiCluster:
  clusterName: west-cluster
network: west-network
```

Execute the following command to update the control-plane installation and enable these features:

```
$ istioctl install -y -f \
    ch13/controlplane/cluster-in-west-network-with-vm-features.yaml
```

The updated control plane configures the service proxies to capture DNS queries and redirect them to the local DNS proxy in the sidecar for resolution. Furthermore, workloads can auto-register and perform and report health status to istiod. There is one further condition for us to use those features: the VM must be able to connect to istiod and receive its configuration and identity. This is what we tackle next!

13.3.1 Exposing istiod and cluster services to the VM

To become part of the mesh, the VM must be able to talk to istiod and initiate connections to the cluster services. This works out of the box when the VM and the cluster are in the same network; but in our case, they are in separate networks and require an east-west gateway to proxy the traffic to the Istio control plane or workloads.

Let's install the east-west gateway as we did in the previous chapter:

```
$ istioctl install -y -f ch13/gateways/cluster-east-west-gw.yaml

✓ Ingress gateways installed
✓ Installation complete
```

With the gateway installed, we can expose the needed ports for the VM to access cluster services and istiod. Figure 13.11 shows the exposed ports that enable the VM to connect to istiod and the cluster services. Let's initially expose the multi-cluster mTLS port (15443) that reverse-proxies requests from the VM to the in-mesh services:

```
$ kubectl apply -f ch13/expose-services.yaml

gateway.networking.istio.io/cross-network-gateway created
```

The east-west gateway routes traffic to the service istiod.istio-system on port 443, which then targets port 15017.

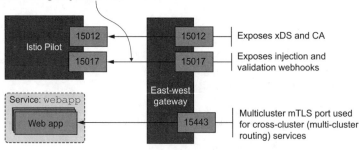

Figure 13.11 The ports that expose istiod and cluster services to the VM

Next, we expose the `istiod` ports by applying a `Gateway` resource and a `Virtual-Service` resource to admit traffic and route it to `istiod`. We configure both by applying the following file:

```
$  kubectl apply -f ch13/expose-istiod.yaml

gateway.networking.istio.io/istiod-gateway created
virtualservice.networking.istio.io/istiod-vs created
```

With the infrastructure created, the updated control plane, and the ability for the proxy to talk to the control plane, we have come a long way toward integrating VMs into the service mesh. What's left is to create a `WorkloadGroup` that represents the group of workloads the VM belongs to.

13.3.2 Representing a group of workloads with a WorkloadGroup

The `WorkloadGroup` defines the common properties of the VMs that are members of it, including application-specific information such as what ports are exposed and how to test the application's readiness to receive traffic. For example, the common properties for the `forum` workloads are defined in this `WorkloadGroup`:

```
apiVersion: networking.istio.io/v1alpha3
kind: WorkloadGroup
metadata:
  name: forum
  namespace: forum-services
spec:
  metadata:
    annotations: {}
    labels:
      app: forum          ◁──┐  Services can target workloads
                               in this group using labels.
  template:
    ports:
      http: 8080                    Validates that workloads possess an
    serviceAccount: forum-sa  ◁──┘  authentication token from forum-sa
                                     to register to this workload group
    network: vm-network   ◁────
  probe:                    ◁──────┐  Enables Istio to configure direct
    periodSeconds: 5                  access between workloads in
    initialDelaySeconds: 1           the same network
    httpGet:                    The istio-agent that runs in the instances of
      port: 8080                this workload group checks the readiness of
      path: /api/healthz        the app by making HTTP GET requests on
                                port 8080 and path /api/healthz.
```

Some of the relevant properties for integrating a VM into the service mesh are as follows:

- `labels`—Enables Kubernetes services to select the workload entries that register to this `WorkloadGroup`.
- `network`—Using this property, the control plane configures service proxies to route traffic to the VM: if it's the same network, use the IP address; otherwise, use the east-west gateway deployed in that network.

- serviceAccount—Represents the identity of the workloads. For a workload to register as a member of this group, it must represent a claim for the service account identity.

Let's create the namespace and service account and then apply the WorkloadGroup configuration to the cluster:

```
$   kubectl create namespace forum-services
$   kubectl create serviceaccount forum-sa -n forum-services
$   kubectl apply -f ch13/workloadgroup.yaml
```

What happens after we apply the WorkloadGroup? Now the cluster is configured to auto-register workloads that can represent a valid token for the service account forum-sa as specified in the WorkloadGroup.

GENERATING THE CONFIGURATION FOR THE VM'S SIDECAR

Besides facilitating workload auto-registration, the WorkloadGroup can be used to generate the common configuration for VMs in this group. Using istioctl, creating the VM configuration is pretty simple. It uses the information in the WorkloadGroup and queries the Kubernetes cluster for additional information needed to generate the configuration for the instances of that WorkloadGroup. For example, the following command generates the configuration for the machines hosting the forum workload:

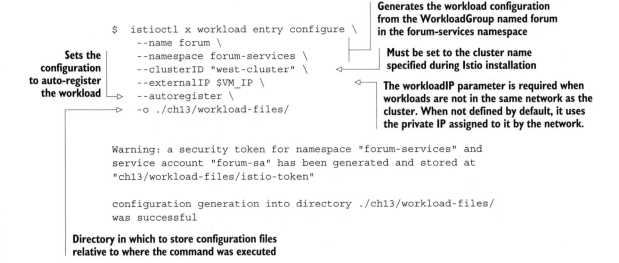

That was easy! If you check the generated configuration, you'll find a number of moving pieces. You don't have to know all of them; however, doing so will simplify troubleshooting issues that you may face. For that reason, we discuss the configuration in more detail in appendix E.

What's important to know at a high level is that the files contain the following:

- The east-west gateway IP address through which istiod is exposed.

- The root certificate to validate the authenticity of the certificate presented by istiod. It's a precursor to initiating a secure connection between the service proxy and istiod.
- The service account token to authenticate as a member of the forum WorkloadGroup, to istiod.
- Configuration about the service mesh, the network, and the common properties, as defined in the WorkloadGroup.

In the presence of this configuration, the service proxy can start a secure connection to the control plane, get its SVID, and receive its Envoy configuration via xDS to become a member of the mesh.

TRANSFERRING THE GENERATED FILES TO THE VM

Because the configuration files contain sensitive data—specifically, the service account token—we must securely transfer them to the VM. For demonstration purposes, we'll use the approach that requires the least effort and copy the files using rsync over SSH, which is secure—but understandably, in production environments, this process must be automated and must not require any manual intervention:

```
$ rsync -e "ssh -i ch13/keys/id_rsa" \
    -avz ch13/workload-files/ azureuser@$VM_IP:~/
```

With the files copied over to the VM, we are ready to install and configure the sidecar to join the service mesh.

13.3.3 *Installing and configuring the istio-agent in the VM*

Open a remote shell session to the machine using the SSH client:

```
$  ssh -i ch13/keys/id_rsa azureuser@$VM_IP
```

> **NOTE** In the following, we indicate when commands are run in the VM using the bash prompt azureuser@forum-vm:~$. For commands run on the local computer, we continue using only the dollar sign ($) symbol.

We need to download and install the istio-agent on the VM. The question is, what options do we have to install the proxy? Istio releases the istio-agent in the following package formats:

- *Debian Software Package (.deb)*, which can be used to install the agent on any of the Debian-based Linux distributions, such as Ubuntu and Linux Mint.
- *Red Hat Package Manager (.rpm)*, which can be used to install the agent in Red Hat-based Linux distributions such as Fedora, RHEL, and CentOS.

Because our VM's operating system is based on Debian, we download and install the istio-agent in the Debian packaging format:

```
azureuser@forum-vm:~$
 curl -LO https://storage.googleapis.com/\
istio-release/releases/1.13.0/deb/istio-sidecar.deb
```

```
azureuser@forum-vm:~$
 sudo dpkg -i istio-sidecar.deb
```

The `istio-agent` reads the configuration files from specific locations, so let's move them and make it happy:

```
azureuser@forum-vm:~$
  sudo mkdir -p /etc/certs
azureuser@forum-vm:~$                                   The root certificate must be
  sudo cp \                                             in the /etc/certs/ directory.
    "${HOME}"/root-cert.pem /etc/certs/root-cert.pem
azureuser@forum-vm:~$
  sudo  mkdir -p /var/run/secrets/tokens
azureuser@forum-vm:~$                                   The service account
  sudo cp "${HOME}"/istio-token \                       token uses the same
    /var/run/secrets/tokens/istio-token                 directory as in Pods.
azureuser@forum-vm:~$
  sudo cp "${HOME}"/cluster.env \
    /var/lib/istio/envoy/cluster.env                    The configuration must be
azureuser@forum-vm:~$                                   moved to the directories
  sudo cp \                                             it is read from.
    "${HOME}"/mesh.yaml /etc/istio/config/mesh
```

We are almost done! Next, we configure the system hosts file with an entry to statically resolve the hostname `istiod.istio-system.svc` to the east-west gateway IP address, which proxies the request to the `istiod` instances. This was generated by the earlier `istioctl` command and stored in a file named `hosts`. We already copied it to the VM. Next, concatenate the contents of the `hosts` file contents to the systems hosts file:

```
azureuser@forum-vm:~$
  cat "${HOME}"/hosts | \
    sudo sh -c 'cat >> /etc/hosts'
```

> **Shouldn't the DNS proxy resolve the in-cluster hostnames?**
>
> Indeed; but at this point, when the sidecar still doesn't connect to the control plane, it will lack the DNS entries known to the pilot.
>
> Additionally, if statically defining the east-west gateway hostname in /etc/hosts is not suitable for your environment, you can stand up a network load balancer to point to the east-west gateway. Refer to your specific cloud or on-premises environment for how to configure and expose a network load balancer.

Next, hardcode the hostname of the machine to the hosts file so that the istio-agent doesn't interfere with its hostname resolution:

```
$ echo "$(hostname --all-ip-addresses | cut -d ' ' -f 1) $(hostname)" | \
  sudo sh -c 'cat >> /etc/hosts'
```

The last step before starting the agent is giving it owner permissions in the directories it reads and writes to:

```
azureuser@forum-vm:~$
  sudo mkdir -p /etc/istio/proxy
azureuser@forum-vm:~$
  sudo chown -R istio-proxy /var/lib/istio \
    /etc/certs /etc/istio/proxy /etc/istio/config \
    /var/run/secrets /etc/certs/root-cert.pem
```

Finally, start the `istio-agent` as a system service:

```
azureuser@forum-vm:~$
  sudo systemctl start istio
```

Verify the status of the service to ensure that it is running:

```
azureuser@forum-vm:~$
  sudo systemctl status istio
```

```
● istio.service - istio-sidecar: The Istio sidecar
   Loaded: loaded (/lib/systemd/system/istio.service; disabled;
  ➥vendor preset: enabled)
   Active: active (running) since Tue 2021-06-01 12:02:40 UTC; 4s ago
     Docs: http://istio.io/
 Main PID: 2826 (su)
    Tasks: 0 (limit: 4074)
   CGroup: /system.slice/istio.service
           ➥2826 su -s /bin/bash -c INSTANCE_IP=138.91.144.131
           ➥POD_NAME=forum-vm POD_NAMESPACE=forum-services
           ➥exec /usr/local/bin/pilot-agent proxy  2> /var/log/ist...
```

The status shows that it is active and running! Next, let's verify that it connected to the control plane by checking the agent logs.

CHECKING THE AGENT LOGS

Istio's agent logs are written in the following two locations:

- The standard output channel is written to the file /var/log/istio/istio.log.
- The standard error channel is written to the file /var/log/istio/istio.err.log.

To verify that the connection to the Istio control plane was successful, we can check the standard output logs:

```
azureuser@forum-vm:~$
  cat /var/log/istio/istio.log | grep xdsproxy

2021-07-15T12:25:20.229041Z     info    xdsproxy
➥Initializing with upstream address "istiod.istio-system.svc:15012"
➥and cluster "west-cluster"                    The istio-agent connected
                                                               to istiod
2021-07-15T12:25:21.405275Z     info    xdsproxy connected to
➥upstream XDS server: istiod.istio-system.svc:15012      ◁
```

Your logs may not be identical but if you look for logs in the `xdsproxy` scope, you will find an entry showing that the connection was successful to the upstream. But what if the log file wasn't created? That can be the case only when the service failed to start.

When that occurs, check the systemd logs using journalctl with the following command (this shows any failures that hindered the startup of the service):

```
journalctl -f -u istio
```

But in our case, the connection was successful, so we don't have to do that.

VERIFYING THAT THE WORKLOAD REGISTERED TO THE MESH

With workload auto-registration enabled, a WorkloadEntry is created as soon as the machine's istio-agent connects to istiod. Let's verify that by listing the workload entries in the forum-services namespace :

```
$ kubectl get workloadentry -n forum-services

NAME                          AGE   ADDRESS
forum-40.83.164.1-vm-network  17s   40.83.164.1
```

As expected, the output shows the registered workload entry for the VM. Additionally, it shows the address where a connection to the instance and the services it provides can be initiated. These are the unique properties for the VM this entry represents. Next, let's see how traffic is routed to in-cluster services and vice versa.

13.3.4 *Routing traffic to cluster services*

To check if traffic is routed to the cluster services, make a curl request from the VM to the webapp workload:

```
azureuser@forum-vm:~$
  curl webapp.istioinaction/api/catalog/items/1

{
  "id": 1,
  "color": "amber",
  "department": "Eyewear",
  "name": "Elinor Glasses",
  "price": "282.00"
}
```

The successful response verifies the traffic routing from the VM to the cluster workload. However, let's dig into the details of what transpired for the request to be served (see figure 13.12):

1. For traffic to leave the application, it must resolve its hostname. For this to occur, the DNS query must be redirected to the DNS proxy.
2. With the name resolved to an IP address, the application can trigger an outbound request that is redirected by Iptable rules to the Envoy proxy.
3. The Envoy proxy routes the traffic to the east-west gateway.
4. The east-west gateway proxies the request to the webapp, which queries the catalog service for the items.

Going over this process at a high level answers questions such as "How is the DNS proxy configured?" and "How does the application interact with it?" and puts it in

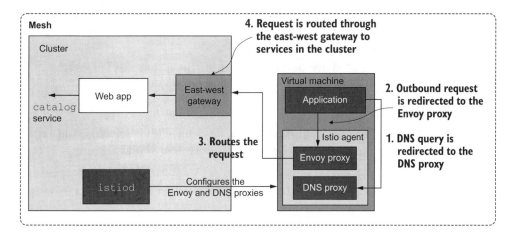

Figure 13.12 How traffic reaches cluster services

context with the entire process of routing traffic to the cluster services from the VM workload. As a user of the service mesh, this suffices; but if you're curious, you can find more details in section 13.4.

13.3.5 *Routing traffic to the WorkloadEntry*

In the previous section, we verified routing from the machine to the in-cluster/in-mesh services. Next, let's verify the opposite: routing from within the cluster to the VM workloads.

How should we make the request to reach services running in the VM? Should we use its IP address, which we saw in the `WorkloadEntry`? Definitely not, for the same reason we don't use static IP addresses of Pods in Kubernetes: to allow the platform to be flexible and replace instances.

As briefly mentioned, we have to create a Kubernetes service that selects the instances using labels and lets Istio dynamically configure all services with the correct IP addresses. For example, to select the `forum` workload entries, we use the following Kubernetes service:

```
apiVersion: v1
kind: Service
metadata:
  labels:
    app: forum
  name: forum
spec:
  ports:
  - name: http
    port: 80
    protocol: TCP
    targetPort: 8080
  selector:
    app: forum
```

This service definition selects the endpoints of all workloads (Pods and Workload-Entries) that match the label selector app: forum. Thus it selects the workload entry for the forum service.

Let's apply this service to the cluster using the following command:

```
$ kubectl apply -f services/forum/kubernetes/forum-svc.yaml \
    -n forum-services
```

With the service created, the WorkloadEntry endpoint is selected, and istiod configures the data plane with it. We can easily verify that by making a request to the forum service:

```
$ EXT_IP=$(kubectl -n istio-system get svc istio-ingressgateway -o \
    jsonpath='{.status.loadBalancer.ingress[0].ip}')
$ curl -is -H "Host: webapp.istioinaction.io" \
    http://$EXT_IP/api/users | grep HTTP

HTTP/1.1 500 Internal Server Error
```

The request failed. Does that mean we did something wrong? We won't know until we do some troubleshooting and find the root cause! The goal of this drill is to give you practice for when things don't work out as you might have planned. Let's begin with the instance that returned an error: the webapp workload. Start looking into its access logs:

```
$ kubectl -n istioinaction logs deploy/webapp -c istio-proxy | tail -2
```

Figure 13.13 shows the output of this command. As covered in chapter 10, the UH response flag stands for "No healthy upstream," which occurs only when a cluster has no healthy endpoints where traffic can be routed. If that's the case, webapp should have no endpoints for the forum service.

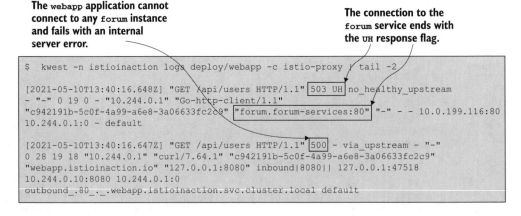

Figure 13.13 The Envoy access logs of the webapp service

> **NOTE** Envoy response flags are documented in the Envoy access logs: http://mng.bz/jyBx.

Verify that using this `istioctl` command:

```
$  istioctl proxy-config endpoints deploy/webapp.istioinaction | \
      grep forum


<empty>
```

The endpoint is definitely missing! We know (and verified) that the `WorkloadEntry` is registered; however, we didn't check whether it's passing the health checks.

VERIFYING THE HEALTH OF THE FORUM WORKLOAD

The health or, to be exact, the readiness of a `WorkloadEntry` to receive traffic is shown when we print its definition in the verbose YAML format:

```
$  WE_NAME=$(kubectl get workloadentry -n "forum-services" \
      -o jsonpath='{.items..metadata.name}')              ⟵───── Gets the workload
                                                                  entry name
$  kubectl get workloadentry $WE_NAME \     Prints the YAML definition
    -n forum-services -o yaml               of the workload entry

apiVersion: networking.istio.io/v1beta1
kind: WorkloadEntry
metadata:
  name: forum-10.0.0.4
  namespace: forum-services
  labels:
    app: forum
    service.istio.io/canonical-name: forum
    service.istio.io/canonical-version: latest
spec:
  address: 138.91.249.118
  labels:
    app: forum
    service.istio.io/canonical-name: forum
    service.istio.io/canonical-version: latest
  network: vm-network
  serviceAccount: forum-sa
status:
  conditions:
  - lastProbeTime: "2021-07-29T09:33:50.281295466Z"
    lastTransitionTime: "2021-07-29T09:33:50.281296166Z"
    message: 'Get "http://40.85.149.87:8080/api/healthz":
    ⟹dial tcp 127.0.0.6:0->40.85.149.87:8080:
      connect: connection refused'
    status: "False"         The False status of the health condition
    type: Healthy           shows that the workload is unhealthy
```

The output shows that the `WorkloadEntry` has failed health checks, as indicated by `status: "False"`. Why could that be the case? Ouch! Recall that when we checked the ports of the machine using Nmap, port 8080 was `closed`, which indicated that there is no application listening for packets on that port. So we still didn't even start the application in the VM! This explains why the application health checks are failing. Let's start the app.

STARTING THE FORUM APPLICATION IN THE VM

To start the application, we have to download the `forum` binary, give it execute permission, and then start it to listen for traffic on port 8080. All of that is done here:

```
azureuser@forum-vm:~$
 wget -O forum https://git.io/J3QrT
azureuser@forum-vm:~$
 chmod +x forum
azureuser@forum-vm:~$
 ./forum
Server is listening on port:8080
```

After starting the application, wait until the health probes succeed and the `istio-agent` informs `istiod` about the newly healthy status of the workload. This usually takes just a few seconds. We can verify the updated status in the verbose YAML format:

```
$  kubectl get workloadentry $WE_NAME -n forum-services -o yaml


apiVersion: networking.istio.io/v1beta1
kind: WorkloadEntry
metadata:
  name: forum-138.91.249.118-vm-network
  namespace: forum-services
spec: <omitted>
status:
  conditions:
  - lastProbeTime: "2021-05-05T12:06:45.474329543Z"
    lastTransitionTime: "2021-05-05T12:06:45.474330043Z"
    status: "True"
    type: Healthy                   ⊢──  The type of the condition is Healthy,
                                         and status is set to True.
```

Now the workload entry is healthy! So `istiod` configures the data plane with its endpoint, which is shown when we print the `webapp` endpoints again:

```
$  istioctl proxy-config endpoints deploy/webapp.istioinaction |\
      grep forum

52.160.67.232:8080  HEALTHY  OK  outbound|80||
forum.forum-services.svc.cluster.local
```

With that fixed, traffic should be routed to the `forum` workload in the VM. Let's trigger another request:

```
$  curl -is -H "Host: webapp.istioinaction.io" \
      http://$EXT_IP/api/users | grep HTTP

HTTP/1.1 200 OK
```

If you also get a successful response, it means that traffic was routed from the cluster and to the forum workload.

With that, we have validated the traffic flow from the cluster services to the workload entry. Additionally, this example has shown you how Istio doesn't send traffic to a workload that isn't ready to receive traffic—by simply not configuring the data plane with its endpoint. The benefits may not be clearly visible in this example, but in a production cluster, this will protect clients from sending traffic to an instance that returns errors and will instead route traffic only to healthy instances.

13.3.6 VMs are configured by the control plane: Enforcing mutual authentication

Because the VM is integrated in the mesh and the sidecar proxy manages the network traffic, we can apply Istio's rich capabilities to the VM. To showcase this, let's create a PeerAuthentication to enforce mutually authenticated traffic and improve security. Currently, because we exposed port 8080 of the VM, anyone who can connect to it can get their requests served. *Anyone*—even unauthorized users! We can verify that by initiating a request to the VM from our local computer, which is *not* integrated into the mesh:

```
$ curl -is $VM_IP:8080/api/users | grep HTTP

HTTP/1.1 200 OK
```

The request was served, which is what we expected but what we will prohibit from now on. To do so, we configure the service mesh with a mesh-wide policy to serve only mutually authenticated traffic and, as a result, protect our service from unauthorized access:

```
$ kubectl apply -f ch13/strict-peer-auth.yaml
```

Wait for some time to pass so the policy is distributed to the data plane. Then validate that non-mutually authenticated traffic is prohibited:

```
$ curl $VM_IP:8080/api/users

curl: (56) Recv failure: Connection reset by peer
```

The request was rejected! Now, let's verify that service-to-service traffic continues to work; there is no reason for it not to, but we'll check for our peace of mind:

```
$ curl -is -H "Host: webapp.istioinaction.io" \
    http://$EXT_IP/api/users | grep HTTP

HTTP/1.1 200 OK
```

The output shows that requests from the webapp were served, meaning that the VM adheres to the configuration applied by the control plane. The PeerAuthentication policy is just one example; and you can similarly use all the Istio APIs to configure the VM's proxy.

13.4   Demystifying the DNS proxy

The DNS proxy is the new component in Istio's sidecar and raises quite a few questions. Let's demystify it by taking a close look under the hood. The goal in this section is for you to understand how the DNS proxy resolves in-cluster service hostnames, but merely to satisfy your curiosity—you will do fine without knowing the concrete details.

13.4.1   How the DNS proxy resolves cluster hostnames

To understand all the steps involved in resolving an in-cluster hostname, we will follow a concrete example of how the `webapp.istioinaction` hostname is resolved. The steps are shown in figure 13.14:

1 The client makes a DNS query to resolve `webapp.istioinaction`.
2 The operating system handles the DNS resolution. It begins by checking whether the hostname matches any entry defined in the hosts file. If there are no matches, the request is forwarded to the default DNS resolver.
3 The default resolver for Ubuntu is `systemd-resolved` (a system service that provides hostname resolution to local applications), and it listens to the loopback address 127.0.0.53 on port 53. However, the request never reaches it because the `istio-agent` configures Iptable rules to redirect it to the DNS proxy.

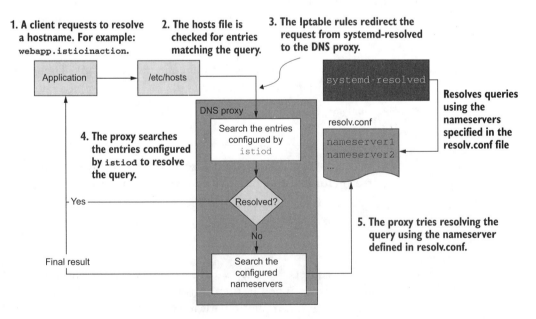

Figure 13.14   The flow of cluster service hostname resolution

4 The DNS proxy contains entries to resolve the services known within the service mesh. If the hostname is matched, it gets resolved, which is the case for `webapp.istioinaction` because it is configured by the control plane using NDS.

5 Otherwise, if it's not a cluster service, the DNS proxy falls back to the nameservers specified in the resolv.conf file, where either it is resolved or resolution fails.

Instead of just theoretically understanding a concept, we prefer to verify each of its steps. Let's begin by verifying that the Iptable rules redirect the queries meant for `systemd-resolved` (which is listening on 127.0.0.53) to the DNS proxy listening for UDP and TCP packets on localhost port 15053. To do so, we print the Iptable rules and grep for traffic routed to port 15053:

```
azureuser@forum-vm:~$
 sudo iptables-save | grep 'to-ports 15053'

-A OUTPUT -d 127.0.0.53/32 -p udp -m udp --dport 53
  ➥-j REDIRECT --to-ports 15053
-A ISTIO_OUTPUT -d 127.0.0.53/32 -p tcp -m tcp --dport 53
  ➥-j REDIRECT --to-ports 15053
```

In the output, we see that traffic is redirected to the DNS proxy port. Let's go full circle and verify that the `istio-agent` started the DNS proxy and is listening on that port, by printing the processes and the ports they use:

```
azureuser@forum-vm:~$
 sudo netstat -ltunp

Active Internet connections (only servers)
Proto Recv-Q Send-Q Local Address      State     PID/Program name
tcp        0      0 0.0.0.0:15021      LISTEN    1553/envoy
tcp        0      0 127.0.0.1:15053    LISTEN    1544/pilot-agent        <-- istio-agent is listening for TCP connections on port 15053.
tcp        0      0 0.0.0.0:15090      LISTEN    1553/envoy
tcp        0      0 127.0.0.53:53      LISTEN    850/systemd-resolve
tcp        0      0 127.0.0.1:15000    LISTEN    1553/envoy
tcp        0      0 0.0.0.0:15001      LISTEN    1553/envoy
tcp        0      0 0.0.0.0:15006      LISTEN    1553/envoy
tcp6       0      0 :::15020           LISTEN    1544/pilot-agent
udp        0      0 127.0.0.53:53                850/systemd-resolve
udp        0      0 10.0.0.4:68                  828/systemd-network
udp        0      0 127.0.0.1:15053              1544/pilot-agent        <-- istio-agent is listening for UDP connections on port 15053.
```

The output shows that the `pilot-agent` (just another way we refer to the `istio-agent`) is listening on port 15053 to resolve DNS queries. If that's the case, we can even manually (using the `dig` command-line utility) make an ad hoc request to resolve an in-cluster hostname:

```
azureuser@forum-vm:~$
 dig +short @localhost -p 15053 webapp.istioinaction
10.0.183.159
```

And as expected, the `pilot-agent` listening to port 15053 resolves the FQDN. In our example, we manually specified the DNS server to resolve the request; however, that's not necessary—when applications resolve hostnames, the request is automatically redirected by the Iptable rules to this port. Next, let's find out what entries the DNS proxy was configured with by the control plane.

13.4.2   *Which hostnames is the DNS proxy aware of?*

To discover all the entries that the DNS proxy is aware of, we need to use the debug endpoints of `istiod` (more about those in appendix D). Using them, we can query the NDS configuration for every workload's sidecar.

Let's begin by picking the workload name we're interested in, which is `forum-vm`:

```
$  iwest proxy-status  | awk '{print $1}'

NAME
webapp-644c89c6bc-c4712.istioinaction
istio-eastwestgateway-8696b67f7f-d4xqf.istio-system
istio-ingressgateway-f7dff857c-f8zgd.istio-system
forum-vm.forum-services
```
◁── **Workload name we're interested in**

We use the name for the `proxyID` parameter when retrieving its NDS configuration. This command needs to be executed from your local computer:

```
$  kubectl -n istio-system exec deploy/istiod \
       -- curl -Ls \
       "localhost:8080/debug/ndsz?proxyID=forum-vm.forum-services"

...
"webapp.istioinaction.svc.cluster.local": {
  "ips": [
    "10.0.183.159"
  ],
  "registry": "Kubernetes",
  "shortname": "webapp",
  "namespace": "istioinaction"
},
...
```

The abridged output shows the entry for the `webapp` service, which contains the list of IP addresses that the name `webapp.istioinaction.svc.cluster.local` resolves to. Checking the output closely, you'll see that there aren't shorter variations such as `webapp.istioinaction`, so how did the resolution work? It's pretty simple: when the `istio-agent` receives the NDS configuration, it generates all variations that would be configured in a Kubernetes cluster, such as

- `webapp.istioinaction`
- `webapp.istioinaction.svc`
- `webapp.istioinaction.svc.cluster`

And all of them resolve to the same list of IP addresses—which, as we see in the previous listing, is `10.0.183.159`.

Here's a summary of the main takeaways:

- The DNS proxy is configured by `istiod` with the services known to it.
- The `istio-agent` generates the shorter variations of the hostnames (to match the experience in Kubernetes).
- Those entries (in the DNS proxy) are used to resolve in-cluster service hostnames.
- For queries of non-cluster hostnames (such as public domains), the resolution falls back to the nameservers the machine was initially configured with.

13.5 Customizing the agent's behavior

The agent has a host of configuration options: what it logs, how it is formatted, and behavior such as configuring the time certificate lifetime that's requested by the agent to get a certificate issued. For example, let's say we want to make two modifications:

- Increase the logging level of the DNS proxy to debug.
- Reduce the certificate lifetime to 12 hours.

We can update the /var/lib/istio/envoy/sidecar.env file, which is meant for a sidecar-specific configuration:

```
ISTIO_AGENT_FLAGS="--log_output_level=dns:debug"
SECRET_TTL="12h0m0s"
```

Restart the Istio service in order for the changes to be picked up:

```
sudo systemctl restart istio
```

You will see the debug logs for the DNS proxy. When the certificate is rotated, you can also verify the expiry of the new certificate, which is stored in the file /etc/certs/cert-chain.pem. For a list of all the configuration options, check Istio's `pilot-agent` documentation: https://istio.io/latest/docs/reference/commands/pilot-agent.

13.6 Removing a WorkloadEntry from the mesh

Just as the VM auto-registers to the mesh, when it is deleted, it gets cleaned up. Let's try that:

```
$ az vm delete \
    --resource-group west-cluster-rg \
    --name forum-vm -y
```

After some time passes, verify that the `WorkloadEntry` was cleaned up:

```
$ kubectl get workloadentries -n forum-services

No resources found in forum-services namespace.
```

Having workload entries automatically cleaned up is just as important as auto-registration, to support the ephemeral nature of cloud-native workloads.

And with that, we conclude this chapter. Because we covered so much, table 13.1 lists the differences between how a Kubernetes Pod and a VM are integrated into the mesh.

Table 13.1   Differences between how a workload in Kubernetes and a workload in a VM are integrated into the mesh

Feature	Kubernetes implementation	Virtual machine implementation
Installing proxy	Manual injection using `istioctl` or automatically with the webhook	Download and install manually
Configuring proxy	Done during sidecar injection	Generate configuration from a `WorkloadGroup` using `istioctl` and transfer to the VM with the proxy
Bootstrap workload identity	Service account token is injected into the Pod by Kubernetes mechanisms	Transfer service account token to the VM manually
Health checking	Readiness and liveness probes are performed by Kubernetes.	Readiness probes are configured in the `WorkloadGroup`.
Registration	Handled by Kubernetes	Auto-registration of VMs as members of a `WorkloadGroup`
DNS resolution	In-cluster DNS server is used to resolve in-cluster FQDNs. The DNS proxy is optional.	The DNS proxy is configured by `istiod` and resolves FQDNs.

We also want to leave you with a word of caution. To be concise, we manually installed and configured the proxy, as this approach permitted us to show all the nooks and crannies of how to integrate workloads into the mesh. But in real projects, this process must be automated. Adding VMs manually into the mesh will result in a very fragile mesh, and inadvertently it will get you paged at 3:00 a.m. to manually rebuild a virtual machine and register it to the mesh to restore service.

The word *automate* may sound daunting. But in reality, most projects nowadays follow good practices and have automation in place to build and deploy VMs, generally using tools such as Packer (packer.io), Ansible (ansible.com), and Terraform (terraform.io). And whenever there is pre-existing automation, it reduces your work to only updating the scripts to install Istio's sidecar alongside the application and providing it with the configuration and the token. And voilà: the VM is integrated into the mesh!

> **NOTE** Remember to clean up resources in the cloud provider. If you are using Azure, you can execute the script `$ az group delete --resource-group west-cluster-rg -y`.

Summary

- Virtual machines graduated to beta as of Istio v1.9. There are further improvements to be expected, and it will be an interesting area of development in the upcoming months. At the same time, it is already mature, and what we covered here is not expected to change.

- `WorkloadGroup` and `WorkloadEntry` enable auto-registration of VMs into the mesh.
- Auto-registration is important to achieve high availability of workloads in VMs.
- `istioctl` can generate VM configuration for it to connect to `istiod`.
- East-west gateways expose `istiod` so that VMs can connect to it.
- The DNS proxy resolves the in-cluster hostnames and is configured by `istiod` using the NDS API.
- The VM machine sidecar adheres to the Istio configuration just as other workloads do.

Extending Istio
on the request path

This chapter covers

- Understanding Envoy filters
- Using Istio's `EnvoyFilter` resource to configure Envoy directly
- Using Lua to customize the request path
- Using WebAssembly to customize the request path

As you've seen throughout this book, Istio can bring a lot of value to organizations with its application-networking functionality. Organizations adopting Istio will likely have other constraints or assumptions that Istio may not fulfill out of the box. You will likely need to extend Istio's capabilities to more nicely fit within these constraints.

As we saw in chapter 3, and reinforced throughout the book, the Envoy proxy is a foundational component of the Istio service mesh. Envoy is the service proxy that lives with the application instance and on the request path between services in a mesh. Although Envoy has a significant set of functionality that can simplify application networking for your services, you will most likely run into scenarios where you need to enhance Envoy for "last-mile" or customized integration. The following are examples of extension:

- Integrating with rate limiting or external authorization services
- Adding, removing, or modifying headers
- Calling out to other services to enrich a request payload
- Implementing custom protocols like HMAC signing/verification
- Non-standard security token handling

Envoy may provide almost everything you need, but eventually, you'll need to customize it for your specific use cases. This chapter covers extending Istio on the request path, which inevitably means extending Envoy.

14.1 Envoy's extension capabilities

One of the Envoy proxy's strengths is that it was built to be extended. A lot of thought and care went into designing Envoy's APIs, and a big reason for its popularity is the extensions others have written for it. A significant way that Envoy can be extended is with its filter extensions. To understand where we can extend Envoy and what will give us the most benefit for applications, we should understand some of Envoy's architecture.

14.1.1 Understanding Envoy's filter chaining

In chapter 3, we introduced Envoy's concepts of *listeners, routes,* and *clusters,* as illustrated in figure 14.1. We made the point that these are high-level concepts but promised to go into more specifics in this chapter. Here, we focus on `Listeners` and how the listener model can be extended with filters and filter chains.

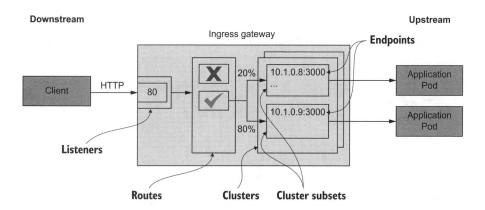

Figure 14.1 A request comes in from a downstream system through the listeners, then goes through the routing rules, and ends up going to a cluster that sends to an upstream service.

A listener in Envoy is a way to open a port on a networking interface and start listening to incoming traffic. Envoy is ultimately a layer 3 and layer 4 (L3/L4) proxy that takes bytes off a network connection and processes them in some way. This brings us to the first important part of the architecture: the filter. A listener reads bytes off the networking stream and processes them through various filters or stages of functionality, as shown in figure 14.2.

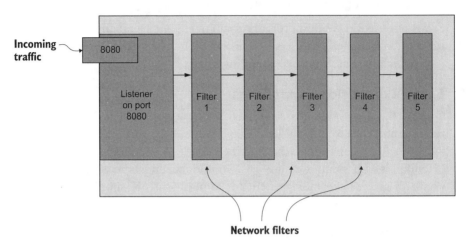

Figure 14.2   Bytes come in from the network through listeners, while listeners process bytes through network filters.

Envoy's most basic filters are *network filters*, which operate on a stream of bytes for either encoding or decoding. You can configure more than one filter to operate on the stream in a sequence called a *filter chain*, and these chains can be used to implement the functionality of the proxy.

For example, out of the box, Envoy has network filters for the following protocols, along with many others:

- MongoDB
- Redis
- Thrift
- Kafka
- HTTP Connection Manager

One of the most commonly used network filters is HttpConnectionManager. This filter is responsible for abstracting away the details of converting a stream of bytes into HTTP headers, body, and trailers for HTTP-based protocols (that is, HTTP 1.1, HTTP 2, gRPC, and recently HTTP 3, and so on) and is shown in figure 14.3.

HttpConnectionManager (sometimes referred to as the HCM) handles HTTP requests as well as things like access logging, request retry, header manipulation, and

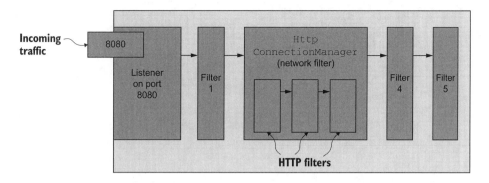

Figure 14.3 `HttpConnectionManager` **is a popular and useful network filter for converting a stream of bytes into HTTP (HTTP/1, HTTP/2, and so on) requests and routing them based on L7 properties like headers or body details.**

request routing based on headers, path prefixes, and other request attributes. The HCM also has a filter-based architecture that allows you to build or configure HTTP filters into a sequence or chain of filters that operate on an HTTP request. Some examples of out-of-the-box HTTP filters include the following:

- Cross-origin resource sharing (CORS)
- Cross-site request forgery prevention (CSRF)
- ExternalAuth
- RateLimit
- Fault injection
- gRPC/JSON transcoding
- Gzip
- Lua
- Role-based access control (RBAC)
- Tap
- Router
- WebAssembly (Wasm)

A full list of HTTP filters can be found at http://mng.bz/BxKJ.

HTTP filters can be configured in a sequence to operate on an HTTP request. The HTTP filters must end in a *terminal filter* that sends the request to an upstream cluster. The HTTP filter responsible for this is the `router` filter, shown in figure 14.4. The router filter matches requests to upstream clusters with configurable timeout and retry parameters. See chapter 6 and the Envoy docs (http://mng.bz/domQ) for more on this functionality.

Users can also write their own filters and layer them on top of the proxy without having to change any of Envoy's core code. For example, Istio's proxy (https://github.com/istio/proxy) adds filters on top of Envoy and builds a custom Envoy for its

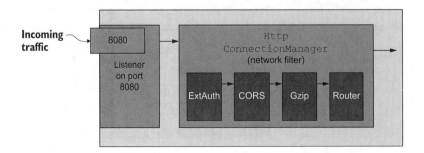

Figure 14.4
HttpConnection-
Manager has a filter
chain that processes
HTTP requests, ending
with a routing filter.

data plane. Other open source projects like Gloo Edge (http://github.com/solo-io/gloo) follow this same approach. However, this introduces a custom Envoy proxy build that can be a lot to maintain and require developers to use C++.

14.1.2 *Filters intended for extension*

Although you can write your own filters in C++ and build them into the proxy, that's beyond the scope of this book. There are ways to extend Envoy's HTTP capabilities, including writing filters, without compiling changes into the Envoy binary itself, by using the following HTTP filters:

- External processing
- Lua
- Wasm (WebAssembly)

With these filters, you can configure calls out to an external service, run a Lua script, or run custom code to enhance the capabilities of the HCM when processing HTTP requests or responses. For calling an external service for processing, we'll focus on the rate-limiting filter. We can also call out for external authorizations, as we covered in chapter 9.

> **NOTE** Envoy has an *external processing filter* for calling out to an external service for generic processing. This filter exists in the code base but does not do anything at the time of writing. We focus on other ways to call out to an external service, such as with the global rate-limiting filter.

14.1.3 *Customizing Istio's data plane*

Armed with a high-level understanding of Envoy's filter architecture, in the next few sections we extend the capabilities of the Envoy data plane using one of the following methods:

- Configuring an Envoy HTTP filter with the `EnvoyFilter` resource from the Istio API
- Calling out to a rate-limit server
- Implementing a Lua script and loading it into the Lua HTTP filter
- Implementing a Wasm module for the Wasm HTTP filter

We need to understand how to configure Envoy's filters directly, and for this, we'll use Istio's `EnvoyFilter` resource. We used this resource in previous chapters, but we dig into it deeper here.

14.2 Configuring an Envoy filter with the EnvoyFilter resource

The first step in extending Istio's data plane is to figure out whether an existing filter in Envoy is sufficient to accomplish the type of extension we're looking for. If one exists, we can use the `EnvoyFilter` resource to directly configure Istio's data plane.

Istio's APIs generally abstract away the underlying Envoy configuration, focusing on specific networking or security scenarios. Resources like `VirtualService`, `DestinationRule`, and `AuthorizationPolicy` all end up getting translated to an Envoy configuration and potentially configure specific HTTP filters in a filter chain. Istio does not try to expose every possible filter or configuration for the underlying Envoy proxy, and there may be cases where we need to configure Envoy directly. Istio's `EnvoyFilter` resource is intended for advanced use cases where a user needs to either tweak or configure a portion of Envoy not exposed by Istio's higher-level APIs. This resource can configure just about anything (with some limitations) in Envoy, including listeners, routes, clusters, and filters.

The `EnvoyFilter` resource is intended for advanced usage of Istio and is a "break glass" solution. The underlying Envoy API may change at any time between releases of Istio, so be sure to validate any `EnvoyFilter` you deploy. Do not assume any backward compatibility here. Bad configuration with this API can potentially take down the entire Istio data plane.

Let's look at an example and understand how it works. If you've followed along from previous chapters, let's reset our workspace, so we can start from scratch:

```
$ kubectl config set-context $(kubectl config current-context) \
 --namespace=istioinaction
$ kubectl delete virtualservice,deployment,service,\
destinationrule,gateway,authorizationpolicy,envoyfilter --all
```

Let's deploy services we'll use for the chapter:

```
$ kubectl apply -f services/catalog/kubernetes/catalog.yaml
$ kubectl apply -f services/webapp/kubernetes/webapp.yaml
$ kubectl apply -f services/webapp/istio/webapp-catalog-gw-vs.yaml
$ kubectl apply -f ch9/sleep.yaml
$ kubectl delete sidecar --all -n istio-system
```

Suppose we want to extend our data plane with tooling to debug certain requests that flow through the webapp service. We can extend Envoy with some custom filters, but if we look thoroughly enough, we see that a `Tap` filter exists for this type of functionality. It is not exposed by Istio's APIs, so we can use the `EnvoyFilter` resource to configure this filter for our webapp service.

The first thing to know about an `EnvoyFilter` resource is that it applies to all workloads in the namespace for which it is declared, unless you specify otherwise. If you create an `EnvoyFilter` resource in the `istio-system` namespace, it will be applied to all workloads in the mesh. If you want to be more specific about the workloads in a namespace to which the custom `EnvoyFilter` configuration applies, you can use a `workloadSelector`, as we'll see in our example.

The second thing to know about an `EnvoyFilter` resource is that it applies after all other Istio resources have been translated and configured. For example, if you have `VirtualService` or `DestinationRule` resources, those configurations are applied to the data plane first.

Finally, you should take great care when configuring a workload with the `Envoy-Filter` resource. You should be familiar with Envoy naming conventions and configuration specifics. This really is an advanced usage of Istio's API and can bring down your mesh if misconfigured.

In our example, we want to configure Envoy's tap filter (http://mng.bz/ramX) to sample messages that go over the data plane for the webapp workload, as shown in figure 14.5. Every time a request or response flows over the tap filter, it streams it out to some listening agent. In this example, we stream it out to the console/CLI.

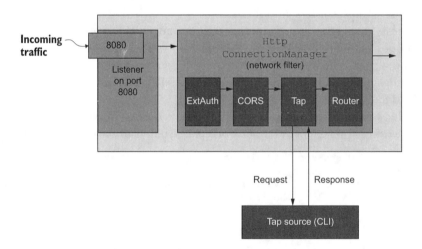

Figure 14.5   The Envoy HTTP tap filter allows you to stream requests and responses unmodified and without impacting the client or upstreams, as a way to debug/introspect the data plane.

We configure an `EnvoyFilter` resource like this:

```
apiVersion: networking.istio.io/v1alpha3
kind: EnvoyFilter
metadata:
  name: tap-filter
  namespace: istioinaction
spec:
  workloadSelector:
```

```
    labels:
      app: webapp          ⤆——┤ Workload selector
  configPatches:
  - applyTo: HTTP_FILTER    ⤆——┐ Where to
    match:                      │ configure
      context: SIDECAR_INBOUND
      listener:
        portNumber: 8080
        filterChain:
          filter:
            name: "envoy.filters.network.http_connection_manager"
            subFilter:
              name: "envoy.filters.http.router"
    patch:                 ⤆——————————┐ Envoy config
      operation: INSERT_BEFORE        │ patch
      value:
       name: envoy.filters.http.tap
       typed_config:
          "@type": "type.googleapis.com/
envoy.extensions.filters.http.tap.v3.Tap"
          commonConfig:
            adminConfig:
              configId: tap_config
```

Let's go through this section by section to make sure we understand the details. The first thing to notice is that we deploy this EnvoyFilter to the istioinaction namespace. As mentioned earlier, this would otherwise apply to the sidecars for all the workloads in that namespace, but we use a workloadSelector to be very specific about the workloads to which this configuration should apply.

Next, we need to specify where in the Envoy configuration to patch the configuration. In this example, we specify that it will be an HTTP_FILTER for an inbound listener (SIDECAR_INBOUND). As mentioned previously, there are network filters for listeners, and one of those is the HCM. The HCM also has a chain of HTTP-specific filters that process HTTP requests. We also specify a particular listener in this example: the HCM on the listener bound to port 8080. Finally, we pick the envoy.filters.http.router HTTP filter in this HCM HTTP filter chain. We pick this specific filter because we will order our new filter right before it, as we'll see in the next section of the configuration.

In the patch section of this EnvoyFilter resource, we specify how we want to patch the configuration. In this case, we merge the configuration *before* the specific filter we selected in the previous configuration section. The filter we add, envoy.filters .http.tap goes *before* the http.filters.http.router in the HCM filter chain. We have to be explicit about the structure of the tap filter configuration, so we give it an explicit type. For the details of the tap configuration format, see the Envoy documentation: http://mng.bz/VlG5.

Let's apply this EnvoyFilter to the webapp workload in the istioinaction namespace:

```
$ kubectl apply -f ch14/tap-envoy-filter.yaml
```

We can verify the Envoy configuration in the webapp sidecar proxy with the following command. Try to find the HTTP filters for the HCM and locate the new tap filter configuration:

```
$  istioctl pc listener deploy/webapp.istioinaction \
--port 15006 --address 0.0.0.0 -o yaml
```

Note that we are reviewing the listener on port 15006 because that's the default ingress port in the sidecar proxy. All other ports reroute to this listener.

You should see something like this when you run the previous command:

```
- name: envoy.filters.http.tap
    typedConfig:
    '@type': type.googleapis.com/envoy.extensions.filters
.http.tap.v3.Tap
    commonConfig:
        adminConfig:
        configId: tap_config
- name: envoy.filters.http.router
    typedConfig:
    '@type': type.googleapis.com/envoy.extensions.filters
.http.router.v3.Router
```

Let's verify that the tap functionality is working. You need two terminal windows for this. In one window, start the tap on the webapp workload by passing in a tap configuration with curl:

```
{
  "config_id": "tap_config",
  "tap_config": {
    "match_config": {
      "http_request_headers_match": {
        "headers": [
          {
            "name": "x-app-tap",
            "exact_match": "true"
          }
        ]
      }
    },
    "output_config": {
      "sinks": [
        {
          "streaming_admin": {}
        }
      ]
    }
  }
}
```

This configuration instructs the tap filter to match on any incoming HTTP requests with the x-app-tap header equal to true. When the tap filter finds a request like this, it streams the request out to a tap handler, which is curl in this case (which is automatically sent to stdout). Before we can reach the admin tap endpoint, we should port-forward the endpoint to localhost in one window:

```
$  kubectl port-forward -n istioinaction deploy/webapp 15000
```

In another window, start the tap:

```
$  curl -X POST -d @./ch14/tap-config.json localhost:15000/tap
```

In another window, call the service like this:

```
$  curl -H "Host: webapp.istioinaction.io" -H "x-app-tap: true" \
http://localhost/api/catalog
```

You should see the tap output in the window where you started the tap. It gives all the information about the request, like headers, body, trailers, and so on. Continue to investigate the Envoy tap filter and how it can be used in Istio to debug requests across the network.

14.3 *Rate-limiting requests with external call-out*

In the previous section, we extended the Istio data plane with functionality that exists in an out-of-the-box HTTP filter. There are also out-of-the-box filters that enhance the data plane with functionality that exists as a *call-out*. With these filters, we call out to an external service and have it perform some functionality that can determine how or whether to continue with a request. In this section, we explore how to configure Istio's data plane to call out to a rate-limiting service to enforce service-side rate-limiting for a particular workload (see figure 14.6).

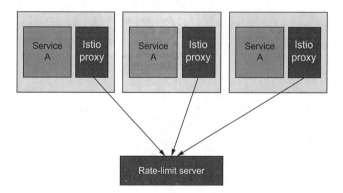

Figure 14.6 Multiple replicas of the same service call the same rate-limit service to get global rate limiting for a particular service.

Just as Istio uses Envoy for the data plane, the specific call-out for rate limiting comes from an Envoy HTTP filter. There are several ways to do rate limiting in Envoy (as a network filter, local rate limiting, and global rate limiting), but we specifically explore the global rate-limiting functionality. With global rate limiting, you have all Envoy proxies for a particular workload calling the same rate-limiting service, which calls a

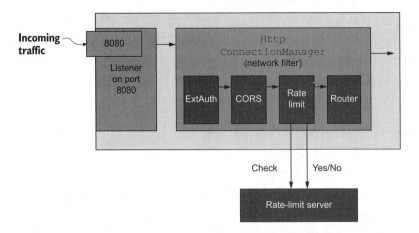

Figure 14.7   With Envoy global rate limiting, we can call out to a rate-limiting server to determine whether we need to rate limit a particular request. Attributes of the request are sent to the rate-limiting server to make a decision.

backend global key-value store as shown in figure 14.7. With this architecture, we can ensure that a rate limit is enforced regardless of how many replicas of a service exist.

To configure rate limiting, we need to deploy the rate-limit server, which comes from the Envoy community (see https://github.com/envoyproxy/ratelimit)—or, more accurately, a rate-limit server that implements the Envoy rate-limiting API (http://mng.bz/xvXB). This server is configured to talk with a backend Redis cache and stores rate-limit counters in Redis (optionally, you can use Memcache). Before we deploy the rate-limit server, we need to configure it with the expected rate-limiting behavior.

14.3.1 *Understanding Envoy rate limiting*

Before configuring the Envoy rate-limit server (RLS), we need to understand how rate limiting works. We are specifically looking at understanding Envoy's HTTP global rate limiting, which exists as an HTTP filter and needs to be configured into the HTTP filter chain on the HCM. When the rate-limit filter processes an HTTP request, it takes certain attributes from the request and sends them out to the RLS for evaluation. Envoy rate-limiting terminology uses the word *descriptors* to refer to attributes or groups of attributes. These descriptors, or attributes, of the request can be things like remote address, request headers, destination, or any other generic attributes about the request.

The RLS evaluates the request attributes that have been sent as part of a request against a set of predefined attributes, as shown in figure 14.8, and increments counters for those attributes. The request attributes may be grouped or defined in a tree to determine what attributes should be counted. If an attribute or set of attributes matches the RLS definitions, then the counts for those limits are incremented. If a count exceeds a threshold, that request is rate-limited.

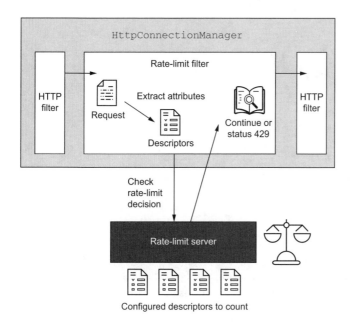

Figure 14.8　Attributes of the request, like remote address, request headers, client ID, and so on, also known as *descriptors* in Envoy terminology, are sent to the rate-limiting server to make a rate-limit decision against a preconfigured set of descriptors.

CONFIGURING THE ENVOY RATE-LIMIT SERVER

Let's configure the RLS with the attribute counters and limits. For our example use case, we want to limit certain groups of users depending on what loyalty tier they have with our example organization. We can determine the loyalty tier in a request by examining the x-loyalty header.

For a particular group of users in the gold tier (x-loyalty: gold), we allow 10 requests per minute. For silver (x-loyalty: silver), we allow five requests per minute; and for bronze (x-loyalty: bronze), we allow three requests per minute. For a loyalty tier that cannot be identified, rate limiting will kick in after one request per minute.

The RLS configuration that captures these attributes of a request (descriptors) can be expressed as follows:

```
apiVersion: v1
kind: ConfigMap
metadata:
  name: catalog-ratelimit-config
  namespace: istioinaction
data:
  config.yaml: |
    domain: catalog-ratelimit
    descriptors:
      - key: header_match
        value: no_loyalty
        rate_limit:
          unit: MINUTE
          requests_per_unit: 1
      - key: header_match
```

```
      value: gold_request
      rate_limit:
        unit: MINUTE
        requests_per_unit: 10
  - key: header_match
    value: silver_request
    rate_limit:
      unit: MINUTE
      requests_per_unit: 5
  - key: header_match
    value: bronze_request
    rate_limit:
      unit: MINUTE
      requests_per_unit: 3
```

Note that we don't deal with the actual request headers directly, just the attributes sent as part of a request. In the next section, we explore how to define these attributes. As mentioned earlier, the RLS configuration defines what rules to follow for rate limiting. When a request is processed through the Istio data plane, attributes are sent to the RLS; and if they match, rate limiting happens accordingly.

CONFIGURING THE REQUEST PATH FOR RATE LIMITING

Once we've configured the RLS, we need to configure Envoy with which attributes to send for a particular request. Envoy terminology refers to this configuration as the rate-limit *actions* taken for a particular request path. For example, if we call the catalog service on path /items, we want to capture whether a request has an x-loyalty header and the group to which it belongs.

To configure the appropriate attributes (actions) sent to the RLS, we need to specify the rate_limit configuration for a particular Envoy route configuration. Istio doesn't have an API for this yet (at the time of this writing), so we have to use Envoy-Filter resources. Here's how we can specify rate-limit actions for any route on the catalog service:

```
apiVersion: networking.istio.io/v1alpha3
kind: EnvoyFilter
metadata:
  name: catalog-ratelimit-actions
  namespace: istioinaction
spec:
  workloadSelector:
    labels:
      app: catalog
  configPatches:
    - applyTo: VIRTUAL_HOST
      match:
        context: SIDECAR_INBOUND
        routeConfiguration:
          vhost:
            route:
              action: ANY
      patch:
        operation: MERGE
```

```
value:                        ┌─ Rate-limit
  rate_limits:          ⟵──┘   actions
    - actions:
      - header_value_match:
          descriptor_value: no_loyalty
          expect_match: false
          headers:
          - name: "x-loyalty"
    - actions:
      - header_value_match:
          descriptor_value: bronze_request
          headers:
          - name: "x-loyalty"
            exact_match: bronze
    - actions:
      - header_value_match:
          descriptor_value: silver_request
          headers:
          - name: "x-loyalty"
            exact_match: silver
    - actions:
      - header_value_match:
          descriptor_value: gold_request
          headers:
          - name: "x-loyalty"
            exact_match: gold
```

Now let's deploy these rules along with the RLS and see how we configure the data plane.

To deploy these rules as a Kubernetes `configmap` and then deploy the RLS with a Redis backend, run the following commands:

```
$  kubectl apply -f ch14/rate-limit/rlsconfig.yaml
$  kubectl apply -f ch14/rate-limit/rls.yaml
```

If we list the Pods in the `istioinaction` namespace, we should see our new rate limit server:

```
NAME                          READY   STATUS    RESTARTS   AGE
webapp-f7bdbcbb5-qk8fx        2/2     Running   0          24h
catalog-68666d4988-qg6v5      2/2     Running   0          24h
ratelimit-7df4b47668-4x2q9    1/1     Running   1          24s
redis-7d757c948f-c84dk        1/1     Running   0          2m26s
```

So far, all we've done is configure and deploy the RLS, but we need to configure Envoy with the attributes to send to the RLS to be counted and rate-limited. To do that, let's apply the `EnvoyFilter` resource that does that, as we've seen:

```
$  kubectl apply -f ch14/rate-limit/catalog-ratelimit.yaml
$  kubectl apply -f ch14/rate-limit/catalog-ratelimit-actions.yaml
```

To test our rate-liming functionality, let's deploy the `sleep` app into the `istioinac-tion` namespace to simulate a client calling the `catalog` service. If you didn't install the `sleep` app earlier in the chapter, run the following command:

```
$  kubectl apply -f ch9/sleep.yaml
```

Once this Pod comes up successfully, let's make a call to the catalog service as in the following example:

```
$  kubectl exec -it deploy/sleep -c sleep -- \
curl http://catalog/items
```

You can run this command only approximately once a minute. This aligns with the rate limits specified for requests with no x-loyalty header. If you change the request to add an x-loyalty header, more requests per minute will be allowed. Experiment with the rate-limit enforcement by passing in different values for the x-loyalty header as in the following example:

```
kubectl exec -it deploy/sleep -c sleep -- \
curl -H "x-loyalty: silver" http://catalog/items
```

If you find that rate limiting is not enforced, you can check that all of the correct EnvoyFilter resources are applied and that the RLS is up and running without any errors in the logs. To double-check that the underlying Envoy configuration has the correct rate-limit actions, you can use istioctl to get the underlying routes for the catalog service:

```
$  istioctl proxy-config routes deploy/catalog.istioinaction -o json \
| grep actions
```

You should see multiple output lines with the word actions. If you don't, something wasn't configured right, and you should double-check that things were applied correctly.

14.4   *Extending Istio's data plane with Lua*

Extending Istio's data plane by configuring existing Envoy filters is convenient, but what if the functionality we want to add doesn't already exist as an out-of-the box Envoy filter? What if we want to implement some custom logic on the request path? In this section, we look at how to extend data-plane behavior with our own custom logic.

We saw in the previous sections that Envoy has a lot of out-of-the-box filters that we can add to a filter chain to enhance the behavior of the Envoy data plane. One of those is the Lua filter, which allows us to customize the behavior of the request or response path by writing Lua scripts and injecting them into the proxy (see figure 14.9). These scripts can be used to manipulate the headers and inspect the body of a request or response. We will continue to use the EnvoyFilter resource to configure the data plane to inject Lua scripts to change the processing of the request path.

Lua programming language

Lua is a powerful, embeddable scripting language that can be used to enhance the capabilities of a system. Lua runs as a dynamically typed and interpreted language with automatic memory management provided by a Lua VM (in Envoy, this is LuaJIT). See https://lua.org and https://luajit.org for more information.

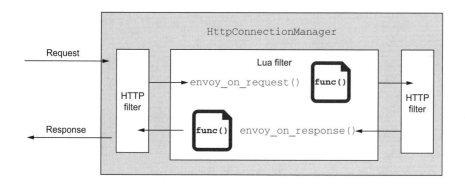

Figure 14.9 Extending request-path functionality with Lua scripting language

NOTE Inspecting the request body can impact how the stream is treated in the proxy. For example, you may run operations on the body that cause it to be fully buffered into memory. This can have performance impacts. See the Envoy proxy documentation on the Lua filter: http://mng.bz/AxOW.

Let's take a common example for customizing the behavior of the request path. Suppose we want to treat every request that comes in as part of an A/B testing group. We can only determine the correct group at run time based on characteristics of the request. To do so, we need to call out to an A/B testing engine to determine the group to which a particular request belongs. The response from this call-out should be added as a header to the request, and any upstream service can use this header to make decisions about routing for A/B testing purposes.

Before we get started, let's remove the configuration from the previous section:

```
$ kubectl delete envoyfilter -n istioinaction --all
```

Let's deploy some supporting services for this example. We deploy a sample `httpbin` service that will echo back the request headers we send into the service. We also deploy our sample A/B testing bucket service. This service evaluates a request's headers and returns a string representing a particular group that request should be in:

```
$ kubectl apply -f ch14/httpbin.yaml
$ kubectl apply -f ch14/bucket-tester-service.yaml
```

Let's look at a Lua script we can write to manipulate the request or response headers and how we can implement this use case. In Envoy, we can implement the `envoy_on_request ()` or `envoy_on_response()` Lua function to inspect and manipulate the request and response, respectively. If we need to make a call to another service from within Lua, we have to use an Envoy-provided function (we should not use a general-purpose Lua library to make RPC calls, because we want Envoy to manage the call correctly with its non-blocking threading architecture). We can use the `http-Call ()` function to communicate with an external service. The following script implements our use case:

```
function envoy_on_request(request_handle)
  local headers, test_bucket = request_handle:httpCall(
  "bucket_tester",
```

```
    {
      [":method"] = "GET",
      [":path"] = "/",
      [":scheme"] = "http",
      [":authority"] = "bucket-tester.istioinaction.svc.cluster.local",
      ["accept"] = "*/*"
    }, "", 5000)

    request_handle:headers():add("x-test-cohort", test_bucket)
end
```

We implement the `envoy_on_request()` function, and we use the `httpCall()` built-in function to communicate with an external service. We take the response and add it to a header called `x-test-cohort`. See the Envoy documentation for more about the built-in functions, including `httpCall ()`: http://mng.bz/mx2r.

We can add this script to an `EnvoyFilter` resource as we did in the previous section:

```
apiVersion: networking.istio.io/v1alpha3
kind: EnvoyFilter
metadata:
  name: webapp-lua-extension
  namespace: istioinaction
spec:
  workloadSelector:
    labels:
      app: httpbin
  configPatches:
  - applyTo: HTTP_FILTER
    match:
      context: SIDECAR_INBOUND
      listener:
        portNumber: 80
        filterChain:
          filter:
            name: "envoy.filters.network.http_connection_manager"
            subFilter:
              name: "envoy.filters.http.router"
    patch:
      operation: INSERT_BEFORE
      value:
       name: envoy.lua
       typed_config:
         "@type": "type.googleapis.com/
envoy.extensions.filters.http.lua.v3.Lua"
          inlineCode: |
            function envoy_on_request(request_handle)
              -- some code here
            end
            function envoy_on_response(response_handle)
              -- some code here
            end
```

We apply this filter to the `httpbin` workloads as defined by the `workloadSelector` in the previous listing:

```
$  kubectl apply -f ch14/lua-filter.yaml
```

If we make a call to our `httpbin` service, we should see a new header `x-test-cohort` that gets added when we make the call-out to the A/B testing service:

```
$  kubectl exec -it deploy/sleep  \
-- curl httpbin.istioinaction:8000/headers

{
  "headers": {
    "Accept": "*/*",
    "Content-Length": "0",
    "Host": "httpbin.istioinaction:8000",
    "User-Agent": "curl/7.69.1",
    "X-B3-Sampled": "1",
    "X-B3-Spanid": "1d066f4b17ee147b",
    "X-B3-Traceid": "1ec27110e4141e131d066f4b17ee147b",
    "X-Test-Cohort": "dark-launch-7"
  }
}
```

You can examine the details more closely in the ch14/lua-filter.yaml file in the book's source code. In this example, we saw how to use a filter that was purposefully built to extend the functionality of the data plane. We used the Lua scripting language to implement this functionality and some built-in functions to make callouts to other services. In the next section, we see how to use other languages to implement our custom functionality with WebAssembly.

14.5 Extending Istio's data plane with WebAssembly

The last approach to extend Istio on the request path that we cover in this chapter is writing new Envoy filters with WebAssembly. In the previous sections, we reused existing Envoy filters and configured them to extend the out-of-the-box Istio capabilities, including injecting our own custom scripts to manipulate the request path. In this section, we explore how we can build our own Envoy filters and dynamically deploy them to the Istio data plane.

14.5.1 Introducing WebAssembly

WebAssembly (Wasm) is a binary instruction format that is intended to be portable across environments and that can be compiled from many different programming languages and run in a VM. Wasm was originally developed to speed up the execution of CPU-intensive operations for web apps in a browser and extend the support for browser-based apps to languages other than JavaScript (see figure 14.10). It became a W3C Recommendation in 2019 and is supported in all major browsers.

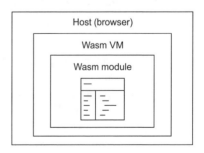

Figure 14.10 WebAssembly is custom code packaged as a module that can run safely in a sandboxed VM within a target host like a web browser.

Wasm is intended to have a compact size and load footprint and execute at near-native speeds. It is also safe to embed in host applications (that is, a browser) because it is memory safe and runs in a sandboxed execution environment (VM). A Wasm module only has access to memory and functionality that the host system allows.

14.5.2 Why WebAssembly for Envoy?

There are two main drawbacks to writing your own native Envoy filter:

- It must be in C++.
- You must statically build the changes into a new Envoy binary, which effectively becomes a "custom" build of Envoy.

Envoy embeds a WebAssembly execution engine that can be used to customize and extend various areas of Envoy, including HTTP filters. You can write Envoy filters in any language supported by Wasm and dynamically load them into the proxy at run time, as shown in figure 14.11. This means you can keep using the out-of-the-box Envoy proxy in Istio and dynamically load your custom filters at run time.

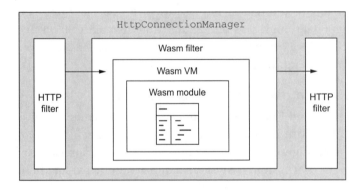

Figure 14.11   A Wasm module can be packaged and run within the Wasm HTTP filter.

14.5.3 Building a new Envoy filter with WebAssembly

To build an Envoy filter with WebAssembly, you need to know what language you want to use, what Envoy version you're on, and what Envoy Abstract Binary Interface (ABI) is supported by that particular version of Envoy. Then you need to pick the correct language SDK and set up the build and dependency toolchain correctly. For this section, we use an open source developer tool called wasme from the folks at Solo.io to create and build Wasm filters for Envoy. With wasme, you can quickly bootstrap a Wasm for the Envoy project and automate any of the boilerplate scaffolding. Let's see how to get started building Envoy filters with Wasm.

At the time of this writing, there are Envoy Wasm SDKs for the following four programming languages:

- C++
- Rust

- AssemblyScript (TypeScript)
- TinyGo

In this section, we build a new Envoy filter with Wasm using the AssemblyScript language (www.assemblyscript.org). AssemblyScript is a variant of TypeScript, so JavaScript developers should be familiar with it. It gives a nice alternative to C++ when building filters for Envoy.

> **NOTE** WebAssembly support in Envoy is considered experimental and subject to change. We recommend thoroughly testing any Wasm modules you create and deploy to Envoy before getting into a production environment.

14.5.4 *Building a new Envoy filter with the meshctl tool*

The meshctl tool is a Docker-like tool for creating, building, publishing, and deploying Wasm modules; it significantly simplifies the user experience when building Wasm filters for Envoy. First, download meshctl and put it on your system path:

```
curl -sL https://run.solo.io/meshctl/install | sh
export PATH=$HOME/.gloo-mesh/bin:$PATH
```

Next, pick a folder to bootstrap a new Wasm project, and then run the following command:

```
$ meshctl wasm init ./hello-wasm --language=assemblyscript
```

This creates a new folder called hello-wasm, all the dependency files, and even an index.ts file with the initial implementation of a filter. This initial implementation shows how to add a header to an HTTP response. If you look into ./hello-wasm/assembly/index.ts, you should see two TypeScript classes created. The first class, AddHeaderRoot, sets up any custom configuration for the Wasm module. The second class, AddHeader, contains the meat of the implementation where you can implement the callback functions that end up processing the request path. In this example, we implement the onResponseHeaders function of the AddHeader class like this:

```
class AddHeader extends Context {
  root_context : AddHeaderRoot;
  constructor(root_context:AddHeaderRoot){
    super();
    this.root_context = root_context;
  }
  onResponseHeaders(a: u32): FilterHeadersStatusValues {
    const root_context = this.root_context;
    if (root_context.configuration == "") {
      stream_context.headers.response.add("hello", "world!");
    } else {
      stream_context.headers.response.add("hello",
        root_context.configuration);
    }
    return FilterHeadersStatusValues.Continue;
  }
}
```

There are also other useful functions for manipulating the request or response:

- onRequestHeaders
- onRequestBody
- onResponseHeaders
- onResponseBody

If we navigate into the hello-wasm folder, we can build the Wasm module with the meshctl wasm tooling like this:

```
$  meshctl wasm build assemblyscript ./hello-wasm/ \
 -t webassemblyhub.io/ceposta/istioinaction-demo:0.1
```

The meshctl wasm tool handles all of the boilerplate tool-chain setup and initiates a build appropriate for the language originally chosen for the module. The output for the build process creates an Open Container Initiative (OCI)-compliant image packaged with the .wasm module as one of the layers in the image.

You can use the meshctl wasm tool to list what modules you have locally:

```
$ meshctl wasm list
NAME                                            TAG SIZE     SHA
webasseblyhub.io/ceposta/cache-example          1.0 12.6 kB  10addc6d
webassemblyhub.io/ceposta/demo-filter           1.0 12.6 kB  a515a5d2
webassemblyhub.io/ceposta/istioinaction-demo    0.1 12.6 kB  a515a5d2
```

You can publish this module to a registry capable of storing OCI images. For example, to use the free webassemblyhub.io repository, you can publish your module like this:

```
$  meshctl wasm push webassemblyhub.io/ceposta/istioinaction-demo:1.0
```

> **WebAssembly Hub**
>
> WebAssembly Hub (webassemblyhub.io) is a free, open, community registry for storing Wasm filters that can then be deployed into Envoy proxy or Istio. See the latest docs for WebAssembly Hub for more information: https://docs.solo.io/web-assembly-hub/latest.

To see the details of a specific OCI image, you can check the ~/.gloo-mesh/wasm/ store folder and find the image that was just built. For example:

```
$ ls -l ~/.gloo-mesh/wasm/store/bc234119a3962de1907a394c186bc486/

total 28
-rw-r--r-- 1 solo solo   224 Jul  2 19:04 descriptor.json
-rw-rw-r-- 1 solo solo 12553 Jul  2 19:04 filter.wasm
-rw-r--r-- 1 solo solo    43 Jul  2 19:04 image_ref
-rw-r--r-- 1 solo solo   221 Jul  2 19:04 runtime-config.json
```

Here you can see the filter.wasm binary along with some metadata files that describe the OCI image and the versions of Envoy (and associated ABIs) that are compatible with the filter. The intention of the image-based packaging is to store it in an existing OCI registry and build tooling to support it.

> **Packaging of Wasm modules**
>
> The Istio community is working on a specification that describes Wasm modules packaged as OCI images. It is based on the work Solo.io contributed (https://github.com/solo-io/wasm/tree/master/spec) and is used in the `meshctl wasm` tooling. This area continues to evolve, and at the time of this writing it is very much in flux.

14.5.5 Deploying a new WebAssembly Envoy filter

Before we get started, let's remove the configuration from the previous section (or any previous attemps to deploy a Wasm filter):

```
$  kubectl delete envoyfilter,wasmplugin -n istioinaction --all
```

Let's deploy some supporting services for this example. We deploy a sample `httpbin` service that will echo back the request headers we send into the service:

```
$  kubectl apply -f ch14/httpbin.yaml
```

In the previous section, we created a new Wasm module from scratch, built and packaged it, and published it to a Wasm registry. In this section, we use Istio's `WasmPlugin` resource to deploy the Wasm filter to workloads running in the service mesh to enhance the capabilities of the request/response path.

Here is a simple `WasmPlugin` resource that selects the `httpbin` workload and specifies the module URL (`oci`, `file` or `https`) to load the Wasm filter into the Istio data plane:

```
apiVersion: extensions.istio.io/v1alpha1
kind: WasmPlugin
metadata:
  name: httpbin-wasm-filter
  namespace: istioinaction
spec:
  selector:
    matchLabels:              ⟵─┐ Workload
      app: httpbin            ⟵─┘ selector
  pluginName: add_header                                        ┐ Module
  url: oci://webassemblyhub.io/ceposta/istioinaction-demo:1.0 ⟵─┘ URL
```

In this example, we pull the module directly from an OCI-compliant registry. We already published our Wasm module to the `webasseblyhub.io` registry in the previous section, and in this configuration we pull it directly down from the registry into the proxy.

Let's apply the Wasm filter:

```
$  kubectl apply -f ch14/wasm/httpbin-wasm-filter.yaml
```

Now, when we make a call to the `httpbin` service, we can verify that we get the expected results. In this case, we expect to see a response header called "hello" with a value of "world":

```
$ kubectl exec -it deploy/sleep -c sleep -- \
curl -v httpbin:8000/status/200

*   Trying 10.102.125.217:8000...
* Connected to httpbin (10.102.125.217) port 8000 (#0)
> GET /status/200 HTTP/1.1
> Host: httpbin:8000
> User-Agent: curl/7.79.1
> Accept: */*
>
* Mark bundle as not supporting multiuse
< HTTP/1.1 200 OK
< server: envoy
< date: Mon, 06 Dec 2021 16:02:37 GMT
< content-type: text/html; charset=utf-8
< access-control-allow-origin: *
< access-control-allow-credentials: true
< content-length: 0
< x-envoy-upstream-service-time: 3          Expected response
< hello: world!                  ◄───────┘  header
<
* Connection #0 to host httpbin left intact
```

Although this example was simple, more complex processing and logic can be built into the filter. With WebAssembly, you can pick the language of your choice to extend Envoy proxy and dynamically load the module at runtime. With Istio the `WasmPlugin` is used to declaratively load the Wasm module.

Summary

- Envoy's internal architecture is built around listeners and filters.
- There are many out-of-the-box Envoy filters.
- We can extend Istio's data plane (Envoy proxy).
- Envoy's HTTP filter architecture can be configured directly with Istio's `Envoy-Filter` resource for more fine-grained configuration or to configure aspects of Envoy not exposed by Istio's API.
- We can extend Envoy's request path for service-to-service communication with functionality like rate limiting or the tap filter.
- Lua and Wasm are available for more advanced customizations to the data plane without having to rebuild Envoy.

appendix A
Customizing the
Istio installation

It may surprise you that we dive into the customization of the Istio installation without initially covering the installation. But installing Istio is easy peasy: you apply the Istio resources to a Kubernetes cluster, and that's it.

There are many ways to apply Istio resources to the cluster:

- helm—The Kubernetes package manager command-line interface can be used to generate and apply the Istio resources to the cluster. All the customization possibilities of the Istio installation are powered by Helm templating.
- istioctl—Exposes a simpler and safer API to install and customizes Istio using the IstioOperator custom resource definition (CRD). Under the hood, it uses Helm to generate the Istio resources.
- istio-operator—An operator running on the cluster side that manages Istio installations in clusters using the IstioOperator API.
- kubectl—Or any tool (ArgoCD, Flux, and so on) that takes Kubernetes resources and applies them to the cluster.

Configuring Istio to run in different environments, such as different cloud providers or networking topology, and to meet different application and security requirements becomes quite complex! Initially, Helm was the main tool to install Istio. But as the number of configuration options grew, it became apparent that Helm's lack of user-input validation led to too many errors, that at best it was annoying to deal with, and that at worst it was a question of time until an indentation error would cause production outages.

A.1   The IstioOperator API

The IstioOperator API (http://mng.bz/PWXP) is a Kubernetes CRD that specifies the desired state of an Istio installation. As a user, you have to define the desired state; then it's up to the tools (such as `istioctl` and `istio-operator`) to use it and figure out how to get from the current installation—or lack thereof—to the new desired state.

The `IstioOperator` API provides two major benefits. The first is user-input validation, which is big! Previously, when the configuration didn't work, you'd have to dig into the source code and reverse engineer the configuration capabilities just to find out that the issue was a typo or an indentation error. The second benefit is that having a well-defined API lets you consult the docs and discover all the configuration possibilities in Istio, which makes coming up with the desired configuration straightforward.

This API was a major improvement; however, to get Istio up and running, there is still a ton of configuration needed. Istio tackles this, too, with ready-to-use installation profiles.

A.2   *The Istio installation profiles*

The installation profiles are predefined configurations that serve as a starting point for installing Istio in a cluster. Recall that throughout the book, we've used the `demo` installation profile. This profile comes with the control plane and the ingress and egress gateways.

In the following listing, we use `istioctl` to print all the built-in profiles. We've added code annotations that explain each profile:

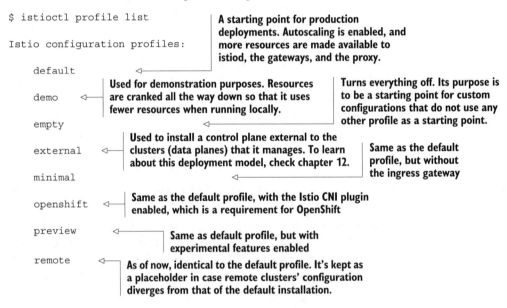

You can view the definition of any of the profiles using the `istioctl profile dump` subcommand:

```
$  istioctl profile dump demo

apiVersion: install.istio.io/v1alpha1
```

```
kind: IstioOperator
spec:
  components:
    egressGateways:           List of egress
    - enabled: true       ◁──┘ gateways
      name: istio-egressgateway   Demo profile comes with
    ingressGateways:              one egress gateway       List of ingress
    - enabled: true             ◁────────────────────┘    gateways
      name: istio-ingressgateway   The demo profile comes
      #...                         with one ingress gateway.
    istiodRemote: {...}
    pilot: {...}
    #...                     The content
  meshConfig: {...}          is collapsed.
  values: {...}
```

It's important to realize that we were using the demo configuration (shown in the list-ing) throughout the book when we installed Istio. Next, let's showcase how to custom-ize the profiles using the IstioOperator API. A good example is to decouple the lifecycle management of the data plane from that of the control plane, which simpli-fies installation and makes control-plane upgrades transparent for the data plane (which is a recommended best practice).

A.3 Installing and customizing Istio using istioctl

To decouple the control-plane and data-plane installation, you need two separate IstioOperator custom resources. The first resource handles the control-plane com-ponents; meanwhile, the second handles the data-plane components.

   To install the control plane without the gateways, we'll use the demo profile as a starting point. Then we will set the gateway components to disabled. This is achieved with the following IstioOperator definition:

```
apiVersion: install.istio.io/v1alpha1
kind: IstioOperator
metadata:
  name: control-plane
spec:                      The demo profile
  profile: demo        ◁──┘ is used as the base.
  components:
    egressGateways:
    - name: istio-egressgateway    The egress gateway defined in
      enabled: false               the demo profile is set to false.
    ingressGateways:
    - name: istio-ingressgateway   The ingress gateway defined in
      enabled: false               the demo profile is set to false.
```

This manifest is stored in the file appendices/demo-profile-without-gateways.yaml. Apply it to the cluster with this command:

```
$ istioctl install -f appendices/demo-profile-without-gateways.yaml
```

You can verify that the control plane is installed without the gateways by querying the Pods in the Istio installation namespace.

With the first step done, we are ready to install the gateways separately. To do so, let's create another IstioOperator definition that defines only one ingress gateway. But which profile should we use as a starting point? If we use the demo profile, it will re-install all the previously applied resources, such as the roles and role bindings, custom resource definitions, and configuration, thus interfering with the previous installation. As we mentioned in the list of configuration profiles, the empty profile turns everything off. Then we can selectively enable the ingress gateway:

```
apiVersion: install.istio.io/v1alpha1
kind: IstioOperator
metadata:
  name: ingress-gateway       ◁┐  The name must be different from the
spec:                             previous installation. Otherwise, it
  profile: empty                  would override the installation and
  components:                     remove the control-plane components.
    ingressGateways:
    - name: ingressgateway
      namespace: istio-system
      enabled: true
      label:
        istio: ingressgateway
      k8s:
        resources:
          requests:
            cpu: 100m
            memory: 160Mi
```

Apply it to the cluster:

```
$  istioctl install -f appendices/ingress-gateway.yaml
```

Query the Istio installation namespace, and verify that the gateways are created. Here, we split the management of the control plane from that of the ingress gateway. Decoupling the control plane from the gateways is the first step to allow for more control when managing and upgrading gateways.

> **NOTE** You can learn more about managing and upgrading gateways at the official docs: http://mng.bz/J16v.

Let's clean up the environment and start with a clean slate when we showcase the same thing using the istio-operator:

```
$  kubectl delete namespace istio-system
```

A.4   *Installing and customizing Istio with the istio-operator*

A Kubernetes Operator is a type of Kubernetes controller that contains operational knowledge about a particular software; it exposes the management of that software through Kubernetes custom resources. In the context of the istio-operator, it manages Istio installations in a cluster and allows the customization of the installation using the IstioOperator API.

The istio-operator (just like any other operator) must be able to talk to the Kubernetes API server to perform its duties. The most straightforward approach is to install the operator in the cluster itself. The operator from within the cluster will authenticate to the API server using Kubernetes RBAC and watch for events of Istio-Operator resources. If a new IstioOperator resource is created, the operator will install Istio according to its definition. If an existing IstioOperator resource is updated, the operator will update the existing Istio installation to match the new IstioOperator definition (see figure A.1).

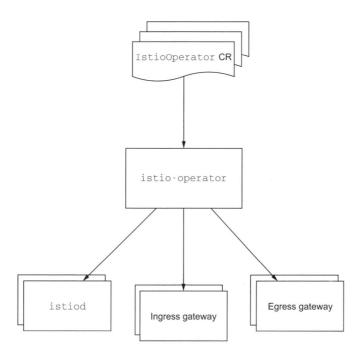

Figure A.1 The istio-operator manages Istio installations in a cluster.

You may worry that introducing another component increases complexity, as it needs to be maintained, and it's another place for bugs to hide. And frankly, you'd be right! However, the promise of the operator is that its benefits outweigh the downsides. It promotes using patterns such as GitOps, where changes committed to Git are propagated to the cluster by continuous delivery pipelines, and the operator updates the Istio installation to match the new desired state.

A.4.1 Installing the istio-operator

We can install the istio-operator using istioctl:

```
$  istioctl operator init

✓ Istio operator installed
✓ Installation complete
```

With the operator installed, we can start and apply `IstioOperator` resources. Let's use the same example with two `IstioOperator` definitions, where one is for the control plane and the other for the data plane:

```
$ kubectl apply -f appendices/demo-profile-without-gateways.yaml \
    -n istio-system

istiooperator.install.istio.io/control-plane created
```

When the operator receives the event that the `IstioOperator` resource is created, it reads the content and, based on it, installs the components: in this case, the control plane. The next step is to install the ingress gateway. This too is just a matter of applying the same `IstioOperator` definition as previously with `istioctl`:

```
$ kubectl apply -f appendices/ingress-gateway.yaml -n istio-system

istiooperator.install.istio.io/ingress-gateway created
```

And we're done!

A.4.2   *Updating the installation of a mesh*

Let's illustrate how the operator enables a fire-and-forget approach, where we make a configuration change and let the operator do the actual work to update the installation and match the desired state. As an example, we'll update the earlier control-plane installation to print access logs in JSON format:

```
apiVersion: install.istio.io/v1alpha1
kind: IstioOperator
metadata:
  name: control-plane        ◁─┐ Must match the installation
spec:                          │ that has to be updated
  profile: demo
  meshConfig:
    accessLogEncoding: JSON   ◁─┐ Access logs are
  components:                   │ formatted as JSON.
    egressGateways:
    - name: istio-egressgateway
      enabled: false
    ingressGateways:
    - name: istio-ingressgateway
      enabled: false
```

Note that it is important for the name of the `IstioOperator` resource to match the name of the installation we want to update. If the names don't match, the operator will assume that the intent is to have a second control plane—which also has its uses for multi-tenancy, canary upgrades, and so on. Apply the updated definition to the cluster:

```
$ kubectl apply -f appendices/demo-profile-without-gateways-json.yaml \
    -n istio-system

istiooperator.install.istio.io/control-plane configured
```

The operator distributes the new configuration to the data plane. In the meantime, you're free to grab a coffee, smoke a cigarette (please, for your health's sake, don't!), or, if you are a control freak, validate that the change was propagated and turn the fire-and-forget process into a "fire-and-meticulously-validate" process.

With all the options, you may be wondering, "What is the right way to install Istio?" Our recommendation is to use either the `istio-operator` or `istioctl`, as they use the `IstioOperator` API, which adds another layer of safety with its user-input validation capabilities. We frequently see enterprises leaning toward the `istio-operator` because it is the GitOps approach and is more fitting to their ideology. In practice, however, the operator adds complexity and requires maintenance. Further, you can use `istioctl` and still adhere to the GitOps approach. Keep in mind that, being pragmatic about its definition, GitOps basically means operations of services and their configuration are sourced from a Git repository. It doesn't matter what tool uses the configuration—`istioctl`, Ansible, or any other tool.

appendix B
Istio's sidecar and its injection options

In this book and in the wider Istio community, we synecdochically refer to Istio's sidecar as the *service proxy* or *Envoy proxy*. This is natural because the proxy does the heavy lifting for most of Istio's features. Yet this is not a one-person show; for example, without supportive components, the proxy cannot place itself in the request path of traffic directed toward apps (shortly, we explain how it does that). There are many other examples where Envoy is helpless, such as getting its identity bootstrapped, certificate rotation, and so on.

The sidecar has these components:

- The Istio agent, often referred to as the *pilot agent*, has important functions such as starting the Envoy proxy within the sidecar container and bootstrapping its identity. Afterward, it maintains a bidirectional connection with the control plane, receives the latest mesh configuration, and applies that configuration to the Envoy proxy.

- The *local DNS proxy* is a recent addition to the Istio agent. It resolves cluster hostnames when integrating virtual machines into the mesh or joining multiple clusters into a single mesh. By default, the DNS proxy is disabled, but it can be enabled during Istio installation.

- The *Envoy proxy* is started as a process and configured within the sidecar container by the Istio agent.

Another integral component of the workload is the `istio-init` container that configures the Pod environment to redirect inbound and outbound traffic from the application to the service proxy. This container uses a Kubernetes feature called *init containers* (http://mng.bz/7WWm) to run before any other container and, as a result, configures Iptable rules and inserts the Envoy proxy into the request path of the application before any traffic reaches the application.

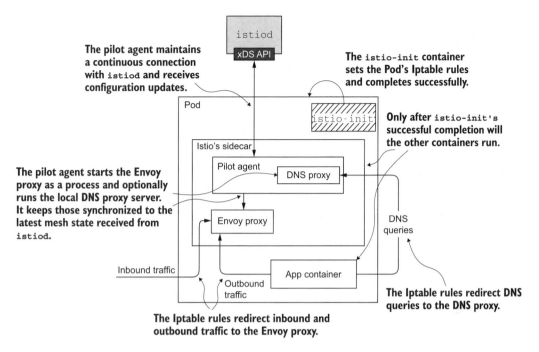

Figure B.1   Istio's data-plane components

Figure B.1 visualizes the relationship between the components of the data plane, how they work together to get the workload identity and configuration to the proxies, and how the configured Iptable rules redirect traffic to go through the proxy. Next, let's elaborate on the options for injecting data-plane components into Kubernetes workloads.

B.1   Sidecar injection

Sidecar injection is the process of updating the Kubernetes application specifications, which are written in YAML to contain the data-plane components. For example, here is a standard Kubernetes app definition that lacks those components:

```
apiVersion: apps/v1
kind: Deployment
metadata:
  name: httpbin
spec:
  selector:
    matchLabels:
      app: httpbin
  template:
    metadata:
      labels:
```

```
      app: httpbin
  spec:
    containers:
    - image: docker.io/kennethreitz/httpbin
      name: httpbin
      ports:
      - containerPort: 80
```

We could manually edit this definition and add the containers. However, updating YAML is notoriously error-prone, and Istio provides us with simpler options.

B.1.1 Manual sidecar injection

In the manual sidecar-injection approach, we feed the app definition to `istioctl` and let it add the data-plane components for us. On second thought, the process isn't that manual, after all! Here, we inject the components in the previous deployment:

```
$  istioctl kube-inject -f deployment.yaml
```

Figure B.2. shows the output after injecting the data-plane components into the deployment. While prototyping you can pipe the output of the above command to `kubectl`

```
$ istioctl kube-inject -f deployment.yaml

apiVersion: apps/v1
kind: Deployment
metadata:
  name: httpbin
spec:
  template:
    spec:
      containers:
      - image: docker.io/kennethreitz/httpbin
        name: httpbin
        ports:
        - containerPort: 80
      - args:
        - proxy
        - sidecar
        # ... more arguments
        image: docker.io/istio/proxyv2:1.11.0
        name: istio-proxy
      initContainers:
      - args:
        - istio-iptables
        # ... even more arguments
        image: docker.io/istio/proxyv2:1.11.0
        name: istio-init
        securityContext:
          capabilities:
            add:
            - NET_ADMIN
            - NET_RAW
            drop:
            - ALL
```

App container

The injected sidecar container

The injected `istio-init` init container

The `istio-init` container requires privileged capabilities. When misused, they can pose a security threat!

Figure B.2 Injecting the data-plane components into the deployment

`apply` (as we do throughout the book) to apply it to the cluster. For real production clusters, you'd manually update every service and store the changes in a Git repository used by your continuous delivery pipelines to apply the changes to the clusters.

With automatic sidecar injection, the manual steps are not needed. Let's take a look.

B.1.2 *Automatic sidecar injection*

Automatic sidecar injection uses Kubernetes mutating admission webhooks to inject data-plane components into the `Pod` definition before it is applied to the Kubernetes datastore (see figure B.3). The modifications are the same as when using `istioctl`. However, app definitions can be applied as is, and the webhook injects the components automatically.

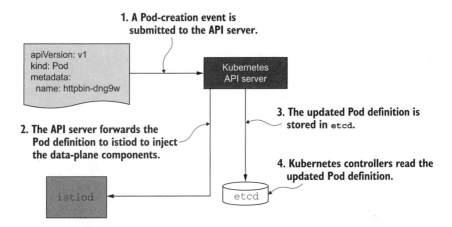

Figure B.3   Automatic sidecar injection using mutating admission webhooks

Automatic sidecar injection is an opt-in feature enabled on a namespace-by-namespace basis. To do this, you label the namespace with `istio-injection=enabled`. Let's create a namespace and label it for automatic injection:

```
$ kubectl create namespace istioinaction
$ kubectl label namespace istioinaction istio-injection=enabled
```

Now, switch to the newly created namespace:

```
$ kubectl config set-context $(kubectl config current-context) \
  --namespace=istioinaction
```

From now on, the data-plane components will be injected into Pods created in this namespace. To verify that, let's create a deployment, which in turn creates the Pods that are intercepted and updated:

```
$ kubectl apply -f services/catalog/kubernetes/catalog.yaml
```

Verify that the Pod definition was updated:

```
$  POD_NAME=$(kubectl get pod -o jsonpath={.items..metadata.name})
$  kubectl get pod $POD_NAME -o yaml
```

```
apiVersion: v1
kind: Pod
metadata:
  name: catalog-68666d4988-mfszp
  namespace: istioinaction
spec:
  containers:
  - image: istioinaction/catalog:latest          The application
    name: catalog
  - args:
    - proxy
    - sidecar                                     The sidecar
    # ... more arguments
    image: docker.io/istio/proxyv2:1.13.0
    name: istio-proxy
  initContainers:
  - args:
    - istio-iptables
    # ... even more arguments                     The istio-init container
    image: docker.io/istio/proxyv2:1.13.0
    name: istio-init
```

The output shows that the webhook made the same changes as when using `istioctl` (shown in the output in figure B.2).

How is Kubernetes configured to route Pod-creation events to the control plane for modification?

The Kubernetes API server is configured by the `MutatingWebhookConfiguration` resource to route matching events to an external service for modification. To list the mutating webhook configuration that injects the sidecar, execute this command:

```
$  kubectl get MutatingWebhookConfiguration

NAME                        WEBHOOKS    AGE
istio-sidecar-injector      4           4d3h
```

To get more details, print the configuration in the verbose YAML format. You'll see the resources and operations that have to match for the request to be sent to Istiod for modification.

Feel free to select whichever option—manual or automatic—makes more sense for your organization. We frequently see organizations adopt automatic sidecar injection because this approach is easier and doesn't require the effort to manually update all service definitions. But it isn't rare for organizations to prefer manual injection as it gives them complete control over what's being deployed.

B.2 *Security issues with istio-init*

The `istio-init` container requires elevated permissions to configure traffic redirection to the Envoy proxy. For some organizations, this requirement is against their security standards. This is frequently the case for organizations that use larger clusters shared by multiple tenants. In such larger clusters, and generally in all multi-tenant environments, an important security standard is that a tenant must not be able to harm another tenant. However, without permissions to run privileged containers, application teams cannot run workloads containing the `istio-init` container. On the other hand, if permissions are given to application teams to run elevated containers, those permissions can be abused and cause harm to other tenants.

To resolve this issue, the Istio Container Network Interface (CNI) plugin was introduced. This plugin moves the `istio-init` container functionality into centralized Pods that run on every node and configure the traffic redirection rules for every Pod. Thus the `istio-init` container is not needed, and neither are the elevated permissions required to run the container. To learn more about this, check out https://istio.io/latest/docs/setup/additional-setup/cni.

appendix C
Istio security: SPIFFE

C.1 Authentication using PKI (public key infrastructure)

Authentication of communicating parties on the World Wide Web is done using digitally signed certificates provisioned by a public key infrastructure (PKI). The PKI is a framework that defines the process of providing the server (such as a web app) with a digital certificate to prove its identity and providing the client with the means of verifying the validity of the digital certificate. To dive deeper into how the PKI works, check out https://www.securew2.com/blog/public-key-infrastructure -explained.

The certificates provisioned by the PKI have a public key and a private key. The public key is contained in the certificate presented to the client as a means of authentication; the client uses it to encrypt data before transmitting the data through the public network back to the server. Only the server with the private key can decrypt the data. In this manner, data is secure in transit.

> **NOTE** The standard format for public key certificates is known as X.509 certificates. In this book, the terms *X.509 certificates* and *digital certificates* are used interchangeably.

The Internet Engineering Task Force defined the Transport Layer Security (TLS) protocol (which uses but is not limited to the PKI) and provisioned X.509 certificates to facilitate authentication and encryption of traffic.

C.1.1 Traffic encryption via TLS and end-user authentication

The TLS protocol uses X.509 certificates as the primary mechanism for authenticating the validity of the servers and securely exchanging keys for symmetric encryption of the traffic in a process known as the *TLS handshake*, shown in figure C.1.

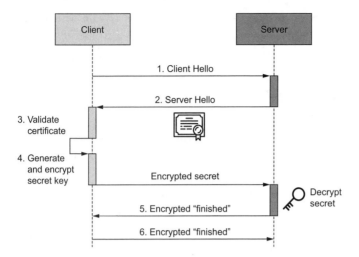

Figure C.1 Steps in a TLS handshake

Let's examine the steps in the figure:

1. The client initiates the handshake with `ClientHello` containing the TLS version and the encryption methods supported by the client.
2. The server responds with `ServerHello` and its X.509 certificate containing server identity data and the public key.
3. The client verifies that the server's certificate data is not tampered with and validates the chain of trust.
4. On a successful validation, the client sends the server a secret key: a randomly generated string encrypted with the server's public key.
5. The server uses its private key to decrypt the secret key and then uses the key to encrypt a "finished" message sent as a response back to the client.
6. The client sends the server an encrypted "finished" message using the secret key, and the TLS handshake is completed.

The result of the TLS handshake is that the client has authenticated the server and has exchanged the symmetric key securely. This symmetric key will be used to encrypt traffic between the client and the server for the duration of this connection, because this approach is more performant than asymmetric encryption. To the end user, this process is done transparently by the browser and denoted by the green lock in the address bar, ensuring that the receiving party is authenticated and that the traffic is encrypted and only the receiving party can decrypt it.

Authenticating the end user to the server is an application detail. There are multiple methods to do this, but all of them revolve around the user knowing a password and then receiving a session cookie or JSON Web Token (JWT), which is preferably short-lived and contains information to authenticate the users' subsequent requests to the server. Istio supports end-user authentication when using JWTs. We saw this in action in section 9.4.

C.2   SPIFFE: Secure Production Identity Framework for Everyone

SPIFFE is a set of open source standards for providing identity to workloads in highly dynamic and heterogeneous environments. To issue and bootstrap identity, SPIFFE defines the following specifications:

- *SPIFFE ID*—uniquely identifies a service within a trust domain.
- *Workload Endpoint*—bootstraps the identity of a workload.
- *Workload API* —signs and issues the certificate containing the SPIFFE ID.
- *SPIFFE Verifiable Identity Document (SVID)*—is represented as the certificate issued by the Workload API.

The SPIFFE specification defines the process of issuing an identity to a workload with the SPIFFE ID format and encoding it in an SVID, as well as how the control-plane component (Workload API) and data-plane component (workload endpoint) work together to verify, assign, and validate the identity of a workload. As those specifications are implemented by Istio, they warrant a deeper investigation.

C.2.1   SPIFFE ID: Workload identity

A SPIFFE ID is an RFC 3986 compliant URI in the following format: spiffe://trust -domain/path. The two variables here are as follows:

- *Trust-domain* represents the issuer of identity, such as an individual or organization.
- *Path* uniquely identifies a workload within the trust domain.

The details of how the path identifies the workload are left open-ended and can be decided by the implementer of the SPIFFE specification. In this appendix, we see how Istio uses Kubernetes service accounts to define the path that identifies the workload.

C.2.2   Workload API

The Workload API represents the control-plane component of the SPIFFE specification that exposes endpoints for workloads to fetch digital certificates that define their identity in a format known as the SVID.

The Workload API's two main functions are

- Issuing certificates to workloads using the certificate authority (CA) private key for signing certificate signing requests (CSRs) made by workloads
- Exposing an API to make its features available to workload endpoints

The specification sets a restriction that workloads must not possess secrets or other information that defines their identity. Otherwise, the system can easily be exploited by a malicious user who gets access to those secrets. As a consequence of the restriction, workloads lack a means of authentication and cannot initiate secure communication with the Workload API. To resolve this situation, SPIFFE defines the Workload Endpoint specification, which represents the data-plane component and performs all activities to bootstrap the identity of a workload, such as initiating secure communication with the Workload API and fetching SVIDs without being susceptible to eavesdropping or man-in-the-middle attacks.

C.2.3 Workload endpoints

A workload endpoint represents the data-plane component of the SPIFFE specification. It is deployed alongside every workload and provides the following functionalities:

- *Workload attestation*—Verifying the identity of a workload using a method such as kernel introspection or orchestrator interrogation.
- *Workload API exposure*—Initiating and maintaining secure communication with the Workload API. This secure communication is used to fetch and rotate SVIDs.

Figure C.2 shows an overview of the steps to issue identities to workloads:

1. The workload endpoint verifies the integrity of the workload (that is, performs workload attestation) and creates a CSR with the SPIFFE ID encoded in it.
2. The workload endpoint submits the CSR to the Workload API for signing.
3. The Workload API signs the CSR and responds with a digitally signed certificate that has the SPIFFE ID in the URI extension of the SAN. This certificate is the SVID that represents the workload identity.

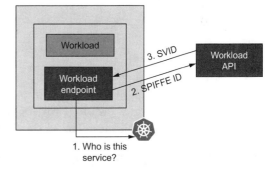

Figure C.2   Issuing an identity for a workload

C.2.4 SPIFFE Verifiable Identity Documents

SVIDs are documents that represent a verifiable workload identity. Being verifiable is the most important property, as otherwise the receiving party could not trust the identity of the workload. The specification defines two types of documents—X.509 certificates and JWTs—that meet the criteria to represent SVIDs, as both are composed of the following components:

- The SPIFFE ID, which represents the workload identity
- A valid signature to ensure that the SPIFFE ID is not tampered with
- (Optional) A public key to build secure communication channels between workloads

Istio implements X.509 certificates for SVIDs. It does so by encoding the SPIFFE ID as a URI in Subject Alternative Name (SAN) extensions. Using X.509 certificates has the additional benefit that workloads can mutually authenticate and encrypt traffic between each other (see figure C.3).

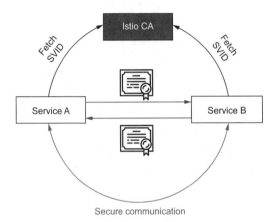

Secure communication

Figure C.3   Workloads fetching their SVIDs and initiating secure communication

By implementing the SPIFFE specification, Istio automatically ensures that all workloads have their identity provisioned and receive certificates as proof of their identity. Those certificates are used for mutual authentication and to encrypt all service-to-service communication. Hence this feature is called *auto mTLS*.

C.2.5   *How Istio implements SPIFFE*

With SPIFFE, the following two components work together to provide workloads with identities:

- The workload endpoint, bootstrapping identity
- The Workload API, issuing certificates

In Istio, the Workload Endpoint specification is implemented by the Istio proxy, as it is deployed alongside the workloads. The Istio proxy bootstraps the identity and fetches certificates from the Istio CA, which is a component of `istiod` and implements the Workload API specification.

Figure C.4 shows how Istio implements the SPIFFE components:

- The workload endpoint is implemented by the Istio Pilot agent that performs identity bootstrapping.
- The Workload API is implemented by Istio CA that issues certificates.
- The workload for which the identity is issued in Istio is the service proxy.

This is the high level of how Istio implements SPIFFE. Let's examine the process step by step to ensure that we understand it and that it sticks with us.

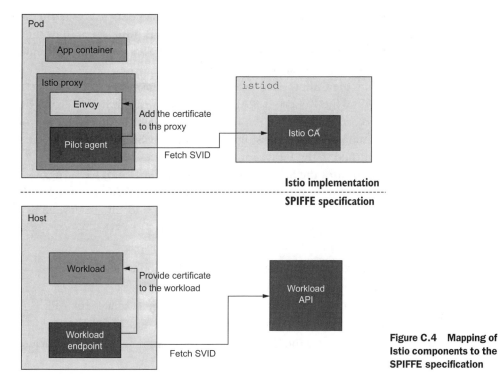

Figure C.4 Mapping of Istio components to the SPIFFE specification

C.2.6   Step-by-step bootstrapping of workload identity

By default, every Pod initialized in Kubernetes has a secret mounted in the path /var/run/secrets/kubernetes.io/serviceaccount/. This secret contains all the data needed to securely talk to the Kubernetes API server:

- The ca.crt validates the certificates that are issued by the Kubernetes API server.
- The namespace represents where the Pod is located.
- The service account token contains a set of claims for the service account representing the Pod.

For the identity-bootstrapping process, the most important element is the token, which is issued by Kubernetes API. Its payload cannot be modified, as otherwise it will fail signature validation. The payload contains data that identifies the application:

```
{
  "iss": "kubernetes/serviceaccount",
  "kubernetes.io/serviceaccount/namespace": "istioinaction",
  "kubernetes.io/serviceaccount/secret.name": "default-token-jl68q",
  "kubernetes.io/serviceaccount/service-account.name": "default",
  "kubernetes.io/serviceaccount/service-account.uid":
    "074055d3-05ca-4968-943a-598b90d1072c",
  "sub": "system:serviceaccount:istioinaction:default"
}
```

The Pilot agent decodes the token and uses the payload data to create the SPIFFE ID (e.g. spiffe://cluster.local/ns/istioinaction/sa/default), which is used in the CSR as a SAN extension of type URI. Both the token and the CSR are sent in the request to the Istio CA to get a certificate issued for the CSR.

Before signing the CSR, the Istio CA uses the `TokenReview` API to validate that the token was issued by the Kubernetes API. (This is a minor deviation from the SPIFFE specification, according to which the workload endpoint [Istio agent] should do the workload attestation.) On a successful validation, the CSR is signed, and the resulting certificate is returned to the Pilot agent.

The Pilot agent uses the Secrets Discovery Service (SDS) to forward the certificate and the key to the Envoy proxy, which marks the end of the Identity bootstrapping process. The proxy can now identify itself to clients and initiate mutually authenticated connections.

Figure C.5 briefly summarizes the steps:

1 A service account token is assigned to the Istio proxy container.
2 The token and a CSR are sent to `istiod`.
3 `istiod` validates the token using the Kubernetes `TokenReview` API.
4 On success, it signs the certificate and provides it as a response.
5 The Pilot agent uses the Envoy SDS to configure it to use the certificate containing the identity.

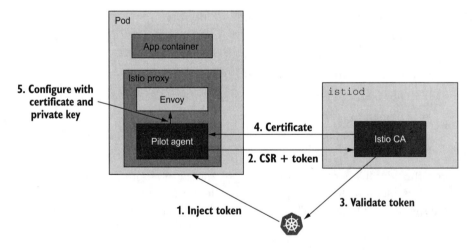

Figure C.5 Issuing an SVID in Kubernetes with Istio

And that's the entire process of how Istio implements the SPIFFE specification to provision workload identity. This process is done automatically for every workload with the Istio proxy sidecar injected.

C.3 *Understanding request identity*

Request identity is represented by the values stored in the filter metadata of the request. This filter metadata contains facts or claims that were extracted from either the JWT or the peer certificate and therefore can be trusted. In chapter 9, we covered how validating the information in the JWT requires a `RequestAuthentication` resource. Similarly, to authenticate the client workload information (such as the namespace it originates), the workloads must mutually authenticate. The `Peer-Authentication` resource can enforce workloads to use only mutual authentication.

After either the JWT is validated or workloads mutually authenticate, the information contained in them is stored as filter metadata. Some of the information stored in the filter metadata is as follows:

- *Principal*—The workload identity defined by the `PeerAuthentication`
- *Namespace*—The workload namespace defined by the `PeerAuthentication`
- *Request principal*—The end-user request principal defined by the `Request-Authentication`
- *Request authentication claims*—The end-user claims extracted from the end-user token

To observe the collected metadata, we can configure the service proxies to log it to standard output.

C.3.1 *Metadata collected by the RequestAuthentication resource*

By default, the Envoy `rbac` logger doesn't print the metadata in the logs. To print it, we need to set the logging level to `debug`:

```
$ istioctl proxy-config log deploy/istio-ingressgateway \
  -n istio-system --level rbac:debug
```

Next, we need a few services to play with. If you are starting from a clean environment with Istio installed and want to follow along, you only have to create the `istioinaction` namespace, deploy the workloads, and configure the ingress gateway to route traffic to it. All of that is done with the following commands:

```
$  kubectl create namespace istioinaction
$  kubectl label namespace istioinaction istio-injection=enabled
$  kubectl config set-context $(kubectl config current-context) \
  --namespace=istioinaction

$  kubectl apply -f services/catalog/kubernetes/catalog.yaml
$  kubectl apply -f services/webapp/kubernetes/webapp.yaml
$  kubectl apply -f services/webapp/istio/webapp-catalog-gw-vs.yaml
$  kubectl apply -f ch9/enduser/ingress-gw-for-webapp.yaml
```

Next, create the `RequestAuthentication` resource and an `AuthorizationPolicy` that uses the filter metadata:

```
$  kubectl apply -f ch9/enduser/jwt-token-request-authn.yaml
$  kubectl apply -f \
    ch9/enduser/allow-all-with-jwt-to-webapp.yaml
```

Make some requests utilizing the admin token, which will generate logs in the ingress gateway:

```
$  ADMIN_TOKEN=$(< ch9/enduser/admin.jwt);
   curl -H "Host: webapp.istioinaction.io" \
     -H "Authorization: Bearer $ADMIN_TOKEN" \
     -s -o /dev/null -w "%{http_code}" localhost/api/catalog

200
```

Now, query the ingress gateway logs to see the filter metadata:

```
$  kubectl -n istio-system logs \
     deploy/istio-ingressgateway -c istio-proxy

# logs omitted
, dynamicMetadata: filter_metadata {
  key: "envoy.filters.http.jwt_authn"
  value {
    fields {
      key: "auth@istioinaction.io"
      value {
        struct_value {
          fields {
            key: "exp"
            value {
              number_value: 4745145071
            }
          }
          fields {
            key: "group"
            value {
              string_value: "admin"
            }
          }
          fields {
            key: "iat"
            value {
              number_value: 1591545071
            }
          }
          fields {
            key: "iss"
            value {
              string_value: "auth@istioinaction.io"
            }
          }
          fields {
            key: "sub"
            value {
              string_value: "218d3fb9-4628-4d20-943c-124281c80e7b"
            }
          }
        }
# further logs omitted
```

The output shows that the RequestAuthentication filter validated the claims of the end-user token and stored the claims as filter metadata. Policies can now act based on this filter metadata.

C.3.2 *Overview of the flow of one request*

Every request targeting a workload goes through the following filters (see figure C.6):

- *JWT authentication filter*—An Envoy filter that does JWT validation based on the JWT specification in authentication policies and extracts claims such as the authentication claims and custom claims, which are stored as filter metadata
- *PeerAuthentication filter*—An Envoy filter that enforces service authentication requirements and extracts authenticated attributes (peer identity such as source namespace and principal)
- *Authorization filter*—The authorization engine that checks the filter metadata collected by the previous filters and authorizes the request based on the policies applied to the workload

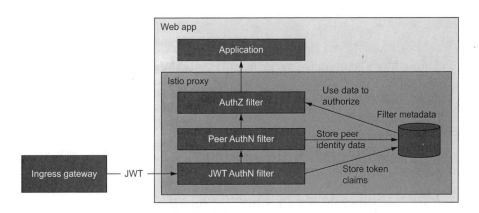

Figure C.6   Collection of validated data in filter metadata

Let's look at a scenario in which a request has to reach the webapp service:

1. The request passes the JWT authentication filter, which extracts the claims from the token and stores them in the filter metadata. This provides the request with an identity.
2. Peer-to-peer authentication is performed between the ingress gateway and the webapp. The peer-to-peer authentication filter extracts the identity data of the client and stores it in the filter metadata.
3. Authorization filters are executed in order:

- *Custom authorization filters*—Reject or allow further evaluation of the request.
- *Deny authorization filters*—Reject or allow further evaluation of the request.
- *Allow authorization filters*—Allow the request if the filter matches.
- *Last (catch-all) authorization filter*—Executed only if no prior filter has handled the request.

And that's how the request is authenticated and authorized for the request to get to the webapp service.

appendix D
Troubleshooting
Istio components

Throughout the book, we frequently query the Istio agent and Pilot to get information such as the configuration of a proxy, metrics exposed by it, and so on. These queries are shown on a use-case by use-case basis and are scattered throughout the book, making it difficult for the reader to recall what port 15000, 15020, or any of the other ports are. This appendix presents all the open ports and the endpoints where you can make requests to debug, troubleshoot, or get information from either the control plane or the service proxy to understand the workings of the mesh.

D.1 Information exposed by the Istio agent

The Istio sidecar provides a lot of functionality:

- *Health checking*—Envoy as a proxy is ready as soon as it can process traffic. But from the perspective of the service mesh, that doesn't suffice. There have to be more checks in place, such as whether the proxy receiving the configuration and being assigned an identity before it can serve traffic.
- *Metrics collection and exposure*—Within a service, three components generate metrics: the application, the agent, and the Envoy proxy. The agent aggregates the metrics from the other components and exposes them.
- DNS resolution, routing inbound and outbound traffic, and much more.

The services are exposed on numerous ports, and they may appear overwhelming when you list all of them:

```
$  kubectl -n istioinaction exec -it deploy/webapp \
     -c istio-proxy -- netstat -tnl

Active Internet connections (only servers)
```

```
Proto Recv-Q Send-Q Local Address      Foreign Address  State
tcp        0      0 0.0.0.0:15021      0.0.0.0:*        LISTEN
tcp        0      0 0.0.0.0:15021      0.0.0.0:*        LISTEN
tcp        0      0 0.0.0.0:15090      0.0.0.0:*        LISTEN
tcp        0      0 0.0.0.0:15090      0.0.0.0:*        LISTEN
tcp        0      0 127.0.0.1:15000    0.0.0.0:*        LISTEN
tcp        0      0 0.0.0.0:15001      0.0.0.0:*        LISTEN
tcp        0      0 0.0.0.0:15001      0.0.0.0:*        LISTEN
tcp        0      0 127.0.0.1:15004    0.0.0.0:*        LISTEN
tcp        0      0 0.0.0.0:15006      0.0.0.0:*        LISTEN
tcp        0      0 0.0.0.0:15006      0.0.0.0:*        LISTEN
tcp6       0      0 :::8080            :::*            LISTEN
tcp6       0      0 :::15020           :::*            LISTEN
```

Figure D.1 visualizes the ports the agent and proxy listen to and the functionality each exposes:

Ports facing other services:

- *15020*—Exposes a variety of functionalities, the main ones being as follows:
  - Aggregating and exposing the metrics of the Envoy proxy by querying metrics from port 15090, application metrics (if configured), and its own metrics.
  - Health-checking the Envoy and DNS proxies. The proxy can be configured to perform health checking of the application on this endpoint as well, but this is generally only used for non-Kubernetes workloads such as virtual machines.
  - Endpoints for debugging the pilot agent—useful for Istio development teams—that expose information such as memory information, CPU profiling, and so on.
- *15021*—Pods with the sidecar injected are configured to check their readiness to receive traffic on this port. As explained previously, the Envoy proxy routes the health checks to the Pilot agent on port 15020, where the actual health-checking occurs.
- *15053*—Local DNS proxy configured by `istiod` to resolve edge cases where Kubernetes DNS resolution doesn't suffice.
- *15001*—Outbound traffic from the application is redirected to this port by Iptable rules, from which point the proxy handles routing the traffic to the services.
- *15006*—Inbound traffic to the application is redirected to this port by Iptable rules, where it is routed to the local application.

Ports that are useful for debugging and introspecting the agent:

- *15000*—Envoy proxy administration interface (this is covered in chapter 10, specifically the section 10.3.1).
- 15090—Exposes Envoy proxy metrics such as xDS stats, connection stats, HTTP stats, outlier stats, health check stats, circuit-breaker stats, and so on.

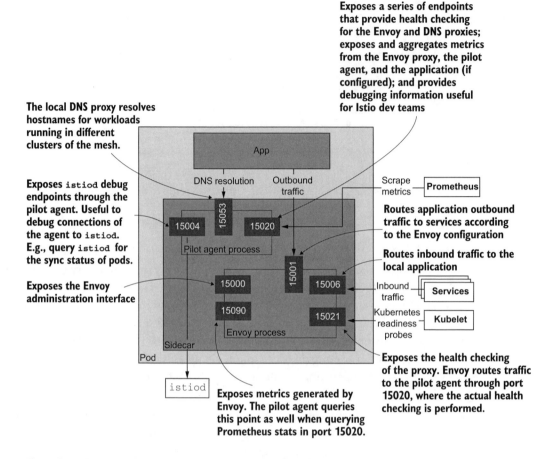

Figure D.1   Agent and Envoy proxy ports and their functionality

- 15004—Exposes the Istio Pilot debug endpoints (more on that later in this appendix) through the agent. Useful to debug connection issues with the Pilot.
- 15020—Exposes endpoints for debugging the Pilot agent (as mentioned for the service-facing ports).

You may have noticed that port 15020 provides multiple functionalities. Let's take a closer look at it.

D.1.1   Endpoints to introspect and troubleshoot the Istio agent

The agent exposes a set of endpoints in port 15020 that aid troubleshooting and introspecting the agent and the proxy. These endpoints are:

- */healthz/ready*—Performs a series of probes on the Envoy and DNS proxies to ensure that the workload is ready to process client requests.

- */stats/prometheus*—Merges the metrics of the Envoy proxy and the application with its own metrics and exposes them for scraping.
- */quitquitquit* —Kills the process of the Pilot agent.
- */app-health/*—Executes the application health probes defined as the environment variable `ISTIO_KUBE_APP_PROBERS` in the Istio proxy sidecar. When an application defines Kubernetes health probes, the `istiod` mutating webhook extracts the information and configures the health checks via this environment variable. (For more, see http://mng.bz/mxxP.) Thus the agent redirects queries on that path to the application.
- */debug/ndsz*—Lists the hostnames for which DNS proxy is configured by `istiod` using the Name Discovery Service (NDS) API.
- */debug/pprof /**—Golang profiling endpoints to help debug performance issues, memory leaks, and so on (see https://golang.org/doc/diagnostics#profiling). You can see the entire list of debug endpoints by querying the base path localhost:15020/debug/pprof. The output is HTML and is best viewed in the browser (remember that you can port-forward the port to your localhost). The profiling endpoints are relevant for Istio developers and not a concern for Istio users.

The easiest way to access these endpoints is using `kubectl exec` to make an HTTP request in any workload that you are interested in. For example, to check the merged stats of the webapp workload we'd execute:

```
kubectl exec deploy/webapp -c istio-proxy -- \
    curl localhost:15020/stats/prometheus
```

In the response, you'll see metrics prefixed with `istio_agent` (originating in the agent) and `envoy` (originating in the proxy), which shows that those are merged. Before going into the next section take some time and investigate the other endpoints listed earlier.

D.1.2 Querying Istio Pilot debug endpoints through the Istio agent

The agent exposes a few `istiod` debug endpoints—you'll learn more about those endpoints later in the appendix—by default on port 15004. Requests on those endpoints are forwarded securely to `istiod` as xDS events, which is a good way to verify connectivity to the control plane from the agent.

For example, one of the endpoints that's exposed allows us to query the synchronization status of workloads. To view that, get a shell connection in one of the proxies, and make a request on the endpoint /debug/syncz on port 15004 of the pilot agent:

```
curl -v localhost:15004/debug/syncz
[
# other items are collapsed
  {
    "@type": "type.googleapis.com/
    ➥envoy.service.status.v3.ClientConfig",
    "node": {
```

```
        "id": "catalog-68666d4988-zjsmn.istioinaction"     ◁─┐ Workload
    },                                                        │ ID
    "genericXdsConfigs": [
        {
            "typeUrl": "type.googleapis.com/
              ⮕envoy.config.listener.v3.Listener",
            "configStatus": "SYNCED"                      ◁─
        },
        {

            "typeUrl": "type.googleapis.com/
              ⮕envoy.config.route.v3.RouteConfiguration",
            "configStatus": "SYNCED"                      ◁─
        },                                                          The xDS APIs are
        {                                                           synchronized to
                                                                    the latest state.
            "typeUrl": "type.googleapis.com/
              ⮕envoy.config.endpoint.v3.ClusterLoadAssignment",
            "configStatus": "SYNCED"                      ◁─
        },
        {

            "typeUrl": "type.googleapis.com/
              ⮕envoy.config.cluster.v3.Cluster",
            "configStatus": "SYNCED"                      ◁─
        }
    ]
}]
```

The exposed information is a subset of the information exposed by the Istio Pilot debug endpoints. The same endpoints are exposed by the `istioctl x internal-debug` command, which is a new addition to `istioctl`.

Knowledge of these ports and the services they expose will make troubleshooting easier. You can query the latest Envoy configuration, manually test DNS resolution, query metrics to learn about the workings of components, and so on. Next, let's look at what the Istio Pilot exposes.

D.2 *Information exposed by the Istio Pilot*

The Pilot also exposes information to introspect and debug the service mesh. This information is useful for external services and as well for service mesh operators.

We can list the ports opened by the Istio Pilot as follows:

```
$  kubectl -n istio-system exec -it deploy/istiod -- netstat -tnl

Active Internet connections (only servers)

Proto Recv-Q Send-Q Local Address          Foreign Address        State
tcp        0      0 127.0.0.1:9876         0.0.0.0:*              LISTEN
tcp6       0      0 :::15017               :::*                  LISTEN
tcp6       0      0 :::8080                :::*                  LISTEN
tcp6       0      0 :::15010               :::*                  LISTEN
tcp6       0      0 :::15012               :::*                  LISTEN
tcp6       0      0 :::15014               :::*                  LISTEN
```

In addition to the ports exposed for workloads to get their configuration and certificates, there are quite a few ports that are useful for you to introspect and debug the control plane. Figure D.2 visualizes the ports and the functionality they expose:

- Service-facing ports:
  - *15010*—Exposes the xDS APIs and the issuance of certificates in plain text. Using this port is not recommended because the traffic can be sniffed.
  - *15012*—Exposes the same information as port 15010 but makes it secure. This port uses TLS for issuing the identity, and subsequent requests are mutually authenticated.
  - *15014*—Exposes control-plane metrics such as those covered in chapter 11.
  - *15017*—Exposes the webhook server that the Kubernetes API server calls to inject the sidecar into newly created pods and validate Istio resources such as Gateways, VirtualServices, and so on.
- Debugging and introspection ports:
  - *8080*—Exposes the Istio Pilot debug endpoints (discussed in the next section).
  - *9876*—Exposes introspection information for the istiod process.

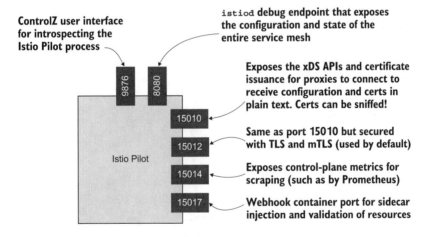

Figure D.2   The exposed Istio Pilot ports and their functionality

D.2.1   The Istio Pilot debug endpoints

The Istio Pilot debug endpoints expose the configuration and state of the entire service mesh—as it is known to the Pilot. The endpoints answer questions such as: Are the proxies synchronized? When was the last push to a proxy performed? What's the state of the xDS APIs? All of these are important for resolving tricky cases and understanding how the proxy is configured.

To access the debug endpoints, port-forward one of istiod instances to your local environment:

```
$ kubectl -n istio-system port-forward deploy/istiod 8080

Forwarding from 127.0.0.1:8080 -> 8080
Forwarding from [::1]:8080 -> 8080
```

Then navigate to http://localhost:8080/debug to see a list of all the debug endpoints, as shown in figure D.3.

Endpoint	Description
/debug/adsz	Status and debug interface for ADS
/debug/adsz?push=true	Initiates push of the current state to all connected endpoints
/debug/authorizationz	Internal authorization policies
/debug/cachez	Info about the internal XDS caches
/debug/config_distribution	Version status of all Envoys connected to this Pilot instance
/debug/config_dump	ConfigDump in the form of the Envoy admin config dump API for passed in proxyID
/debug/configz	Debug support for config
/debug/edsz	Status and debug interface for EDS
/debug/endpointShardz	Info about the endpoint shards
/debug/endpointz	Debug support for endpoints
/debug/inject	Active inject template
/debug/instancesz	Debug support for service instances
/debug/ndsz	Status and debug interface for NDS
/debug/pprof/	Displays pprof index
/debug/pprof/cmdline	The command line invocation of the current program
/debug/pprof/profile	CPU profile
/debug/pprof/symbol	Symbol looks up the program counters listed in the request
/debug/pprof/trace	A trace of execution of the current program.
/debug/push_status	Last PushContext Details
/debug/registryz	Debug support for registry
/debug/resourcesz	Debug support for watched resources
/debug/syncz	Synchronization status of all Envoys connected to this Pilot instance

Figure D.3   The Istio Pilot debug endpoints

NOTE   The debug endpoints contain sensitive information that could be misused if exposed. We recommend disabling the debug endpoints in production by setting the environment variable ENABLE_DEBUG_ON_HTTP to false during Istio installation. Doing so will break the functionality of tools dependent on those endpoints; however, in future releases, these endpoints will be exposed securely over xDS.

These endpoints can be logically grouped as follows:

- Endpoints that represent the service mesh state as known to the Pilot:
  - */debug/adsz*—Configuration for clusters, routes, and listeners
  - */debug/adsz?push=true*—Trigger a push to all proxies managed by this Pilot
  - */debug/edsz=proxyID=<pod>.<namespace>*—Endpoints known to a proxy
  - */debug/authorizationz*—List of authorization policies as applied to namespaces
- Endpoints that represent the data-plane configuration as known to the Pilot:
  - */debug/config_distribution*—Version status of all Envoys connected to this Pilot instance.
  - */debug/config_dump?proxyID=<pod>.<namespace>*—Generates the Envoy configuration according to the current known state of Istio Pilot.
  - */debug/syncz*—Displays the proxies managed by this Pilot. Additionally, it shows the latest nonce sent to the proxy and the latest nonce acknowledged. When those are the same, the proxy has the latest configuration.

As a service mesh operator, you will usually use the endpoints indirectly through other tools such as Kiali, `istioctl`, and so on. For example, the `istioctl proxy-status` command uses the */debug/syncz* endpoint to check whether the proxies are synchronized. However, when the information provided by these tools is not enough, you can dig deeper using the debug endpoints on your own.

D.2.2 *The ControlZ interface*

The Istio Pilot comes bundled with an administrative user interface that enables inspecting the current state of the Pilot process and some minor configuration possibilities. This interface provides a quick lookup of information related to the Istio Pilot instance, as covered in table D.1.

Table D.1 Content in the ControlZ interface

Page	Description
Logging Scopes	Logging for this process is organized in scopes, enabling us to configure the logging level separately for every scope.
Memory Usage	This information is gathered from the Go runtime and represents the ongoing memory consumption of this process.
Environment Variables	The set of environment variables defined for this process.
Process Information	Information about this process.
Command-Line Arguments	The set of command-line arguments used when starting this process.
Version Info	Version information about the binary (such as Istio Pilot 1.7.3) and Go runtime (go1.14.7).
Metrics	Another way of retrieving metrics exposed by the Pilot.
Signals	Enables sending a SIGUSR1 signal to the running process.

To access the dashboard, port-forward it to your local environment using `istioctl`, and open it in your browser:

```
$ istioctl dashboard controlz deploy/istiod.istio-system
```

```
http://localhost:9876
```

Besides looking up information related to the Istio Pilot in a simple web interface, the most common usage of the ControlZ dashboard is to change the logging scopes when you have to debug the Istio Pilot.

appendix E
How the virtual machine is configured to join the mesh

In this appendix, we take a closer look at the configuration generated by `istioctl` for virtual machines (VMs) when we want to register them to the mesh. Specifically, the files were generated when we executed the following command in chapter 13:

```
$  tree ch13/workload-files

istioctl x workload entry configure \
    --name forum \
    --namespace forum-services \
    --clusterID "west-cluster" \
    --externalIP $VM_IP \
    --autoregister \
    -o ./ch13/workload-files/
```

Quite a few files were generated, with a lot of structured configuration. If users had to come up with it, a lot of trial and error would be required to get it right. That's why this process is automated with `istioctl`.

To learn more about the generated configuration, start by listing all the files.

```
$  tree ch13/workload-files

ch13/workload-files
├── cluster.env
├── hosts
├── istio-token
├── mesh.yaml
├── root-cert.pem
```

The files are as follows:

- The hosts file is configured with the host entry `istiod.istio-system.svc`, which resolves to the IP of the east-west gateway. By default, this host entry uses the IP of the gateway named `istio-eastwestgateway`. However, you can change that by specifying the name with the flag `--ingressService` or the IP directly with `--ingressIP`.

- The istio-token file contains a short-lived token (by default, 1 hour) that the workload uses to identify itself to `istiod`. You can specify the expiry duration with the flag `--tokenDuration`.

- The root-cert.pem file is the public certificate of the root certificate authority (CA) that enables the workload to validate the control-plane certificate.

- The cluster.env file contains metadata for the workload such as the namespace, service accounts, network, workload group it belongs to, and so on. To get a better idea, let's print the configured values:

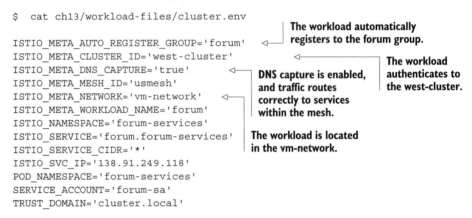

```
$ cat ch13/workload-files/cluster.env

ISTIO_META_AUTO_REGISTER_GROUP='forum'
ISTIO_META_CLUSTER_ID='west-cluster'
ISTIO_META_DNS_CAPTURE='true'
ISTIO_META_MESH_ID='usmesh'
ISTIO_META_NETWORK='vm-network'
ISTIO_META_WORKLOAD_NAME='forum'
ISTIO_NAMESPACE='forum-services'
ISTIO_SERVICE='forum.forum-services'
ISTIO_SERVICE_CIDR='*'
ISTIO_SVC_IP='138.91.249.118'
POD_NAMESPACE='forum-services'
SERVICE_ACCOUNT='forum-sa'
TRUST_DOMAIN='cluster.local'
```

The workload automatically registers to the forum group.

The workload authenticates to the west-cluster.

DNS capture is enabled, and traffic routes correctly to services within the mesh.

The workload is located in the vm-network.

- The mesh.yaml file configures the discovery address and the probes by which the sidecar tests the application's readiness to receive traffic.

This is all the configuration needed to integrate one VM into the service mesh. It's preferable to always use `istioctl` to generate the configuration; but when troubleshooting why a workload is not connecting to the mesh, you will iterate faster by making changes directly to the files and restarting the service proxy to pick up the changes.

index